International Investment Law and Soft Law

International Investment Law and Soft Law

Edited by

Andrea K. Bjorklund
University of California, Davis, USA

August Reinisch
University of Vienna, Austria

Edward Elgar
Cheltenham, UK • Northampton, MA, USA

Published by
Edward Elgar Publishing Limited
The Lypiatts
15 Lansdown Road
Cheltenham
Glos GL50 2JA
UK

Edward Elgar Publishing, Inc.
William Pratt House
9 Dewey Court
Northampton
Massachusetts 01060
USA

A catalogue record for this book
is available from the British Library

Library of Congress Control Number: 2012935320

FSC
www.fsc.org
MIX
Paper from
responsible sources
FSC® C018575

ISBN 978 1 78100 321 3

Printed and bound by MPG Books Group, UK

Contents

Acknowledgements

We are most grateful to the individual authors of the chapters of this book who have made our jobs easy by producing outstanding work and with whom it has been a pleasure to meet to discuss the intersection of soft law and the law of international investment. Books like this do not come together without a great deal of assistance. Jamin Horn at the University of California, Davis, provided excellent assistance with citations. Florian Dunkel at the University of Vienna was indispensable – he provided outstanding help at all stages of the project and we could not have completed the work without his diligence.

As always we acknowledge our families for their assistance and their forbearance.

Andrea K. Bjorklund
Davis, California

August Reinisch
Vienna, Austria

Contributors

Andrea K. Bjorklund is Professor of Law at the University of California, Davis, USA; Visiting Professor (Guest of the L. Yves Fortier Chair in International Arbitration and International Commercial Law) at McGill University School of Law, Montreal, Canada.

Giuditta Cordero-Moss is Professor at the Department of Private Law at the University of Oslo, Norway; honorary lecturer and principal research fellow at the Centre for Energy, Petroleum and Mineral Law & Policy, University of Dundee, UK.

Melaku Geboye Desta is Reader in International Economic Law at the Centre for Energy, Petroleum and Mineral Law & Policy, University of Dundee, UK.

Moshe Hirsch holds the Maria von Hofmannsthal Chair in International Law, Faculty of Law and Department of International Relations, Hebrew University of Jerusalem, Israel.

Kate Miles is Senior Lecturer in International Law at the Faculty of Law, University of Sydney, Australia.

August Reinisch is Professor of International and European Law at the University of Vienna, Austria and Professorial Lecturer at the Bologna Center of SAIS/Johns Hopkins University in Bologna, Italy.

Emily Sipiorski is senior researcher and lecturer at the Institute of Economic Law and the Transnational Economic Law Research Center (TELC) at the Law School of Martin-Luther-University Halle Wittenberg, Germany.

Christian Tietje is Professor of Public, European and International Economic Law, Director of the Institute of Economic Law and Director of the Transnational Economic Law Research Center (TELC) at the Law School of Martin-Luther-University Halle Wittenberg, Germany.

Andreas R. Ziegler is Professor and Director of the LLM Programme in International and European Economic and Commercial Law at the University of Lausanne, Switzerland; Conjoint Professor at the University of New South Wales in Sydney, Australia and Guest Professor at the University of St. Gallen and the Swiss Institute of Technology, Zurich.

1. Introduction: the ILA Study Group on the role of soft law instruments in international investment law[1]

Andrea K. Bjorklund and August Reinisch

The Study Group was established by the International Law Association (ILA) Executive Council in November 2008 for a three-year period with the express mandate 'to study the development of soft law instruments in international investment law and the feasibility of a "codification" of the present state of this field of international economic law'.

The Executive Council appointed Sir Franklin Berman (UK ILA Branch) as Chairman, as well as Andrea K Bjorklund (US ILA Branch) and August Reinisch (Austrian ILA Branch) as Co-Rapporteurs of the Study Group. As of Spring 2010, further members of the Group were Yas Banifatemi (French ILA Branch), Giuditta Cordero-Moss (Norwegian ILA Branch), Melaku Desta (UK ILA Branch), Moshe Hirsch (Israeli ILA Branch), Daniel Magraw (US ILA Branch), Kate Miles (Australian ILA Branch), Audley Sheppard (UK ILA Branch), Christian Tietje (German ILA Branch), Matthew Weiniger (UK ILA Branch), Catherine Yannaca-Small (Greek ILA Branch), Andreas Ziegler (Swiss ILA Branch).

The establishment of the Study Group was initiated by a proposal elaborated jointly by Thomas Wälde (deceased, formerly UK ILA Branch) and August Reinisch after the ILA Committee on the International Law on Foreign Investment had come to an end at the Rio Conference in 2008. It had concluded its work with the publication of the *Oxford Handbook on International Investment Law*,[2] which addressed major issues of both substantive and procedural investment law. In the

[1] The bulk of this introduction was presented as the Study Group's interim report at the ILA Biennial Conference in The Hague in 2010.

[2] P Muchlinski, F Ortino and C Schreuer (eds), *Oxford Handbook of International Investment Law* (Oxford University Press 2008).

course of that Committee's work it had become evident that the growing arbitral case law was contributing to an increasingly elaborate body of international investment law. The proponents of the Study Group thus considered it timely to suggest the establishment of a study group to investigate whether the time was ripe for an attempt to formulate and summarize the main rules relating to investment law in a 'codification'-type instrument. Their initial proposal made it very clear that the Study Group's mandate should not extend to an attempt to partially or exhaustively codify rules of investment law. Rather, the focus of the Group's work should be on the assessment of the ripeness of such an undertaking. Thus, the Study Group's mandate concentrates on the elaboration of a 'feasibility study'.

After the untimely death of Professor Wälde in late summer 2008, Professor Bjorklund agreed to serve as Co-Rapporteur of the Study Group. The Group was formally established in November 2008. It had working meetings in June 2009 in Vienna, in November 2009 in London, in August 2010 in The Hague and in March 2011 in Vienna.

At these meetings crucial decisions concerning the work and working methods of the Group were taken. In addition to the periodic reports due for ILA Conferences, the Group decided that it would work towards the publication of a book containing the contributions of the Group's members. The Group focused on identifying the main issues surrounding a potential 'codification' of investment law and investigating whether and in what form investment law may be 'codified'. The contributions in this book, which contains the major output of the Study Group's work, could lead to a recommendation that the ILA pursue the elaboration of an international soft law instrument on international investment.

The ILA has a long-standing tradition of formulating 'Rules', 'Recommended Practices', 'Draft Articles' and the like in an attempt to contribute to the codification and development of various fields of international law.

In the field of investment law, such a soft law instrument could provide a contemporary view of the state of the emerging and in several areas already settled jurisprudence of international investment law. Indeed, a significant contribution would be to identify those areas in which one can identify a *jurisprudence constante*. It could thereby serve tribunals, parties and counsel in helping to identify the current state of investment arbitral jurisprudence and scholarship (in the sense of Article 38 of the ICJ Statute). By objectively describing the current state of international investment law it could facilitate the identification of customary international law. Such an instrument could also assist governments in the negotiation and renegotiation of existing bilateral investment treaties where the trend is to incorporate (or react to) investment arbitral jurisprudence by adding much more detail to the hitherto quite open-ended treaty obligations. Finally it could, if a window of political opportunity emerged, provide an early model and drafting text for another attempt at a legally binding multilateral investment convention.

The Study Group's book is, however, also intended to analyse the potential disadvantages of soft law instruments. It is evident that in situations where there is no established case law a soft law instrument would leave a gap or would have to state a principle by endorsing an approach that had not earned consistent or near-universal support. In the case of conflicting approaches, choices made at the drafting stage might result in wording that would not necessarily be representative of any leading approach. Finally, a soft law instrument might have to be formulated so generally to be representative of all various approaches that it could not induce harmonization when specific questions have to be decided.

Furthermore, the variety of potential end-users described above could prove to be a challenge should the Study Group conclude that drafting a soft law instrument is feasible. A precise descriptive statement of existing law might be of most use to counsel and arbitrators, whereas a more prescriptive approach suggesting innovative practices might be more appropriately addressed to legislative bodies. In either case, a clear and objective assessment of purpose is essential to establish the credibility of the drafters and the reliability of the product.

The 'feasibility' study of the Study Group contained in this book is intended to address these issues head-on. For that purpose, a number of its members were asked to analyse previous experiences in other fields. This involves, among others, a discussion of soft codifications in the area of commercial law, addressing the scope of the relevant instruments (e.g. the specificity of INCOTERMS[3] vs the generalized nature of the UNIDROIT Principles of International Commercial Contracts[4]), language problems that may arise in the course of such 'codification' exercises, as well as the difficulties involved when ascertaining whether there is true or merely apparent consensus. In commercial law, soft law instruments have been very successful in practice by leading to predictable results, in particular where they are sufficiently precise so that they can be interpreted without being influenced by the legal tradition of the interpreter.

---

3 ICC, *Incoterms 2000* (ICC Pub 1999).

4 *UNIDROIT Principles of International Commercial Contracts 2004*, endorsed by the UN Commission on International Trade Law, UN Doc A/62/17 (Part I) (23 July 2007), 52–4.

Similar experience in other fields like environmental law, as well as GATT/WTO law, is considered in this book. The latter field demonstrates that a fruitful approach need not be uniform, but could include binding treaties, such as the Antidumping[5] and Subsidies[6] Agreements, the Agreement on Technical Barriers to Trade,[7] and the Agreement on the Application of Sanitary and Phytosanitary Measures,[8] as well as the interactions of those treaties with non-binding standards set by various institutions, like the International Organization for Standardization (ISO).[9]

Finally, experiences taken from general public international law provide useful material to assess the feasibility of a 'codification' of investment law. In this context, the ILC codification efforts, including those on State responsibility,[10] the iterative Law of the Sea conventions,[11] State

---

[5] Agreement on Implementation of Article VI of the General Agreement on Tariffs and Trade 1994 (Anti-dumping Agreement), 15 April 1994, entered into force 1 January 1995, Marrakesh Agreement Establishing the World Trade Organization, Annex 1A, 1868 UNTS 201.

[6] Agreement on Subsidies and Countervailing Measures, 15 April 1994, entered into force 1 January 1995, Marrakesh Agreement Establishing the World Trade Organization, Annex 1A, 1869 UNTS 14.

[7] Agreement on Technical Barriers to Trade, 15 April 1994, entered into force 1 January 1995, Marrakesh Agreement Establishing the World Trade Organization, Annex 1A, 1868 UNTS 120.

[8] *Agreement on the Application of Sanitary and Phytosanitary Measures*, 15 April 1994, Marrakesh Agreement Establishing the World Trade Organization, Annex 1A, 1867 UNTS 493.

[9] The Agreement on Technical Barriers to Trade encourages State Parties to comply with a Code of Good Practice; local governments, non-governmental and other standardizing bodies, including the ISO, can also accept the Code of Good Practice. This cooperative approach contributes to a uniformity of technical regulations that facilitates, rather than impedes, trade. The Agreement on the Application of Sanitary and Phytosanitary Measures encourages members to use international standards, guidelines and recommendations, such as those set out by the ISO.

[10] In 2001, the Commission completed its second reading of the Draft Articles on the Responsibility of States for Internationally Wrongful Acts. The Commission adopted the text of the articles and submitted them to the General Assembly with the recommendation that it take note of the articles in a resolution and that it annex the articles to the resolution. The Commission further suggested that the General Assembly consider, at a later stage, convening an international conference with a view towards adopting a convention on the topic. *Report of the Commission at its Fifty-third Session*, UN Doc A/56/10 (2001), para 11.

[11] The ILC's work on the Law of the Sea has resulted in several multilateral conventions regulating the law of the high seas, of the continental shelf, and of the

succession,[12] and State immunity[13] provide an interesting point of departure. At the same time scholarly attempts to offer broad annotated commentaries on core public international law topics, such as Judge Bruno Simma's UN Charter Commentary,[14] or the Commentary on the Statute of the ICJ,[15] provide useful techniques for investment purposes.

Also former attempts to codify investment law, such as the OECD projects of the 1960s[16] and 1990s[17] and related projects, as well as different generations of BITs and other international investment agreements, may equally be viewed as representing forays into codification.

---

territorial seas and the contiguous zone. The Convention on the High Seas entered into force on 30 September 1962, while the second and current UN Convention on the Law of the Sea entered into force 16 November 1994. UN Convention on the Law of the Sea, 10 December 1982, 1833 UNTS 3. See also Convention on the High Seas, 29 April 1968, 450 UNTS 11; Convention on the Continental Shelf, 29 April 1958, 499 UNTS 311; Convention on the Territorial Sea and the Contiguous Zone, 29 April 1958, 516 UNTS 205.

[12] The ILC initially considered succession in respect of treaties, succession in respect of rights and duties resulting from sources other than treaties, and succession in respect of membership in international organizations. The ILC set aside the latter topic and appointed a special rapporteur to explore the first two. The ILC has never acted on the topic, but has prepared several reports summarizing state practice: *The succession of States in relation to membership in the United Nations*, UN Doc A/CN.4/149 and Add. 1 (3 December 1962), 101 *et seq.*; *Succession of States in relation to general multilateral treaties of which the Secretary-General is the depositary*, UN Doc A/CN.4/150 (10 December 1962), 106 *et seq*; *Digest of decisions of international tribunals relating to State succession*, UN Doc A/CN.4/151 (3 December 1962), 131 et seq; *Digest of decisions of national courts relating to succession of States and Governments*, UN Doc A/CN.4/157 (18 April 1963), 95 et seq.

[13] The ILC project on State Immunity has resulted in the adoption by the General Assembly of the *United Nations Convention on Jurisdictional Immunities of States and Their Property*, UN Doc A/RES/59/38 (16 December 2004). As of 29 May 2010 ten States had ratified the Convention but it had not yet entered into force.

[14] B Simma, *The Charter of the United Nations: A Commentary* (Oxford University Press 1994).

[15] A Zimmerman, C Tomuschat and K Oellers-Frahm (eds), *The Statute of the International Court of Justice: A Commentary* (Oxford University Press 2006).

[16] The OECD Council published a *Draft Convention on the Protection of Foreign Property* in 1967, but the draft was never formally adopted. Resolution of the OECD Council, 12 October 1967, 7 ILM 117.

[17] From 1995 to 1998 the OECD hosted a series of negotiations designed to produce a multilateral agreement on investment (MAI). The negotiating group produced a draft text, but the negotiations stalled. For a draft text, see *The Multilateral Agreement on Investment: Draft Consolidated Text*, DAFFE/MAI(98)7/REV1 (22 April 1998).

Special attention is given to different forms of soft law instruments and their advantages and disadvantages. National samples, like the US Restatements,[18] Dicey and Morris,[19] etc., as well as international ones, like the UNIDROIT Principles,[20] the OECD Guidelines for Multinational Enterprises,[21] ILA resolutions,[22] Institut de Droit International resolutions,[23] OECD Model Tax treaties,[24] the Ruggie-commissioned study on stabilization clauses,[25] the Association of International Petroleum Negotiators standardized oil and gas contracts,[26] Energy Charter Treaty Secretariat model agreements,[27] etc., are scrutinized with a view to their adaptability for investment law purposes.

A central question to be clarified for the purpose of the formulation of a soft law instrument is the issue of the breadth of the investment law that might be subject to soft law instruments or other forms of 'codification'; in other words, whether a 'codification' should comprise only core standards or also include broader 'investment and . . . ' issues, such as human rights protections and environmental norms.

---

[18] For a complete list of US Restatements of the Law, see <http://tinyurl.com/24vm7rr>. A current Restatement project of interest for the Study Group project is the proposed Restatement on the US Law of International Commercial Arbitration. Chapter 6 of that Restatement will address investor-state dispute settlement as it interacts with US courts.

[19] L Collins, *Dicey, Morris and Collins on the Conflict of Laws* (Sweet & Maxwell 2006).

[20] *UNIDROIT Principles of International Commercial Contracts 2004*, endorsed by the UN Commission on International Trade Law, UN Doc A/62/17 (Part I) (23 July 2007) 52–4.

[21] OECD, *OECD Guidelines for Multinational Enterprises*, DAFFE/IME/WPG(2000)15/FINAL (31 October 2001).

[22] Reports of all ILA Conferences, including the text of the Resolutions adopted by the Association, are available on HeinOnline.

[23] A chronological index of the resolutions adopted by the Institut de Droit International is available at <http://www.idi-iil.org/idiE/navig_res_chon.html>.

[24] The latest version is the *Articles of the Model Convention with Respect to Taxes on Income and Capital* (17 July 2008), available at <http://www.oecd.org/dataoecd/43/57/42219418.pdf>.

[25] Andrea Shemberg, *Stabilization Clauses and Human Rights: A research project conducted for IFC and the United Nations Special Representative to the Secretary General on Business and Human Rights* (11 March 2008), available at <http://tinyurl.com/2excemo>.

[26] For a list of model contracts available from the AIPN, see <http://www.aipn.org/modelagreements>.

[27] Energy Charter Secretariat, *Model Intergovernmental and Host Government Agreements for Cross-Border Pipelines* (2nd edn, Energy Charter Secretariat 2007).

Equally important is a clarification of the sources of investment law, the extent to which there is a hierarchy of sources, fragmentation issues resulting from the problem of inconsistent treaties, the use of *ad hoc* arbitral bodies, and the lack of any kind of system of precedent or top-down control mechanism to impose consistency on tribunal decision-making, and the relationship between investment law and other bodies of international law.

This study investigates also various techniques and the practical problems of 'codification'. The fact that there is an exponentially growing law and that there are increasing instances of inconsistencies, etc., makes it more difficult to ascertain commonalities of approach. The present book thus identifies areas where there is homogeneous case law and where there are divergent approaches by individual tribunals, including the debate over the most-favoured-nation clause, the 'umbrella' clause, and the notion of investment. It also attempts to identify applicable principles in those situations in order to achieve predictability.

Of significant interest is the role of arbitrators in whatever 'codification' process is under way in the area of investment law. The identification of sources from which tribunals should draw in coming to their conclusions and the identification of sources that ought properly to provide the basis for a codification will pose serious problems.

Two specific studies will test sample codification approaches. In particular, the non-discrimination standard of in expropriation and most-favoured-nation (MFN) treatment lend themselves to further exploration.

A chapter on MFN will try to give an overview on the practice of tribunals in this field and derive answers as to whether it seems likely that a common understanding on the scope of the MFN clause could be agreed upon for use in a multilateral system and, if so, what it should be. The main types of MFN clauses, currently found in the bilateral investment treaties (BITs) of major players in this field and the topical arbitration awards, will be analysed.

Finally, a chapter will deal with expropriation, a topic that has already formed the basis for a substantial amount of case-law based on customary international law principles and on treaty provisions. By way of a 'sample codification' a specific aspect of expropriation – the legality requirement of non-discrimination – will be addressed. In this field, the practice of international tribunals strongly supports the assumption that non-discrimination is a requirement for the legality of an expropriation both under customary international law as well as under specifically applicable IIAs. While tribunals tend to qualify politically motivated or other egregious forms of discrimination as unlawful, they do apply a more nuanced approach to expropriations which affect only some foreigners if such discrimination may be the result of legitimate government policies. These fairly uniform interpretations may lend themselves to an interpretation apt for codification.

One of the threshold questions we needed to consider was what, at least in broad terms, we mean by soft law for the purposes of this study. While we did not find it necessary to adopt, as a Group, a specific definition of soft law or its role in international investment law, we have chosen to devote a short early chapter to provide an overview of the large body of literature on the subject. The purpose of this chapter is to inform the rest of the book rather than to limit the scope of each contribution – indeed, each contributor wrote his or her chapter without reference to this introductory chapter or any constraint imposed by a Group-level understanding of what exactly we mean by soft law.

This book containing the papers forming the foundation of the ILA Study Group's project is organized as follows. After this introductory chapter, three chapters discuss different facets of 'soft law'. Chapter 2, written by Moshe Hirsch, introduces the primary sources of international law and describes their relationship with soft law. Chapter 3, authored by Melaku Desta, addresses soft law generally, while Chapter 4, written by Andrea Bjorklund, examines the factors that lead soft law instruments to be successful and critically appraises the advantages and disadvantages of various instruments with an eye towards their efficacy in the field of international investment law.

The following three chapters are studies of the ways that soft law has been used in various fields. Chapter 5, written by Kate Miles, examines the important influence soft law instruments have had in the field of international environmental law. In Chapter 6 Giuditta Cordero-Moss assesses the effectiveness of various soft law manifestations in international commercial law. In Chapter 7, Melaku Desta turns to the innovative ways in which the WTO Agreements have encouraged the mingling of hard and soft law.

The next three chapters look more specifically at international law's ripeness for codification. In Chapter 8, Christian Tietje and Emily Sipiorski explore the development of international investment treaties and examine the common strands that unify the current generation of investment treaties. Chapter 9, written by Andreas Ziegler, assesses whether the most-favoured-nation obligation is ripe for codification or multilateralization. In Chapter 10, August Reinisch examines particularly the 'legality' requirement in the standard of expropriation and attempts a sample codification. Finally, a concluding chapter written by August Reinisch and Andrea Bjorklund addresses the ripeness of international investment law for concretization in a soft law instrument.

2. Sources of international investment law

Moshe Hirsch

The point of departure for a discussion on sources of investment law is the recognized list of sources of general international law according to Article 38 of the Statute of the International Court of Justice (ICJ).[1] It is noteworthy, however, that not all rules of public international law are relevant to relationships between host states and foreign investors.[2] This chapter emphasizes the distinctive features of the sources of international investment law and briefly discusses the interactions between non-binding instruments ('soft law') and the recognized sources of investment law. Soft law rules are not legally binding and legal decision-makers have discretion whether to apply them to a particular dispute or not. Though not mandatory, these norms often influence investment arbitrators. As elaborated below, the recognized sources included in Article 38 interact

[1] This approach was also undertaken by the Report of the Executive Directors on the ICSID Convention. The Report provides as follows: '40. . . . The term "international law" as used in this context should be understood in the sense given to it by Article 38(1) of the Statute of the International Court of Justice, allowance being made for the fact that Article 38 was designed to apply to inter-State disputes.' ICSID, 'Report of the Executive Directors on the Convention' (ICSID 2006) <http://icsid.worldbank.org/ICSID/StaticFiles/basicdoc/CRR_English-final.pdf>; see also *Inceysa Vallisoletana S.L. v Republic of El Salvador*, Award of 2 August 2006, ICSID Case No ARB/03/26, para 225 <http://italaw.com/documents/Inceysa_Vallisoletana_en_001.pdf>; *Methanex v United States*, Final Award of 3 August 2005, NAFTA, Part II, Chapter B, para 3 <http://www.state.gov/documents/organization/51052.pdf>.

[2] It is clear that certain rules regarding inter-state relations (such as diplomatic immunities) do not apply to such relationships. The applicability of some concepts of public international law is controversial in certain cases. See e.g. with regard to the ILC Articles on State Responsibility on 'necessity', Stephan W Schill, 'German Constitutional Court Rules on Necessity in Argentine Bondholder Case' (2007) 11 ASIL Insight (31 July 2007) <http://www.asil.org/insights070731.cfm>.

with diverse soft law instruments in various manners. The interaction between binding legal rules and non-binding (but influential) norms enriches investment law and allows legal decision-makers resorting to soft law instruments to clarify open-textured terms included in treaties or customary law. Furthermore, the fact that non-binding instruments may provide evidence for both elements of international customary law somewhat assimilates soft law into 'hard' law. Thus, while it is analytically possible to disentangle 'soft' from 'hard' laws, they are almost seamlessly interwoven in the fabric of international investment law.

I. TREATIES

One of the exceptional features of international investment law relates to the major role of bilateral treaties in investment relations. In addition to their forming the basis for more than 2,600 bilateral treaties, some rules on foreign investments are included in regional[3] and multilateral[4] treaties. Thus, it is not surprising that in the majority of contemporary investment disputes, bilateral investment treaties' rules are the centerpiece of the law applied by investment tribunals.[5]

The considerable number of bilateral treaties, as well as the ongoing process of concluding treaties in other spheres of international law, increases the likelihood that the rules included in investment treaties will not be consistent with other treaties, thus raising the intricate question as to the normative relationships between these treaties. Where rules emanating from two (or more) treaties are incompatible, it is clear that the *specific treaty* trumps the general one.[6] Additional rules regarding the

---

[3] The notable regional treaties are the Energy Charter Treaty, 34 ILM 360 (1995); Chapter 11 of the North American Free Trade Agreement (NAFTA), 32 ILM 289 (1993); the Framework Agreement on the ASEAN Investment Area (1998); the ASEAN Comprehensive Investment Agreement (2009) <http://www.aseansec.org/documents/FINAL-SIGNED-ACIA.pdf>; Protocol of Colonia for the Promotion and Reciprocal Protection of Investments in Mercosur <http://www.cvm.gov.br/ingl/inter/mercosul/coloni-e.asp>; MERCOSUR Protocol on Promotion and Protection of Investments Coming from Non-MERCOSUR State Parties (1994) <http://www.sice.oas.org/trade/mrcsrs/decisions/dec1194e.asp>.

[4] See e.g. the 1994 WTO Agreement on Trade Related Investment Measures <http://www.wto.org/english/docs_e/legal_e/18-trims.pdf>.

[5] Christoph Schreuer, Loretta Malintoppi, August Reinisch and Anthony Sinclair, *The ICSID Convention: A Commentary* (2nd edn, CUP 2009) 605.

[6] See e.g. Paul Reuter, *Introduction to the Law of Treaties* (Kegan Paul International 1995) 132–3.

interaction between inconsistent treaties are included in Article 30 and Article 59 of the Vienna Convention on the Law of Treaties.[7]

Subject to the superior status of the United Nations Charter's obligations,[8] Article 30(2) of the Vienna Convention provides as follows: 'When a treaty specifies that it is subject to, or that it is not to be considered as incompatible with, an earlier or later treaty, the provisions of that other treaty prevail.'

Consequently, if the two treaties address a subject matter in a comparable degree of generality, and the *parties' preference* in favor of one of the treaties is expressed in the treaty, this article directs us to accept the normative order as specified by the contracting parties. Thus, for instance, Article 103 of the NAFTA reflects the parties' intention regarding the relationships between this treaty and the GATT (and other agreements):

> 1. The Parties affirm their existing rights and obligations with respect to each other under the General Agreement on Tariffs and Trade and other agreements to which such Parties are party.
> 2. In the event of any *inconsistency between this Agreement and such other agreements, this Agreement shall prevail* to the extent of the inconsistency, except as otherwise provided in this Agreement.[9] [emphasis added]

Similarly, the Canadian[10] and US[11] model BITs include several provisions that explicitly clarify the relationships between bilateral agreements and other international treaties.[12]

The principle of respecting the parties' intentions is also reflected (though more implicitly) in Article 59 of the Vienna Convention. If all the

---

[7] Vienna Convention on the Law of Treaties (opened for signature 23 May 1969, entry into force 27 January 1980), 8 ILM 679 (1969). Article 31(3) of the Vienna Convention is discussed further below.

[8] On Article 103 of the United Nations Charter, see Section VII below.

[9] North American Free Trade Agreement (NAFTA), 32 ILM 289 (1993).

[10] See, for instance, Annex III of the Canadian Model BIT (regarding the most-favored principle, MFP) and Articles 9(1) and 10(4)(3) of this Model BIT. Agreement Between Canada And – For The Promotion And Protection of Investments <http://www.sice.oas.org/investment/NatLeg/Can/2004-FIPA-model-en.pdf>.

[11] See, for instance, Articles 13 and 16 of the 2004 US Model BIT, Treaty Between the Government of the United States of America and the Government of [Country] Concerning the Encouragement and Reciprocal Protection of Investment 2004 <http://www.state.gov/documents/organization/117601.pdf>.

[12] For additional examples, see Marie-France Houde and Katia Yannaca-Small, *Relationships between International Investment Agreements* (OECD Publishing 2004) 9–10.

contracting parties to a particular treaty conclude later another treaty relating to the same subject matter, and it appears from the later treaty (or is otherwise established) that the parties intended that the subject matter should be governed by the latter treaty, the latter treaty shall prevail (and the prior treaty shall be considered as terminated).[13] The same rule applies where the provisions of the latter treaty are incompatible with those of the earlier one and the two treaties are not capable of being applied at the same time.[14] Where the inconsistent treaties do not indicate any precedence ordering, and all the parties to the earlier treaty are also parties to the latter treaty, and the earlier treaty is not terminated under Article 59, Article 30(3) of the Vienna Convention applies the *lex posterior* principle and accords precedence to the latter treaty.[15] Arguments regarding inconsistencies between BITs and the EU treaties were carefully analyzed by investment tribunals in two cases involving Slovakia and the Czech Republic but these arguments were eventually rejected.[16]

The most intricate question arises where the parties to two conflicting treaties are not identical: e.g. one party is a contracting party to both treaties and the other party is a contracting party to only one of them. Article 30(4)(b) of the Vienna Convention provides that: 'as between a State party to both treaties and a State party to only one of the treaties, the treaty to which both States are parties governs their mutual rights and obligations'.

This rule does not set a preference ordering between the incompatible treaties and it does not absolve the contracting party that undertook inconsistent treaty obligations from its obligation to comply with both treaties. This provision leaves the latter party with the choice regarding which treaty to honor and which to breach, and as hinted in 30(5),[17] this

---

[13] Article 59(1)(a) of the Vienna Convention, above n 7.

[14] Article 59(1)(b) of the Vienna Convention, above n 7.

[15] Article 30(3) of the Vienna Convention provides as follows: 'When all the parties to the earlier treaty are parties also to the later treaty but the earlier treaty is not terminated or suspended in operation under article 59, the earlier treaty applies only to the extent that its provisions are compatible with those of the latter treaty.' See also Reuter, above n 6, 132.

[16] *Eureko v Slovakia*, Award on Jurisdiction, Arbitrability and Suspension of 26 October 2010, UNCITRAL, paras 270 <http://ita.law.uvic.ca/documents/EurekovSlovakRepublicAwardonJurisdiction.pdf>; *Eastern Sugar v Czech Republic*, Partial Award of 27 March 2007, SCC Case No 088/2004, paras 159–66 <http://ita.law.uvic.ca/documents/EasternSugar.pdf>.

[17] Article 30(5) of the Vienna Convention: 'Paragraph 4 is without prejudice to article 41, or to any question of the termination or suspension of the operation of a treaty under article 60 or to any question of responsibility which may arise for a

party is likely to incur international responsibility *vis-à-vis* the injured party.[18]

Investment tribunals that have faced arguments regarding inconsistent treaties have yet to resort to the above mentioned Article 30(4) of the Vienna Convention. The few tribunals that have faced such arguments regarding inconsistencies between environmental and investment treaties have carefully examined the provisions of both conventions, aiming to find whether the relevant international instruments contradict each other.[19] Though investment tribunals have seriously examined arguments regarding the interactions between such treaties, thus far no investment tribunal has absolved a party to an investment dispute from its investment obligations (or significantly reduced its responsibility to compensate the injured investor) on the grounds that it was excused by a conflicting obligation in such cases. Investment tribunals have taken a more reserved approach with regard to the relationships between investment and human rights treaties.[20]

Thus, for example, the *Siemens* award addressed arguments regarding inconsistent investment and human rights obligations, as well as the relevance of the jurisprudence of the European Court of Human Rights (ECHR) to investment disputes. Regarding the amount of compensation, Argentina argued that when a state expropriated for social or economic reasons, the regular 'fair market value' could not apply, because this would limit the sovereignty of a country to introduce reforms.[21] Argentina relied here on a statement of the ECHR in the *Tecmed* award[22] as an

---

State from the conclusion or application of a treaty the provisions of which are incompatible with its obligations towards another State under another treaty.'

[18] See also Reuter, above n 6, 133–4.

[19] See e.g. *SD Myers v Canada*, 40 ILM 1408 (2001), paras 213–21; *SPP (ME) v Egypt*, 19 YB of Comm Arb 51 (1994), paras 154–7. Compare *Santa Elena v Costa Rica*, 15 ICSID Review-FILJ 169 (2000), paras 71-2.

[20] For an analysis of the approach undertaken by investment tribunals regarding the relationships between human rights and investment treaties, see Moshe Hirsch, 'Investment Tribunals and Human Rights: Divergent Paths' in Pierre-Marie Dupuy, Francesco Francioni and Ernst-Ulrich Petersmann (eds), *Human Rights in International Investment Law and Arbitration* (OUP 2008) 97–114.

[21] *Siemens A.G. v Argentine Republic* Award of 6 February 2007, ICSID Case No ARB/02/08, para 356.

[22] The *Tecmed* tribunal discussed the particular vulnerability of foreign investors to bearing an excessive share of the burden involved in the realization of public aims, and cited with approval the Judgment of the ECHR in *James v UK*: 'Especially as regards a taking of property effected in the context of a social reform, there may well be good grounds for drawing a distinction between nationals and non-nationals as far as compensation is concerned. [. . .] Non-nationals are more

example to follow in terms of considering the purpose and proportionality of the measure taken *vis-à-vis* the private investor.[23] The tribunal observed that Argentina did not develop this argument, that the consideration mentioned by the *Tecmed* tribunal was part of the latter's determination of whether an expropriation had occurred and not of its determination of compensation,[24] and emphasized the difference between the two branches of international law. In this respect, the *Siemens* tribunal noted that Article I of the First Protocol to the European Convention on Human Rights (which addresses the right to property) permitted a 'margin of appreciation' not found in customary international law or the investment treaty.[25]

The trigger for the application of the above regulatory rules necessitates a prior determination that the rules deriving from different treaties or sources of international law are inconsistent. Such a determination depends to a significant extent on the interpretation given to the international rules involved; certain interpretations might render the two agreements reconcilable, while others would not. A softer approach that avoids setting a hierarchical order between the different legal rules lies in the harmonious interpretation of the relevant treaties. Such harmonious (or 'systemic') approach strives to interpret one treaty in light of the other treaty or international customary rules.[26] Article 31(3) of the Vienna Convention, which sets out the general principles of treaty interpretation, supports this interpretation method: 'There shall be taken into account, together with the context: . . . (c) any relevant rules of international law applicable in the relations between the parties.'

---

vulnerable to domestic legislation: [. . .] although a taking of property must always be effected in the public interest, different considerations may apply to nationals and non-nationals and there may well be legitimate reason for requiring nationals to bear a greater burden in the public interest than non- nationals.' *Tecmed v Mexico*, Award of 29 May 2003, ICSID Case No 00/2, 43 ILM 133 (2004), para 122. For the ECHR's decision, see *James v United Kingdom* (1986) 8 EHRR 123, para 50.

23 *Siemens v Argentina*, above n 21, paras 354 and 346.

24 Ibid, para 354.

25 Ibid; on this part of the award, see Lahra Liberti, 'The Relevance of Non-Investment Treaty Obligations in the Assessment of Compensation' (2007) 6 Transnational Dispute Management 4.

26 On this method of interpretation, see Andrew Newcombe and Lluís Paradell, *Law and Practice of Investment Treaties* (Kluwer 2009) 109–10; Campbell McLachlan, 'The Principle of Systemic Integration and Article 31(3)(c) of the Vienna Convention' (2005) 54 ICLQ 279; International Law Commission, *Report on the Work of its Fifty-Seventh Session* (2 May to 3 June and 11 July to 5 August 2005), UN GAOR, 60th Session, Supp No 10 (A/60/10) 214–20.

Treaty rules and soft law interact in various manners. In some cases, the adoption of non-binding instruments constitutes the basis for later international treaties. Thus, for example,[27] the 1967 Outer Space Treaty[28] was largely based on the Declaration of Legal Principles Governing the Activities of States in the Exploration and Use of Outer Space, which had been unanimously adopted by the United Nations General Assembly on 13 December 1963.[29] Furthermore, international tribunals occasionally employ non-binding instruments to interpret provisions included in binding international treaties. Thus, for example, the 1970 General Assembly Declaration on Principles of International Law Concerning Friendly Relations is regarded as constituting an authoritative interpretation of several provisions of the UN Charter.[30]

II. INTERNATIONAL CUSTOMARY LAW

The important role of treaties in international investment law should not lead to an underestimation of the significance of non-treaty rules in investment disputes. Unlike the situation prevalent in many branches of international law, most rules of investment law are included in treaties.[31] Although more than 2,600 treaties (mostly bilateral) regulate investment relations, customary rules of international law play an important role in numerous cases. They are particularly significant where the relations between the host state and the investor are not subject to an investment treaty.[32]

Even where certain treaties are being applied to a particular investment

---

[27] For additional cases, see Alan Boyle and Christine Chinkin, *The Making of International Law* (OUP 2007) 216.

[28] 1966 Treaty on Principles Governing the Activities of States in the Exploration and Use of Outer Space, including the Moon and Other Celestial Bodies (Outer Space Treaty) <http://www.oosa.unvienna.org/pdf/publications/STSPACE11E.pdf>.

[29] Outer Space Treaty, above n 28.

[30] See e.g. Malcolm Shaw, *International Law* (6th edn, CUP 2008) 253.

[31] See e.g. Christoph Schreuer, 'Diversity and Harmonization of Treaty Interpretation in Investment Arbitration' (2006) 3 *Transnational Dispute Management* 1; Jeswald W Salacuse, 'The Treatification of International Investment Law: A Victory of Form Over Life? A Crossroads Crossed?' (2006) 3 *Transnational Dispute Management*.

[32] See e.g. *Case Concerning Diallo* (*Guinea v Congo*), Judgment of 24 May 2007, ICJ General List No 103 (2007) <http://www.icj-cij.org/docket/files/103/13856.pdf>.

dispute, these treaties often do not regulate all specific questions arising in the particular dispute. Thus, in cases of *lacunae*, investment treaty rules are supplemented by rules of customary law[33] (such as those included in the 2001 ILC Articles on Responsibility of States).[34] For instance, where the *Enron* tribunal encountered arguments regarding 'necessity', the arbitrators examined the relevant treaty provisions, and then stated:[35]

> [A] treaty regime specifically dealing with a given matter will prevail over more general rules of customary law. Had this been the case here the Tribunal would have started out its considerations on the basis of the Treaty provision and would have resorted to the Articles on State Responsibility only as a supplementary means. But the problem is that the Treaty itself did not deal with these elements. *The Treaty thus becomes inseparable from the customary law standard insofar as the conditions for the operation of state of necessity are concerned.*[36] [emphasis added]

In addition, certain investment treaties explicitly refer to international customary law.[37] Thus, for instance,[38] Article 1105(1) of the NAFTA

---

[33] See e.g. Rudolf Dolzer and Christoph Schreuer, *Principles of International Investment Law* (OUP 2008) 153–62; Tarcisio Gazzini, 'The Role of Customary International Law in the Field of Foreign Investment' (2007) 8 *Journal of World Investment and Trade* 691.

[34] International Law Commission, Draft Articles on Responsibility of States for Internationally Wrongful Acts, with commentaries <http://untreaty.un.org/ilc/texts/instruments/english/commentaries/9_6_2001.pdf>.

[35] For additional examples of investment awards, see Gazzini, above n 33, 711.

[36] *Enron and Ponderosa v Argentina*, Award of 22 May 2007, ICSID Case No ARB/01/3, para 334 <http://ita.law.uvic.ca/documents/Enron-Award.pdf>; and see the tribunal's analysis of the elements of Article 25 of the ILC rules on state responsibility in paras 303–13; see also *Amoco v Iran*, 15 Iran–US Claims Tribunal Reports (1987) 189, 222.

[37] See Campbell McLachlan, Laurence Shore and Matthew Weiniger, *International Investment Arbitration: Substantive Principles* (OUP 2007) 16–17.

[38] See also Article 12(1) of the 1990 investment treaty between Italy and Bangladesh that provides as follows: 'Whenever any issue is governed both by this Agreement and by another International Agreement to which both the Contracting Parties are parties, or whenever it is governed otherwise by general international law, the most favorable provisions, case by case, shall be applied to the Contracting Parties and to their investors.' Agreement Between the Government of the Republic of Italy and the Government of the People's Republic of Bangladesh on the Promotion and Protection of Investments of 20 March 1990. And see *Saipem v Bangladesh*, Decision on Jurisdiction of 21 March 2007, ICSID Case No ARB/05/07, para 99 <http://italaw.com/documents/Saipem-Bangladesh-Jurisdiction.pdf>; see also *Pantechniki v Albania*, Award of 30 July 2009, ICSID Case No ARB/07/21, para 69 <http://ita.law.uvic.ca/documents/PantechnikiAward.pdf>.

(regarding minimum standard of treatment) provides that '[e]ach Party shall accord to investments of investors of another Party treatment in accordance with international law, including fair and equitable treatment and full protection and security'.[39] In 2001, the NAFTA Free Trade Commission stated that 'Article 1105(1) prescribes the customary international law minimum standard of treatment of aliens as the minimum standard of treatment to be afforded to investments of investors of another Party'.[40]

Even where the particular legal question is addressed by specific treaty provisions, those treaty rules are frequently subject to different interpretations.[41] In such cases, international tribunals[42] (including investment tribunals) often interpret the particular treaty provisions in light of international customary law.[43] The *Phoenix* tribunal noted in that regard that:

> [i]t is evident to the Tribunal that the same holds true in international investment law and that the ICSID Convention's jurisdictional requirements – as well as those of *the BIT – cannot be read and interpreted in isolation from public international law, and its general principles.*[44] [emphasis added]

Article 38(1)(b) of the ICJ Statute presents the two traditional elements of international customary law: general practice and *opinio juris*. As for the first (objective) component, in addition to physical acts, international tribunals often consider various non-physical acts as 'practice'. Such acts

---

39 See also Article 5(1) of the 2004 US Model BIT, above n 11.

40 Article B, Notes of Interpretation of Certain Chapter 11 Provisions (NAFTA Free Trade Commission 2001) <http://www.naftaclaims.com/files/NAFTA_Comm_1105_Transparency.pdf>.

41 See e.g, Gazzini, above n 33, 710–12.

42 See e.g, McLachlan, Shore and Weiniger, above n 37, 15.

43 The *Saipem* tribunal stated in that regard: 'Since *Saipem*'s claim is based on Article 5 of the BIT, the Tribunal will primarily apply the BIT as the applicable rule of international law. The Tribunal will also apply the general rules of international law that may be applicable, either because an issue of international law is not directly dealt with in the BIT or, if necessary, to interpret the BIT.' *Saipem v Bangladesh*, above n 38, para 99.

44 *Phoenix v the Czech Republic*, below n 77, para 78; see also paras 99, 106–7. The tribunal also stated in that regard: 'It is not disputed that the interpretation of the ICSID Convention and of the BIT is governed by international law, including the customary principles of interpretation embodied in the Vienna Convention on the Law of Treaties and the general principles of international law.' *Phoenix* Award, below n 77, para 75.

include diverse verbal acts[45] (such as declarations) and domestic legislation.[46]

Practice alone cannot lead to the formation of customary law and a subjective element (*opinio juris*) is needed to establish a new rule of international law.[47] The absence of a sense of obligation has led some scholars and tribunals to reject arguments that a series of similar investment treaties give rise to new customary rules.[48] A sense of obligation (i.e. whether a certain behavior is considered as legally obligatory or not) may be manifested by various means, including states' declarations, resolutions of international organizations, international treaties and decisions of international tribunals.[49]

'Soft' declarations of international institutions may provide evidence for establishing the existence of *opinio juris*.[50] Thus, the ICJ clarified in the *Legality of Nuclear Weapon Advisory Opinion*:

> The Court notes that *General Assembly resolutions,* even if they are not binding, may sometimes have normative value. They *can, in certain circumstances, provide evidence important for establishing the existence of a rule or the emergence of an opinio juris.* To establish whether this is true of a given General Assembly resolution, it is necessary to look at its content and the conditions of

---

45 See e.g. Article 4, ILA Statement of Principles Applicable to the Formation of General Customary International Law (2000).

46 See e.g. *Prosecutor v Norman*, Judgement of 31 May 2004, Special Court for Sierra Leone, at 1–27, <http://www.unhcr.org/refworld/publisher,SC-SL,,,49abc0a22,0.html>; see also Gazzini, above n 34, 692.

47 See e.g. Article 16 of the ILA Statement, above n 45.

48 See e.g. Article 25 of the ILA Statement, above n 45; see also the Commentary on this article at 48; also see *UPS v Canada*, Award on Jurisdiction of 22 November 2002, UNCITRAL, para 97, <http://italaw.com/documents/UPS-Jurisdiction.pdf>; Gazzini, above n 33, at 694; Patrick Dumberry, 'Are BITs Representing the "New" Customary International Law in International Investment Law?' <http://kluwerarbitrationblog.com/blog/2009/09/02/are-bits-representing-the-%E2%80%9Cnew%E2%80%9D-customary-international-law-in-international-investment-law/>.

49 See e.g. Malcolm Shaw, *International Law* (6th edn, CUP 2008) 88–9; Gazzini, above n 33, 693.

50 The ICJ stated in the Nicaragua case in that regard: 'This opinio juris may, though with all due caution, be deduced from, inter alia, the attitude of the Parties and the attitude of States towards certain General Assembly resolutions, and particularly resolution 2625 (XXV) entitled "Declaration on Principles of International Law concerning Friendly Relations and Co-operation among States in accordance with the Charter of the United Nations".' *Case Concerning Military and Paramilitary in and against Nicaragua*, Judgment of 27 June 1986, (1986) ICJ Rep 14, para 188.

its adoption; it is also necessary to see whether an opinio juris exists as to its normative character.[51] [emphasis added]

Some experts emphasize the 'compensatory' relationships between the objective and subjective elements.[52] As the ILA Committee on the Formation of Customary Law noted, international tribunals' decisions indicate that 'a substantial manifestation of acceptance (consent or belief) by States that a customary rule exists may compensate for a relative lack of practice, and vice versa'.[53]

An examination of decisions by international tribunals (including the ICJ) and the legal literature indicates that international tribunals do not undertake a uniform approach regarding the determination of the above two elements of customary law. International tribunals often pronounce international customary rules without referring to these two components or without distinguishing between the two elements. The absence of discussion on the objective and subjective components may be explained by the unclear distinction between these two elements (e.g. statements of states and international organizations may be considered as 'practice' as well as '*opinio juris*').

Recent research and scholarship on international customary law indicates that the subjective element is increasingly emphasized at the expense of the objective element (general practice). Weisburd's comprehensive examination of the decisions of the ICJ reveals, for instance, that the Court rarely relies on actual practice to determine the content of customary rules; and that it frequently bases its conclusions in this regard on non-binding resolutions of international bodies (such as the ILC) and on its own decisions.[54] Other scholars highlight the contrast between the 'traditional custom' that emphasizes the role of state practice

---

51 *The Legality of the Threat or Use of Nuclear Weapons*, Advisory Opinion of 8 July 1996 (1996) ICJ Rep 226, para 70. See also, *Filartiga v Peña-Irala*, 630 Fed 2nd 876 (2nd Cir, 1980).

52 For a discussion of this relationship, see Frederic L Kirgis Jr, 'Custom on a Sliding Scale' (1987) 81 *AJIL* 146; Tullio Treves, 'Customary International Law', *Max Planck Encyclopedia of Public International Law*, at 12–13, and the references therein <http://www.mpepil.com/sample_article?id=/epil/entries/law-9780199231690-e1393&recno=29&>.

53 Article 19 of the ILA Statement, above n 45. Also see the ILA Commentary on Article 19, at 41–2 (and the references therein).

54 Arthur M Weisburd, 'The International Court of Justice and the Concept of State Practice', UNC Legal Studies Research Paper No 1282684 <http://ssrn.com/abstract=1282684> <http://papers.ssrn.com/sol3/papers.cfm?abstract_id=1282684>.

and 'modern custom' that emphasizes *opinio juris*.[55] Damrosch *et al.* state in their textbook that '[t]he tendency to "find" new customary law based mainly on *opinio juris* (i.e., statements that a legal rule has now been recognized) without demonstrating uniform conduct among states in general is especially evident in regard to human rights, environmental protection, and economic development.'[56]

In light of the above trend in general international law, the question arises whether, and to what extent, this trend of downplaying the role of physical acts and emphasizing the role of non-physical acts (that are more related to *opinio juris*) influences investment tribunals. An examination of most decisions rendered by investment tribunals during 2009 (awards on merit) indicates that tribunals which pronounce various customary rules are inclined *not* to discuss the existence (or lack) of general practice; and that they frequently rely on decisions of international courts and tribunals as well as 'soft' decisions by international bodies.[57]

Thus, for instance,[58] the *Total* tribunal stated that the ILC rules on State Responsibility reflect a principle of international customary law:

> *This principle reflects the general principle of customary international law* according to which, for the purpose of State responsibility for the commission of an internationally wrongful act, the characterization of an act as lawful under the State's internal law is irrelevant. *This principle has been restated at Article 3 of the Articles on Responsibility of States for Internationally Wrongful Acts* drafted by the International Law Commission and annexed to General Assembly Resolution A/RES/56/83.[59] [emphasis added]

---

[55] Anthea E Roberts, 'Traditional and Modern Approaches to Customary International Law: A Reconciliation' (2001) 95 *AJIL* 756.

[56] Lori F Damrosch, Louis Henkin, Richard C Pough, Oscar Schachter and Hans Smit, *International Law* (4th edn, West 2001) 96.

[57] For investment awards that infer the existence of customary rules from rules adopted by the International Law Commission, see e.g. *Saipem v Bangladesh*, above n 38, para 165; *Funnekotter v Zimbabwe*, below n 61, para 47; *Renta A v Russia*, above n 61, para 77; *Bayindir v Pakistan*, below n 61, para 129; *EDF v Romania*, Award and Dissenting Opinion of 8 October 2009, ICSID Case No ARB/05/13, para 213 <http://ita.law.uvic.ca/documents/EDFAwardandDissent.pdf>.

[58] See also the statement of the *Impreglio* tribunal statement regarding the ILC rules on state responsibility: 'The Arbitral Tribunal therefore must evaluate Argentina's necessity plea under the standard set by customary international law, which the Parties agree has been codified in Article 25 of the International Law Commission's Articles on Responsibility of States for Internationally Wrongful Acts.' *Impregilo v Argentina*, Award of 21 June 2011, ICSID Case No ARB/07/17 para 344 <http://icsid.worldbank.org/ICSID/FrontServlet?requestType=CasesRH&actionVal=showDoc&docId=DC2171_En&caseId=C109>.

[59] *Total v Argentina*, Decision on Liability of 21 December 2010, ICSID Case

Similarly, the tribunal stated that the ILC rules on unilateral declarations 'were formulated by the International Law Commission in 2006 as a restatement of international (interstate) case law in the subject matter'.[60]

The examination of most investment awards rendered in 2009 reveals that investment tribunals often cite decisions of the ICJ as proving the existence of international customary law.[61] Investment arbitrators also often infer the existence of customary rules from the awards of other investment tribunals,[62] and sometimes from rules adopted by the International Law Commission[63] or experts' publications.[64] In certain cases, investment awards do not elaborate on the evidence leading to statements regarding international customary rules.[65]

Thus, soft instruments of international law may provide evidence for both elements of international customary law. As discussed above, international tribunals often consider 'verbal acts' that include various declarations as 'practice'. Similarly, non-binding declarations of international institutions (prominently the General Assembly's resolutions and ILC's decisions) may fulfill the second element of *opinio juris*.

No ARB/04/1, para 40, note 21 <http://italaw.com/documents/TotalvArgentina_DecisionOnLiabilty.pdf>.

[60] *Total v Argentina*, above n 59, para 132.

[61] See e.g. *Funnekotter v Zimbabwe*, Award of 22 April 2009, ICSID Case No ARB/05/6, para 105 (necessity), at para 108, <http://ita.law.uvic.ca/documents/ZimbabweAward.pdf>; *Saipem v Bangladesh*, above n 38, para 201 (remedies); *Romak v Uzbekistan*, Award of 26 November 2009, UNCITRAL, para 169, para 195; *Phoenix v the Czech Republic*, below n 77, para 76; *Cementownia v Turkey*, Award of 17 September 2009, ICSID Case No ARB(AF)/06/2, para 155 <http://ita.law.uvic.ca/documents/CementowniaAward.pdf>; *Renta 4 SVSA et al. v Russian Federation*, Award on Preliminary Objections of 20 March 2009, SCC No 24/2007, paras 80, 88 <http://ita.law.uvic.ca/documents/Renta.pdf>; *Bayindir v Pakistan*, Award of 27 August 2009, ICSID Case No ARB/03/29, para 136, <http://ita.law.uvic.ca/documents/Bayandiraward.pdf>.

[62] See, e.g., *Funnekotter v Zimbabwe*, above n 61, para 124; *Pantechniki v Albania*, above n 38, para 78; *European Cement v Turkey*, Award of 30 August 2009, ICSID Case No ARB(AF)/07/2, para 171 <http://italaw.com/documents/EuropeCementAward.PDF>; *Phoenix v the Czech Republic*, below n 77, para 108, *Cementownia v Turkey*, above n 61, paras 153, 155.

[63] See above on awards that infer the existence of customary rules from rules adopted by the International Law Commission.

[64] See e.g. *Pantechniki v Albania*, above n 38, paras 79–81, 94; *Saipem v Bangladesh*, above n 38, para 160; *Renta v Russia*, above n 61, para 100 ; *Bayindir v Pakistan*, above n 57, para 136.

[65] See e.g. *Funnekotter v Zimbabwe*, above n 61, paras 115, 123; *Saipem* v *Bangladesh*, above n 38, para 175.

Finally, some 'soft' resolutions of the International Law Association are widely accepted by the international community as customary international law; Salman notes with regard to the ILA Helsinki Rules on the Uses of the Waters of International Rivers:[66]

> *Like other IIL and ILA rules and resolutions, the Helsinki Rules have no formal standing or legally binding effect per se. However, until the adoption of the UN Convention 30 years later, they remained the single most authoritative and widely quoted set of rules* for regulating the use and protection of international watercourses. Indeed, those Rules are the first general codification of the law of international watercourses. As noted by Charles Bourne, *the Helsinki Rules were soon accepted by the international community as customary international law* (Bourne, 1996). The Rules have been referred to or adopted by a number of organizations and countries.[67] [emphasis added]

III. GENERAL PRINCIPLES OF LAW

This source of international law, established by Article 38(1)(c) of the ICJ statute, was adopted by the drafters in response to the need for completeness of law, and to avoid *non-liquet* situations.[68] Thus, this source of law is often considered as a residual reservoir of legal rules that may fill gaps where no applicable treaty provision or international customary rule exists.[69] General principles of law appear in Article 38(1) after international treaties and customs that both reflect states' consent in a more direct fashion. Consequently, proponents of the voluntarist/positivist approach to international law seeking to base international legal rules on states' consent tend to undervalue the role of general principles as a source of international law.[70] The recourse to this vague source was a characteristic feature of arbitral awards in the early stages of international

[66] The Helsinki Rules on the Uses of the Waters of International Rivers, Adopted by the International Law Association at the 52nd conference <http://www.internationalwaterlaw.org/documents/intldocs/helsinki_rules .html>.

[67] MA Salman, 'The Helsinki Rules, the UN Watercourses Convention and the Berlin Rules: Perspectives on International Water Law' (2007) 23 *Water Resources Development* 625, 630.

[68] Alain Pellet, 'Article 38' in Andreas Zimmermann *et al.* (eds), *The Statute of the International Court of Justice* (OUP 2006) 677, 764–5.

[69] See e.g. Jeswald W Salacuse, *The Law of Investment Treaties* (OUP 2010) 46; Schreuer *et al.*, above n 5, 608; Vaughan Lowe, *International Law* (OUP 2007) 87.

[70] See e.g. Boyle and Chinkin, above n 27, at 12. See also Pellet, above n 68, at 767; Ian Brownlie, *The Principles of Public International Law* (6th edn, OUP 2003) 15; Sornarajah, below n 82, 93.

law[71] but, as discussed below, these principles have largely been neglected by contemporary investment tribunals.[72]

Though there are some controversies in legal literature, the prevailing view today is that 'general principles of law' are characterized by the three following prerequisite elements:

1. Wide-ranging character – the words 'general principles' indicate that this source has to relate to broad legal principles (rather than specific rules).[73]
2. Recognition in states' municipal legal systems (*foro domestico*) – though there is a need to resort to comparative research, it is not necessary to examine all states' domestic systems. Since all modern domestic laws can be gathered into a few family systems of law (and since only general principles are to be taken into account), it is sufficient to ascertain that such principles are present in the laws belonging to the principal families of laws. The term 'civilized nations' mentioned in Article 38(1)(c) is not relevant today and all states are considered to be 'civilized nations'.[74]
3. Transposability to international law – the principle has to be appropriate for application in the international community. This requirement indicates that even if all municipal systems include a particular legal rule, this rule is not automatically recognized as a 'general principle of law'.[75] This requirement reminds us that the conditions in the international system are occasionally very different from those prevailing in domestic systems, and that some legal rules, even when shared by numerous domestic statutes, cannot be mechanically imported into the international legal realm.[76]

---

[71] The ICJ and other international tribunals do not frequently resort to this source of international law; Pellet, above n 68, 765, 771; Salacuse, above n 69, 46; on the practice of international tribunals regarding general principles of law, see Boyle and Chinkin, above n 27, 286–8.

[72] On the factors explaining this state of affairs, see further below.

[73] Pellet, above n 68, at 767.

[74] Pellet, above n 68, at 768–70.

[75] Oscar Schachter, 'International Law in Theory and Practice' (1982) 178 *Recueil des cours* 9, 78–80; Pellet, above n 68, 772; Lowe, above n 69, 88; on the controversy regarding the applicability of the domestic rule on 'limited liability' corporations to intergovernmental organizations, see Moshe Hirsch, *The Responsibility of International Organizations Toward Third Parties; Some Basic Principles* (Kluwer-Nijhoff 1995) 132.

[76] McNair stated in that regard: 'The way in which international law borrows from this source [. . .] is not by means of importing private law institutions "lock,

International investment tribunals have occasionally resorted to general principles of law. The *Phoenix* tribunal, for instance, stated:

> Also, international agreements like the ICSID Convention and the BIT have to be analyzed with due regard to the requirements of the *general principles of law*, such as the principle of non-retroactivity or the principle of *good faith*, also referred to by the Vienna Convention.[77]

Investment tribunals have stated that some legal principles, such as good faith,[78] unjust enrichment,[79] and *res judicata*[80] constitute 'general principles of law'[81] and applied them.[82] The principle of 'fair and equitable treatment' is also often discussed in the context of general principles of law derived from domestic legal systems.[83]

---

stock and barrel", ready-made and fully equipped with a set of rules [. . .] [T]he true view of the duty of international tribunals in this matter is to regard any features or terminology which are reminiscent of the rules and institutions of private law as an indication of policy and principles rather than as directly importing these rules and institutions.' As cited in Pellet, above n 68, 772.

77 *Phoenix v the Czech Republic*, Award of 15 April 2009, ICSID Case No ARB/06/5, para 77; see also paras 75, 78 <http://ita.law.uvic.ca/documents/PhoenixAward.pdf>; see also *Inceysa Vallisoletana SL v Republic of El Salvador*, Award of 2 August 2006, ICSID Case No ARB/03/26, para 226 <http://ita.law.uvic.ca/documents/Inceysa_Vallisoletana_en_000.pdf>.

78 See e.g. *Sempra Energy International v Argentina*, Award of 28 September 2007, ICSID Case No ARB/02/16, para 297 <http://ita.law.uvic.ca/documents/SempraAward.pdf>; *Phoenix v the Czech Republic*, above n 77, para 77.

79 *Saluka Investments BV (The Netherlands) v Czech Republic*, Partial Award of 17 March 2006, UNCITRAL, para 449 <http://ita.law.uvic.ca/documents/Saluka-PartialawardFinal.pdf>.

80 *Waste Management v Mexico* (ii), Decision on Jurisdiction of 26 June 2002, ICSID Case No ARB(AF)/00/3, paras 39 and 43 <http://ita.law.uvic.ca/documents/WastMgmt2-Jurisdiction.pdf>.

81 On the prohibition on bribery in investment relations as a general principle of international law, see Richard Kreindler, 'Corruption in International Investment Arbitration: Jurisdiction and Unclean Hands Doctrine' in Kaj Hober *et al.* (eds), *Between East and West: Essays in Honor of Ulf Franke* (Juris 2010) 309, 311.

82 For additional examples of general principles of international law recognized by investment tribunals, see Schreuer *et al.*, above n 5, 608–9 and the references therein; Tarcisio Gazzini 'General Principles of Law in the Field of Foreign Investment' (2009) 10 *Journal of World Investment and Trade* 103, 111–12. See also Sergey Ripinsky and Kevin Williams, *Damages in International Investment Law* (British Institute of International and Comparative Law 2008) 322; Muthucumaraswamy Sornarajah, *The International Law on Foreign Investment* (2nd edn, CUP 2004) 93–5.

83 On the close relationships between the principle of 'fair and equitable

The *ad hoc* committee in the *Klöckner* case annulled the decision of the ICSID tribunal, *inter alia*, because of an error regarding its pronouncement on a general principle of law relating to the duty of full disclosure. The Committee emphasized that investment tribunals are not allowed to base their rulings on 'general principles of law' on the basis of a single domestic legal system (in that case the French law), without examining legal principles applicable in additional legal systems.[84]

The celebrated *Texaco* arbitration well illustrates the importance of the second requirement concerning wide recognition in states' municipal legal systems. Dupuy, the sole arbitrator, provided two main explanations for declining to apply the concept of administrative contracts to the agreement between the host state and foreign investor. The first reason related to the underlying unequal character of administrative contracts and the parties' clear intention to contract on equal footing.[85] The second reason concerned the question of whether the domestic rules regarding administrative contracts were considered as 'general principles of international law'. Dupuy explained that the doctrine of administrative contracts was adopted by French law and several other domestic legal systems

> [b]ut it is unknown in many other legal systems which are as important as the French system and it has not been accepted by international law notwithstanding wishes which *de lege ferenda* may have been expressed in this field. The distinction made by certain legal systems between 'civil contracts' and 'administrative contracts' cannot therefore be regarded as corresponding to a 'general principle of law' [. . . .][86]

As Gazzini notes, investment tribunals have often not clearly distinguished between rules derived from 'general principles of law' and

---

treatment' in international investment law and general principles of law, see Sornarajah, above n 82, 341; Gazzini, above n 82, 116–17; on the potential of this source of law to clarify the particular rules deriving from fair and equitable treatment in international investment law, see e.g. Stephan W Schill *et al.*, 'International Investment Law and General Principles of Law' in Jürgen Bering *et al.* (eds), *General Public International Law and International Investment Law: A Research Sketch on Selected Issues* (ILA German Branch 2009) 9 <http://www.50yearsofbits.com/docs/0912211342_ILA_Working_Group_IIL_PIL.pdf>.

84 *Klöckner v Cameroon*, Decision on Annulment of 3 May 1985, ICSID Case No Arb/81/2, paras 69–73 <http://icsid.worldbank.org/ICSID/FrontServlet?requestType=CasesRH&actionVal=showDoc&docId=DC665_En&caseId=C127>.

85 *Texaco v Libya*, Ad Hoc Award of 19 January 1977, 17 ILM 1 (1978), paras 54–6.

86 *Texaco v Libya*, above n 85, at para 57 (footnote omitted).

international customary law, prominently when stating rules regarding reparation for expropriation.[87] A similar (somewhat confusing) approach was also undertaken in several awards rendered by the Iran-US Claims Tribunal.[88]

General principles of law are certainly considered a legitimate source of law in contemporary international investment law[89] but some authors have criticized their application by investment tribunals as being biased in favor of investors, and working to the detriment of developing countries.[90] General principles of law played a significant role in the formative period of international investment law, prominently in the oil concession arbitrations and in the pre-BIT era[91] (such as in the Iran-US Claims Tribunal)[92] but contemporary arbitral tribunals seem to have largely neglected them.[93] An empirical study conducted by Fauchald on ICSID case law[94] indicates that those tribunals have paid relatively little attention to this source of law as an interpretative source.[95] As stated in Fauchald's study:

> Contrary to what was expected, the tribunals examined general principles of law as a separate legal basis in only eight of the 98 decisions.[96]
>
> [. . .] Tribunals made use of general principles of law as an interpretive argument in only four decisions. Hence, even if international investment law is an area of law where there are close links between domestic and international law and where general principles derived from domestic legal systems may be expected to be of importance to the interpretation and application of international law, *there were few instances where such principles had practical significance.*

---

87 Gazzini, above n 82, 110; the *Phoenix* tribunal, for instance, refers several times to 'general principles of international law', *Phoenix v the Czech Republic*, above n 77, paras 80, 106.

88 Grant Hanessian, 'General Principles of Law in the Iran-U.S. Claims Tribunal' (1989) 27 *Columbia Journal of Transnational Law* 309, 323.

89 Gazzini, above n 82, 103 and 109–10; Schreuer *et al.*, above n 5, at 178–82.

90 See e.g. Sornarajah, above n 82, 94.

91 Schill, above n 83, 10.

92 On the importance of 'general principles of law' in Iran-US claims Tribunal's jurisprudence, see e.g. John R Crook, 'Applicable Law in International Arbitration: The Iran-US Claims Tribunal Experience' (1983) 83 *AJIL* 278, 292–9.

93 Schill, above n 83, 9.

94 Fauchalds analysis includes decisions rendered by ICSID tribunals in the period between 1 January 1998 and 31 December 2006 (98 decisions in 72 different cases); Ole K Fauchald, 'The Legal Reasoning of ICSID Tribunals – An Empirical Analysis' (2008) 19 *EJIL* 301, 304.

95 Ibid, at 326.

96 Ibid, at 312.

> Moreover, there was no thorough analysis of the content of the principles in any of the decisions, and the principles were not used as essential interpretive arguments, but rather as non-essential arguments or as general starting points for the subsequent analysis.[97] [emphasis added, footnotes omitted]

The relatively insignificant role of general principles of law in contemporary investment jurisprudence may be explained by the interrelationships between the various sources of international investment law and the general character of this source of law. As noted above, general principles have a residual nature and international tribunals tend to use them to fill remaining gaps in treaty and customary law. Thus, there is a clear trade-off between the number of rules existing in treaty/customary law and the resorting to general principles of law. The dramatic proliferation of investment treaties in recent decades, as well as the significant increase of investment awards pronouncing numerous customary norms, explain the diminishing need to apply the residual rules drawn from general principles of law. This factor indicates that investment tribunals are more likely to apply general principles of law to disputes that are not covered by treaty provisions or customary rules.

The second factor explaining the diminishing role of general principles of law in contemporary investment law relates to the vague nature of this source of law. As noted by some authors, the employment of general principles of law is accompanied by a high degree of subjectivity[98] and it generally grants considerable latitude to international tribunals. As Schwarzenberger noted in that regard, there is a concern that this source of law lends itself 'too readily to abuse'.[99] These concerns and the need for certainty and predictability in international investment relations lead to decreased resorting to this less certain source of law. Still, it is clear that there remain numerous vague rules in international investment law, and they may be clarified by application of general principles of law.

Certain soft law instruments, such as the UNCITRAL Model Law on Commercial Arbitration, have influenced states' legislation.[100] Such non-

---

97 Ibid, at 326.

98 Sornarajah, above n 82, 93.

99 Asif H Qureshi and Andreas H Ziegler, *International Economic Law* (2nd edn, Sweet & Maxwell 2007) 28.

100 On the impact of the UNCITRAL Model Law on Commercial Arbitration on states' domestic legislation, see e.g. Tan Leng Cheo & Partners, *International Commercial Arbitration: Singapore As A UNCITRAL Model Law Jurisdiction* (2002) <http://www.accountlaw-tax.com.sg/Website_tlc/ws-international%20arbitration.htm>; on the impact of other UNCITRAL model laws on domestic legislation, see e.g. Amelia H Boss, 'Electronic Commerce and the Symbiotic

binding instruments may, where adopted by numerous states, influence in turn the emergence of general principles of law.

IV. JUDICIAL DECISIONS

Article 38(1)(d) of the ICJ Statute provides that judicial decisions (along with scholarly writings) constitute 'subsidiary means for the determination of rules of law'. Though this provision indicates that judicial decisions play only a secondary role, international courts (and remarkably the ICJ) take part in the law-making process and significantly influence the development of international law. As Pellet stated:

> [T]here is no doubt that, in reality, the international jurisprudence and, primarily, the case law of the Court has been a powerful tool of consolidation and of evolution of international law.[101]

Decisions of international tribunals also play a significant role in the reality of international investment jurisprudence.[102] Accordingly, almost all investment awards in the past two decades include numerous references to prior decisions of investment tribunals.[103] As discussed above,[104] investment tribunals often cite decisions of the ICJ as authoritative statements of existing international legal rules, most prominently ICJ decisions regarding reparations,[105] state responsibility[106] and the law of

---

Relationship between International and Domestic Law Reform' (1998) 72 *Tulane Law Review* 1931, 1942, 1993–94; on the limits of such attempts to harmonize domestic laws, see Katharina Pistor, *The Standardization of Law and Its Effect on Developing Economies* (2000) <http://www.g24.org/PDF/g24-dp4.pdf>.

[101] Pellet, above n 68, 789; and see some prominent examples regarding the ICJ decisions in Pellet, 789–90, see also Boyle and Chinkin, above n 27, 268–9.

[102] See e.g. Andrea K Bjorklund, 'Investment Treaty Arbitral Decisions as Jurisprudence Constante' in Colin Picker, Isabella Bunn and Douglas Arner (eds), *International Economic Law: The State and Future of the Discipline* (Hart 2008) 265, 269 and the references therein.

[103] See e.g. Schreuer *et al.*, above n 5, 610–11; for more details, see e.g. Fauchald, above n 94, 339–42; Jeffery P Commission, 'Precedent in Investment Treaty Arbitration – A Citation Analysis of a Developing Jurisprudence' (2007) 24 *Journal of International Arbitration* 129.

[104] See Section II above.

[105] The *Chorzow Factory* Case, Judgment of 13 September 1928, (1928) PCIJ Series A, No 17.

[106] *Elettronica Sicula S.p.A. (ELSI) (United States v Italy)*, Judgment of 20 July 1989, (1989) ICJ Rep 15.

treaties.[107]

The role of judicial decisions in investment law brings to the fore the sensitive question of the precedential value of previous decisions by investment tribunals. Article 59 of the ICJ Statute[108] (also mentioned in Article 38(1)(d)), as well as Article 1136 of the NAFTA,[109] clearly reject the doctrine of precedent in international law[110] and investment tribunals have emphasized that they are not bound by awards rendered by other tribunals. Thus, for instance, the *AES* tribunal (Jurisdiction) stated in that regard:

> The provisions of Article 25 of the ICSID Convention together with fundamental principles of public international law dictate, among others, that the Tribunal respects: [. . .]d) the rule according to which each decision or award delivered by an ICSID Tribunal is only binding on the parties to the dispute settled by this decision or award. *There is so far no rule of precedent in general international law;* nor is there any within the specific ICSID system for the settlement of disputes between one State party to the Convention and the National of another State Party.[111] [emphasis added, footnote omitted]

Notwithstanding such statements regarding the absence of the doctrine of precedent in international investment law,[112] investment tribunals are likely to follow an accretion of rulings on the same subject matter (in similar circumstances) and develop *jurisprudence constante* to enhance stability and predictability in this sphere.[113] Thus, it is clear that 'a *de facto*

---

[107] See e.g. Schreuer *et al.*, above n 5, 610; Sornarajah, above n 82, at 95–6; Fauchald, above n 94, 341–42.

[108] Article 59 of the ICJ statute provides as follows: 'The decision of the Court has no binding force except between the parties and in respect of that particular case.'

[109] Article 1136 of the NAFTA provides as follows: 'An award made by a Tribunal shall have no binding force except between the disputing parties and in respect of the particular case.' North American Free Trade Agreement (NAFTA), 32 ILM 289 (1993).

[110] Article 53 of the ICSID Convention does not make specific mention of precedent, instead providing only that '[t]he award shall be binding on the parties and shall not be subject to any appeal or to any other remedy except those provided for in this Convention.'

[111] *AES Corporation v Argentina*, Decision on Jurisdiction of 26 April 2005, ICSID Case No ARB/02/17, para 23 <http://ita.law.uvic.ca/documents/AES-Argentina-Jurisdiction_001.pdf>.

[112] See additional citations in Peter Muchlinski, Federico Ortino and Christoph Schreuer (eds), *Oxford Handbook of International Investment Law* (OUP 2008) 1191–5.

[113] Bjorklund, above n 102, 265; thus, for instance, the *Impreglio* tribunal

practice of precedent certainly'[114] exists in international investment law, and most tribunals carefully examine earlier decisions and accept these as authority most of the time.[115]

Summarizing the existing state of affairs in investment jurisprudence, the *Suez* tribunal stated as follows:

> In interpreting this vague, flexible, basic, and widely used treaty term, this *Tribunal has the benefit of decisions by prior tribunals that have struggled strenuously, knowledgeably, and sometimes painfully, to interpret the words 'fair and equitable' in a wide variety of factual situations and investment relationships.* Many of these cases arose out of Argentina's economic crisis of 2001–2003. *Although this tribunal is not bound by such prior decisions, they do constitute 'a subsidiary means for the determination of the rules of [international] law.'* Moreover, considerations of basic justice would lead tribunals to be guided by the basic judicial principle that 'like cases should be decided alike,' unless a strong reason exists to distinguish the current case from previous ones. In addition, a recognized goal of international investment law is to establish a predictable, stable legal framework for investments, a factor that justifies tribunals in giving due regard to previous decisions on similar issues. *Thus, absent compelling reasons to the contrary, a tribunal should always consider heavily solutions established in a series of consistent cases.*[116] [emphasis added, footnotes omitted]

The investment tribunals' extensive reliance on previous decisions by other investment tribunals led Fauchald, after an empirical study of the case law[117] of the ICSID tribunals, to observe that 'it was quite common for tribunals to use case law as a means to establish a presumption in favor

---

stated as follows: '[T]he Arbitral Tribunal finds it unfortunate if the assessment of these issues would in each case be dependent on the personal opinions of individual arbitrators. The best way to avoid such a result is *to make the determination on the basis of case law whenever a clear case law can be discerned.*' (emphasis added), *Impregilo v Argentina*, Decision on Liability of 21 June 2011, ICSID Case No ARB/04/1, para 108 <http://icsid.worldbank.org/ICSID/FrontServlet?requestType=CasesRH&actionVal=showDoc&docId=DC2171_En&caseId=C109>.

114 Christoph Schreuer and Matthew Weiniger, 'A Doctrine of Precedent?' in Muchlinski *et al.*, above n 112, 1188.

115 Ibid, 119.

116 *Suez v Argentina*, Decision on Liability of 30 July 2010, ICSID Case No ARB/03/19, para 189 <http://ita.law.uvic.ca/documents/SuezVivendiAWGDecisiononLiability.pdf>.

117 On the impact of Iran-US Claims Tribunal's awards on ICSID tribunals, see Christopher S Gibson and Christopher R Drahozal, 'Iran-U.S. Claims Tribunal Precedent in Investor-State Arbitration' in Christopher R Drahozal and Christopher S Gibson, *The Iran-U.S. Claims Tribunal at 25* (OUP 2007) 1, 22.

of one result, and thus for placing a burden of proof on one of the parties'.[118]

Still, it is important to emphasize that the above pattern of *jurisprudence constante* in most spheres of investment law does not imply that investment tribunals always adopt the same position expressed by previous tribunals. This is particularly true with regards to inconsistent interpretations of similar treaty provisions regarding umbrella clauses,[119] the defense of 'necessity' (under the ILC rules on state responsibility),[120] and the applicability of BITs' MFN (most-favored-nation) clauses to dispute settlement provisions.[121]

'Soft law' rules are not legally binding and investment arbitrators have discretion whether to apply them in a particular dispute or not. Though not mandatory, the preceding sections on treaties and customary law show that such soft norms often influence investment tribunals.[122] These non-binding instruments fulfill three major functions in investment jurisprudence: interpreting ambiguous provisions included in international treaties,[123] filling gaps in existing international investment law, and supporting legal findings arising from other sources of investment law (e.g. deriving from treaty or customary law).

The gap-filling function was prominent, for instance, in the *OPIC* decision on the proposal to disqualify one of the arbitrators (Professor

---

[118] Fauchald, above n 94, 336–7, see also at 335.

[119] See e.g. *Eureko v Poland*, Partial Award on Liability of 19 August 2005, at 78–85 <http://www.eureko.net/press/eureko/archives/2005-09-05.asp>; *SGS v Pakistan*, Decision on Jurisdiction of 6 August 2003, ICSID Case No ARB/01/13, paras 166–8; *Duke v Ecuador*, Award of 18 August 2008, ICSID Case No ARB/04/19 <http://icsid.worldbank.org/ICSID/FrontServlet?requestType=CasesRH&actionVal=showDoc&docId=DC792_En&caseId=C44>.

[120] See e.g. *Enron v Argentina*, above n 36, at paras 288, 345; *LG&E International v Argentina*, Decision on Liability of 3 October 2006, ICSID Case No ARB/02/1, paras 201–66 <http://www.worldbank.org/icsid/cases/pdf/09_LGE_Liability_e.pdf>.

[121] See e.g. *Wintershall Aktiengesellschaft v Argentina*, Award of 8 December 2008, ICSID Case No ARB/04/14, para 193 <http://ita.law.uvic.ca/documents/Wintershall.pdf>; *Maffezini v Spain*, Award on Jurisdiction of 25 January 2000, ICSID Case No ARB/97/7, paras 56, 63 <http://ita.law.uvic.ca/documents/Maffezini-Jurisdiction-English_001.pdf>.

[122] On the factors that motivate legal decision-makers to follow soft law, see Gabrielle Kaufmann-Kohler, 'Soft Law in International Arbitration: Codification and Normativity' (2010) 1 *Journal of International Dispute Settlement* 1, 2–3 (and see the references therein).

[123] See Section II above.

Sands). The *OPIC* tribunal faced here a novel question regarding multiple appointments and disqualification of arbitrators. Since this question was not addressed in Article 14(1) of the ICSID Convention (regarding independence and impartiality of arbitrators), the tribunal resorted[124] to the IBA Guidelines on Conflicts of Interests in International Arbitration.[125] As to the function of supporting legal findings derived from the 'recognized sources' of investment law, the *World Duty Free* tribunal, for instance, cited the UN General Assembly Declaration against Corruption and Bribery in International Commercial Transactions (1996)[126] to support its conclusion that bribery is contrary to international public policy.[127]

V. SCHOLARLY WRITINGS

'Teachings of the most highly qualified publicists of the various nations' constitute the last source of international law mentioned in Article 38(1)(d) of the ICJ Statute, and they are referred to as a subsidiary means for the determination of international legal rules. The ICJ rarely refers to the opinions of writers[128] in its decisions (although more references appear in

---

[124] The tribunal stated in that regard: 'We accept that the IBA Guidelines are not conclusive for the purposes of the decision that we are required to make on this challenge, and that the examples contained in the IBA Guidelines are both non-exhaustive and not in themselves decisive of whether or not the standards set out in the guidelines for impartiality and independence of arbitrators have been met. The IBA Guidelines do, however, indicate that multiple appointments represent an issue relevant to impartiality and independence and, in our opinion, are correct in so doing.' *OPIC v Venezuela*, Decision of 5 May 2010, ICSID Case No ARB/10/14, para 48 <http://italaw.com/documents/OPICKarimumDisqualificationDecision.pdf>.

[125] IBA Guidelines on Conflicts of Interest in International Arbitration, Approved on 22 May 2004 by the Council of the International Bar Association (2004) <http://www.ibanet.org/Publications/publications_IBA_guides_and_free_materials.aspx#conflictsofinterest>.

[126] United Nations Declaration against Corruption and Bribery in International Commercial Transactions, 16 December 1996, 36 ILM 1043 (1997).

[127] *World Duty Free v Kenya*, Award of 31 August 2006, ICSID Case No ARB/00/7, para 145 <http://italaw.com/documents/WDFv.KenyaAward.pdf>; and see UN General Assembly Resolution 1803 on Permanent Sovereignty over Natural Resources, UN Doc A/5217 (14 December 1962) that was cited in the *Desert Line v Yemen*, Award of 6 February 2008, ICSID Case No ARB/05/17, para 157 <http://italaw.com/documents/DesertLine.pdf>.

[128] The rare exceptions are the references to *Oppenheim's International Law*, Hersch Lauterpacht and Gilbert Gidel; Pellet, above n 68, 791.

the opinions of individual judges).[129] Nevertheless, scholarly writings are an important source for organizing and analyzing the structure and content of international law; and for elucidating the nature, history and practice of the rules of law,[130] and they certainly influence tribunals' decisions.

In stark contrast to the practice of the ICJ, the WTO Appellate Body and the European Court of Human Rights (which rarely refer to writers' opinions), investment arbitrators refer to scholarly writings in almost all instances. Writers' publications are extensively used with regard to specific treaty interpretation and questions concerning rules of international customary law. Scholarly writings are often used to establish a point of departure for further legal analysis and tribunals frequently employ experts' writings to define 'tests' to be later utilized as conditions for applying rules.[131]

Scholarly writings include numerous references to soft law instruments, and preparatory works leading to non-binding instruments (such as the ILC rules on state responsibility) extensively cite a wide range of scholarly works.[132]

VI. RELATIONSHIPS BETWEEN SOURCES OF INVESTMENT LAW

Different rules deriving from various sources of investment law may contradict each other, and the proliferation of BITs as well as the increasing number of investment tribunals' awards are likely to engender more inconsistent rules. This section will briefly address the principal rules that regulate the relationship between the sources of international investment law.[133] International norms that are considered as *jus cogens* (peremptory norms)[134] prevail over all other inconsistent rules of international law.[135] Article 53 of the 1969 Vienna Convention on the Law

---

[129] Pellet, above n 68, 792.

[130] Shaw, above n 30, 113.

[131] Fauchald, above n 94, 152.

[132] See e.g. Draft articles on State Responsibility, above n 35, at 33 (note 49 *et seq.*).

[133] On the relationships between inconsistent treaties, see Section II above.

[134] Art 53 of the Vienna Convention defines rules of *jus cogens* as follows: 'For the purposes of the present Convention, a peremptory norm of general international law is a norm accepted and recognized by the international community of States as a whole as a norm from which no derogation is permitted and which can be modified only by a subsequent norm of general international law having the same character'. Vienna Convention on the Law of Treaties, above n 7.

[135] Art 53 of the Vienna Convention, above n 7; Robert Jennings and Arthur Watts, *Oppenheim's International Law* (9th edn, Longman 1996) 7–8.

of Treaties further establishes that such a conflicting treaty is void. The superior normative status of *jus cogens* rules[136] has also been confirmed in several investment awards.[137]

Unless peremptory rules of international law are involved, Article 103 of the United Nations Charter provides that the Charter's provisions prevail over other incompatible treaties.[138] The special status of the UN Charter's provisions was affirmed by the ICJ's decision in the *Lockerbie* case regarding the relationship between Article 25 of the Charter and the 1971 Montreal Convention for the Suppression of Unlawful Acts against the Safety of Civil Aviation.[139]

International investment tribunals have extensively cited various provisions of the Vienna Convention but they have yet to effectively resort to Article 53 regarding the primacy of the rules of *jus cogens* or UN Charter provisions over investment treaties. Still, these well-known principles of public international law may be applied by future investment tribunals. This is particularly true with regard to arguments regarding inconsistencies between human right treaties and investment treaties' obligations.[140]

---

[136] See also Conclusions 32–33 of Conclusions of the work of the Study Group on the Fragmentation of International Law, UN Doc A/61/10 (2006), para 251; the question regarding which rules of international law are considered *jus cogens* is not settled. The prominent examples that are mentioned in the International Law Commission's Commentary on Article 53 are the unlawful use of force contrary to the principles of the UN Charter, a treaty contemplating the performance of any other act criminal under international law, and a treaty contemplating or conniving at the commission of acts, such as trade in slaves, piracy, or genocide; *Yearbook of the International Law Commission* (1966, Vol. II(2)) 247–8; see also Dinah Shelton, 'Normative Hierarchy in International Law' (2006) 100 *AJIL* 297; David J Harris, *Cases and Materials on International Law* (6th edn, Sweet & Maxwell 2004) 856–8.

[137] *Phoenix v the Czech Republic*, above n 77, para 77; *Corn Products v Mexico*, Decision on Responsibility of 15 January2008, ICSID Case No ARB(AF)/04/1, para 149 <http://www.worldtradelaw.net/nafta11/CornProducts(Award).pdf>.

[138] Art 103 of the UN Charter provides as follows: 'In the event of a conflict between the obligations of the Members of the United Nations under the present Charter and their obligations under any other international agreement, their obligations under the present Charter shall prevail.' See also Art 30(1) of the Vienna Convention, above n 7, see also Conclusion 34 of the work of the Study Group on the Fragmentation of International Law, above n 136.

[139] *Questions of Interpretation and Application of the 1971 Montreal Convention arising from the Aerial Incident at Lockerbie (Libyan Arab Jamahiriya v United States of America)*, Order of 14 April 1992, (1992) ICJ Rep 3, para 39.

[140] On arguments regarding inconsistencies between BITs' provisions and human rights treaties, see Hirsch, above n 20, 21, 97–114.

Where rules of *jus cogens* or UN Charter provisions are not involved, different rules regulate the relationships between inconsistent rules of international law. Where the incompatible rules derive from *different* sources of international law (e.g. treaty rule vs customary law), an embedded hierarchy is apparent: Treaty and customary rules are regarded as *primary* sources of international law,[141] general principles of law are viewed as *complementary* rules and are applied in cases where the dispute cannot be settled either on the basis of treaties or custom,[142] and the judicial decisions and writings of authors are considered as *subsidiary* sources of international law.[143] Consequently, where a legal rule derives from either treaty or custom, it will generally prevail over rules derived from other sources of international law.

A more frequent and difficult question arises where different international rules derived from customary and treaty law. Such a contradiction may arise, for instance, where a rule included in an investment treaty is inconsistent with a customary rule regarding environmental protection. Under international law, treaty and custom generally have equal weight,[144] and inconsistencies are regulated by three interrelated principles: (i) *lex specialis derogat legi generali* – i.e. a specific rule prevails over a general one; (ii) *lex posterior derogat legi priori* – a later rule prevails over a prior one; and (iii) respecting the parties' intentions – where the parties intended to replace a rule deriving from one source of international law with another rule included in another source of law (e.g. replacing a customary rule with a treaty rule), the rule preferred by the parties will prevail.[145] The above principle regarding the priority of a specific rule over a general one was confirmed[146] by the *Enron* case in which the tribunal addressed the relationship between a rule included in the Argentina-US BIT (regarding emergency cases) and rule of customary

---

[141] Jennings and Watts, above n 135, at 24, 36; but Pellet expresses the view that in reality there is a priority of consideration given to treaty rules over customary rules, Pellet, above n 68, 773–5.

[142] See e.g. Pellet, above n 68, 776.

[143] Jennings and Watts, above n 135, 41–2; see also the discussion above on judicial decisions and scholarly writings (Sections IV and V).

[144] Damrosch *et al.*, above n 56, 109; but see Pellet, above n 68, 773–5.

[145] Conclusions 5, 10 and 24 of the work of the Study Group on the Fragmentation of International Law, above n 136; Damrosch *et al.*, above n 56 at 109.

[146] See also *Amoco v Iran*, above n 36, 222 (see also para 112); see some discussion on '*lex specialis*' in *CMS v Argentina*, Award on Jurisdiction of 17 July 2003, ICSID Case No ARB/01/8, para 48 <http://ita.law.uvic.ca/documents/cms-argentina_000.pdf>.

international law (article 25 of the ILC on state responsibility). The tribunal stated in that regard:

> The expert opinion of Dean Slaughter and Professor Burke-White expresses the view that the treaty regime is different and separate from customary law as it is *lex specialis. This is no doubt correct in terms that a treaty regime specifically dealing with a given matter will prevail over more general rules of customary law.* Had this been the case here the Tribunal would have started out its considerations on the basis of the Treaty provision and would have resorted to the Articles on State Responsibility only as a supplementary means. But the problem is that the Treaty itself did not deal with these elements.[147] [emphasis added]

VII. CONCLUDING REMARKS

The preceding sections discussed the sources of investment law and highlighted the distinctive features of this branch of international law *vis-à-vis* general international law, and also briefly elaborated on the interactions between non-binding instruments ('soft law') and the recognized sources of investment law. Bilateral investment treaties have a predominant role in investment disputes, a fact that raises several questions regarding the relationships between investment and non-investment treaties. Though investment tribunals have seriously examined arguments regarding the interactions between such treaties, thus far no investment tribunal has absolved a party to an investment dispute from its investment obligations (or significantly reduced the amount of compensation to be paid to the injured party) in such cases. Despite the major role of treaties, customary rules of international law play a significant role in investment disputes, prominently to fill gaps in existing treaty law (*lacunae*) and to assist tribunals in interpreting the particular treaty provisions in their light. An examination of decisions rendered by investment tribunals indicates that investment tribunals which pronounce various customary rules are inclined *not* to discuss the existence (or lack) of the separate components of 'practice' and '*opinio juris*', and that they frequently rely on decisions of international courts and tribunals as well as decisions of international bodies.

General principles of law played a significant role in the formative period of international investment law, prominently in the oil concession arbitrations and in the pre-BIT era (such as in the Iran-US Claims

---

147 *Enron v Argentina*, above n 36, para 334.

Tribunal) but recent empirical studies indicate that contemporary arbitral tribunals have largely neglected them. The relatively insignificant role of general principles of law in contemporary investment jurisprudence may be explained by the interrelationships between the various sources of international investment law (the growing numbers of treaties and tribunals' pronouncements regarding customary rules) as well as the inherently vague character of this source of law.

Though 'judicial decisions' are only considered as a 'subsidiary' source of public international law, almost all investment awards include numerous references to prior decisions of investment tribunals. Notwithstanding tribunals' statements regarding the absence of the doctrine of precedent in international investment law, investment tribunals are likely to follow the accretion of rulings on the same subject matter (in similar circumstances) and to develop *jurisprudence constante* to enhance stability and predictability in this sphere. Writers' publications are also merely considered as a 'subsidiary' source of international law but are often cited by investment tribunals. In stark contrast to the practice of the ICJ, the WTO Appellate Body and the European Court of Human Rights (which rarely refer to writers' opinions), investment arbitrators refer to scholarly writings in almost all instances.

Different rules deriving from various sources of investment law may contradict each other, and the proliferation of BITs as well as the increasing number of investment tribunals' awards are likely to engender more inconsistent rules. Investment tribunals have resorted to some rules of public international law regarding such inconsistencies (prominently the principle of '*lex specialis*'); but they have effectively not applied the hierarchical rules embodied in Article 53 of the Vienna Convention regarding *jus cogens* and Article 103 of the UN Charter regarding the superiority of the Charter's obligations *vis-à-vis* investment treaties.

Soft law rules are not legally binding but they often influence investment arbitrators. As elaborated above, the recognized sources included in Article 38 of the ICJ Statute interact with diverse soft law instruments in various manners. Non-binding instruments are occasionally employed by investment tribunals to interpret vague provisions included in binding international treaties. Furthermore, soft law instruments may provide evidence for both elements of international customary law ('practice' and '*opinio juris*'). International tribunals often consider 'verbal acts' that include various non-binding declarations as 'practice'. Similarly, soft declarations of international institutions (prominently General Assembly resolutions and ILC declarations) may fulfill the second element of *opinio juris*. Non-binding instruments often influence states' legislation and, where such instruments are adopted by numerous states, these pieces of legislation may in turn influence the emergence of general principles of law.

Judicial decisions by investment tribunals often resort to soft law rules. Such non-binding instruments fulfill three major functions in investment jurisprudence: interpreting open-textured provisions included in treaties, filling gaps in existing international investment law, and supporting legal findings arising from other sources of investment law (e.g. deriving from treaty or customary law). Scholarly writings include numerous references to soft law instruments and preparatory work leading to non-binding instruments (such as the ILC rules on state responsibility) extensively cite a wide range of scholarly works.

The above discussion on the diverse interactions between 'hard' and 'soft' law rules leads to the conclusion that binding legal rules and influential non-binding norms complement each other in the fabric of international investment law. This interaction enriches investment law and allows legal decision-makers (including arbitrators) resorting to soft instruments to shed light on open-textured terms included in treaties or customary law. Furthermore, the fact that non-binding instruments may provide evidence for both elements of international customary law ('practice' and '*opinio juris*') somewhat assimilates soft law into 'hard' law. Thus, the interactions between non-binding and binding rules (and particularly those derived from treaties or customary law) make it almost impossible to disentangle between 'soft' and 'hard' rules in the real life of international investment law.

3. Soft law in international law: an overview

Melaku Geboye Desta

I. CONTEXT

When the ILA Study Group on the Role of Soft Law Instruments in International Investment Law was established by the ILA Executive Council in November 2008, its mandate was 'to study the development of soft law instruments in international investment law and the feasibility of a "codification" of the present state of this field of international economic law'. The purpose of this chapter is to provide a broad, and far from comprehensive, overview of the large body of literature on soft law and its role in international law generally. While this chapter thus informs the rest of the book, it does not purport to provide a shared understanding of the concept or set limits to the scope of each contribution – indeed, each contributor wrote their chapter without reference to this introductory chapter or any constraint imposed by a Group-level understanding of what exactly we mean by soft law.

II. A BRIEF LOOK AT THE SOFT LAW LITERATURE

Concept

The question of whether there is any normative instrument or arrangement that lies somewhere below what is law, but above what is not law, in international relations, or more broadly whether there are different degrees of normativity in international law,[1] has generated a

[1] International law is often described as a normative system (with broadly three types of norms: prescriptive, prohibitive and permissive) and an operational system. See e.g. Rosalyn Higgins, *Problems and Process: International Law and How We Use It* (Clarendon Press 1993) 1; see also Prosper Weil, 'Towards Relative Normativity in International Law' (1983) 77 *AJIL* 413–42.

fascinating academic debate and a voluminous literature – a 'cottage industry', as Daniel Bodansky calls it[2] – over the past three decades in particular.[3] The binary image of a world in which a certain set of norms is either law or not law at all is increasingly being challenged, paving the way for the growing acceptance of a mid-way concept of 'soft law' that would occupy some space in between. It is a measure of the success of this debate that the use of adjectives like 'soft' and 'hard' before the word 'law' has become a part of the international lawyer's standard vocabulary.[4]

Different scholars define the term 'soft law' to mean many different things but there is a widely shared understanding that soft law refers to norms that are neither law, nor mere political or moral statements, but lie somewhere in between. In very general terms, Reisman's recent description of soft law as 'intentionally non-binding arrangements'[5] appears to be shared by most writers.[6] However, not all 'intentionally non-binding arrangements' can be called soft law, as otherwise the very concept would be too broad to serve any useful purpose. We thus need some way of differentiating between intentionally non-binding arrangements that are

---

[2] See Daniel Bodansky, 'Prologue to a Theory of Non-Treaty Norms' in Mahnoush H Arsanjani, Jacob Katz Cogan, Robert D Sloane and Siegfried Wiessner (eds), *Looking to the Future: Essays on International Law in Honor of W. Michael Reisman* (Martinus Nijhoff 2011) 122.

[3] For a comprehensive look at the issue of soft law, see Dinah Shelton (ed), *Commitment and Compliance: The Role of Non-Binding Norms in the International Legal System* (OUP 2000).

[4] See Mary Footer, 'The (Re)turn to "Soft Law" in Reconciling the Antinomies in WTO Law' (2010) 11 *Melbourne Journal of International Law* 241–76, 246 (arguing that the functionalist approach to soft law, which accords an important role for soft law in global governance, 'has won the day').

[5] See W Michael Reisman, 'Soft Law and Law Jobs' (2011) 2:1 *Journal of International Dispute Settlement* 25–30, 25.

[6] Boyle and Chinkin also present 'soft law' as 'a convenient description for a variety of non-legally binding instruments used in contemporary international relations'. Alan Boyle and Christine Chinkin, *The Making of International Law* (OUP 2007) 212. According to Shaw, the term soft law 'is meant to indicate that the instrument or provision in question is not of itself "law", but its importance within the general framework of international legal development is such that particular attention requires to be paid to it'. Malcolm N Shaw, *International Law* (4th edn, Cambridge 1997) 494–5. But note also Bruno Simma, 'A Hard Look at Soft Law' (1988) 82 *American Society of International Law Proceedings* 380 (arguing that in fields such as international human rights law, soft law plays roles as significant as defining the precise content of hard law and it is 'quite imprecise' to regard it as legally nonbinding).

meant to remain mere political statements[7] and those that are created with some form of expectation of legal relevance or that later acquire such attributes. Joseph Gold captured this point well when he said, 'the essential ingredient of soft law is an expectation that the states accepting these instruments will take their content seriously and will give them some measure of respect'.[8] More recently, Timothy Meyer took a similar view when he defined soft law obligations as 'those international obligations that, while not legally binding themselves, are created with the expectation that they will be given some indirect legal effect through related binding obligations under either international or domestic law'.[9] Lowe's description of soft law as 'norms that are not themselves legally binding but form part of the broader normative context within which expectations of what is reasonable or proper State behaviour are formed'[10] also appears to emphasize this element of expectation of legal or normative relevance. It is in this broad sense of non-binding arrangements with the expectation, or effect, of legal relevance that we use the term 'soft law' in this chapter.[11]

---

[7] In an older article, Reisman called them 'statements in the subjunctive mood'. W Michael Reisman, 'A Hard Look at Soft Law' (1988) 82 *American Society of International Law Proceedings* 373.

[8] See Joseph Gold, 'Strengthening the Soft International Law of Exchange Arrangements' (1983) 77 *AJIL* 443.

[9] Timothy Meyer, 'Soft Law as Delegation' (2009) 32:3 *Fordham International Law Journal* 888, 889–90.

[10] See Vaughan Lowe, *International Law* (OUP 2007) 95–6. Lowe helpfully uses technical standards set by such international institutions as the World Health Organization (WHO) and the Codex Alimentarius Commission as examples of soft law instruments that are 'increasingly relied upon in order to give precise substance to international rules that are framed in general terms.' Ibid, 95.

[11] At the same time, this understanding of soft law is also narrower than the way some scholars define it. For example, Guzman and Meyer define soft law simply as 'quasi-legal rules that are not legally binding on states', but they explicitly extend the scope of this concept to cover what is traditionally called 'case law', i.e. the judgments and awards rendered by international tribunals. See Andrew T Guzman and Timothy L Meyer, 'International Common Law: The Soft Law of International Tribunals' (2009) 9:2 *Chicago Journal of International Law* 518. Guzman and Meyer now call these 'international common law' and describe them as another form of soft law in that while a judgment of the ICJ, a report of the WTO Appellate Body or an international investment arbitration award is strictly binding only on the parties to the particular case to the exclusion of all other parties to the underlying treaties, in fact, the decisions of international tribunals have their 'broadest effect' as soft law: 'the decisions of international tribunals at most bind the parties to the dispute before the tribunal on the facts of the case, but their nonbinding interpretation of hard legal obligations affects the legal expectations of all states subject to the underlying obligation.' Ibid, 535. While I recognize the role

Understood in this sense, the term soft law applies, for example, to international standards, guidelines and recommendations created by intergovernmental institutions in their spheres of competence;[12] vague, weak or exhortative provisions contained in international treaties; non-binding declarations and resolutions of the organs of international treaty bodies; treaty interpretations by non-judicial treaty bodies, such as the 'comments' of the UN Human Rights Committee;[13] and, increasingly, the standards, guidelines and codes of conduct issued by international private, professional or other trade bodies.[14]

Role of Soft Law

The broad consensus on the general meaning of soft law does not extend to its utility or role within the international law system. There is a wide spectrum of views held by scholars on this issue, which ranges from those who consider soft law to be an essential element of international law (soft law advocates), to those who are highly sceptical, even dismissive, of the very concept of soft law (soft law sceptics); there is also a third and significant group of scholars in the middle who take more nuanced approaches to soft law, dismissing it as irrelevant for certain purposes while in the same breath considering it useful for other purposes (the third group).[15] In the rest of this chapter, I will highlight these different views

---

of case law in influencing the legal expectations of states parties to a particular treaty or other legal relationship, I do not see the utility of extending the soft law concept to capture an already well-defined and reasonably well-understood 'source' of international law.

12 For more on this, see Desta, Chapter 7, this volume.

13 See <http://www2.ohchr.org/english/bodies/hrc/>.

14 For a useful tool in understanding the different degrees of softness and hardness in international law norms, see Kenneth W Abbott and Duncan Snidal, 'Hard and Soft Law in International Governance' (2000) 54:3 *International Organization* 421–56. Abbott and Snidal define international hard law as 'legally binding obligations that are precise (or can be made precise through adjudication or the issuance of detailed regulations) and that delegate authority for interpreting and implementing the law.' Ibid, 421. Any agreement that lacks in any one or more of the three dimensions of legalization falls under the category of soft law, but its degree of softness varies depending on how many of these dimensions is missing and so on.

15 Shaffer and Pollack put the existing literature relating to soft law in three camps: the legal positivists (who 'tend to favour hard law and view hard and soft law in binary terms'), the rationalists (who contend that 'hard and soft law have different attributes that states choose for different contexts') and the constructivists (who maintain that 'state interests are formed through socialization processes of

under these three broad groupings.[16]

The Soft Law Advocates

According to Joseph Gold, it is 'easy to be too condescending toward soft law'[17] but soft law serves a number of important functions in the international system. Soft law, argues Gold, helps overcome deadlocks in inter-state relations; its application can produce over time an accretion of hard law; and in certain circumstances, soft law may be 'the only alternative to anarchy'.[18]

Christine Chinkin rejects the binary approach that an instrument is either law or not law.[19] For Chinkin, the reality is that both traditional international legal forms and soft law instruments 'play a major role in the development of international law and both are needed for the regulation of States' activities and for the creation of expectations'.[20]

Fastenrath argues that relative normativity[21] in international law, including recognition of soft law as distinct from hard law, is 'unavoidable'.[22] According to Fastenrath, soft law performs a number of highly valuable functions, such as helping generate better understanding of international hard law through more detailed definitions and legal standards and serving as an early version of future hard law. For Fastenrath, soft law plays such an important role in international law that, in its absence, 'the law would founder on the rocks of divergent legal concepts and modes of interpretation'.[23]

Dinah Shelton argues that soft law is an important part of the international legal system which works in dynamic interaction with hard

---

interstate interaction which hard and soft law can facilitate'). See Gregory C Shaffer and Mark A Pollack, 'Hard vs. Soft Law: Alternatives, Complements, and Antagonists in International Governance' (2010) 94 *Minnesota Law Review* 706, 707–8.

16 I need to point out here that I use these categories with a significant degree of simplification for illustrative purposes only; otherwise, it is clear that some authors probably fall in more than category.

17 Gold, above n 8, 443.

18 Gold, above n 8, 444.

19 See Christine M Chinkin, 'The Challenge of Soft Law: Development and Change in International Law' (1989) 38 *ICLQ* (1989) 850–66.

20 Ibid, 866.

21 For a discussion on this, see Weil, above n 1, 413–42.

22 See Ulrich Fastenrath, 'Relative Normativity in International Law' (1993) 4 *EJIL* 305–40.

23 Ibid, 324.

law and exercises a 'complex and potentially large impact in the development of international law'.[24] According to Shelton, several reasons may explain the choice of soft law over hard law instruments, including respect for hard law, the use of soft law as tools to induce non-participating states to conform, a state of uncertainty about underlying issues, its suitability for non-state actor involvement, and the ease with which it can be adopted and adapted.[25]

Kirton and Trebilcock also argue that the world has increasingly turned to soft law in order to make 'hard choices' because soft law offers several advantages over hard law, such as the possibility for action when governments are not ready for hard law commitments and the opportunities for civil society to have a say in global governance.[26]

O'Connell views soft law as one of the instruments we have developed to deal with a complex and globalized world.[27] Boyle and Chinkin, in their 2007 book, make the case for soft law in more comprehensive terms, arguing that soft law facilitates progressive evolution of international law and presents alternatives to law-making by treaty and at times complements it.[28] Guzman sees the difference between soft law and the traditional sources of international law as merely 'a matter of degree rather than of kind'; for Guzman, soft law 'must be part of the discussion about international law if we are to make any sense of how the international legal system influences state behavior.[29]

---

[24] Shelton, above n 3, 1, 11. Shelton noted that 'the international legal system appears to be a complex, dynamic web of interrelationships between hard and soft law, national and international regulation, and various institutions that seek to promote the rule of law. In this system, soft law is playing increasingly important and varied roles.' Ibid, 18.

[25] Ibid, 12–13.

[26] See John J Kirton and Michael J Trebilcock (eds), *Hard Choices, Soft Law: Voluntary Standards in Global Trade, Environment and Social Governance* (Aldershot 2004) 5. In a review of this volume, Sindico sees soft law as 'a very useful instrument in those cases in which hard law is still not feasible because states are not yet willing to commit to binding international legal norms, or in those cases in which hard law has proved to be ineffective.' See Francesco Sindico, 'Soft Law and the Elusive Quest for Sustainable Global Governance' (2006) 19 *Leiden Journal of International Law* 829–846, 832.

[27] O'Connell argues that soft law is a device that is 'already playing a key role' in our 'transition to a global society under law'. Mary E O'Connell, 'The Role of Soft Law in a Global Order' in Shelton, above n 3, 100.

[28] See Boyle and Chinkin, above n 6, 229; see also Alan Boyle, 'Some Reflections on the Relationship of Soft Law and Treaties' (1999) 48 *ICLQ* 901–13.

[29] See Andrew T Guzman, *How International Law Works: A Rational Choice Theory* (OUP 2008) 9.

More recently, in an article that discussed the concept and role of mainly private-sector-generated procedural soft law in international commercial arbitration, Kaufmann-Kohler argued that soft law 'carries a certain normative weight' and that codification of soft law 'serves a useful purpose in increasing certainty and predictability'.[30] Slaughter goes even further and argues that soft law, compared to hard law, 'is emerging as an equally powerful, if not more powerful, form of regulation'.[31]

The Soft Law Sceptics

This group mainly, though not exclusively, covers those scholars who perceive law in binary terms; something is either law or is not law at all; there is nothing in the middle. However, there are different types of scepticism represented here, ranging from those who simply avoid the use of the term soft law altogether to those who would be prepared to recognize it, but only for the *soft content* of formally international law instruments.

Prosper Weil believes that before we use the adjectives 'soft' and 'hard' before the word 'law', we must first ensure that we are referring to 'law' in the strict sense, as determined by the form that a normative act is contained in. Once we have a normative act, such as a treaty, we can talk about the hardness or softness of its content. In the absence of a normative act, however, such as when we deal with the resolutions of some international organizations, we are in a sub-legal world where there is no room to talk about law, and the adjectives qualifying it would not make sense. From this, Weil proceeds to advise that:

> It would seem better to reserve the term 'soft law' for rules that are imprecise and not really compelling, since *sublegal obligations are neither 'soft law' nor 'hard law': they are simply not law at all.* Two basically different categories are involved here; for while there are, on the one hand, legal norms that are not in practice compelling, because too vague, there are also, on the other hand, provisions that are precise, yet remain at the pre- or subnormative stage. To discuss both of these categories in terms of 'soft law' or 'hard law' is to foster confusion.[32]

---

[30] See Gabrielle Kaufmann-Kohler, 'Soft Law in International Arbitration: Codification and Normativity' (2010) 1:2 *Journal of International Dispute Settlement* 283, 299.

[31] See Anna-Marie Slaughter, *A New World Order* (Princeton University Press 2005) 178.

[32] Weil, above n 1, 414–15 (emphasis added).

Klabbers recognizes only a binary system in which norms are either law or not law at all and dismisses 'soft law' as redundant.[33] For Klabbers, 'within the binary mode, law can be more or less specific, more or less determinate, more or less wide in scope, more or less pressing, more or less serious, more or less far-reaching; the only thing it cannot be is more or less binding'.[34]

Raustiala agrees that '[t]here is no such thing as "soft law." The concept of soft law purports to identify something between binding law and no law. Yet as an analytic or practical matter no meaningful intermediate category exists. . . . soft law agreement is not a coherent concept; nor does it accord with state practice.'[35] In order to more accurately demarcate between what is law and what is law-like but not law, Raustiala suggests that we distinguish instead between pledges and contracts in international law, where contracts 'create legally binding obligations for states, while pledges create only political or moral obligations'.[36] This, according to Raustiala, is a distinction 'between the use of law and the avoidance of law'.[37] Like Raustiala, Goldsmith and Posner avoid the term 'soft law' altogether 'because nonlegal agreements are not binding under international (or any other) law, so it is confusing to call them law, soft or otherwise'.[38]

More recently, Jean d'Aspremont focused on what he calls the 'fundamental flaw of the softness theory', which in his view results from the inability of some scholars to distinguish between legal acts and legal facts.[39] According to d'Aspremont, an act is considered a 'legal act' when its legal effects originate directly 'in the will of the legal subject to whom the behaviour is attributed and not to any pre-existing rule in the system', while 'those acts which yield legal effects but which are not a direct consequence of the will of legal persons' or 'whose legal effects originate in

---

33 See Jan Klabbers, 'The Redundancy of Soft Law' (1996) 65 *Nordic Journal of International Law* 167–82.

34 Ibid, 181.

35 Kal Raustiala, 'Form and Substance in International Agreements' (2005) 99 *AJIL* 586–7.

36 Ibid, 586.

37 Ibid.

38 See Jack L Goldsmith and Eric A Posner, *The Limits of International Law* (OUP 2005) 81–2.

39 Jean d'Aspremont, 'Softness in International Law: A Self-Serving Quest for New Legal Materials' (2008) 9:5 *EJIL* 1075–93. Indeed, d'Aspremont goes as far as accusing the proponents of soft law of harbouring a hidden agenda 'to broaden the international law discipline beyond its original ambit with a view to expanding the potential objects that they can seize and study'. Ibid.

the legal system itself, which provides for such an effect prior to the adoption of the act' are called legal facts. According to d'Aspremont, it is the legal act that 'usually allows legal subjects to create new rules'. Putting all these premises together, d'Aspremont concludes:

> the claim of the softness of international law does not pertain to those behaviours which create legal effects irrespective of the will of the state (*fait juridique*). There is no such thing as a soft international legal fact. In a positivist logic, although contested, softness can be envisaged only in connection with legal acts in the strict sense, as it is necessarily the outcome of the intention of the subjects, not the result of a pre-existing rule of the international legal system. In other words, softness is not programmed by the international legal order but is simply determined by its subjects and, for that reason, only legal acts can prove soft.[40]

Pursuing this a step further, d'Aspremont then distinguishes between rules with a *soft instrumentum*, in the sense of rules contained in a non-legal instrument, i.e. neither a treaty nor a binding unilateral promise, and rules with a *soft negotium*, i.e. rules contained in a legal instrument but without imposing a specific legal obligation.[41] He then concludes effectively that there can be soft content contained in a hard law instrument but there cannot be a soft law instrument as such. In his own words: 'The only softness which law can accommodate is the softness of the *negotium*, that is when a rule undoubtedly constitutes a legal rule but fails, because it lacks precision or hinges on the adoption of complementary legal instruments, to provide any precise directive as to which behaviours the addressees must live up to.'[42] What is also interesting is that d'Aspremont himself does not deny that those same instruments that do not meet the requirements to be called soft law, i.e. those contained in a soft *instrumentum*, still produce legal consequences: 'It is undisputed, even by positivists, that acts with a soft *instrumentum* still produce legal effects. For instance, they can play a role in the internationalization of the subject-matter, provide guidelines for the interpretation of other legal acts, or pave the way for further subsequent practice which may one day be taken into account for the emergence of customary international norm.'[43] To this extent at least d'Aspremont's

---

40 Ibid, 1077–81.

41 See ibid, 1081–7.

42 See Jean d'Aspremont, 'Softness in International Law: A Self-Serving Quest for New Legal Materials: A Rejoinder to Tony D'Amato' (2009) 20:3 *EJIL* 911–17, 914 (footnotes omitted).

43 See d'Aspremont, above n 39, 1082.

approach is much more nuanced than many other critics of the soft law thesis.

The Third Group

Professor Michael Reisman has been an enthusiastic advocate of the soft law thesis for a very long time. Defining law in terms of the three elements of content (what law asks us to do or not do), authority signal (which distinguishes it from, e.g., moral statements) and control intention to make it effective (which others would call a sanction), Reisman argued in 1988 that 'law can be soft in all its dimensions: in terms of its content, in terms of its authority, and in terms of its control intention'.[44] More recently, Reisman argued that soft law is 'a useful tool for some international law jobs', such as '[t]hose who are trying to understand the complex and phased international law-making processes'.[45] Reisman could thus easily fit in under the first category, but his approach is much more nuanced than many of the advocates. In his 2011 article, Reisman went further and argued that, for certain types of 'law jobs', such as those of adjudication and arbitration, the term soft law is unsuitable:

> The adjective 'soft', when used to modify the word 'law', brings to mind the adverb 'slightly', when used to modify the word 'pregnant'. The trader, the investor, the executive signing off on her company's balance sheet and the soldier on the battlefield, must all be able to incorporate into their respective decision-making what the law prohibits and permits, lest they suffer penalties or jail. For all of these law jobs, the notion that, besides 'law', there is also something out there called 'soft' or 'slightly' law is not helpful.[46]

Shaffer and Pollack also take a similarly nuanced, but much more developed, approach that examines soft law at two different stages – *ex ante* at the negotiation stage and *ex post* at the enforcement stage. From an *ex post* enforcement perspective, they argue that 'to a judge, a given instrument is either legally binding or non-binding', but they add: 'a formally non-binding instrument can normatively affect a judge's interpretation of the meaning of the terms of a formally binding instrument'.[47] While this brings them closer to positivists like d'Aspremont, they also go further and argue that, 'from an *ex ante*

---

44 See Reisman, above n 7, 374.
45 See Reisman, above n 5, 25.
46 See ibid, 26.
47 Shaffer and Pollack, above n 15, 716.

negotiating perspective, actors have choices that, in practice, can render agreements relatively more or less binding'.[48] They conclude that hard and soft law 'are best seen not as binary categories but rather as choices arrayed along a continuum'.[49] Reisman's binary approach and dismissal of the concept of soft law for the 'law jobs' of the judge and the arbitrator appears to closely follow the approach taken by Shaffer and Pollack who call it the '*ex post* enforcement perspective' of soft law, whereas Reisman's readiness to see the benefits of soft law for the law jobs of the academic or lobbyist interested in the international rule-making process appears in line with Shaffer and Pollack's '*ex ante* negotiating perspective' of soft law. Shaffer and Pollack's most original contribution to the debate lies in their insight that hard and soft law can operate not only as alternatives and complements but also, and often, as 'antagonists'[50] and their hypotheses about the different scenarios in which this interaction can assume a particular form.[51]

Conclusion

The preceding brief survey of the literature supports the following broad conclusions about soft law and its role in the international law system.

---

48 Ibid.

49 Ibid.

50 Shaffer and Pollack argue that the interaction between hard and soft law instruments is 'not necessarily mutually supportive but also can counteract and undermine each other under certain conditions.' Shaffer and Pollack (2010), above n 15, 744.

51 Shaffer and Pollack hypothesize that the positions assumed by powerful states in international negotiations are crucial in determining the type of interaction between hard law and soft law in a particular area. Their five hypotheses thus go as follows: 1. where powerful states agree on a common policy, hard and soft law are more likely to work as complements in an evolutionary manner; 2. where these states disagree on policy, hard and soft law are likely to work in opposition to each other; 3. even where powerful states agree on a regulatory approach, smaller states that are adversely affected can use international hard and soft law strategies to attempt to thwart powerful states' aims, with the result that hard and soft law are likely to act as antagonists; 4. even where powerful states prevail in negotiations at the international level *vis-à-vis* third countries, domestic actors aiming to frustrate the implementation of agreements can mobilize to seek the adoption of new international hard or soft law instruments designed to act as antagonists to existing ones; and 5. while states have a spectrum from which they may choose in using hard and soft law instruments to counter existing international law, more powerful states are more likely to be able to obtain the adoption of new hard law provisions, while less powerful states are more likely to rely solely on soft-law provisions in their attempts to counter existing international law. Ibid, 765–90.

First, a significant majority of the scholars who have published on the subject recognize that soft law plays some role in the making, interpretation and development of international law. Second, following Shaffer and Pollack's distinction between *ex post* and *ex ante* perspective of international law, it appears that everyone who recognizes soft law recognizes its role *ex ante* at the negotiation and development phase of international law while most deny a role for soft law *ex post* at the enforcement stage of international law. On the latter, both the literature and the jurisprudence appear to revert to the binary world of international law where something is either law or not law, and only law can be enforced through courts and other tribunals. Once they have identified the relevant law, judges and arbitrators are likely to resort to soft law in their efforts to interpret and apply the law, just as they would refer to a dictionary to determine the meaning of a term or prior judicial or arbitral decisions on similar cases so as to learn any lessons without being bound to follow them.[52] Finally, even when judges and arbitrators do not explicitly refer to them, soft law instruments are also likely to play a part in their reasoning and decision-making.[53]

---

[52] See e.g. *Chemtura Corporation v Canada* (Arbitration Award 2010), available at <http://www.international.gc.ca/trade-agreements-accords-commerciaux/assets/pdfs/Chemtura_Award_Aug_2010.pdf> para 109.

[53] It is this approach that I develop in Chapter 7 of this volume.

4. Assessing the effectiveness of soft law instruments in international investment law

Andrea K. Bjorklund[*]

The term 'soft law' entered the international lexicon in the 1970s as a descriptive and differentiating phrase:[1] soft law was anything that was not, in fact, hard law promulgated by a governmental body authorized to enact it, but that nonetheless was designed to affect, or actually did affect, behavior and that might in time solidify into hard law or otherwise affect the development of hard law.[2] Though the phraseology was perhaps new, the existence of non-binding written instruments designed to influence the development of the law or designed themselves to become law at an

* I thank Lee Ann Bambach and Seán Duggan for helpful suggestions.

1 Lord McNair is usually credited with the first use of the expression. Dinah Shelton, 'Introduction: Law, Non-Law and the Problem of "Soft Law"' in Dinah Shelton (ed), *Commitment and Compliance: The Role of Non-Binding Norms in the International Legal System* (OUP 2000) 1, 22. See also Jan Klabbers, 'Reflections on Soft International Law in a Privatized World' (2005) XVI *Finnish YB Int'l L* 313, 314 (noting that prior to the introduction of 'soft' law one did not need to describe law as 'hard'.).

2 There are numerous definitions of soft law. Francis Snyder describes soft law as 'rules of conduct which, in principle, have no legally binding force but which nevertheless may have practical effects'. Francis Snyder, 'Soft Law and Institutional Practice in the European Community' in Steve Martin (ed), *The Construction of Europe – Essays in Honour of Emile Noël* (Kluwer 1993) 198. Ulrika Mörth has described soft law as 'the well-known phenomenon in global politics – governance without government'. Ulrika Mörth, 'Preface' in Ulrika Mörth, *Soft Law in Governance and Regulation* (Edward Elgar 2004) ix; Timothy Meyer writes: '[S]oft legal obligations are those international obligations that, while not legally binding themselves, are created with the expectation that they will be given some indirect legal effect through related binding obligations under either international or domestic law.' Timothy Meyer, 'Soft Law as Delegation' (2009) 32:3 *Fordham International Law Journal* 888, 889–90.

appropriate stage existed in both municipal and international law long before 'soft law' achieved currency of use.[3]

The very idea of soft law has engendered controversy and criticism. An initial question is one of nomenclature; should instruments that fall outside the category of 'hard' law be in any way dignified with the term 'law', even or especially when allied to the word 'soft'?[4] This chapter will not address the desirability of the coinage of the phrase 'soft law'; rather, it will assume the existence of instruments that on the international plane fall outside the sources of law as defined in Article 38 of the Statute of the International Court of Justice,[5] and that on the municipal plane have not been promulgated by official law-makers, e.g. legislative bodies, but that can and do have an effect on behavior, and will accept that those instruments are commonly described as embodying 'soft law'.[6] Nor will the chapter grapple with the larger question of whether soft law has a destabilizing effect on the viability of international law generally. Those

---

[3] For example, the Institut de Droit International was founded in 1873 to contribute to the development of international law and its subsequent implementation. Once the plenary Assembly receives the work of a Commission entrusted with studying a particular area of law, the Institute, when appropriate, adopts resolutions 'of a normative character', which are then brought to the attention of governmental authorities, international organizations, and the general community, in order to 'highlight the characteristics of the lex lata in order to promote its respect. Sometimes [the Institute] makes determinations de lege ferenda in order to contribute to the development of international law'. Institut de Droit International, 'History' <http://www.idi-iil.org/idiE/navig_history.html> accessed 28 October 2011.

[4] Klabbers, above n 1, 314; Richard B Bilder, 'Beyond Compliance: Helping Nations Cooperate', in Shelton, above n. 1, 65, 71 (questioning coherence and usefulness of the term 'soft international law' but noting pervasiveness of distinctions between binding and non-binding arrangements in municipal and international law).

[5] Article 38 identifies the sources of international law as: 'a. international conventions, whether general or particular, establishing rules expressly recognized by the contesting states; b. international custom, as evidence of a general practice accepted as law; c. the general principles of law recognized by civilized nations; d. subject to the provisions of Article 59, judicial decisions and the teachings of the most highly qualified publicists of the various nations, as subsidiary means for the determination of rules of law.'

[6] Andrew Guzman argues that international law should be viewed as incorporating soft law, as well as the traditional categories found in the Statute, because many 'soft-law' instruments nonetheless represent commitments by a State which, if breached, will have a reputational effect. Andrew Guzman, 'A Compliance-Based Theory of International Law' (2002) 90 *Cal Law Rev* 1823, 1825.

issues have been thoroughly and ably canvassed elsewhere.[7]

This chapter will analyze the likely effectiveness of different types of soft law instruments in the area of investment law. Section I discusses the role of soft law instruments generally and surveys those characteristics that make them successful. It addresses the relationship between form and function, and their effect on the type of instrument one uses, as well as the relationship between form and substance, and their effect on the precision of the principles sought to be concretized. It examines the process used to identify soft law and define its contours, as well as the effect the participants in the process of formulating soft law instruments have on the outcome of any given exercise. Finally it examines the influence of the identity of the projected consumer of the product on an instrument's ultimate form and content. Section II surveys three categories of soft law instruments in light of their primary purposes and analyzes significant forms of soft law instruments – both municipal and international – *vis-à-vis* their ability to further those goals. This is a daunting task given the plethora of soft law instruments, but I have focused on those most commonly used and most likely to have characteristics making them attractive or useful in the international investment context. The chapter will assess the strengths and weakness of the form of instrument in light of the factors identified in Section 1 in discussing the advantages and disadvantages of attempting to craft soft law instruments in the area of international investment law.

I. IDENTIFYING THE ROLES PLAYED BY 'SOFT LAW' INSTRUMENTS AND ASSESSING THEIR EFFECTIVENESS

As Michael Reisman has noted, soft law is a concept, and concepts are tools to be used in the performance of various jobs.[8] The concept of soft

---

7 A small sampling includes Christine M Chinkin, 'The Challenge of Soft Law; Development and Change in International Law' (1989) 38 *ICLQ* 8501; Prosper Weil, 'Towards Relative Normativity in International Law?' (1983) 77 *AJIL* 413, 414–18; Gregory C Shaffer and Mark A Pollack, 'Hard vs. Soft Law: Alternatives, Complements and Antagonists in International Governance' (2010) 94 *Minnesota Law Review* 706, 712–27; Salem H Nasser, *Sources and Norms of International Law: A study on soft law* (Galda Wilch Verlag 2008); Catherine Kessedjian, 'Codification du Droit Commercial International et Droit International Privé' (2002) 300 Recueil des Cours 79; W Michael Reisman, 'A Hard Look at Soft Law' (1988) *American Society of International Law Proceedings* 373.

8 W Michael Reisman, 'Soft Law and Law Jobs' (2011) 2 *JIDS* 25, 25.

law is effective in alerting users 'to the possibility of different levels in the three components of any legal formulation:

- Degrees of clarity or lack of clarity in the normative content of a legal formulation and, perforce, the degree of discretion that will be deployed by whatever court or tribunal is called upon to apply it;
- Degrees of authority that attach to a legal formulation;
- Degrees to which the legal formulation, upon which users may be about to rely, enjoys political support and is controlling.'[9]

Using the term 'soft law' might give extra legitimacy to instruments that lack formal legal status. To the extent that the word 'law' is deemed to have concrete effect, the phrase 'soft law' gives more weight to the instrument it describes. For example, using the term soft law enables proponents of yet-to-be-enacted legislation, such as members of civil society, various interest groups, or even government officials, to attach the word 'law' to their proposals in advance of their concrete adoption.[10] To the extent that soft law is viewed as an intermediate step in the transmission of an idea into a law, it suggests some advancement along that continuum.[11]

Soft law instruments are created for multiple reasons and are designed to serve various functions.[12] The variety of soft law instruments is virtually endless. I identify three main categories in light of the focus of this book on preparing a feasibility study of the preparation of a soft law instrument on international investment. Some soft law might be described as emergent hard law, leading either to the formalization of a binding instrument or to the formation of customary international law.[13] Soft law might also build upon or fill gaps in hard law, elaborating upon framework commitments or otherwise filling *lacunae* in existing regulation.[14] Soft law might also be intended to describe and possibly to influence the development of hard

---

9 Ibid, 25. See also Bilder, above n 4, 66–7.

10 Reisman, above n 8, 26–7.

11 Guzman, above n 6, 1828 ('[soft law] should be recognized as part of a spectrum of commitment along which states choose to locate their promises').

12 See e.g. Dinah Shelton, 'Introduction: Law, Non-Law and the Problem of "Soft Law"' in Shelton, above n 1, 10 (noting that soft law is used most frequently as a precursor to hard law or as a supplement to a hard law instrument).

13 Christine Chinkin, 'Normative Development in the International Legal System' in Shelton, above n 1, 30–1.

14 Ibid.

law; treatises, annotations, commentaries and restatements often encapsulate existing disparate principles and also seek to influence the development of the law.[15] In these classic examples, soft law and hard law are often thought of as acting either as complements or as alternatives to each other; recently Greg Shaffer and Mark Pollack have suggested that soft and hard law can act as antagonists as well should actors seek to undermine existing hard law with which they disagree by resorting to the promulgation of competing soft law instruments.[16]

A soft law instrument will be accounted successful if it has achieved its desired effect, or possibly even if it has achieved a portion of its desired effect. It would be expecting too much to think that all soft law instruments should coalesce into 'hard' law in order to serve useful purposes. Some instruments might influence the development of law without themselves ever becoming law. Some instruments might influence the behavior of decision-makers without their effect being publicly acknowledged. 'Social systems utilize both binding principles and substrata of non-binding principles that are not and need not be incorporated within formal law-making processes, but still create normative standards and expectations of appropriate behavior.'[17]

Several factors will determine whether a particular soft law instrument is the proper tool to perform the job envisioned by its drafters. First is the suitability of the instrument's form to achieving its desired goal. Second is the suitability of the legal area – its ripeness – for incorporation into the particular soft law instrument chosen. Third is the rigor of the process used to formulate the soft law instrument. Fourth is the identity of the drafters and their ability to command respect. Fifth are the characteristics of the targets of the soft law, and the suitability of the type of instrument chosen for *their* purposes. These areas are, of course, interrelated.

A. Suitability of Form for Intended Purpose

The purpose the instrument is intended to serve should dictate what form of instrument is selected. Some instruments are meant to serve as templates for hard law, in which case the appropriate form to effectuate that purpose is likely to be a model treaty or a model law. While using

---

[15] Other examples include soft law that parallels hard law and act as a fall-back provision or that serves, through acquiescence and estoppel, as a source of legal obligation. Ibid.

[16] Shaffer and Pollack, above n 7, 727–43.

[17] Chinkin, above n 13, 24–5.

these forms can help ease the transition from the soft law instrument to the hard law instrument, often the transition may result in changes to particular articles or sections. If uniformity in obligation is the goal, a multilateral treaty is the most suitable form of instrument to minimize the chance of change upon implementation.[18]

Some soft law instruments help to regulate behavior that spans national boundaries and that is not easily controlled by a single state's laws; soft law can fill in the gap. The *OECD Guidelines for Multinational Enterprises* seek to provide voluntary principles and standards for responsible business conduct; they seek to control behavior that might otherwise escape oversight because no single jurisdiction clearly has authority over some of the activities engaged in by multinational corporations.[19] An influential arbitration soft law instrument is the *IBA Guidelines on Conflicts of Interest in International Arbitration*.[20] The Guidelines are used as a stand-alone instrument and as a supplement to otherwise applicable arbitration rules. The guidelines are useful precisely because they are an attempt to distill transnational principles regarding the ethical obligations to which international arbitrators should adhere. Their very flexibility, however, sometimes leads to charges that they are not stringent enough.

Some soft processes might be desirable for the very reason that they are in fact 'soft'. Christine Chinkin notes that certain forms of soft dispute resolution processes, such as negotiation, mediation and conciliation, can be beneficial precisely because they avoid an adversarial process that results in a binary win or lose outcome; soft sanctions might be useful when a party's real goal is a change in behavior rather than redress for past wrongs.[21] In terms of soft law instruments, governments sometimes

---

[18] Even a multilateral treaty can be implemented in domestic law in ways that do not accurately reflect the intent of the treaty drafters. For example, the US legislation implementing the WTO Agreements, the Uruguay Round Agreements Act, did not mirror perfectly the language in the agreements themselves. See Homer E Moyer, Jr, 'How Will the Uruguay Round Change the Practice of Trade Law in the United States: U.S. Institutions, Not the WTO, May Hold the Answer' in Terence P Stewart (ed), *The World Trade Organization: Multilateral Trade Framework for the 21st Century and U.S. Implementing Legislation* (ABA 1996) 727, 729.

[19] OECD, *OECD Guidelines for Multinational Enterprises* (OECD 2011), <http://www.oecd.org/document/28/0,3746,en_2649_34889_2397532_1_1_1_1,00.html> accessed 27 September 2011.

[20] *IBA Guidelines on the Taking of Evidence in International Arbitration* (2004), <http://www.ibanet.org/Publications/publications_IBA_guides_and_free_materials.aspx> accessed 7 November 2011.

[21] Chinkin, above n 13, 40.

participate in non-binding cooperative arrangements when they would not adopt a hard law obligation because they have competing national interests or because they lack the technical or fiscal ability to participate.[22]

One example is the Montreal Protocol to the Vienna Convention for the Protection of the Ozone Layer, whose implementation was entrusted to an Implementation Committee.[23] Another is the Antarctic Treaty Consultative Meeting process, through which the Antarctic Treaty's obligations have been expanded though the treaty itself has never been amended.[24] Participants in the meetings, who are representatives of states, recommend 'measures' that become effective once they are approved by all of the consultative parties, but that approval process is an intermediate step before the measures are approved by the governments themselves and then implemented in municipal law.[25] 'As non-binding norms, the obligations contained in recommendations can be formulated in a more precise, distinct, and restrictive manner than is acceptable in a formally binding international agreement.'[26]

Many instruments seek to develop the content of or otherwise influence international law. Sometimes these are scholarly publications, such as treatises, annotations, commentaries, or restatements;[27] sometimes these are learned society resolutions or reports. Often the purpose of these documents is to compile and analytically describe existing practice, a particularly important contribution to learning when the relevant information, such as the state practice that leads to the formation of customary international law, is found in disparate places.

Each of the foregoing examples demonstrates the link between specific forms of soft law and the purposes they serve. These are not compartmentalized categories; parts of a treatise or a restatement might be adopted as law, which might comport with the drafters' hope but not their primary goal in writing the document. Soft regulation might eventually

---

22 Christopher C Joyner, 'The Legal Status and Effect of Antarctic Recommended Measures' in Shelton, above n 1, 163, 177.

23 Chinkin, above n 13, 27.

24 Joyner, above n 22, 164–5.

25 Ibid, 165–6.

26 Ibid, 183.

27 It is true that the writings of the best-known publicists are a subsidiary source of international law and thus could qualify as 'hard' law, though the traditional view of the subsidiary sources is that they capture otherwise-existing hard law, and they are not themselves creating hard law. Yet in the descriptive process or by virtue of normative critique they will conceivably influence international law.

become hard; gap-filling instruments might be adopted by municipal legal systems.

B. Ripeness of Legal Field for Incorporation into the Chosen Instrument

One of the reasons that one has soft law is that there is a lack of agreement on what the hard law should be. The greater the agreement about the principles involved, the more likely it is that a 'harder' form of soft law instrument would be appropriate. There are numerous examples of failure stemming from attempts to shoehorn unripe legal principles into a too-'hard' instrument and the resultant failure of the exercise. Balancing ripeness with 'hardness' can be a difficult tightrope to walk, however. Principles at too high a level of abstraction are ineffective because states can either comply or claim to comply with them and their vagueness precludes objective verification. Yet forcing through more specific obligations can also backfire, however, because if the relevant actors, whether they be states or private parties, do not adopt them or do not abide by them, the exercise will be deemed a failure and might even have a chilling effect on future attempts to regulate. Thus, deep-seated differences of opinion about appropriate legal standards can affect or even derail a 'soft' codification exercise.[28]

Two examples illustrate each end of the ripeness spectrum, and the ease, or lack thereof, in reaching agreement. The International Law Commission started to consider codifying the law of state responsibility for injuries to aliens in 1925.[29] The exercise continued for approximately 70 years, with some periods of little activity. The initial exercise was unsuccessful at least partly because members of the ILC did not agree on substantive norms. By 1971, the focus of the project shifted to general principles of state responsibility and attribution. Finally, only when James Crawford was appointed special rapporteur and the orientation of the project shifted from primary rules to secondary rules was the exercise successful.[30] By contrast, negotiating the second Law of the Sea Convention was a relatively speedy exercise, taking roughly nine years.[31]

---

[28] See, for example, the discussion of the MAI, *infra* at 67.

[29] United Nations, 'Documents on the Development and Codification of International Law', 41 *AJIL* 29 (Supp 1947) 102–3.

[30] The International Law Commission adopted the articles on 9 August 2001. The Articles still reflect lack of consensus on certain provisions. For example, Article 27 states that a state's invocation of a circumstance precluding wrongfulness is 'without prejudice' to the question of compensation due the injured state. See August Reinisch, 'Necessity in International Investment Arbitration – An Unnecessary Split of Opinions in Recent ICSID Cases?' (2007) 8 *JWIT* 191, 207–8.

A related issue is whether an instrument is meant to fit within or explain or elaborate upon already existing law, or whether it is designed to create new obligations. Effectuating or at least influencing the 'progressive development' of the law is not incompatible with the promulgation of a soft law instrument; indeed, this is one of the ways soft law instruments can influence most the development of the law. In order to be effective, however, instruments suggesting progressive development of the law should distinguish carefully between those norms that have already been widely accepted and those that would constitute a move beyond well-accepted principles. Overstating the solidity of principles advocated by the drafters risks undermining the value of the entire project. Again, this issue might well affect the type of instrument chosen in order that such distinctions can be readily made so that the end users can objectively assess the desirability of the suggested progressive development.

C. Rigor of the Process used to Formulate the Instrument

Soft law can occupy any point along a continuum ranging from precise controlling norms that are not technically binding but are universally observed to vague recommended principles that very few recognize. Most falls somewhere between these two extremes. Some soft law purports to reflect existing law, while other soft law very clearly reflects non-binding aspirational goals. Many instruments might include a mix of generally agreed upon principles and nascent concepts that have not yet garnered widespread acceptance.

The more that a soft law instrument purports to reflect or codify existing international law, the more rigorous the process of identifying that law needs to be. International law is often derided for its lack of specificity. These charges are especially cogent when levied against the difficulty to substantiate customary international law or the disparate and dispersed general principles of law, two of the classic sources of international law. Treaty provisions can be vague – sometimes deliberately so – but are at least easily identifiable. Identifying with precision non-treaty-based sources of law is difficult. In order for a soft law 'codification' to garner widespread respect, comprehensive reach and objective assessment are paramount, as is the accurate identification and explanation of anomalies. The process also needs to distinguish between

---

[31] The 1982 Convention on the Law of the Sea was negotiated from 1973 to 1982. See generally Philip Allott, 'Power Sharing in the Law of the Sea' (1983) 77 *AJIL* 1.

those principles that are generally accepted and those that seek to engage in the 'progressive development' of the law.

The process used to formulate a US 'Restatement' is a good example of an attempt to identify 'black-letter' law distilled from decisions taken by multiple courts in specific areas of the law. Restatements are successful largely because of the careful, but cumbersome and time-consuming, approach taken to drafting them. Generally a reporter or reporters with outstanding reputations in their fields are chosen to begin the drafting process. The American Law Institute (ALI) then assembles a group of advisers (usually 25 to 30) who are duty bound to review drafts and offer critical comments. A second group of ALI members also has the opportunity to weigh in on early drafts. Tentative drafts are then presented both to the entire ALI membership and to the ALI Executive Council; any draft has to be approved by each body before it has the Restatement imprimatur. The result tends to be an extremely thorough, thoughtful and well-weighed conclusion on major issues. Yet reaching that point can take years; the Project on Wills and Donative Transfers has been 21 years in the making, and the drafting of the Restatement on the US Law of International Commercial Arbitration is projected to last between six and ten years.

On the international front, codification challenges are even greater. Identifying and assessing *opinio juris* is a daunting task, and ensuring that the investigation is comprehensive is paramount both to ensuring validity and to achieving acceptance. The same would hold true for an attempt to distill rules from general principles of law.

Soft law instruments that promulgate non-binding standards can be more flexible in approach. Yet the manner of their formulation can have a significant effect on the breadth of their acceptance. Though standards might be vague, they are likely to be more broadly accepted if the target group has had some say in creating them and they reflect general agreement about the appropriate direction to take. One thing about which to be wary when one is discussing non-binding codes of conduct is that it is extremely easy for entities to sign on given that the sanctions for non-compliance are small to non-existent. This has to some degree happened in the area of corporate social responsibility. One counsel to an MNE said that his company has signed on to more than 30 codes of conduct or best practices type obligations; he confessed to have little idea in practice what his company needed to do to comply with all of them.[32]

---

[32] This statement was made at a conference, 'Corporations and International Law', held at Santa Clara University School of Law in March 2010; see also John J

D. Identity of the Drafters

The identity of the participants in the drafting of a soft law instrument is a key component to its acceptance. A soft law instrument will generally reflect some kind of consensus, at least on the part of a possibly influential group of elites. Yet that consensus might be broad or narrow, depending on those who played a role in the drafting. The expertise of the drafters, their reputations for quality and objectivity, and of course the work they produce, will all affect how widely the work's influence is felt.

The UN General Assembly adopts resolutions that are non-binding but quite possibly influential, depending on the breadth of agreement they attract. Breadth is measured not just in numbers (though that can be important) but in terms of measures such as the regions' supporters represent, the diversity of economic development levels among supporters, and the like.

Ideally the drafters of any instrument will have both expertise in the topic the instrument seeks to address and objectivity in their approach to it. These factors can be difficult to balance; experts will often tend to hold strong and even passionate views, and their objectivity might suffer as a result. Achieving this balance does not mean that experts cannot somehow be participants in the process they seek to regulate – indeed, they might be engaged in drafting the instruments precisely because of their knowledge and expertise in a particular topic. But there must be safeguards against self-serving activity. A group such as an NGO might be expert, yet it might also be motivated to show its constituency – particularly if the constituency is composed of dues-paying members – that it is engaged in some kind of activity. An international technocrat might be expert, but her job description might encourage quantity over quality.

The reputation of the drafters can significantly enhance the influence of an instrument. Learned organizations, such as the International Law Association, the Institute of International Law, or the American Law Institute, can use their institutional reputation and that of their members to give an imprimatur of quality and objectivity to a project, and those projects can be enormously influential. The Hague Conference on Private

---

Kirton and Michael J Trebilcock, 'Introduction: 'Hard Choices and Soft Law in Sustainable Global Governance' in John J Kirton and Michael J Trebilcock (eds), *Hard Choices, Soft Law: Voluntary Standards in Global Trade, Environment and Social Governance* (Ashgate 2004) 3, 11 (noting that 'the world may be approaching the point where there are too many, often competing codes, rather than too few').

International Law has expertise in drafting conventions that 'respond to global needs' in the areas of international protection of children, family and property relations, international legal cooperation and litigation, and international commercial and finance law.[33]

Non-governmental organizations are prominent forces in the international legal sphere. They participate, often informally, in the drafting of resolutions, declarations and other documents and often have a significant influence in their content. Usually their participation is not formal and the degree to which they are influential in formulating policy is uncertain. Yet their participation during the drafting equates to steady pressure on states to consider their views and might also play a role in maintaining pressure on states to comply with the end result.[34]

The influence of judicial and arbitral decisions means that judges and arbitrators play a role in the creation and formulation of both hard and soft international law.[35] The judges on the International Court of Justice have sometimes been accused of letting politics triumph over law. Yet ICJ judges sit for a defined term. Arbitrators are rather more dependent on their reputations. Thus, the influence of a decision from a sole arbitrator will depend very much on that arbitrator's expertise, reputation and the quality of the opinion. Tribunal opinions from 'strong' tribunals might carry more weight than those comprising lesser-known arbitrators. The background of the arbitrators might very well influence the way they approach a legal question. In international investment law it is often alleged that whether arbitrators have commercial law backgrounds or public international law backgrounds has a decisive effect on their method of approaching any case and very likely on its outcome.[36]

---

33 <http://www.hcch.net/index_en.php?act=text.display&tid=1> accessed 10 November 2011.

34 Chinkin, above n 13, 28–9.

35 Like the writings of publicists, the decisions of international tribunals have some status as a subsidiary source of international law, though the classic view is that they identify otherwise-existing international law. Shabtei Rosenne, III *The Law and Practice of the International Court 1920–2005* (M Nijhoff 2006) 1550–1; Alain Pellet, 'Article 38' in Andreas Zimmermann, Christian Tomuschat and Karin Oellers-Frahm (eds), *The Statute of the International Court of Justice: A Commentary* (OUP 2006) 677, 788–90. For a fuller discussion of the impact of international tribunal decisions, see *infra* 77–75.

36 See Anthea Roberts, 'Power and Persuasion in Investment Treaty Interpretation: The Dual Role of States' (2010) 104 *AJIL* 179, 197–8; Michael Waibel and Yanhui Wu, 'Are Arbitrators Political?', *ASIL* Research Forum, UCLA (5 November 2011) (unpublished paper on file with author); Jan Paulsson, 'Arbitration Without Privity' (1995) 10 ICSID Rev 232, 257 (noting need for

E. Identity of the Intended Users

Decisions about the form of the instrument and who should be responsible for its drafting must be made in light of the intended users of the soft law. A soft law instrument in the form of a multilateral convention might be readily adoptable. Yet ease of adoption may prove insufficient, especially if those responsible for treaty signing and ratification, or the states that they represent, had little to nothing to do with the treaty's creation or content. Indeed, as mentioned above, the participation of the users is often key to the success of an instrument. Both voluntary standards and aspiring hard law norms are more likely to be accepted if their targets played a role in their creation.[37] One of the reasons underpinning the failure of the MAI negotiations was their negotiation by only OECD members; less wealthy states did not play a role in the instrument's drafting.

Some instruments are directed at more than one set of users. The MacBride Principles, which required adhering corporations doing business in Northern Ireland to agree to try to improve employment of the historically disadvantaged Catholic population, were designed for both direct and indirect end-users. They were directed primarily at US companies with affiliates in Northern Ireland because of the likelihood of a favorable reception and the potential for adverse publicity should corporations refuse to sign;[38] however, their indirect audience was the UK government, which opposed the Principles but which eventually adopted legislation requiring improved labor conditions for Catholics in Northern Ireland.[39]

Other instruments are directed towards a more specific audience. The

---

arbitrators to show a degree of sophistication when assessing governmental actions).

37 When non-state actors are one of the end users it can be useful to have an informal instrument to facilitate mutual evaluation; for example, in the money laundering context the FATF permits all participating entities to evaluate the effectiveness of the recommendations. Such an evaluation would likely be less possible in the context of a treaty situation where certainly private actors would be discouraged (at least formally) from evaluating sovereign governments. David A Wirth, 'Compliance with Non-Binding Norms of Trade and Finance' in Shelton, above n 1, 330, 331.

38 Christopher McCrudden, 'Human Rights Codes for Transnational Corporations: The Sullivan and MacBride Principles' in Shelton, above n 1, 418, 443.

39 Ibid, 446. Even after the adoption of the Fair Employment Act 1989, the MacBride Principles continued to fill cracks in existing 'hard' law, particularly with respect to gaps in enforcement.

voluntary international standards of the International Organization for Standardization, for example, are created by both state agencies and private entities, but are intended for use by private actors. The ISO is a federation of national standards bodies, whose composition varies but which often comprises government representatives as well as trade association officials.[40] ISO standards often serve a gap-filling function. 'By far the strongest factor leading to success in terms of the actors involved in creating the standard was the participation of the targets of the norm in the standard-setting and implementation processes.'[41] (ISO as a technical non-political result best left to standards professionals.) In the standards-setting context end-users – manufacturers – often have the incentive to comply in order for the product to be widely usable.

Frequent targets for using soft law instruments are judges and arbitrators. The suitability of their using soft law, and the manner in which they ought to use soft law, is a matter of some debate. Professor Reisman suggests that soft law is off limits as a rule of decision for those performing the job of international judges or arbitrators.[42] Yet as Professor Klabbers has observed, '[t]ribunals will always try and find legal authority for their statements, regardless of the existence of a formal doctrine of precedent, and regardless of whether the authority invoked forms part of the same legal system.'[43] Klabbers was in particular talking about the tendency of tribunals to cite other judicial decisions, including those from different legal systems, if those decisions support the outcome sought by the decision maker in the given case.

The factors identified above do not operate in isolation. The drafters of an instrument are usually the driving force behind assessing the state of the law, selecting the appropriate instrument given the desired end-user, and designing the appropriate process to conclude the instrument. But their goals might be altered once they discover limitations in one of the factors. The purpose and function of the instrument will affect the model adopted; several different instruments could be directed towards the same end-user in order to effectuate different purposes. One might have a draft convention directed towards governments; one might also have a

---

40 Naomi Roht-Arriaza, '"Soft Law" in a "Hybrid" Organization: The International Organization for Standardization' in Shelton, above n 1, 263, 265.

41 Ibid, 279 (speaking of the drafting of the ISO 14001).

42 Reisman, above n 8, 26–7.

43 Jan Klabbers, 'Precedent and Principles' (2001) 3 *Turku Law Journal* 71, 72.

summary of practice designed to help governments negotiate treaties in a knowledgeable fashion.

II. SOFT LAW INSTRUMENTS AND INTERNATIONAL INVESTMENT LAW

Having briefly addressed the factors that measure the success of any soft law instrument, the discussion below focuses on three categories of soft law instruments: first, it looks at instruments created with the deliberate hope that they should some day become hard law; second it looks at soft law that builds upon or fills gaps in existing hard law and thus might be said to fulfill a complementary and regulatory function; and third, it looks at instruments that seek to influence the development of both hard and soft law. These categories are not mutually exclusive; a soft law instrument might be meant to serve as a template for future treaty or legislative activity but in the meantime be used to fill *lacunae* in existing laws. The subsections below deal with each of these categories in turn, examining the most commonly used and useful types of soft law instruments in each category with an eye towards their applicability to international investment law.

A. Soft Law as Emergent Hard Law

Many organizations, particularly those concerned with governance, might deliberately draft conventions or model laws designed to be adopted by law-makers. This activity is the *raison d'être* of some organizations, such as the International Law Commission and the Hague Conference on Private International Law. These organizations are often but not always inter-governmental. In other words, sometimes the drafters of the instrument encompass the States who would be responsible for turning the draft soft law instrument into a hard law treaty, but that is not inevitably the case. NGOs or other interested parties can also draft model treaties in the hope that they may be adopted as is or that at least they may be influential in the treaty-making process.[44] The same groups, as well as States themselves, whether individually or as part of a group of like-minded States, may also issue soft law instruments over and over again in the hope of influencing customary international law.

---

44 The IISD's Model International Agreement on Investment is a prominent example in the investment law arena. Howard Mann *et al.*, *IISD Model International Agreement on Investment for Sustainable Development* (IISD 2005).

1. Multilateral treaties

The International Law Commission has drafted several model multilateral Conventions that have been ultimately approved by the United Nations and acceded to by a sufficient number of States to enter into force.[45] Other groups, including the International Law Association and the Harvard Research in International Law, have taken a similar approach with those areas of law they have viewed as ripe for codification.[46]

International investment law has seen its share of codification efforts aimed to result in a multilateral instrument. As early as 1929 the Harvard Research proposed a codification of the law of state responsibility for injuries to aliens, to be used by the International Law Commission in its codification efforts.[47] In the middle of the twentieth century, Hermann Abs and Hartley Shawcross proposed a draft Convention that, though never formally adopted, would prove influential in the negotiation of subsequent bilateral investment treaties.[48] In addition, the Abs-Shawcross Convention attempted to encapsulate the drafters' view of then current customary international law. 'The draft presented itself as a "restatement" of such "principles of conduct," meaning that it was intended to reflect rules of customary international law regarding the treatment of aliens.'[49] The Abs-Shawcross draft was followed in short order in 1962 by the German-initiated OECD Draft Convention on the Protection of Foreign Property, a document containing similar but not identical provisions, though both envisioned the settlement of investor-State disputes by

---

45 August Reinisch and Andrea K Bjorklund, Chapter 11, this volume (describing the codification exercises conducted by the International Law Commission).

46 For example, the International Law Association has, *inter alia*, drafted articles for a Convention on State Immunity (1983) 22 ILM 287 and on the Protection of Civilian Populations Against New Engines of War. See <http://www.icrc.org/ihl.nsf/INTRO/345?OpenDocument> accessed 28 October 2011; Research in International Law at Harvard Law School, 'The Law of Responsibility of States for Damage Done in Their Territory to the Person or Property of Foreigners' (1929) 23 (Special Supp) *AJIL* 131.

47 Harvard Research Draft, above n 1.

48 Draft Convention on Investments Abroad (1960) 9 *Journal of Public Law* 115; see also Louis B Sohn and RR Baxter, 'Convention on the International Responsibility of States for Injuries to Aliens' in FV Garcia-Amador, Louis B Sohn and RR Baxter (eds), *Recent Codification of the Law of State Responsibility for Injuries to Aliens* (Oceana 1974) 133.

49 Antonio R Parra, *The World Bank Group's Centre for Settlement of Investment Disputes: A History* (draft of September 19, 2011) (OUP 2012 forthcoming).

50 Organization for Economic Cooperation and Development, Draft

arbitration.[50] Neither entered into force. Both were intended to be multilateral treaties, but though they failed to achieve acceptance in that guise, they had a significant influence on the bilateral treaty negotiations that followed their introduction.[51]

A different agreement limited to encouraging the settlement of investment disputes, rather than regulating foreign investment generally, was proposed by the World Bank in the early 1960s. Painstaking negotiations under the aegis of the General Counsel of the Bank, Aron Broches, led to the negotiation of the Convention on Settlement of International Investment Disputes, also known as the Washington or the ICSID Convention.[52]

Most recently, and perhaps most notoriously, the Organization for Economic Cooperation and Development Ministerial Council approved the commencement of the negotiation of a multilateral investment agreement (MAI) in 1995.[53] The MAI was to be negotiated first by OECD members, but once finalized would have been opened for signature by non-OECD countries as well. The MAI text as drafted was strongly influenced by NAFTA Chapter 11 and US BITs, though there were differences among the negotiators with respect to several issues.[54] External criticism was perhaps even more vociferous as NGOs protested the opacity and lack of accountability in the proposed arbitral process.[55] By early 1998, the OECD had decided that there should be a 'period of assessment' during which the member States consulted their constituencies about the desirability of continuing negotiations, which resulted in France's decision not to take part in any further negotiations because of '"fundamental problems with respect to the sovereignty of States".'[56] The MAI negotiations were abandoned in December 1998, and could be said to have foundered on the same tide of anti-globalization activism that would disrupt the WTO's Seattle Ministerial in 1999.

2. Model treaties

Some instruments are specifically designed to serve as models for draft

---

Convention on the Protection of Foreign Property, 2 ILM 241 (1963); see generally Parra, above n 49, 21–2.

51 Ibid, 27–9.

52 Convention on the Settlement of International Investment Disputes Between States and Nationals of Other States, 18 March 1965, 575 UNTS 159.

53 Parra, above n 49, 269–70.

54 Parra, above n 49, 270.

55 Ibid, 271–2.

56 Ibid, 272–3.

bilateral conventions. The OECD has, for example, promulgated a series of draft model double taxation treaties that have served as the bases for numerous bilateral agreements.[57] Many States have model investment treaties from which they commence negotiations for bilateral investment treaties.[58]

Model treaties can be useful for facilitating the efficient negotiation of an agreement. They provide a starting point from which to commence negotiations. These treaties become hard law once they are adopted, but even as models they might influence negotiations and subsequent treaties entered into even by States who do not sign on to a treaty that precisely replicates the model, and might even affect one that strays far from the model. Indeed, this influence could be positive as well as negative; i.e. states could deliberately follow the model or deliberately reject it.

A State that drafts a model treaty might have a strong interest in having all of its treaties on the same subject follow the model precisely. The model would in many cases encapsulate the State's views about ideal policies, and the negotiators for the State might have little authority to depart from the model. To the extent that similar treaties have most-favored-nation clauses, departure from the model might be ineffective, anyway. A model, whether drafted by the State or not, might exert even more of a constraining effect if the States feared that departing from the model, even in ways that might seem insignificant, could have an effect on the interpretation of that treaty, or of prior treaties. One sees, for example, a continuity of approach in the US approach to negotiating investment chapters in FTAs, in which the language in the agreement itself is nearly identical to the language in the 2004 US Model BIT and even to prior model treaties, yet 'annexes' are attached to clarify and elaborate on those obligations.[59]

The existence of multiple model investment treaties drafted by multiple States could have an influence beyond each state's individual treaty negotiations. To the extent that there are multiple models, most of which

---

[57] Peter Carroll and Aynsley Kellow, *The OECD: A Study of Organisational Adapation* (Edward Elgar 2011) 139–40.

[58] For a compilation of and commentary on significant models, see Chester Brown and Devashish Krishan, *Commentaries on Selected Model Investment Treaties* (OUP 2012 forthcoming).

[59] For an example of the treatment of expropriation by both the United States and Canada, see Andrea K Bjorklund, 'NAFTA Chapter 11 and the Environment: An Assessment After Fifteen Years' in Emmanuel Gaillard and Frédéric Bachand (eds), *Fifteen Years of NAFTA Chapter 11 Arbitration* (Juris 2011) 195–201.

contain similar obligations, their cumulative effect could have a strong influence on non-model-based treaties.[60]

3. Model laws

Model laws share some characteristics with model treaties. A model law can be adopted by the law-making authorities in those States that wish to take the approach recommended by the model. The benefit of this approach is that implementation of the international norms is likely to be uniform and consistent. Yet there is always the danger that the law will be changed in implementation. In countries following the dualist approach to international law, ratification of a treaty often precedes and is separate from the enactment of implementing legislation. The legislation, once drafted and approved by the applicable legislative process, might vary somewhat from the treaty itself. A departure from the model law's language is, of course, also possible, but as the relevant language is drafted as a Code the likelihood of significant differences is diminished. An excellent example is the UNCITRAL Model Law on Arbitration.[61]

Federal states are likely to use model laws on the municipal plane to effectuate common policy while nonetheless respecting state sovereignty. In the United States, the National Conference of Commissioners on Uniform State Laws drafts model laws that can be adopted by individual states.

The benefit of the model law approach is that it helps to lead to harmonization but respects state sovereignty because states can modify the model in transforming it into municipal law. The drawback to the model law approach is the same; the goal of harmonization can be defeated by the enactment of similar but not identical laws. The drawbacks should not be overstated, however; because as Giuditta Cordero-Moss convincingly demonstrates, even identical laws or treaties can be interpreted by law-makers differently, especially if those law-makers represent different legal traditions. Thus, if uniformity of interpretation is a key goal, constraining that discretion is paramount.[62]

---

[60] For discussion of the identifiable common strands of obligations in multiple investment treaties, see Christian Tietje and Emily Sipiorski, Chapter 8, this volume, *infra* 192 *et seq.*

[61] William W Park, 'The Procedural Soft Law of International Arbitration' in Loukas Mistelis and Julian Lew (eds), *Pervasive Problems in International Arbitration* (2006) 141.

[62] Giuditta Cordero-Moss, Chapter 6, this volume, *infra* 112–125.

4. Customary international law

The perennially elusive customary international law might well be affected by soft law. The promulgation of soft law instruments is often part of a long-term struggle to achieve recognition of particular principles; as state practice incorporates the soft law those principles may one day achieve hard law status. Kate Miles' contribution illustrates the important roles soft law instruments have played in international environmental law.[63] Soft law might also be used to affect the content of possibly emerging customary international law. The mid-twentieth-century battle over the appropriate standard of compensation for expropriation under international law, with iterative General Assembly resolutions influenced by the New International Economic Order, demonstrates the strategic use of soft law to forestall what might have been viewed as an emerging norm of compensation based on the Hull formula requiring prompt, adequate and effective compensation for expropriation.

In the investment law realm, the question of transparency has been an issue for some time. The movement towards transparency started in NAFTA cases at the behest of NGOs who sought both access to documents about the proceedings and the ability to participate as *amici curiae*. Though the most significant openness is still found in NAFTA and in treaties negotiated by Canada and the United States after 2000, a more limited version of transparency has made inroads in other areas as well, although it has not been universally accepted.[64] ICSID, for example, amended its Convention Arbitration Rules and its Additional Facility Rules to permit the participation of *amici curiae* in appropriate circumstances and to provide for the publication of the legal *ratio* of ICSID awards, even if the parties do not consent to release of the entire award. The UNCITRAL Arbitration Rules, which are often used to govern investor-state disputes, were updated in 2010 without significant changes to the provisions regarding confidentiality in arbitration, but the Commission entrusted the Working Group with the task of preparing a legal standard on the question of transparency in investor-state arbitration. The assumption was that it was too early to prepare a formal instrument, but that the Working Group should prepare 'rules of uniform law on transparency in treaty-based investor-State arbitration'.[65] The

---

63 Kate Miles, Chapter 5, this volume, *infra* 82 *et seq*.

64 Andrea K Bjorklund, 'The Emerging Civilization of Investment Arbitration' (2009) 113 *Penn State Law Review* 1269, 1286–94; Bjorklund, above n 59, 211–16.

65 Settlement of commercial disputes: Preparation of a legal standard on

mandate to the Working Group did not require that the rules take any particular form and suggested that the rules not be limited to UNCITRAL disputes. Thus, the Working Group's project might involve 'the preparation of instruments such as model clauses, specific rules or guidelines, an annex to the UNCITRAL Arbitration Rules in their generic form, separate arbitration rules or optional clauses for adoption in specific treaties.'[66]

It is too early to say that there is a customary international law norm of transparency in investment arbitration, yet the abundance of instruments, both soft and hard, recognizing a need for greater transparency, might well contribute to its emergence.

B. Instruments Designed to Fill *Lacunae* in Official Regulation or to Supplement it

Soft law instruments sometimes fill *lacunae* in official regulation.[67] These instruments might stem from various groups, including international government organizations, non-governmental organizations, or even private entities. They might be used to fill gaps deliberately left in hard law instruments or to fill unanticipated gaps, or to capture agreement on issues that represents an important moment in negotiations but is too vague to be reduced to a legal instrument. They might elaborate on vague or abstract principles. They might be used to forestall formal regulation out of fear it would be more restrictive and less desirable. They might be designed to influence policy though they do not lend themselves to adoption as principles or to incorporation in contracts.

1. Resolutions

International and inter-governmental organizations cannot make formal law; they lack the power to ratify conventions. Thus, the UN General Assembly is not a law-making entity and its resolutions by definition do not have the status of law. Any emanation from an IGO or the General Assembly will, strictly speaking, be a soft law instrument prior to its ratification by states. The General Assembly does adopt Conventions that are then sent round for signature, yet it also adopts instruments, such as declarations and resolutions, that are deliberately intended to be only 'soft law', often offered in that guise because the states are unable to agree to

---

transparency in treaty-based investor-State arbitration, A/CN.9/WG11/WP.162 (9 December 2010), para 1.

66 Ibid, para 5.

67 Weil, above n 7, 414.

formalize the arrangement in the form of a convention. A classic example would be a UN General Assembly resolution or a proclamation after a conference, such as the Rio Declaration that emanated from the United Nations Conference on Environment and Development.[68] Notwithstanding their formal soft law status, General Assembly resolutions can encapsulate customary international law or serve as precursors to the formation of customary international law, or serve as templates for the negotiation of future conventions.[69]

Inability to come to agreement on a formal convention might result from disagreement about the specific terms that any such agreement would include. A soft law instrument might be designed to symbolize and publicize the results of a conference at which there was insufficient time to negotiate specific commitments to underpin a binding treaty. The negotiating parties might fear that agreement could only be reached on anodyne terms that effectively create no agreement at all. They will thus resist formalizing a document that contains only minimal obligations, but might agree to a non-binding resolution, for example, to show that negotiations were not entirely unsuccessful or to serve as a starting point for future negotiations. The soft law instrument could capture general principles on which the relevant parties agree and could be used to prevent backsliding when negotiations recommenced in future. In the event the agreement did contain more solid principles, it might one day concretize into hard law.

States might also be concerned about the acceptability of such agreements by domestic constituencies. Promulgating a soft law instrument permits ideas to be encapsulated in writing and that document to be used to educate important stakeholders prior to the adoption of any binding rule.

One goal of some soft law promulgation can be to forestall formal regulation that would likely be more cumbersome and intrusive and thus less welcome. Such a document must be rigorous enough to stave off the undesired formal regulation yet sufficiently attuned to the degree of cooperation those involved are willing to offer. The problem of international legal and soft law approaches to combating money laundering is a good example where private actors such as banking

---

68 *Rio Declaration on Environment and Development*, 3–14 June 1992 <http://www.unep.org/Documents.Multilingual/Default.asp?documentid = 78&articleid = 1163?> accessed 19 September 2011.

69 The General Assembly can, of course, adopt Conventions and recommend their adoption to the UN Member States.

institutions have the political power to prevent the conclusion of binding obligation but shared concerns nonetheless may be facilitated by the passage of soft law instruments.[70] The Financial Action Task Force (a group composed of representatives from government ministries, law enforcement authorities, and bank supervisory and regulatory agencies) issued Forty Recommendations to secure some coordination with respect to financial disclosure rules in order to combat money laundering.[71] The recommendations are addressed to two parties: state financial regulators and financial institutions.[72] So long as they are effective, more stringent and variable state-specific regulation can be avoided.

2. Principles and guidelines

Codes of conduct have been useful instruments for setting out standards to be followed by those who are not traditional subjects of international law and whose activities are not readily located in a single jurisdiction. Corporations have taken some steps to regulate themselves as globalization places them beyond the reach of individual nation states.[73] Private actors such as NGOs, consumers, shareholders and trade unions also seek to take more of a role when they believe the traditional regulatory approach is ineffective.[74] Prominent examples of such regulatory initiatives include the Equator Principles[75] and the OECD's Guidelines on Multinational Enterprises.[76]

---

70 Beth Simmons, 'International Efforts against Money Laundering' in Shelton, above n 1, 245.

71 Ibid, 255–6.

72 Ibid. Another body recently convened in the aftermath of the 2007–08 financial crisis is the European Systemic Risk Board, an entity that lacks formal status but which may nonetheless prove influential as it recommends action without the constraint allied to cumbersome and multiplicitous law-making procedures ('Alternative modes of [international financial] regulation and supervision have flourished by necessity at the international level because the capacity for formal law-making and enforcement is restricted.'). Ellis Ferran, 'Can Soft Law Bodies be Effective? The Special Case of the European Systemic Risk Board' (2010) 6 *European Law Review* 751, 753.

73 Wolfgang H Reinicke and Jan M Witte, 'Interdependence, Globalization, and Sovereignty: The Role of Non-binding International Legal Accords' in Shelton, above n 1, 75, 80.

74 McCrudden, above n 38, 423.

75 <http://www.equator-principles.com/index.php/about-ep/about> accessed 31 October 2011.

76 OECD, *OECD Guidelines for Multinational Enterprises* (OECD 2011), <http://www.oecd.org/document/28/0,3746,en_2649_34889_2397532_1_1_1_1,00.html> accessed 27 September 2011.

Another area where soft law has been particularly influential is in the development of ethical standards applicable to the international judiciary and to international arbitrators.[77] The instruments applicable to the international judiciary have been described as 'gather[ing] the wisdom of domestic laws over the years and across borders'.[78] The IBA Guidelines on Conflicts of Interest have been noted above.[79] Soft law instruments might be particularly useful in areas viewed as properly subject to municipal sovereign authority such that an externally imposed 'hard law' instrument would not be accepted, yet in which for various reasons municipal law has not developed adequately or is too parochial for use in an international context.

Other initiatives seek to regularize activity in an area that is largely entrusted to private legal ordering but in which repeated use suggests that there would be efficiencies in promulgating default rules. The IBA Rules on the Taking of Evidence in International Arbitration[80] fall within this category, as do the AIPN's model petroleum contracts.[81] To the extent that sample contracts are replicated numerous times, they may be a kind of 'soft law'; parties will tend to favour the same forms partly because they have been successful and partly because they are there and hard to displace, even if they are not especially helpful or useful. Of course, when the instruments are adopted by parties they can even be transformed into 'hard' law for purposes of an individual transaction.

Another reason soft law is desirable is its flexibility. It is therefore not surprising that a process such as international arbitration, whose flexibility is one of its advantages, uses various forms of soft law instruments, such as rules and guidelines, to help manage the arbitral process. Ensuring that the instrument not only contains flexibility but also adopts the requisite level of specificity will facilitate its success. The International Bar Association's Rules on the Taking of Evidence, for example, are frequently used to govern evidentiary matters in international arbitrations.[82] Though a soft

---

77 Fabien Gélinas, 'Independence and Impartiality in International Adjudication' in Adam Dodek and Lorne Sossin (eds), *Judicial Independence in Context* (Irwin Law 2010) 499, 501.

78 Ibid.

79 See *supra* p56.

80 IBA Rules on the Taking of Evidence in International Arbitration 2010 <http://www.ibanet.org/Publications/publications_IBA_guides_and_free_materials.aspx#takingevidence> accessed 31 October 2011.

81 <http://www.aipn.org/mcvisitors.aspx> accessed 31 October 2011.

82 IBA Rules on the Taking of Evidence in International Arbitration (2010), <http://www.ibanet.org/Publications/publications_IBA_guides_and_free_materials.aspx#takingevidence> accessed 7 November 2011.

law instrument, they are extremely specific to their purpose, and once they are adopted by the parties to an arbitration they harden to become part of the rules governing the arbitration. Yet they can also be adopted in amended form, and in that respect their flexibility makes them even more suitable for the purpose they are intended to serve.

3. 'Delegated' soft law

International agreements can generate what Christine Chinkin terms 'secondary' or 'delegated' soft law: 'statements and practice that develop around a treaty to supplement or correct the text'.[83] The traditional international law making process is not well suited to coming to agreement about how to regulate highly detailed, fast-changing areas. The formal law-making process is cumbersome, and in areas characterized by rapid development, such as technological growth, innovation outstrips regulation. (This is true even on a municipal law plane.) Without a Constitution there can be no delegation to an administrative agency, but the task for formulating non-binding regulations or standards can be entrusted to a sub-group. Rules emanating from the sub-group will likely be soft law, but could nonetheless prove persuasive if not authoritative.[84]

Certain methods of adoption of non-binding standards could even render that soft law hard. The reference to the Codex Alimentarius Commission in the Uruguay Round Agreement on Sanitary and Phytosanitary Measures has meant decisions of that body have enhanced status.[85] States are not necessarily well suited to regulating in highly technical specific areas. Memoranda of Understanding concluded by the states party to the Convention on the Conservation of Migratory Species of Wild Animals set out specific, targeted actions that are subject to ready verification; they 'can provide swift coordinated international action for very highly endangered species'.[86]

4. 'Secondary' soft law – *jurisprudence constante and inconstante*

Both international and domestic tribunals issue decisions that apply international legal norms. Article 38 of the ICJ Statute assumes that court decisions will be a source of customary international law insofar as they

---

[83] Chinkin, above n 13, 27.

[84] Reinicke and Witte, above n 73, 88 (noting potential lack of legitimacy and accountability of supranational regulatory authorities).

[85] Melaku Desta, Chapter 7, this volume, *infra* 160.

[86] Clare Shine, 'Selected Agreements Concluded Pursuant to the Convention on the Conservation of Migratory Species of Wild Animals' in Shelton, above n 1, 196, 222.

identify state practice that has crystallized into customary international law. To a lesser extent, and somewhat controversially, they issue decisions that could be said to make norms. In one respect, then, tribunal decisions are recognized as a source of law, yet the jurisgenerative function of international tribunals is not universally accepted. For this reason, Andrew Guzman and Timothy Meyer place tribunal decisions in the category of soft law; this study will accept this designation.[87]

Investment tribunal decision making illustrates a process that Dinah Shelton has also called 'secondary soft law':

> Probably even more common is the 'secondary' soft law that is not preliminary or declaratory in nature, but is intended to be the ultimate and authoritative determination of a legal question. In this regard, hard law and soft law interact to shape the content of international obligations. Soft law formulates and reformulates the hard law of human rights treaties in the application of this law to specific states and cases. Paradoxically, this secondary soft law may be harder than the primary soft law declaring new standards.[88]

Indeed, the extent to which arbitral decisions can be said to make international investment law has been the subject of a great deal of scholarly commentary,[89] and the undoubted influence of tribunal decisions is one of the catalysts of this feasibility study. In practice it seems that investment tribunal decisions are sometimes treated as direct sources of law, especially as they accrete around one particular approach. To the extent tribunal decisions are adopted and argued by states themselves,

---

[87] Andrew T Guzman and Timothy L Meyer, 'International Common Law: The Soft Law of International Tribunals' (2009) 9 *Chicago Journal of International Law* 515, 516.

[88] Dinah Shelton, 'Commentary and Conclusions', in Shelton, above n57, 449, 461.

[89] Andrea K Bjorklund, 'Investment Treaty Arbitral Awards as *Jurisprudence Constante*' in Douglas Arner, Isabella Bunn and Colin Pickers (eds), *International Economic Law: The State and Future of the Discipline* (Hart 2008) 265; Tai-Heng Cheng, 'Precedent and Control in Investment Treaty Arbitration' (2007) 30 *Fordham Journal of International Law* 1014; Jeffery P Commission, 'Precedent in Investment Treaty Arbitration: A Citation Analysis of a Developing Jurisprudence' (2007) 24 *Journal of International Arbitration* 129; Gabrielle Kaufmann-Kohler, 'The 2006 Freshfields Lecture – Arbitral Precedent: Dream, Necessity, or Excuse?' (2007) 23 *Arbitration International* 357; Jan Paulsson, 'Awards – and Awards' in Andrea K Bjorklund, Ian A Laird and Sergey Ripinsky (eds), *Investment Treaty Law: Current Issues III* (BIICL 2008) 95; Christoph Schreuer and Matthew Weiniger, 'A Doctrine of Precedent' in Christoph Schreuer, Peter Muchlinski and Federico Ortino (eds), *The Oxford Handbook of International Investment Law* (2008).

they might be an example of state practice. In any event it is clear that they influence states.

C. Instruments designed to facilitate legal practice and to influence its development

Multiple scholars have contributed to the development of international law through the elaboration of treatises on particularized topics and the painstaking compilation of practice in various areas. Indeed, Article 38 of the ICJ statute contemplates the writings of publicists as a subsidiary source of international law.

Municipal law instruments, particularly from common-law countries, also offer useful examples of attempts to identify and describe general principles from disparate sources of law. Some, such as US Restatements of the Law, act at times as quasi-legal instruments. Treatises, often the work of one or two people, attempt to gather all relevant practice in a particular area and to derive lessons and principles from them. Annotations are similar to treatises, but are organized according to statutory provision or rule. Learned societies might also issue reports, resolutions, or the like in the hope of influencing legal development.

1. Restatements

The American Law Institute's Restatements create a 'black letter' rule of what it has assessed to be the most accurate and important statement of the law in a given area. After the affirmative statement, each principle is elaborated upon in the form of notes and comments to describe the genesis of the provision, offer illustrations of it in practice, and finally offer reporters' notes that give more information about specific sources. The Restatements are frequently cited by US courts as authoritative expositions of the law in the various areas they cover. But in some instances they have had a law-making function as well. The Restatement (Second) of Conflict of Laws adopted choice-of-law rules that had not been promulgated by any particular court but was an amalgam of different approaches; as of 2009, 24 jurisdictions had adopted the approach in the Second Restatement for torts, and 23 had done so for contracts.[90]

Some Restatements have been more controversial than others. The amount of controversy has tended to escalate when juridical practice is far from uniform, the content of the particular volume becomes more prescriptive and there is no uniform agreement about the desirability of recommending one approach over others. The Restatement of the Law

---

[90] Symeon Symeonides, *Choice of Law in the American Courts in 2009: Twenty-Third Annual Survey*, 58 *American Journal of Comparative Law* 1, 5–6 (2010).

(Third) of the Foreign Relations Law of the United States is one example of contentious negotiation among drafters. Some Restatements illustrate the problem of trying to reconcile disparate approaches. The Restatement (Second) of Conflict of Laws is one example; it adopts pieces of the territorial approach advocated by the Restatement (First) of Conflict of Laws and insights gleaned from Brainerd Currie's interest analysis along with a smattering of other approaches. By some measures it is very successful; judges like it because they have a great deal of flexibility in applying it in any given case, but critics point to the lack of predictability inherent in giving broad choice to those applying it.

2. Treatises

Treatises are usually compendia of practice interlaced with observations and opinions. Outstanding treatises may be every bit as influential as Restatements. Because they are often the work of only one or two authors, however, they are also able to engage in progressive development of the law without the need of convincing some hundreds of other people – or even thousands – to agree with them. Their influence should not be discounted; one thinks of *Dicey & Morris on the Conflict of Laws*,[91] Lady Hazel Fox on *State Immunity*[92] and *Oppenheim's International Law*,[93] to name just a few.

3. Annotations and commentaries

Annotations and commentaries take a particular set of rules, such as the Federal Court Rules in Canada,[94] or the Federal Rules of Civil Procedure in the United States,[95] or the Statute of the International Court of Justice,[96] the ICSID Convention[97] or NAFTA Chapter XI,[98] and

---

[91] Sir Lawrence Collins (ed), *Dicey & Morris on the Conflict of Laws* (14th edn, Sweet & Maxwell 2006).

[92] Hazel Fox, *The Law of State Immunity* (2nd edn, OUP 2008).

[93] Robert Jennings and Arthur Watts (eds), I & II *Oppenheim's International Law* (Longman 1996).

[94] Roger T Hughes, Arthur B Renaud and LE Trent Horne, *Canadian Federal Courts Practice, 2012 Edition* (LexisNexis 2011).

[95] Lee H Rosenthal (ed), *Moore's Federal Practice* (LexisNexis 2007).

[96] Andreas Zimmermann, Christian Tomuschat and Karin Oellers-Frahm (eds) *The Statute of the International Court of Justice: A Commentary* (OUP 2006).

[97] Christoph Schreuer, with August Reinisch, Loretta Malintoppi and Anthony Sinclair, *The ICSID Convention: A Commentary* (2nd edn, CUP 2009).

[98] Meg Kinnear, Andrea K Bjorklund and John FG Hannaford, *Investment Disputes Under NAFTA: An Annotated Guide to NAFTA Chapter 11* (Kluwer 2006; updated 2008, 2009).

exhaustively collect decisions and practice related to each Code provision. They can assist attorneys to prepare their clients' cases. They might also help judges, or judicial clerks, familiarize themselves with a specialized area of practice. An annotation is an excellent way to collect practice related to a single concept and identify competing approaches to contested questions, even if finding one single 'best' practice remains illusive. Depending on the approach of the authors an annotation might or might not be critical and prescriptive.

4. Learned society resolutions and recommendations.

The Institut de Droit International is perhaps the best-known learned society that promulgates resolutions on important topics of international law. The stature of the group's membership ensures that the resolutions carry weight and authority. The International Law Association, too, has been influential in soft law-making. For example, the International Law Association's Helsinki Rules on the use of waters in international rivers, drafted in 1966, have served as guidelines for state practice, have been incorporated into bilateral agreements, and have been recognized by the ILC.[99]

III. A NEW SOFT LAW INSTRUMENT ON INTERNATIONAL INVESTMENT LAW?

What do the foregoing analyses suggest about how soft law should interact with the international investment regime? The classic description of an international regime is that of Stephen Krasner: '[r]egimes constrain and regularize the behavior of participants, affect which issues among protagonists move on and off the agendas, determine which activities are legitimized or condemned, and influence whether, when, and how conflicts are resolved.'[100] The international investment regime is a loose network of some 2,800 investment agreements, mostly bilateral in nature, which usually contain similar but not identical obligations and similar but not identical methods of dispute settlement. It is clear that there is no single type of soft law that can best influence it; activity on all fronts will continue and will react to issues that arise within the regime itself.

---

99 Alexandre Kiss, 'Commentary and Conclusions' in Shelton, above n 1, 223, 226.

100 Stephen D Krasner, 'Structural Causes and Regime Consequences: Regimes as Intervening Variables' in Stephen D Krasner (ed), *International Regimes* (Cornell University Press 1983) 1, 2.

'Form ever follows function': Louis Sullivan's words can guide those engaged in endeavours other than architecture.[101] As discussed in Section I, the purpose of a soft law instrument should dictate its form. Thus, individuals or organizations aspiring to draft a soft law instrument should first decide what function they hope the instrument will perform in light of the likely users of it and the capabilities of the drafters themselves. The issues that arise in the investment law regime and that attract 'legitimation' or 'condemnation' often arise in the decisions of tribunals convened under the treaties. The dispersed nature of issue generation in international investment law suggests that one particularly useful contribution soft law might make would be to distill the state of the law, identify areas of agreement and disagreement, and identify the policy implications of selecting different routes of decision.

The precise form this distillation might take would depend on the primary intended user and the capabilities and status of the drafters. To the extent those users are projected to be States, the siren call of harmonization and multilateralization makes the drafting of a new multilateral agreement on investment appealing. Yet one of the lessons of the MAI is that the drafters of any such instrument must include the intended users of the instrument – this means States themselves must be involved, and a diverse range of States at that. The fact of the OECD's having taken the lead in negotiations and the perception that emerging economies had no influence on the resulting draft was one of the reasons for its failure. It is possible that multilateralization will come via regional convergence, as the European Union has asserted competence over investment with the passage of the Lisbon Treaty and the Trans-Pacific Partnership negotiations are projected to include investment. But it seems that a non-State-generated instrument is unlikely to achieve acceptance.

The study undertaken by Christian Tietje and Emily Sipiorski suggests a degree of convergence – of 'ripeness' – in the legal standards incorporated in the current generation of investment treaties that might make it possible to draft a soft law investment instrument that captures standards and practices commonly found in investment treaties.[102] Yet the

---

[101] Louis Sullivan, 'The Tall Office Building Artistically Considered' (March 1896) *Lippincott's Magazine*; for the principle's application to international investment law, see Andrea K Bjorklund, 'Improving the International Investment Law and Policy System: Report of the Rapporteur, Second Columbia International Investment Conference: What's Next in International Investment Law and Policy?' in José E Alvarez and Karl Sauvant, *The Evolving International Investment Regime* (OUP 2011) 213, 213–14, 244–5.

[102] Tietje and Sipiorski, above n 60, 236–37.

trend towards convergence stops short of uniformity; differences in interpretation of the scope of matters such as the meaning of an 'umbrella clause', the proper interpretation of 'most-favored-nation clauses', and the definition of 'investment' with regard to ICSID Convention cases are matters that continue to divide investment tribunals and commentators. Moreover, the spectacular failure of the MAI, the difficulty states such as Norway and the United States have had in revising their model treaties due to deep divisions in the polities over the appropriate balance between investor protection and investor responsibility, and the general criticism levied at international investment treaties suggest that launching a 'codification' exercise would be premature.

Given uncertainty about certain areas of investment law, and agreement about others, rigor in any drafting process will be essential. The concern in investment law might not be so much about distinguishing between 'black letter' law and its progressive development as guarding against suggesting a premature coalescence around a particular legal principle, but rather identifying and acknowledging divergent lines of analysis.

The feasibility study undertaken by the International Law Association is in part directed to considering what contribution the ILA itself could make to drafting a soft law investment instrument. It is a well-respected organization that can draw on the expertise of contributors representing a broad range of States. Given the reservations about codification expressed above, the distillation would more likely take the form of a commentary, annotation or treatise, and would be directed towards a wider audience than just States, though it could help to guide treaty negotiators and decision-makers, including States and arbitrators. In fact, negotiation of a multilateral instrument might be facilitated and influenced by a soft law instrument that brings together investment law practice in an objective manner, that sets forth areas of convergence and divergence and the choices that need to be made by drafters, and that clearly sets out the policy implications of each of those choices.

The International Law Association would appear to be ideally situated to draft such an instrument.

5. Soft law instruments in environmental law: models for international investment law?

Kate Miles

I. INTRODUCTION

The changing nature of the international legal system over the last 50 years has generated novel approaches to law-making, innumerable rules, and a variety of institutions, mechanisms, and new actors within international law.[1] Reflecting these trends, there has also been an increased use of 'soft law' instruments during this period.[2] In part, this recent proliferation of soft law instruments and non-state actor initiatives is due to the manifold nature of the functions they can fulfil within international law, both as an end mechanism in themselves and as a precursor to the development of 'hard law'. Nevertheless, certain fields within international law have not utilized soft law instruments to the same degree as others, international investment law being just such an area. Recent developments in investment law, however, together with the trends in international law more generally, suggest that it is now appropriate to consider the potential use of soft law instruments within international investment law, and, indeed, the feasibility of the narrower task of codification of its principles and rules.

---

[1] See Philippe Sands, 'Turtles and Torturers: The Transformation of International Law' (2001) 33 *New York University Journal of International Law and Politics* 527; Anne-Marie Slaughter, *A New World Order* (2004); Nico Krisch and Benedict Kingsbury, 'Introduction: Global Governance and Global Administrative Law in the International Legal Order' (2006) 17:1 *The European Journal of International Law* 1; Frank Garcia, 'Globalization and the Theory of International Law' (2005) 11 *International Legal Theory* 9.

[2] Pierre-Marie Dupuy, 'Soft Law and the International Law of the Environment' (1991) 12 *Michigan Journal of International Law* 420; Kevin T Jackson, 'Global Corporate Governance: Soft Law and Reputational Accountability' (2010) 35 *Brooklyn Journal of International Law* 41, 44–7.

In exploring such issues, it also seems prudent to examine other fields of international law in which there has been extensive use of soft law instruments and where attempts have been made to codify principles and rules within discrete areas of international law. Adopting such an approach has the advantage of bringing insights from the experiences in these other areas into the examination of soft law instruments within international investment law. Accordingly, this chapter considers these issues with a particular focus on international environmental law, a field in which there has been a wide-ranging use of soft law instruments. However, in looking to the practices of another discipline within international law, the hazards of doing so – primarily that of the actual transferability of the experiences – must also be considered. For this reason, the similarities and differences between the target areas are also emphasized so as to assess the applicability of the experiences in the environmental field to that of investment.

II. SOFT LAW INSTRUMENTS IN INTERNATIONAL ENVIRONMENTAL LAW

Over recent decades, explorations into new techniques of law-making within international environmental law have produced numerous soft law initiatives.[3] These have taken a variety of forms, including aspirational framework-type documents, practical process-oriented standards, and detailed codification of specific subject areas.[4] In examining these instruments, what is particularly striking is the sheer volume of soft law

---

[3] Pierre-Marie Dupuy, 'Formation of Customary International Law and General Principles' in Bodansky, Brunnée and Hey (eds), *The Oxford Handbook of International Environmental Law* (2007) 458.

[4] See Neil Gunningham and Darren Sinclair, *Voluntary Approaches to Environmental Protection: Lessons from the Mining and Forestry Sectors*, OECD Global Forum on International Investment, OECD Conference on Foreign Direct Investment and the Environment: Lessons to be Learned from the Mining Sector (Paris, February 2002) 2 <http://www.oecd.org/dataoecd/46/1/1819792.pdf> accessed 24 February 2011; see also Stepan Wood, 'Voluntary Environmental Codes and Sustainability' in Benjamin J Richardson and Stepan Wood (eds), *Environmental Law for Sustainability* (2006) 229, 232–3; Kevin T Jackson, 'Global Corporate Governance: Soft Law and Reputational Accountability' (2010) 35 *Brooklyn Journal of International Law* 41, 70–85; see e.g. International Law Association, *Montreal Rules on Transfrontier Pollution*; *Rio Declaration on Environment and Development, Report of the UNCED*, 31 ILM 874, UN Doc A/CONF.151/6/Rev.1 (1992); *Equator Principles* (Washington, DC, 4 June 2003) <http://www.equator-principles.com> accessed 22 February 2011.

initiatives within the international environmental field. Individually, of course, there are those that are regarded as having achieved greater degrees of strength, influence or success than others, but it is also clear that such perceptions are linked to the particular functions of the instrument – and that those functions are largely determinative of many aspects of the instrument's form, substance and, ultimately, perceived success. In other words, the particular model adopted for any one instrument tends to be dependent on the purpose of the initiative. These elements then, in turn, shape the expectations of the instrument's likely outcomes or influence on the conduct of relevant actors.

In the context of the enquiries in this book, this experience with environmental instruments points to an important preliminary issue for consideration – what functions do we want soft law instruments to fulfil within the investment sector? As the possible functions identified will likely shape the type of instruments designed, this question should remain at the forefront of assessments of potential soft law models for use in international investment law. Accordingly, there is a need to ascertain whether the investment sector should (i) focus solely on codification of international investment law; (ii) consider a mixture of codification and progressive development of the law; (iii) explore other forms of law-making instruments that could be useful in the context of investment law; or (iv) adopt a combination of these options.

A. Codification Attempts within International Environmental Law

In examining the feasibility of codifying international investment law, insights can be drawn from several codification attempts within international environmental law. In particular, two key points can be discerned. First, successful codification requires a discrete subject area. For example, when attempts were made to ascertain the general rules and principles of the international law on the environment as a whole, as the International Law Association (ILA) sought to do during the 1970s,[5] significant disagreement emerged and the scope of the investigation had to be scaled down to a more manageable topic.[6] Thus, rather than the full

---

[5] International Law Association, *Report of the 50th Conference* (1972) 468–500; International Law Association, *Report of the 54th Conference* (1976) 564–87; International Law Association, *Report of the 56th Conference* (1978) 383–422.

[6] Alan Boyle, 'Codification of International Environmental Law and the International Law Commission: Injurious Consequences Revisited' in Alan E Boyle and David Freestone (eds), *International Law and Sustainable Development: Past Achievements and Future Challenges* (1999) 61, 64–5.

breadth of international environmental law, the focus of the study instead became that of transboundary issues and led to the drafting of the *Montreal Rules on Transfrontier Pollution.*[7] With this type of experience in mind, it would seem advisable to determine at the outset whether the entirety of international investment law is ripe for codification, and if not, whether perhaps instead certain discrete topics within the field currently lend themselves to the process of codification more than others.

The drawback to this more limited approach in striving solely for codification, however, is that its very character of consensus indicates that the instrument is not breaking new ground. In this regard, a criticism that has been levied at the *Montreal Rules on Transfrontier Pollution,*[8] as well as at other codification attempts within the environmental field,[9] is that where they have been restricted to codification of existing law only, the result has been exceedingly conservative.[10] Indeed, the lack of controversy, perhaps, indicates that the instrument is too 'safe' and is, therefore, less useful as it merely reproduces information of which experts are already aware and upon which they all agree.

The second key point to note reinforces these inferences from the first regarding the limitations of codification as an approach. In contrast to the *Montreal Rules on Transfrontier Pollution,*[11] many codification-type instruments in international environmental law have tended not to be restricted solely to crystallized rules of international law, but have also engaged in the progressive development of the law in the specific sectors examined, including emerging rules within the field or seeking to create new rules.[12] Combinations of this kind can be seen in the International Law Commission's work on the law of the sea,[13] the *Stockholm Declaration,*[14]

---

7 International Law Association, *Report of the 60th Conference* (1982) 1.

8 Ibid.

9 See e.g. the sectoral work of the International Law Association on water pollution.

10 Boyle, above n 6, 65.

11 International Law Association, *Report of the 60th Conference* (1982) 1.

12 Boyle, above n 6, 61–4; see also, Dupuy, above n 3, discussing the role of soft law instruments in the development of new rules of customary law; see also Ian Brownlie, *Principles of Public International Law* (7th edn, 2008) 278–80 (discussing 'Emergent Legal Principles', sustainable development, and 'soft law').

13 The International Law Commission (ILC) worked on the codification of the law of the sea from 1950 until the adoption of the *United Nations Convention on the Law of the Sea*, which was opened for signature 10 December 1982, (1982) 21 ILM 1261 (entered into force 16 November 1994).

14 *Declaration of the United Nations Conference on the Human Environment*, 16 June 1972, UN Doc A/CONF.48/14 (1972), 11 ILM 1416 (1972).

the 1986 *Draft Convention on Environmental Protection and Sustainable Development*,[15] the United Nation's *Rio Declaration*,[16] or the IUCN's (International Union for Conservation of Nature) *Draft Covenant on Environment and Development*.[17] It is quite clear from the impact of such instruments that even if some aspects do not immediately reflect existing law, the document itself can come to take on an authoritative role. In these particular instances, the instruments influenced the direction of the law significantly and many elements considered controversial at the time of drafting often later became a settled part of the law.[18]

Reflecting on these experiences within the environmental field, a central issue for the investment sector clearly involves the scope of the material to be included in a codification project. In fact, decisions on content will largely be determined by the intended purpose of the instrument. In other words, do we want an instrument that focuses solely on codification of existing law, or one that also shapes the law of the future and expressly engages in the progressive development of the rules? While there are advantages in limiting the project to those principles around which there is consensus – not the least of which is the timely completion of the project – I am very much of the view that the more progressive approach is the preferable one, both generally and as specifically applied to international investment law. Such a project in the investment field could afford to be somewhat adventurous and to seek to shape the rules. And indeed, if it does not, it may run the risk of being dismissed, first, as irrelevant because it states the obvious, or second, as a thinly veiled attempt to resurrect the rules embodied in the *Multilateral Agreement on Investment*[19] without

---

15 R D Munro and J A Lammers (eds), *Environmental Protection and Sustainable Development: Legal Principles and Recommendations* (1986).

16 *Rio Declaration on Environment and Development, Report of the UNCED*, UN Doc A/CONF.151/6/Rev.1 (1992), 31 ILM 874 (1992).

17 IUCN, *Draft Covenant on Environment and Development* (3rd edn, 2004) <http://www.i-c-e-l.org/english/EPLP31EN_rev2.pdf > accessed 26 January 2011.

18 For example, the Rio Declaration's statements on sustainable development were not established principles of international environmental law at the time, but now form part of the accepted principles of international environmental law, if not of international law more generally; see also the ILC's draft articles on the law of the sea, which formed the basis for the *United Nations Convention on the Law of the Sea*, opened for signature 10 December 1982, (1982) 21 ILM 1261 (entered into force 16 November 1994).

19 See the draft *Multilateral Agreement on Investment* (MAI) at OECD Negotiating Group on the Multilateral Agreement on Investment, Draft Consolidated Text, 22 April 1998, <http://www1.oecd.org/daf/mai/pdf/ng/ng987r1e.pdf> accessed 25 January 2011.

addressing the more controversial issues that contributed to the collapse of those negotiations.[20]

Codification, together with progressive development, of investment law would certainly be the more difficult path to pursue as there is a disparate and passionately held range of views. However, it would also be the more appropriate model for this field precisely because a number of key areas of the law are still in a state of flux and continue to cause controversy, notable examples being the constituent elements of the fair and equitable treatment standard and the use of non-treaty-based rules such as the defence of necessity. While some areas are now well settled, acknowledging that controversy is, in my view, important to the credibility of the instrument. Furthermore, this dual purpose model would make for a more interesting, constructive, and ultimately more useful option, as it would constitute a 'living' instrument rather than one solely seeking to capture a moment in time that has, in fact, already passed.

B. Beyond Codification: Other Forms of Soft Law Instrument in International Environmental Law

In addition to treaties and rules of customary international law, international environmental law-making has manifested itself through a vast array of soft law instruments.[21] Accordingly, it is also worth considering whether instruments other than codification models could be of value to international investment law. In this regard, it is fair to say that international environmental law has been, and continues to be, shaped in fundamental ways by soft law instruments and other initiatives. In part because of its non-binding and flexible character, soft law is being used to perform a number of central functions in international environmental relations and law-making. In contrast to the lengthy processes entailed in the conclusion of treaties and the crystallization of rules of customary international law, the relative ease with which soft law instruments can be negotiated and altered renders them ideal mechanisms when a rapid response to global environmental issues is required.[22] At times considered

---

20 See M Sornarajah, *The International Law on Foreign Investment* (3rd edn, 2010) 3, 258–62 (discussing the contributing causes of the collapse of the MAI negotiations).

21 Philippe Sands, *Principles of International Environmental Law* (2nd edn, 2003) 124, 231–2; Dupuy, above n 2; see also Brownlie, above n 12.

22 Geoffrey Palmer, 'New Ways to Make International Environmental Law' (1992) 86 *AJIL* 259, 269–70; Kenneth W Abbott and Duncan Snidal, 'Hard and Soft Law in International Governance' (2000) 54 *International Organization* 421,

as evidence of state practice or *opinio juris* or even as an intermediary signal of future 'hard law', the norms contained within soft law instruments interact closely with treaty obligations and custom.[23] And, as a reflection of these dynamic processes, fluidity in the exchange of concepts among disciplines is also common in the substance of soft law instruments within the environmental field.[24]

1. Concept formation

One key role for soft law is in the introduction and progressive development of new concepts and principles. For example, within international environmental law, soft law has been instrumental in the appearance of the concept of sustainable development, the particular form it has ultimately taken, and its evolution into a principle of international environmental law.[25] Much the same can also be said of the precautionary principle. Through an ongoing process of utilization in soft law instruments,[26] fierce debate among commentators,[27] submissions in

---

421–423; Andrew T Guzman, 'A Compliance-Based Theory of International Law' (2002) 90 *California Law Review* 1823, 1879–81; Dinah Shelton, 'Normative Hierarchy in International Law' (2006) 100 *AJIL* 291, 319–20; Anne-Marie Slaughter, Andrew S Tulumello and Stepan Wood, 'International Law and International Relations Theory: A New Generation of Interdisciplinary Scholarship' (1998) 92 *AJIL* 367, 370–1.

[23] Palmer, above n 22, 269–70; Shelton, above n 22, 319–20; see also David Weissbrodt and Muria Kruger, 'Norms on the Responsibilities of Transnational Corporations and Other Business Enterprises with Regard to Human Rights' (2003) 97 *AJIL* 901, 914–15.

[24] Philippe Sands, 'Treaty, Custom and the Cross-Fertilization of International Law' (1998) 1 *Yale Human Rights and Development Law Journal* 85, 88–91; see generally Milena Sterio, 'The Evolution of International Law' (2008) 31 *Boston College International and Comparative Law Review* 213, 215–20; see also Alhaji B Marong, 'From Rio to Johannesburg: Reflections on the Role of International Legal Norms in Sustainable Development' (2003) 16 *Georgetown International Environmental Law Review* 21, 30–2 (discussing sustainable development and soft law instruments).

[25] See Sands, above n 21, 252–66; for example, the Rio Declaration was particularly influential in the development of the principle of sustainable development, as was the 'Brundtland Report', *Rio Declaration on Environment and Development, Report of the UNCED*, UN Doc A/CONF.151/6/Rev.1 (1992), (1992) 31 ILM 874; World Commission on Environment and Development, *Our Common Future: The Report of the World Commission on Environment and Development* (1987).

[26] See e.g. *Rio Declaration on Environment and Development, Report of the UNCED*, UN Doc A/CONF.151/6/Rev.1 (1992), (1992) 31 ILM 874.

[27] See Jacqueline Peel, *The Precautionary Principle in Practice: Environmental Decision-Making and Scientific Uncertainty* (2005) (analysing discourses and

international disputes,[28] and appearance in environment-related treaties,[29] precaution, in its many forms, has evolved into a principle of international environmental law.[30] Its interaction with other fields of international law and possible application in other contexts, such as trade regulation, is, of course, a separate and far less conclusive matter.[31] For the purposes of this study, however, it is particularly useful to note the role played by soft law in the embryonic stages of concept development. With respect to sustainable development and the precautionary principle, soft law initiatives were central in proposing particular formulations of the concepts, generating debate, triggering the design of alternative phrasing, and contributing to their transition into core principles of international environmental law.[32] Although significant disagreement still surrounds the implications of these principles and their application in specific circumstances, it is clear that soft law performed an important role in creating space for both the development of the concepts' key elements and the discourse surrounding their progression – and this is a valuable lesson in considering the uses to which soft law could be put in the investment field.

In this regard, soft law instruments could well provide an experimental forum in which new concepts can be proposed or existing ones fleshed out and remodelled. They could also be a useful means through which states could express an affinity with principles or viewpoints to which they were not quite ready to commit in bilateral investment treaties. In some respects, this would almost serve as a 'bridging' function, giving states time

---

disagreements); see e.g. Julian Morris (ed), *Rethinking Risk and the Precautionary Principle* (2000) (discussing critical perspectives on the precautionary principle).

28 See, for example, the reliance on precaution by state parties in the following trade disputes: *European Communities – Measures Concerning Meat and Meat Products (Hormones)*, WT/DS26/AB/R (1998); Panel Report, *European Communities – Measures Affecting the Approval and Marketing of Biotech Products*, WT/DS291/R (2006).

29 See e.g. *United Nations Convention on Biological Diversity*, opened for signature 5 June 1992, (1992) 31 ILM 822 (entered into force 29 December 1993).

30 Sands, above n 21, 267–79.

31 See Peel, above n 27 (discussing the interaction between principles of trade law and environmental law); see also Jacqueline Peel, *Science and Risk Regulation in International Law* (2010).

32 See *Rio Declaration on Environment and Development, Report of the UNCED*, UN Doc A/CONF.151/6/Rev.1 (1992), (1992) 31 ILM 874 (discussing in particular, the influential appearance of the precautionary principle and sustainable development).

to become comfortable with controversial ideas before actually assuming such obligations in a 'hard law' form. Such a mechanism could be particularly useful in promoting the more general application of features that have appeared in the so-called 'new generation BITs', a term that has been adopted to refer to recent treaties that have included express references to sustainable development, protection of the environment, and the health and safety of the public.[33] This bridging function could, perhaps, take form within international investment law as a Declaration of Principles, a Code of Conduct, or Guidelines under the auspices of international organizations such as the United Nations.[34] In this way, not only could provisions from new generation BITs be included in the instrument, but more controversial proposals that have not yet featured in treaties could also be introduced. Such an approach would certainly generate the discourse necessary to explore concepts more fully and would also give an indication of possible future directions for the rules to develop.

A fairly hefty proviso to the utilization of this function of soft law, however, is that there needs to be the requisite desire for such instruments within the investment context. Furthermore, once drafted, there would also need to be a conviction among the relevant decision-makers, such as states and arbitrators, that the instrument is both applicable and useful in individual instances of treaty negotiation or interpretation. These aspects could prove to be hurdles to the realization and use of investment soft law instruments styled in the image of the environmental law experience. Indeed, in some quarters, there remains a strong sense that the field is

---

[33] See Andrew Newcombe, 'Sustainable Development and Investment Treaty Law' (2007) 8 *Journal of World Investment & Trade* 357, 399 (using the term 'new generation BITs'); Wenhua Shan, 'From "North–South Divide" to "Private–Public Debate": Revival of the Calvo Doctrine and the Changing Landscape in International Investment Law' (2007) 27 *Northwestern Journal of International Law & Business* 631, 652, 656; see, for examples of such treaties, the United States–Uruguay BIT, *Treaty between the United States of America and the Oriental Republic of Uruguay Concerning the Encouragement and Reciprocal Protection of Investment* (2005) <http://www.unctad.org/sections/dite/iia/docs/bits/US_Uru guay.pdf> accessed 15 February 2011; see also the Canada–Peru BIT, *Agreement between Canada and the Republic of Peru for the Promotion and Protection of Investments* (2006) <http://www.international.gc.ca/trade-agreements-accords-commerciaux/assets/pdfs/Canada-Peru10nov06-en.pdf> accessed 4 February 2011.

[34] Precedents for such approaches include the United Nations Economic and Social Council, *Norms on the Responsibilities of Transnational Corporations and Other Business Enterprises with Regard to Human Rights*, UN ESCOR, 55th Sess, Agenda item 4, UN Doc E/CN.4/Sub.2/2003/12/Rev.2 (2003).

already well served by the existing network of investment treaties and its fundamentally treaty-based structure. For this reason, in particular, investment-related soft law instruments in the mode of a 'Declaration of Principles' may not emerge organically from within the sector in the way they have in international environmental law.

There are also significant structural differences between the environmental and investment areas and their law-making processes that may also impact upon the use of such instruments within international investment law. For example, historically, international environmental law has developed in an essentially *ad hoc* manner, arising out of complex interactive processes between states, non-state actors, and the occurrence of particular environmental events, and it is an area of law that continues to be drawn from disparate sources.[35] As a field, it has a strong reliance on customary international law, general principles and soft law, in addition to a number of key environmental treaties addressing individual substantive topics.[36] The principles of international investment law developed in the nineteenth century as a branch of the law on diplomatic protection of alien property, before evolving into a primarily treaty-based system with the advent of bilateral investment treaties, the first of which was concluded between Germany and Pakistan in 1959.[37] There is now a network of close to 3,000 bilateral investment treaties and, although each treaty might vary in the exact wording of the provisions, most involve variations of the same core obligations, namely national treatment, most-favoured-nation

---

[35] Sands, above n 21, 25–45; 169–70.

[36] For examples of key environmental treaties, see *United Nations Convention on the Law of the Sea*, opened for signature 10 December 1982, (1982) 21 ILM 1261 (entered into force 16 November 1994); *United Nations Framework Convention on Climate Change*, opened for signature 9 May 1992, 31 ILM 849 (entered into force 24 March 1994); *United Nations Convention on Biological Diversity*, opened for signature 5 June 1992, (1992) 31 ILM 822 (entered into force 29 December 1993); *Convention on International Trade in Endangered Species of Wild Fauna and Flora*, opened for signature 3 March 1973, 993 UNTS 243 (entered into force 1 July 1975); *Convention on the Control of Transboundary Movement of Hazardous Wastes and their Disposal*, opened for signature 22 March 1989, (1989) 28 ILM 657 (entered into force 1992).

[37] *Treaty between the Federal Republic of Germany and Pakistan for the Promotion and Protection of Investments*, signed 25 November 1959, (1963) 457 UNTS 23 (entered into force 28 April 1962); Charles Lipson, *Standing Guard: Protecting Foreign Capital in the Nineteenth and Twentieth Centuries* (1985) 11–12, 37–38; see Andrew Newcombe and Lluís Paradell, *Law and Practice of Investment Treaties: Standards of Treatment* (2009) 3–18 (discussing the historical development of international investment law).

treatment, fair and equitable treatment, full protection and security, and prohibitions on uncompensated expropriation.[38] In more recent treaty negotiations, the nature of certain obligations has been expanded upon; in addition, nuances have emerged in the course of arbitral proceedings.[39] Although influenced by the ongoing discourse in the field, these have been the primary methods of structured concept formation within international investment law. There has not, traditionally, been a reliance on soft law for the formation of concepts similar to that seen in international environmental law, and this difference in approach may well impact significantly on the field's interest in utilizing soft law in this fashion.

The different ways in which these areas of international law are enforced is also relevant for assessing the transferability of the environmental law model to investment. In particular, it should be noted that the investor-state arbitration mechanism and the central role of investors in invoking investment protection treaties has led to a highly utilized dispute settlement system, the effect of which is that, in recent years, a large number of awards have been published.[40] One effect of this increase has been the development of a quasi-jurisprudential approach to the application of the law, in which the reasoning in many awards appears to have assumed the additional function of the exploration and expansion of concepts in international investment law.[41] In contrast to this more litigation-based model, international environmental dispute resolution has generally featured a more regulatory approach, in which treaties have established monitoring procedures and compliance mechanisms.[42]

---

[38] See generally Stephan W Schill, *The Multilateralization of International Investment Law* (2009).

[39] See e.g. Canada–Peru BIT, *Agreement between Canada and the Republic of Peru for the Promotion and Protection of Investments* (2006) <http://www.international.gc.ca/trade-agreements-accords-commerciaux/assets/pdfs/Canada-Peru10nov06-en.pdf> accessed 4 February 2011; see *In the Matter of a NAFTA Arbitration under UNCITRAL Arbitration Rules between International Thunderbird Gaming Corp v United Mexican States*, Award, 26 January 2006 (discussing fair and equitable treatment and 'legitimate expectations').

[40] Newcombe and Paradell, above n 37, 57–9.

[41] See e.g. Thomas Wälde in *In the Matter of a NAFTA Arbitration under UNCITRAL Arbitration Rules between International Thunderbird Gaming Corp v United Mexican States*, Award, 26 January 2006 <http://www.naftaclaims.com/Disputes/Mexico/Thunderbird/Thunderbird_Dissent.pdf> accessed 27 September 2011 (discussing 'legitimate expectation' in Thomas Wälde's separate opinion).

[42] See generally Tim Stephens, *International Courts and Environmental Protection* (2009); see e.g. *Kyoto Protocol to the United Nations Framework Convention on Climate Change*, opened for signature 11 December 1997, (1998) 37 ILM 22 (entered into force 16 February 2005).

Although there are, of course, environmental-related state-to-state disputes in which treaties are interpreted and concepts are analysed,[43] they occur relatively infrequently compared to the rapid growth in investor-state disputes. In this respect, the opportunities for exploration of concepts in the course of proceedings are, perhaps, fewer than those afforded to international investment law. To meet such a need, soft law has provided an avenue for the regular consideration of concepts within international environmental law. However, a comparable 'gap' within international investment law-making may not be present, rendering the need for soft law less pressing.

2. Norm-creation, non-state actors and influencing state behaviour

The role played by soft law in concept formation is also closely interrelated with two of its other key functions – norm-creation and influencing state behaviour. Recently within the international sphere, there has been a willingness to explore new governance options and a marked expansion of the role of non-state actors.[44] The combined effect of these elements has had a profound impact on law-making within the environmental field, and it is possible that such processes could also influence law-making within foreign investment protection. Certainly, the recent activities of non-state actors traditionally concerned with environmental issues have stretched beyond that field into the cross-sectoral framing of issues. This bringing together of seemingly disparate issues in trade, investment, development, environmental protection and human rights, together with the focus on interdisciplinary initiatives and the promotion of integrated approaches within soft law instruments, has promoted a novel cross-fertilization of concepts and principles among various fields of international law.[45] In contrast, soft law has not, to date, tended to play such a significant role in the formation of concepts within investment law. As discussed above, in the modern context, this function has largely been performed through

---

43 Notable examples include the *Case Concerning the Gabĉíkovo-Nagymaros Project (Hungary/Slovakia)* (1997) ICJ Rep 7; see also *United States-Import Prohibition of Certain Shrimp and Shrimp Products, Report of the Appellate Body* (1999) 38 ILM 118.

44 Sands, above n 21, 112–22; S Jacob Scherr and R Juge Gregg, 'Johannesburg and Beyond: The 2002 World Summit on Sustainable Development and the Rise of Partnerships' (2006) 18 *Georgetown International Environmental Law Review* 425; see also Sands, above n 1.

45 Sands, above n 1; see Sands, above n 24 (discussing the transfer of concepts and principles and using the term 'cross-fertilization' for the transfer of principles within international law for the first time in this 1998 article).

treaty negotiation processes and the published reasoning of arbitral awards. However, it may not be possible for investment law to remain immune from these more general developments in international law-making and governance as multiple areas of international law are increasingly linked. Accordingly, the experience of soft law instruments within the environmental field may not only have analogous lessons for international investment law, but may also result in direct engagement between these areas of law. Indeed, drawing on constructivist international relations theory, the early stages of just such a possibility are explored in the remainder of this chapter. To this end, it examines the interaction between soft law instruments, the emergence of corporate social responsibility initiatives, environmental codes of conduct in the financing and investment sectors, and potential law-making implications for international investment law.

a. Norm-creation in international environmental law

Exploring the role of soft law instruments in norm-creation, it becomes clear that the emergence of norms is an interactive process involving the assertion of principles, identification of behaviour reflecting their content, and a belief in the legal character of the new principles.[46] It is a gradual, continuous process of evolution and reinforcement of concepts, expected conduct, dialogue amongst actors on the international plane and assimilation of international principles into domestic law, policy and practices.[47] Traditionally, of course, norm-creation has been solely the realm of states.[48] A rule of customary international law crystallizes as such when

---

[46] Brownlie, above n 12, 6–10; Claire Moore Dickerson, 'How Do Norms and Empathy Affect Corporation Law and Corporate Behavior? Human Rights: The Emerging Norm of Corporate Social Responsibility' (2002) 76 *Tulane Law Review* 1431, 1433–4; see Anthony Clark Arend, 'Do Legal Rules Matter? International Law and International Politics' (1998) 38 *Virginia Journal of International Law* 107, 128–40 (using a constructivist account of the emergence of norms in international law).

[47] Brownlie, above n 12, 6–10; Arend, above n 37, 128–40; John Braithwaite and Peter Drahos, *Global Business Regulation* (2000) 32; Harold Hongju Koh, 'Review Essay: Why Do Nations Obey Law?' (1997) 106 *Yale Law Journal* 2599, 2603; Eibe Riedel, 'Standards and Sources: Farewell to the Exclusivity of the Sources Triad in International Law?' (1991) 2:2 *EJIL* 58; Abram Chayes and Antonia Handler Chayes, *The New Sovereignty: Compliance with International Regulatory Agreements* (1995) 112–34.

[48] Sands, above n 1; JL Brierly, *The Law of Nations: An Introduction to the International Law of Peace* (6th edn, 1963) 1; Gillian D Triggs, *International Law: Contemporary Principles and Practices* (2006) 11–12, 23; Gennady M Danilenko, *Law-Making in the International Community* (1993) 75–87.

there is consistent state practice accompanied by *opinio juris*, being the belief that states are legally obligated to so act.[49]

Although it remains the case that states ultimately confer legal status on a concept either through its acceptance as a rule of customary international law or its inclusion in treaties, recent transformations in international law-making have seen non-state actors impacting on the evolution of principles of international law.[50] With respect to international environmental law and its reach into the investment field, complex processes have become engaged, in which the activities of international organizations, non-governmental organizations (NGOs), multinational corporations and international financial institutions are contributing to the development of emerging principles of corporate social and environmental responsibility for the financing and investment sectors.[51]

i. Soft law instruments, CSR and international investment law

In considering the significance of corporate social responsibility (CSR) as it pertains to international investment law, it is useful to draw on the work of international relations scholars, and, in particular, those working in the

---

[49] Brierly, above n 39, 59–62; Brownlie, above n 37, 6–10; Jennifer A Zerk, *Multinationals and Corporate Social Responsibility: Limitations and Opportunities in International Law* (2006) 262; Theodor Meron, 'The Continuing Role of Custom in the Formation of International Humanitarian Law' (1996) 90 *AJIL* 238, 239.

[50] Sands, above n 1; James Crawford, *International Law as an Open System: Selected Essays* (2002) 19–22; Philippe Sands, 'The Environment, Community and International Law' (1989) 30 *Harvard International Law Journal* 393; Peter J Spiro, 'Globalization, International Law and the Academy' (2000) 32 *New York University Journal of International Law and Politics* 567; Isabelle R Gunning, 'Modernizing Customary International Law: The Challenge of Human Rights' (1991) 31 *Virginia Journal of International Law* 211, 221; Julie Mertus, 'Considering Nonstate Actors in the New Millennium: Toward Expanded Participation in Norm Generation and Norm Application' (2000) 32(2) *New York University Journal of International Law and Politics* 537, 537, 562; Harold Hongju Koh, 'Transnational Legal Process' (1996) 75 *Nebraska Law Review* 181, 203–4; Julie Mertus, 'Doing Democracy Differently: The Transformative Potential of Human Rights NGOs in Transnational Civil Society' (1998) *Third World Legal Studies* 205.

[51] Moore Dickerson, above n 37, 1433–34; see also Sol Picciotto, 'Rights, Responsibilities and Regulation of International Business' (2003) 42 *Columbia Journal of Transnational Law* 131; David B Hunter, 'Civil Society Networks and the Development of Environmental Standards at International Financial Institutions' (2008) 8 *Chicago Journal of International Law* 437, 437–8, 467–9.

constructivist school, to gain a sense of emerging trends.[52] From a constructivist perspective, soft law instruments and other CSR initiatives, whether originating from states, NGOs, industry or international organizations, are creating pre-normative 'noise'.[53] The multitude of instruments, codes, concepts, standards, and policies related to CSR specifications have not only firmly placed the issue on the international agenda, but are also part of the process of exploring the most effective mechanisms to bring about more socially and environmentally responsible corporate conduct. At the same time, this interplay of actors, instruments and differing forms of CSR implementation is leading to the normalization or mainstreaming of CSR within the private sector.[54] It also constitutes a mutually reinforcing mode of interaction between emerging norms and corporate conduct.[55] Of course, the significance of this trend should not be overstated. CSR has not yet crystallized into a rule of customary international law. The conduct of states does not consistently reflect the existence of such a rule.[56] On a number of levels, however, it does appear that state behaviour is being influenced by the pre-normative CSR activities of non-state actors – and this points to the future emergence of international customary rules on CSR.[57] What can be said is that CSR principles are in the process of emerging; they are shaping the discourse;

[52] Jutta Brunnée and Stephen J Toope, 'International Law and Constructivism: Elements of an Interactional Theory of International Law' (2000) 39 *Columbia Journal of Transnational Law* 19. The constructivist international law/international relations position examines the role of processes, actors, interests, contextual understandings, and shifting perspectives in norm-creation. See further for an account of the constructivist view, Kenneth WAbbott, 'International Relations Theory, International Law, and the Regime Governing Atrocities in Internal Conflicts' (1999) 93 *AJIL* 361, 362–77.

[53] See, Zerk, above n 40, 101–2; see also Brunnée and Toope, above n 43; for a discussion on the role of soft law, states and non-state actors in the process of international legalization, see Abbott and Snidal, above n 22, 421–3.

[54] Amiram Gill, 'Corporate Governance as Social Responsibility: A Research Agenda' (2008) 26 *Berkeley Journal of International Law* 452, 461–2; Kenneth W Abbott and Duncan Snidal, 'Strengthening International Regulation Through Transnational New Governance: Overcoming the Orchestration Deficit' (2009) 42 *Vanderbilt Journal of Transnational Law* 501.

[55] Moore Dickerson, above n 37, 1433; Gregory C Shaffer, 'How Business Shapes Law: A Socio-Legal Framework' (2009) 42 *Connecticut Law Review* 147; Ralph G Steinhardt, 'Soft Law, Hard Norms: Competitive Self-Interest and the Emergence of Human Rights Responsibilities for Multinational Corporations' (2008) 33 *Brooklyn Journal of International Law* 933, 934–6.

[56] Zerk, above n 40, 276, 299–300.

[57] Ibid, 243, 262–3; Moore Dickerson, above n 37, 1433, 1460.

they are creating expectations of state and corporate conduct; and they are underpinning calls for a multilateral treaty on CSR.[58]

The development of CSR as a concept and its rapid progression as an emerging principle provides a startling example of the impact that soft law and other related instruments can have on the evolution of norms. It is also a particularly significant mode of interaction for the investment sector as these concepts are concerned with the way in which transnational business is conducted, although it entails the emergence of norms from outside the investment field. These trends indicate shifting expectations and understandings in the wider environment in which transnational business operates and point to the potential for a spill-over of these developments into what is expected from the international investment field and the law that governs it.

ii Soft law instruments, non-state actors and the cross-fertilization of concepts

As discussed above, the recent activities of non-state actors, and new methods of engagement between states and non-state actors, have been instrumental in the cross-sectoral infusion of concepts, principles and issues. In particular, within the environmental field, there has been an emphasis on the use of soft law instruments to promote this approach and on the fostering of 'partnerships' and new collaborations.[59] For example, a significant feature of the 2002 World Summit on Sustainable Development was the focus on partnerships to promote sustainable development.[60] Illustrative of this approach to global governance, the *Johannesburg Plan of Implementation* provides that:[61]

> [...] the implementation [of the outcomes of the Summit] should involve all relevant actors through partnerships, especially between Governments of the

---

58 Zerk, above n 40, 243–4, 262–3; see Isabella D Bunn, 'Global Advocacy for Corporate Accountability: Transatlantic Perspectives from the NGO Community' (2004) 19 *American University International Law Review* 1265, 1304–6; Robert McCorquodale, 'Human Rights and Global Business' in Stephen Bottomley and David Kinley (eds), *Commercial Law and Human Rights* (2002) 89, 111–14; for an example of a CSR treaty proposal, see Friends of the Earth, *Towards Binding Corporate Accountability* (2002) <www.foe.co.uk/resource/briefings/corporate_accountability.pdf> accessed 23 January 2011.

59 Sands, above n 21, 12–122; Scherr and Gregg, above n 44.

60 Scherr and Gregg, above n 44, 439–40.

61 *Johannesburg Plan of Implementation, Report of the World Summit on Sustainable Development*, UN Doc A/CONF.199/20 (2002) para 3, <www.un.org/esa/sustdev/documents/WSSD.../WSSD_PlanImpl. pdf> accessed 25 February 2011.

North and South, on the one hand, and between Governments and major groups, on the other, to achieve the widely shared goals of sustainable development. As reflected in the Monterrey Consensus, such partnerships are key to pursuing sustainable development in a globalizing world.

The *United Nations Global Compact* (*UN Global Compact*) provides another example of this emphasis on collaborative engagement, combining new institutional techniques with a cross-sectoral approach. It promotes voluntary partnerships between governments, corporations, NGOs and United Nations agencies to address issues related to human rights, the environment, economic activity, developing markets, labour rights and anti-corruption measures.[62] In fact, the field of international development law and policy, in particular, is illustrative of this integrated approach within both soft law instruments and other programmes. A range of different types of international instruments exemplify the contextual consideration of development issues, such as the *Rio Declaration on Environment and Development*,[63] *Agenda 21*,[64] the World Bank's 'safeguard policies' on social and environmental issues in project finance for developing states,[65] the *United Nations Millennium Development Goals*,[66] the *Monterrey Consensus on Financing for Development*,[67] the *Johannesburg Declaration on Sustainable Develop-*

---

62 United Nations Global Compact, *Corporate Citizenship in the World Economy* (2008) <http://www.unglobalcompact.org/docs/news_events/8.1/GC_brochure_FINAL.pdf> accessed 1 March 2011; see Benjamin J Richardson, *Socially Responsible Investment Law: Regulating the Unseen Polluters* (2008) 409–10; Michael Barnett and Raymond Duvall, 'Power in International Politics' (2005) 59 *International Organization* 39; see also Dilek Cetindamar and Kristoffer Husoy, 'Corporate Social Responsibility Practices and Environmentally Responsible Behavior: The Case of the United Nations Global Compact' (2007) 76 *Journal of Business Ethics* 163; Lisa Whitehouse, 'Corporate Social Responsibility, Corporate Citizenship and the Global Compact: A New Approach to Regulating Corporate Social Power?' (2003) 3:3 *Global Social Policy* 299.

63 *Rio Declaration on Environment and Development, Report of the UNCED*, UN Doc A/CONF.151/6/Rev.1 (1992), 31 ILM 874 (1992).

64 *Agenda 21, Report of the UNCED*, UN Doc A/CONF.151/26/Rev.1 (vol.I) (1992), 31 ILM 874.

65 The World Bank, *Operational Manual: Operational Policies: Environmental Assessment*, World Bank OP 4.01 (January 1999).

66 *United Nations Millennium Declaration*, UNGA Res. A/55/2 (2000); *United Nations Development Goals*, <http://www.un.org/millenniumgoals/> accessed 15 February 2011.

67 *Monterrey Consensus of the International Conference on Financing for Development*, UN Doc A/AC.257/32 (2002) <http://www.un.org/esa/ffd/monterrey/MonterreyConsensus.pdf> accessed 5 February 2011.

ment,[68] the *Doha Ministerial Declaration* linking trade and environmental protection,[69] the *Conference on the World Financial and Economic Crisis and its Impact on Development*,[70] and the *UN Global Compact*.[71] In practice, this approach means that while the focus of these instruments is on development, the issues are not considered in artificial isolation from other relevant factors. The wider impact over time, of course, is that the influence of these instruments stretches beyond the immediate context of development and affects the way in which other related issues, such as foreign investment, are perceived.

Reinforcing the integrated approach seen in such soft law instruments, a number of environmental NGOs and research organizations have specifically focused on integrating issues and facilitating the cross-fertilization of principles between fields of international law.[72] For example, the Washington-based Center for International Environmental Law has a specific programme dedicated to the intersection of human rights law and international environmental law.[73] The International Union for Conservation of Nature (IUCN), as a hybrid organization of governmental and non-governmental members, has several cross-cutting programmes, including 'Business and Biodiversity',[74] 'Social Policy in Conservation',[75] and 'Species Trade and Use'.[76] The IUCN has also issued a statement on armed conflict

---

68 *Johannesburg Declaration on Sustainable Development, Report of the United Nations World Summit on Sustainable Development*, UN Doc A/CONF. 199/20 (2002) <http://www.un.org/esa/sustdev/documents/WSSD_POI_PD/English/POI_PD.htm> accessed 5 February 2011.

69 *Declaration of the Fourth Ministerial Conference*, Doha, Qatar, WT/MIN(01)/DEC/1, 20 November 2001, paras 31–3.

70 *Conference on the World Financial and Economic Crisis, Report of the Secretary-General*, UN Doc. A/CONF.214/4 (2009) <http://www.un.org/ga/search/view_doc.asp?symbol=A/CONF.214/4&Lang=E> accessed 15 February 2011.

71 United Nations Global Compact (2000) <http://www.unglobalcompact.org/> accessed 15 February 2011.

72 Sands, above n 24; see Sands, above n 1, 527, 530, 556–7 (discussing the role of non-state actors in new trends in international law).

73 Center for International Environmental Law, *Human Rights and the Environment* (2005) <http://www.ciel.org/Hre/programhre.html> accessed 10 February 2011.

74 IUCN, *Business and Biodiversity* <http://www.iucn.org/about/work/programmes/business/> accessed 10 February 2011.

75 IUCN, *Social Policy* <http://www.iucn.org/about/work/programmes/social_policy/> accessed 11 February 2011.

76 IUCN, *Our Work Programmes: Species Trade and Use Programme* <http://www.iucn.org/ about/work/programmes/species/our_work/species_trade_use/> accessed 11 February 2011.

and principles of environmental protection and included provisions on military activities and the environment in its Draft Covenant on Environment and Development.[77] The London-based NGO Foundation for International Environmental Law and Development (FIELD) has three work streams, one of which is devoted to 'Trade, Investment and Sustainable Development'.[78] The rationale for the International Institute for Sustainable Development (IISD) is necessarily the integration of social, economic and environmental issues, with key research themes encompassing 'Climate Change and Energy', 'Governance', 'Foreign Investment for Sustainable Development', 'Networks and Partnerships' and 'Sustainable Markets'.[79] And the Centre for International Sustainable Development Law (CISDL) further exemplifies an integrated approach with its multi-pronged international legal research agenda designed to 'promote sustainable societies and the protection of ecosystems'[80] through diverse programmes such as 'Trade, Investment and Financial Law for Sustainable Development', 'Biodiversity and Biosafety', 'Health and Hazards', 'Climate Change', 'Natural Resources' and 'Human Rights and Poverty Eradication in Sustainable Development Law'.[81]

From an interactive and process-oriented perspective on international law and international relations, this type of engagement from environmental NGOs has contributed to the framing of international issues in an integrated fashion.[82] In reinforcing the approach taken in soft

---

[77] IUCN, *Statement: Armed Conflict and the Environment* (2003) <http://www.iucn.org/en/news/ archive/2001_2005/press/iraqstatement210303.pdf> accessed 26 July 2007; IUCN, *Draft Covenant on Environment and Development*, (3rd edn, 2004) Art 32, Commentary 101–6, <http://www.i-c-e-l.org/english/EPLP31EN_ rev2.pdf > accessed 12 February 2011.

[78] Foundation for International Environmental Law and Development, *Trade, Investment and Sustainable Development* <http://www.field.org.uk/work-areas/trade-investment-and-sustainable-development/trade-investment-and-sustainable-development> accessed 12 February 2011.

[79] International Institute for Sustainable Development, *Our Knowledge: Themes* <http://www.iisd.org/> accessed 11 February 2011.

[80] Centre for International Sustainable Development Law, *About the CISDL* <http://www.cisdl.org/ about.html> accessed 11 February 2011.

[81] Centre for International Sustainable Development Law, *CISDL Legal Programmes* <http://www.cisdl.org/ programmes.html> accessed 18 February 2011.

[82] See further discussion *supra* in chapter 3 on the role of environmental NGOs in global politico-legal issues and the development of international law and policy. In particular, see, Sands, above n 1, 527, 530, 556–7 (discussing the influence of NGOs in international law and politics); Stephan Hobe, 'Global Challenges to Statehood: The Increasingly Important Role of Nongovernmental Organizations'

law instruments, it has been a factor in normalizing the idea of transferring principles as among previously isolated fields of international law, and, in particular, it has extended the reach of the concept of sustainable development well beyond international environmental law. With respect to the investment sector, the work of NGOs such as FIELD, IISD and CISDL has specifically directed attention to the wider implications of foreign investment practices and has advocated the application of an integrated approach to international investment law.[83] By locating foreign investment law and policy within a framework of sustainability, these NGOs have not only placed pressure on the investment sector to incorporate principles from other areas of international law, but, at the same time, have also provided channels through which reshaping of the law could occur. For example, their work points to those areas considered most in need of reform, illustrates the way in which socially and environmentally responsible investment principles could play a role in resolving investment disputes, and provides templates for the adoption of an integrated approach in international investment instruments.[84]

(1997) 5 *Indiana Journal of Global Legal Studies* 191; see generally, Thomas Princen and Matthias Finger, *Environmental NGOs in World Politics: Linking the Local and the Global* (1994); Michele M Betsill and Elisabeth Corell, 'Introduction to NGO Diplomacy' in Michele M Betsill and Elisabeth Corell (eds), *NGO Diplomacy: The Influence of Nongovernmental Organizations in International Environmental Negotiations* (2008) 2–3.

[83] See e.g. Howard Mann and Konrad von Moltke, *NAFTA's Chapter 11 and the Environment: Addressing the Impacts of the Investor-State Process on the Environment*, International Institute for Sustainable Development, 6 (1999) <http://www.iisd.org/pdf/nafta.pdf> accessed 20 February 2011; Konrad von Moltke, *An International Investment Regime? Issues of Sustainability*, International Institute for Sustainable Development (2000) 50 <http://www.iisd.org/pdf/invest ment.pdf> accessed 5 April 2009; Marie-Claire Cordonier-Segger, Markus Gehring and Andrew Newcombe (eds), *Sustainable Development in International Investment Law* (2011); Foundation for International Environmental Law and Development and International Institute for Environment and Development, *Governance of Oil and Gas Contracts in Kazakhstan* (2008) <http://www.field.org.uk/work-areas/trade-investment-and-sustainable-development/ investment/governance-oil-and-gas-contracts-kazakhstan> accessed 19 February 2011.

[84] See e.g. Cordonier-Segger, Gehring and Newcombe, above n 83; Foundation for International Environmental Law and Development and International Institute for Environment and Development, above n 83; Howard Mann *et al.*, *IISD Model International Agreement on Investment for Sustainable Development* (2nd edn, 2006) x–xi, International Institute for Sustainable Development <http://www.iisd.org/pdf/2005/investment_model_int_hand book.pdf> accessed 5 February 2011; Aaron Cosbey *et al.*, *Investment and*

There is a clear message to be taken from the use of soft law instruments within international environmental law to promote the integrated consideration of multiple issues and from the activities of non-state actors that reinforce that approach: international investment law will continue to come under pressure to adopt a more contextual consideration of investment issues. There is also, perhaps, a further lesson for the investment field. Advocates of environmental protection issues and their integration within other contexts have been successful in promoting such an approach through soft law instruments. In this sense, soft law has very clearly contributed to the normalization of particular perspectives within the discourse. At this point, it could quite rightly be suggested that the circumstances of the two fields, environment and investment, are very different in that investment law is heavily based on bilateral treaties and therefore there is not such a reliance on soft law for norm-creation. Indeed, this is a valid point of distinction. The insight that I am suggesting could be taken from the environmental experience is, however, a subtle one. In much the same way as has been witnessed in environmental law-making, specific positions within international investment law could also be promoted through the targeted use of soft law instruments. Any such soft law instruments would not, of course, replace relevant treaties as the source of law governing investment disputes, but they may influence the 'shared understandings' of those treaties, particularly in the way in which they are interpreted. The question then becomes one of substance – what view of international investment law should be proffered? Given the potential influence of such instruments, it is a question of some importance.

III. ENVIRONMENTAL CODES IN THE FINANCING AND INVESTMENT SECTORS

Interestingly, several voluntary codes that merge the lines between environmental protection, human rights, transnational financing and international investment have recently been developed. These initiatives could potentially influence the development of soft law instruments for

---

Sustainable Development: A Guide to the Use and Potential of International Investment Agreements (2004) International Institute for Sustainable Development <http://www.iisd.org/pdf/2004/investment_invest_and_sd.pdf> accessed 5 February 2011; International Institute for Sustainable Development, *Revising the UNCITRAL Arbitration Rules to Address Investor-State Arbitrations* (2007) <http://www.iisd.org/pdf/2007/investment_revising_uncitral_arbitration_september.pdf> accessed 5 February 2011.

international investment law. And, although these instruments are directed at private sector actors and have clearly experienced difficulties with implementation, it would be worth looking closely at these codes in designing soft law instruments for states and, perhaps, also in considering initiatives applicable to private actors as well.

A. United Nations Principles for Responsible Investment

The *United Nations Principles for Responsible Investment* (UNPRI) is a normative code for corporate conduct, specifically targeting institutional investors.[85] Established in April 2006 under the auspices of the UN Global Compact and UNEP Finance Initiative,[86] the UNPRI was signed at its launch by major financial institutions responsible for US$2 trillion in assets. By 2008, more than 250 investment entities, controlling over US$10 trillion in assets, had joined the UNPRI.[87]

The UNPRI consists of six principles and 35 'possible actions' through which investors can integrate environmental, social and corporate governance matters into their operations.[88] These directives address internal investment analysis and decision-making policies, a function which should, simultaneously, also promote cultural change within signatory institutions. Additionally, the principles and actions encourage active ownership activities, such as filing shareholder resolutions to promote long-term environmentally and socially responsible corporate conduct. UNPRI signatories also pledge to request appropriate disclosure from the companies in which they invest. Furthermore, the UNPRI points to education initiatives, reporting requirements and the need to infuse a culture

---

[85] Normative codes are described by Richardson as those providing 'substantive principles and guidance toward desirable performance'. They 'set goals or benchmarks to move financiers from perpetuating or mere tinkering of existing unsustainable practices.' Benjamin J Richardson, *Socially Responsible Investment Law: Regulating the Unseen Polluters* (2008) 381–2.

[86] United Nations Principles for Responsible Investment (UNPRI) <http://www.unpri.org/principles/> accessed 12 February 2011; United Nations Global Compact, 'United Nations Secretary-General Launches "Principles for Responsible Investment"' (April 2006) <http://www.unglobalcompact.org/NewsAndEvents/news_archives/2006_04_27.html> accessed 1 March 2011.

[87] See, Richardson, above n 85, 399–402; see also, Michael R Siebecker, 'Trust & Transparency: Promoting Efficient Corporate Disclosure Through Fiduciary-Based Disclosure' (2009) 87 *Washington University Law Review* 115, 123–4.

[88] UNPRI, above n 86; see also, Janet E Kerr, 'A New Era of Responsibility: A Modern American Mandate for Corporate Social Responsibility' (2009) 78 *UMKC Law Review* 327, 359 (discussing the UNPRI).

of acceptance of the Principles throughout the investment industry.[89]

Critics query the capacity of the UNPRI to effect change in the practices of target companies. It is very much embedded within a business case approach to responsible investment, does not require its signatories to provide formal, public reporting of their implementation progress, does not require CSR and ecological sustainability factors to be determinative of any ultimate investment decisions, and does not require specific quotas of socially and environmentally responsible companies within their investment portfolios.[90] Again, however, like the CSR movement as a whole and initiatives such as the UN Global Compact, the UNPRI is effective in a cultural sense, normalizing the consideration of social and environmental factors in corporate decision-making in the investment sector – and, in this sense, it is contributing to the development of international CSR norms for financiers and investors.[91]

B. Equator Principles

A key voluntary code directed at the private equity sector is the *Equator Principles*.[92] It has a different format, focus and audience from the UNPRI, and, as it sets out the specific procedures to be followed in financing proposed projects, it is an example of what Richardson has termed 'process standards'.[93] The *Equator Principles* were developed by

---

[89] UNPRI, above n 86.

[90] Richardson, above n 85, 400–1; Surya Deva, 'Global Compact: A Critique of the U.N.'s "Public-Private" Partnership for Promoting Corporate Citizenship' (2006) 34 *Syracuse Journal of International Law and Commerce* 107, 127–8; Benjamin J Richardson, 'Keeping Ethical Investment Ethical: Regulatory Issues for Investing for Sustainability' (2009) 87(4) *Journal of Business Ethics* 555, 559; see Joakim Sandberg et al, 'The Heterogeneity of Socially Responsible Investment' (2009) 87(4) *Journal of Business Ethics* 519 (discussing the variance in approach of UNPRI signatories); see a general critique of the UNPRI in Robert Howell, 'Globalization and the Good Corporation: Whither Socially Responsible Investment?' (2008) 27 *Human Systems Management* 243, 246–7; see the criticisms in Global Compact Critics, *Seriousness of Firms' Commitment to the UN Principles for Responsible Investment Questioned*, 10 February 2010 <http://globalcompactcritics.blogspot. com/2010/02/seriousness-of-firms-commitment-to-un.html> at 1 March 2011.

[91] See Richardson, above n 76, 401–2, 448 (discussing the UNPRI becoming a key 'benchmark' for socially responsible investment).

[92] Equator Principles (Washington, DC, 4 June 2003) <http://www.equator-principles.com> at 1 March 2011.

[93] Richardson, above n 85, 411; Benjamin J Richardson, 'Financing Sustainability: The New Transnational Governance of Socially Responsible Investment' (2007) 17 *Yearbook of International Environmental Law* 73, 89.

the World Bank's International Finance Corporation (IFC) and a number of key private investment banking houses as a response to increasing pressure from NGOs and the public to refrain from funding socially and environmentally harmful projects.[94] The resulting initiative is a voluntary code setting out criteria by which loan applications are to be assessed and ongoing management of projects is to be conducted.

The *Equator Principles* were launched with the goal of becoming the industry standard for project financing assessment processes. As 68 financial institutions have adopted the *Equator Principles* to date, including banks which account for over 85 per cent of global project financing, the *Principles* are close to fulfilling that intention.[95] In many respects, however, the *Equator Principles* have remained controversial. In particular, NGOs have expressed concern that the mode of implementation of the *Principles* will be the determinative factor in their success and they have queried the implementation record of the signatories, so-called '*Equator Principles* Financial Institutions' or EPFIs.[96]

C. Implications for International Investment Law

Implementation is likely to remain a significant issue for the *Equator*

---

[94] Richardson, above n 85, 411; Benjamin J Richardson, 'The Equator Principles: The Voluntary Approach to Environmentally Sustainable Finance' (2005) *European Environmental Law Review* 280, 285; Christopher Wright and Alexis Rwabizambuga, 'Institutional Pressures, Corporate Reputation, and Voluntary Codes of Conduct: An Examination of the Equator Principles' (2006) 111 *Business and Society Review* 89, 97–9; Niamh O'Sullivan and Brendan O'Dwyer, 'Stakeholder Perspectives on a Financial Sector Legitimation Process: The Case of NGOs and the Equator Principles' (2009) 22 *Accounting, Auditing and Accountability Journal* 553.

[95] The *Equator Principles* <http://www.equator-principles.com/documents/About_the_Equator_Principles.pdf> accessed 3 March 2011; see the discussion in Richardson, above n 85, 413–14.

[96] Richardson, above n 85, 287; Richardson, above n 93, 92–3; BankTrack, *Going Round in Circles: An Overview of BankTrack–EPFI Engagement on the Equator Principles, 2003–2010* (February 2010) <http://www.banktrack.org/download/going_around_in_circles/100210_going_around_in_circles_post_mtg_version.pdf> accessed 2 March 2011; see also the critique in Steven Herz *et al.*, *The International Finance Corporation's Performance Standards and the Equator Principles: Respecting Human Rights and Remedying Violations?* (2008) <http://www.banktrack.org/download/the_international_finance_corporation_s_performance_standards_and_the_equator_principles_respecting_human_rights_and_remedying_violations_/0_final_ruggie_submission_august_6_.pdf> accessed 2 March 2011.

Principles. As with other process-oriented soft law instruments within the environmental field,[97] its regulatory-type approach requires specific steps to be taken and 'success' or otherwise can measured against those benchmarks. However, key functions of both the UNPRI and the *Equator Principles* have been to redefine market considerations and to bring about cultural shifts in the acceptability of their core concepts. This would be an interesting aspect to explore in the context of international investment law – essentially considering the use of soft law instruments as a mechanism for cultural shaping, either to bring about or resist change. In that regard, such an approach could be applied to many different normative elements within international investment law, depending on the perspective adopted.

Indeed, although any aspect within the field could be selected for emphasis, for the moment I will use the example of seeking to introduce more socially and environmentally responsible principles into the law. For such a purpose, various types of instruments could be employed to facilitate the promotion of particular concepts. Drawing on the models of the UNPRI and *Equator Principles*, possible avenues to pursue would be the more general Declaration of Principles or, at the other end of the spectrum, perhaps a detailed code setting out specific requirements on the chosen topic.

From a substantive point of view, it would also be useful to consider the material contained within a range of other instruments that are not strictly 'environmental', but which are related to the field and should also be consulted in designing either a codification-type model or a declaration of principles model for international investment law. In this vein, the expansively entitled *United Nations Norms on the Responsibilities of Transnational Corporations and Other Business Entities with Regard to Human Rights*, or as they are more commonly called, the *UN Norms*,[98] would be an interesting source of information in both form and content.

---

[97] See e.g. the Food and Agriculture Organization Code of Conduct for Responsible Fisheries, the failure of which to ensure its signatory states to voluntarily reduce fisheries subsidies is discussed in Margaret Young, 'Fragmentation or Interaction: the WTO, Fisheries Subsidies, and International Law' (2009) *World Trade Review* 477; Food and Agriculture Organization Code of Conduct for Responsible Fisheries <http://www.fao.org/DOCREP/005/v9878e/v9878e00.htm#BAC> accessed 10 February 2011.

[98] United Nations Economic and Social Council, *Norms on the Responsibilities of Transnational Corporations and Other Business Enterprises with Regard to Human Rights*, UN ESCOR, 55th sess, Agenda item 4, UN Doc E/CN.4/Sub.2/2003/12/Rev.2 (2003).

Attention should also be given to the *OECD Guidelines on Multinational Enterprises*[99] for inspiration on subject matter or formulation of particular provisions, so that the produced document does not simply employ a 'lowest common denominator' approach and replicate the most uncontroversial elements of several bilateral investment treaties.

IV. CONCLUSION

From the analysis in this chapter, it can be seen that, within international environmental law, soft law instruments have served important roles on several levels, but most particularly in the development of new concepts, principles, and mechanisms within the field, and as innovative tools pointing towards the possibility of hard law obligations. Gradually, such instruments have become a central part of an interactive process of engagement with new ideas, new actors and the exploration of possible forms that principles and rules might take. Although the precise character of normativity of soft law remains a contested subject, what can be said is that the evolution, proliferation and deepening influence of soft law instruments reflects both the changing nature of the international legal system and the range of factors that now shape state behaviour.

Whether or not codification of principles and rules of international investment law is currently feasible, there is a range of other useful forms and functions for soft law instruments. However, the differences in law-making processes between the investment and environmental fields may render the environmental experience of soft law largely inapplicable to the investment sector. In other words, it may be that there is no comparable 'space' for soft law instruments as there is within international environmental law and that similar functions for soft law are not presenting themselves within the investment field. Certainly, however, what can be taken from the environmental field is that the function of the instrument shapes its form and substance, as well as the expectations surrounding its operation. In this regard, perhaps greater consideration could be given to the particular soft law functions which might be envisaged within international investment law, as 'function' will not only be determinative of the model and subject adopted in any such instruments, but also, ultimately, of their acceptance and usefulness. Certainly, a 'restatement of the rules' type model or codification of discrete

---

[99] OECD, *OECD Guidelines for Multinational Enterprises* (2011) <http://www.oecd.org/dataoecd/43/29/48004323.pdf> accessed 30 October 2011.

areas of investment law is most likely to be widely accepted rather than instruments seeking to develop the law. However, in many respects, it would be regrettable for the field to ignore additional processes to influence the future direction of the law and to not benefit from the dynamism, fluidity and experimentation that can emerge from a variety of soft law instruments.

6. Soft law codifications in the area of commercial law

Giuditta Cordero-Moss

In the process of evaluating whether, to what extent and in what form investment law may usefully be the subject of soft law codifications, it may be relevant to look to the experience in soft codification in the field of commercial contracts.

After a short introduction to the structural differences between contract law and investment law (section 1 below), this chapter will analyse the effectiveness of various soft codifications in the field of contract law mainly from the point of view of whether they achieve their intended purposes, which I have defined as ensuring predictability (section 2 below), and compatibility with enforceability (section 3 below). I will also consider whether soft codifications may be addressed to any user or need to be tailored to the intended user, and whether their effectiveness may be affected by the descriptive or prescriptive character of the soft rules or by the drafting process (section 4 below).

At the end of each section I will present my considerations on the relevance that the experience in soft codification of contract rules may have to soft codification of investment law.

1. PARALLELS BETWEEN CONTRACT LAW AND INVESTMENT LAW?

There are similarities but also structural differences between the regulation of the parties' interests in a commercial setting and the regulation of foreign investment.

Commercial law regulates obligations of private law as between private parties (or, at least, entities acting as private parties). It mainly addresses contractual conduct and interests of which the parties may freely dispose. The parties have typically regulated the interests involved in the contract and the judge or arbitrator is requested to apply the contract and the governing law to solve a dispute. The question that may arise regarding a state's law is whether it is applicable, and this will be solved by choice of law rules contained in private international law. Beyond the matter of applicability of the law, commercial disputes do not usually require that a court review a state's use of its own sovereign powers.

In contrast, investment treaty disputes[1] between a foreign investor and the host state are mainly based on an alleged breach by the state of a rule of international law, be it a treaty-based standard of treatment or a customary principle. The point of these allegations is that the host state has used its sovereign powers in a manner that violates rules and principles binding on states. This is the only, or the most effective, recourse available to a foreign investor against the host country: in the absence of rules and principles of public international law, the state would be free from any restrictions on the use of its public powers because it could pass legislation that renders any abusive or discriminatory act legal within its territory. Public international law is the dimension above national sovereignty that sets fundamental and generally recognized (or agreed to) criteria limiting national states' otherwise unrestricted use of their respective sovereign powers.

To put it bluntly, the main purpose of a commercial dispute is to ascertain which company has violated the agreement and owes reimbursement to the other party under the applicable law; the main purpose of an investment dispute is to review the host country's exercise of its sovereign powers and to review the legitimacy of, among other things, its law against parameters of public international law – with varying degrees of interference with domestic law depending on various issues such as the application of the proportionality principle or how an investor's legitimate expectations should take into account the development level and capabilities of the host state. The former type of dispute is simply an economic settlement between participants in business activity and does not affect third parties. The latter involves public interests of various kinds.

This leads to another structural difference between commercial and investment law, namely that the former is ultimately based on national law, whereas the latter is based on public international law and its interaction with domestic law.

As will be seen below, the instances where the borders of domestic law are successfully overcome and a transnational law for international commercial contracts is created are quite restricted; whenever a harmonized transnational commercial law is not available, it will be

---

[1] Investment disputes also include disputes arising out of concession contracts, which may also raise issues of private law relating to alleged breaches of contract.

possible to identify the applicable domestic law and this will supply a systematic context for the regulation of the matters that are left uncovered. As a consequence, soft codifications of commercial law interplay with the applicable domestic law.

Investment law does not rely on specific domestic legal systems, but is a part of public international law. The general sources of public international law supply a context for investment law, and so do, with respect to certain areas, specific sources of investment law. However, it is doubtful whether this may be considered an exhaustive, unitary system that may serve as a context for soft codification in the same way as domestic law does within the area of commercial law.[2]

The question is to what extent these differences between commercial and investment law affect the applicability to investment law of the criteria that will be used below to evaluate the effectiveness of soft codification in the field of commercial law.

Most soft codifications within contract law are meant to regulate interests of the parties in a transaction, either as integration of the contract terms, or as a body of rules on the basis of which a difference between the parties may be decided, typically in connection with the interpretation or application of the contract. The main aim of these codifications is to overcome the diversity in regulation contained in the various jurisdictions that may be relevant for an international transaction, and thus ensure a uniform regulation irrespective of which law governs. Another purpose for these soft codifications is to create certainty regarding rights and obligations of the parties in specific situations that are not regulated by law and are typically left to the autonomy of the parties – either because of their very specific and technical character, or because they reflect trade usages and the need to adapt to changing circumstances.

There are many soft law codifications in the area of contract law, some of them more successful than others. Successful codifications contain principles and rules that, if relied upon by the parties when writing the contract or by the arbitral tribunal when rendering the award, ensure predictable application and do not prevent enforceability of the contract or of the award. This chapter highlights the main elements that favour or affect such predictable enforceability and illustrates them with some of the best-known soft law codifications.

---

2 See G. Kaufmann-Kohler, 'Arbitral precedent: dream, necessity or excuse?', (2007) *23 Arbitration International 357, 373 et seq* (explaining how international law, as a body of rules, is in an earlier stage of development compared to national states' law).

The analysis will show that predictability and uniformity are easier to achieve when the codification has a specific scope of application and does not have ambitions to codify general principles. The latter approach would require that the soft codification bridge different legal traditions or have recourse to general clauses or principles that need concretization. If the purpose of soft codification is to avoid multiplicity of regulations and create uniformity across legal systems, it is intuitive that the soft rules should be formulated so precisely that they may be applied without leaving too much to the interpretation of the user. This is because interpretation is influenced by the legal tradition of the user and may lead to differing legal effects for the same formulation. Uniformity of application of imprecise rules may be achieved only if the rules are ultimately subject to interpretation by a centralized body such as a Supreme Court, which may over time ensure a coherent jurisprudence. As long as case law within international contract law is produced by a multiplicity of courts and arbitral tribunals each following a different legal tradition, and there is no centralized institution ensuring consistent jurisprudence, imprecise soft rules will not be the basis for uniform application of the law.

To the extent that soft codifications are used as a basis for integrating contracts or solving disputes, it seems that the requirement of precision is relevant irrespective of whether the field of application is contract law or investment law. If soft codification is used as a tool in the process of law-making, however, other criteria may be relevant. If soft law is intended as a step in the course of a gradual formation of consensus among the various stakeholders, it may benefit from a certain flexibility. This would permit reaching an initial compromise among the various interests without defining the respective positions in a too clear or definitive way. This, in turn, may be the basis for adjustments and learning processes that may eventually lead to a reconciled position.

Soft law as a model for legislative activity is not the main subject of the analysis here, and this chapter deals with soft codifications of the first-mentioned kind, aimed at being adopted in a contract by the parties or used by tribunals to solve disputes.

2. PREDICTABILITY

Soft law instruments support predictable results when they can be interpreted without being influenced by the legal tradition of the interpreter, and applied without being affected by the governing law.

2.1 Soft Codification with Precise Scope Fosters Predictability

Soft law instruments that are (i) precise, and (ii) have a specific scope of application have proven to be very successful in practice.

Specific areas of international commercial law have proven to be particularly favourable for harmonization. Harmonization can be achieved in various ways: (i) through binding instruments, such as the 1980 Vienna Convention on Contracts for the International Sale of Goods (CISG), which creates a uniform law for certain aspects of sale contracts; (ii) through instruments issued by international bodies but without binding effect, such as the 1985 UNCITRAL Model Law on International Commercial Arbitration, revised in 2006,[3] or the UNCITRAL Arbitration Rules of 1976, revised in 2010; and (iii) through instruments issued by private organizations such as the International Chamber of Commerce (ICC) and without binding effect unless the parties to the contract adopt them – such as the INCOTERMS or the UCP 600 (formerly 500). Common to these instruments is the fact that they have a specific scope of application: certain aspects of the contract of sale for the CISG, the procedural aspects of arbitration for the Model Law on Arbitration and the UNCITRAL Arbitration Rules, the passage of risk from seller to buyer and other specific obligations between the parties for the INCOTERMS, and the mechanism of documentary credits for the UCP 600. These instruments do not have the goal of regulating all aspects of the relationship between the parties, such as the validity of the contract, its interpretation, or all remedies for breach of contract.

These matters do not need to be interpreted in the light of general principles and do not interfere with the fundamental characteristics of the various legal systems. Hence, these instruments can be applied autonomously.

Thanks to this specific scope of application, the enforceability of these instruments is easy to predict and achieve: if they are incorporated into the contract, they will be binding on the parties and enforceable as long as they do not violate mandatory rules of the applicable law. Because their area of application is specified and usually well within the scope of the freedom of contract, they are generally enforced without any difficulties. If the instruments are not incorporated by the parties, they may nevertheless be applicable as expression of trade usages. In spite of the undeniably wide recognition of these sources, however, they are not unanimously

---

3 This instrument is not binding, as it is a model for legislators. If adopted, it will be binding in the system that has enacted it.

considered as trade usages; in some countries, they are considered as standard terms of contract that become effective between the parties only if they are expressly incorporated.[4] Furthermore, not all publications issued, e.g. by the ICC, enjoy the same degree of recognition as the INCOTERMS and the UCP 600; thus, the simple fact that there is an ICC publication is not sufficient evidence that there is a corresponding trade usage.

2.1.1. The International Commercial Terms (INCOTERMS)

The International Commercial Terms (INCOTERMS), a publication by the International Chamber of Commerce, illustrate transnational harmonization supplementing national law. The INCOTERMS apply to cross-border delivery of goods, and list 11 different terms of delivery, all expressed by three-letter acronyms. Each of these abbreviations corresponds to an allocation between the seller and the buyer regarding responsibility for customs clearance, the arranging and paying of transportation and insurance, the definition of the place of delivery, and the consequent passage of risk from the seller to the buyer. By writing the abbreviation in the contract and specifying the place of delivery, the parties incorporate the corresponding allocation of obligations, and do not need to regulate all these matters in the contract.

A dispute regarding whether the seller is obliged to clear the goods for export, who bears the risk of loss until delivery or who was supposed to pay for the insurance under transportation, will be easily solved by verifying which term of the INCOTERMS the parties have chosen. Other disputed matters, such as the validity of the contract or what remedies are available in case of default, are not regulated by the INCOTERMS. Even matters that are within the scope of the INCOTERMS may be subject to different regulation by the governing law. For example, the question of liability for damages to the goods under transportation, normally directly regulated by the INCOTERMS, may be decided differently under the governing law under specific circumstances which discharge one party from the obligations that the contract (and the INCOTERMS) has imposed on it (such as, for example, Article 66 of the CISG, in case of damage due to an act or omission of the seller).

---

[4] See for references, H van Houtte, *The Law of International Trade* (2nd edn, Sweet and Maxwell 2002) Section 8.15. On the challenges that courts may face in applying the UCP in spite of their general acknowledgement, see C Twigg-Flesner, 'Standard Terms in International Commercial Law – The Example of Documentary Credits' in R Schulze (ed), *New Features in Contract Law*, (Sellier 2007), 325–39.

2.1.2 The Uniform Customs and Practices for Documentary Credits (UCP 600)

The Uniform Customs and Practices for Documentary Credits (UCP 600), a publication by the ICC regulating the payment mechanism of letters of credit, are another example of soft law supplementing the governing law. Like the INCOTERMS, they regulate a specific mechanism and do not have the goal of covering general matters of contract law. However, they have a broader scope of application and in some situations they may conflict with mandatory rules of the governing law, as will be seen in section 3 below.

Letters of credit are a widely used method of payment applied when the creditor does not intend to take the commercial risk connected with the creditworthiness of the debtor. A letter of credit is structured as follows: the debtor (applicant) requests a bank (the issuing bank) to issue a letter of credit in favour of the creditor (the beneficiary). The application contains the instructions for the issuing bank, and must state the precise amount of money that has to be paid, as well as the documents upon the presentation of which the bank has to effect payment. This is the main characteristic of a letter of credit: the bank has to effect payment upon presentation by the beneficiary of the documents that are named in the instructions. The bank has simply to verify the facial conformity of the presented documents, and is not requested to assess the proper performance of the underlying transaction, or any other matter. The autonomous character of the bank's payment obligation is one of the most characteristic aspects of a letter of credit, and is codified in the UCP 600, Articles 4 and 5. The UCP 600 contain a series of technicalities on the relationship between the parties and the mechanism of payment, such as the involvement of an advising or a confirming bank, the modalities of payment, and the examination of the presented documents.

The UCP 600 enjoy a general recognition as regulation of letters of credits; they are, at the same time, a source of regulation, and codification of generally acknowledged practices within that area.

2.1.3 The Convention on Contracts for the International Sale of Goods (CISG)

The Convention on Contracts for the International Sale of Goods was drafted by the United Nations Commission on International Trade Law (UNCITRAL) and adopted in Vienna in 1980.[5]

---

[5] The full text can be found on the UNCITRAL's homepage <http://www.uncitral.org> which also contains an updated list of the countries that have ratified it, the reservations that were made, etc.

The CISG has been signed by 74 parties, and it is looked upon with extreme interest, especially in academic circles,[6] as the first example of uniform law that, in addition to creating binding law as an international convention, gives recognition to the spontaneous rules born out of commercial practice,[7] and has itself become an autonomous body of international regulation that adapts to changing circumstances independently of the legal systems of the ratifying States.[8] For the sake of completeness, however, it must be mentioned here that the CISG has not been ratified by such an important country in international commerce as the United Kingdom, nor by several States in Central and South America, nor by most Arabic and African countries, nor by India and other South Asian countries.

The CISG is a binding instrument; therefore, its rules are the prevailing law in the countries that have ratified it – unless the parties made use of the possibility, contained in Article 6, of excluding application of the Convention. The CISG covers the formation of contracts and the substantive rights and obligations of the buyer and the seller arising out of contract of sale, such as delivery, conformity of the goods, payment and remedies for breach of the related obligations.

In spite of its binding nature and specific scope of application, the CISG is sometimes referred to as having, in addition to its direct binding effect, an authoritative effect that goes beyond its territorial and substantive scope of application and makes it one of the most important sources of soft law for general contract law. The CISG is often mentioned together with two instruments that will be analysed immediately below: the UNIDROIT Principles of International Commercial Contracts and the Principles of European Contract Law. These three instruments are sometimes referred to as constituting a 'Troika', a body of transnational law particularly apt to govern commercial contracts.[9] If seen as a soft source of general contract law, the CISG has to be analysed along the same lines set forth in the next section.

---

6 See, for example, B Audit, 'The Vienna Sales Convention and the Lex Mercatoria' in T Carbonneau (ed), *Lex Mercatoria and Arbitration* (Juris Publishing 1998) 173–94.

7 This is because of the convention's many references to trade usages.

8 This is because of the particular rules on the convention's interpretation laid down in its Article 7, that require an autonomous interpretation based on the principles underlying the convention. On the opinion that the CISG is so widely recognized that it is applicable even without having been ratified, see below.

9 See, for example, O Lando, 'CISG and Its Followers: A Proposal to Adopt Some International Principles of Contract Law' (2005) 53 *American Journal of Comparative Law*, 379–401, 379 *et seq.*

2.2 Soft Codification of General Law does not Foster Predictability

Soft law instruments that cover general areas of the law are subject to the principles underlying those areas in any given legal system and will therefore have different effects depending on the legal system within which they are implemented. To the extent they contain general principles or vague formulations, they will be interpreted differently in the various legal traditions. Examples mentioned below include the UNIDROIT Principles of International Commercial Contracts, the Principles of European Contract Law and the academic Draft Common Frame of Reference – all covering general contract law and containing principles on interpretation of contracts, good faith in performance and similar general rules that are not sufficiently precise to permit an autonomous interpretation.

Even specific formulations may be interpreted differently depending on the legal tradition within which they are included. Examples mentioned below include certain contract clauses often recurring in international commercial contracts. Clauses on termination or on exclusion of liability for unjustified break-off of negotiations interact with the governing law's principles on interpretation according to good faith, duty of loyalty between the parties, etc., which are regulated differently in the various systems. Hence, the clauses will have different effects depending on the governing law.

2.2.1 Soft codification of general contract law

Various soft codifications of general principles of contract law have been produced in the past decades, and some of them have attracted considerable interest in academic circles.

The Principles of International Commercial Contracts (UPICC)[10] were published first in 1994 by UNIDROIT, an international organization established in 1926 with the purpose of unifying private law. The work on the UPICC had started in 1981, in a working group under the direction of the Italian professor Joachim Bonell.

The Principles of European Contract Law (PECL) were published in three volumes, from 1995 to 2002, by the so-called Commission on European Contract Law, a group of academics established in 1982 under

---

10 *UNIDROIT Principles of International Commercial Contracts*, International Institute for the Unification of Private Law, Rome (3rd edn, 2010) available at <http://www.unidroit.org/english/principles/contracts/principles2010/blackletter2010-english.pdf>.

the leadership of the Danish professor Ole Lando.[11] The work on the PECL proceeded largely in parallel with the work on the UPICC and many members of one working group were also members of the other.

As a result of the partial overlap in these academic groups, the content and the structure and terminology of these two collections of principles are largely similar to each other, with certain main differences that will be seen below.

Neither the PECL nor the UPICC are international conventions or have binding effect. They are meant to formulate systematically the main rules prevailing in the field of cross-border contracts in a way that may be interpreted equally in all countries where they are applied. They are not merely a record of existing practices: they are in part a codification of generally adopted principles of international contracts, and in part new rules ('best solutions') developed by a large group of experts from around the world.

There are several purposes which PECL and the UPICC could serve, as is apparent from their respective preambles. As they are the result of an extensive comparative study and offer modern and functional solutions, they may be a source of inspiration to legislators for legislation on general contract law. Because of their persuasive authority based on the professional standing of the working group that prepared them, they could be used by courts or arbitrators to interpret existing international instruments. Moreover, they may be used by contracting parties during the preparation of their contract as a guide to the drafting. The parties to an international contract might decide to subject their contract to the PECL or the UPICC as an expression of a balanced, international set of rules, rather than choose a national applicable law. They might be useful for arbitrators, especially if the dispute is decided on the basis of transnational law: rather than having to search for what could constitute international usages of trade, or similar undefined concepts, the arbitrators could rely on a ready available set of rules. They might be used by courts or arbitrators instead of the applicable law, should the content of the law be impossible or extremely difficult to establish.

A significant difference between the two instruments is that the UPICC have no specific territorial scope and apply to any international contract, whereas the PECL have defined Europe as their scope of application. This prompted a higher degree of aspirations for the PECL: in addition to

---

[11] O Lando and H Beale (eds), *Principles of European Contract Law*, parts 1 and 2 (Kluwer Law International 2002) and *Principles of European Contract Law*, part 3 (Kluwer Law International, 2003).

aspiring to the status of source of soft law as described above, the PECL aspire to become the prevailing (and in the long term binding) contract law within the European Union and to replace the national laws that prevail today in every state. On this basis, the PECL could not ignore the fact that one of the major areas of concern for European contract law is the protection of the consumer. The PECL, therefore, extend their object to contract law in general, i.e. including both commercial and consumer law.

In the framework of a process initiated in the beginning of this millennium,[12] the European Commission (EC) is presently encouraging the preparation of an instrument called the *Common Frame of Reference* (CFR).[13] The CFR is intended to be a set of non-binding guidelines used on a voluntary basis by law-makers at the Community level, either as a common source of inspiration or as a reference in the law-making process. It is intended to be a set of definitions, general principles and model rules in the field of contract law, and is to be derived from a variety of sources – such as a systematization of existing EC law and a comparative analysis of the member states' laws.

The ongoing work has resulted so far in the so-called Draft Frame of Reference,[14] referred to as 'academic' to underline that it is the result of the work of two academic groups (the Study Group on a European Civil Code and the European Research Group on the Existing EC Private Law ('Acquis Group'))[15] and is not to be confused with what will be the final result of the political European process.

This academic DCFR is largely based on the PECL and looks like a codification of the law of obligations. Its scope is significantly more extensive than the consumer legislation issued so far by the EC: the draft

---

[12] Resolution of the European Parliament of 16 March 2000, OJ C 377, 323.

[13] Communication by the European Commission 'European contract law and the revision of the acquis: the way forward', COM(2004) 651 final.

[14] C Von Bar, E Clive, H Schulte-Nölke *et al.* (eds), *Principles, Definitions and Model Rules of European Private Law Draft Common Frame of Reference (DCFR)* (Sellier 2008). After this chapter was concluded, the commission issued a proposal for a regulation on a common European sales law, COM(2011) 635 final, requiring member states to enact a sales law (ESL). If the regulation is issued, the ESL would act as a second regime besides the state's own law, and it would be an optional instrument, i.e. it would become applicable only if the parties have chosen it. The text of the ESL is largely based on the DCFR.

[15] The Acquis Group also published the Acquis Principles, a systematization of the existing European law: Research group on the Existing EC Private Law (Acquis Group), *Principles of the Existing EC Contract Law (Acquis Principles) Contract II: General Provisions, Delivery of Goods, Package Travel and Payment Services*, Munich 2009.

covers also non-contractual obligations and parts of property law. Contract law is covered in its generality, i.e. both consumer and commercial contracts. The extensive scope of the draft has been noted and is subject to debate, by both politicians[16] and scholars.[17] In addition, the Commission has launched a public consultation on the matter.[18]

To test the ability of the UPICC to ensure predictability in the interpretation and application of contracts by harmonizing general contract law, it is interesting to examine the case law collected in respect of Article 2.1.17 of the UPICC. This Article recognizes the so-called merger clause (also known as an Entire Agreement clause), according to which the document signed by the parties is deemed to contain their whole agreement and may not be supplemented by evidence of prior statements or agreements. This is a recurrent clause in commercial contracts and is intended to render the contract self-sufficient by avoiding any interference from external elements. Under English law this clause is deemed to exclude any possibility of integrating the text of the contract with other elements, be it as implied terms or arguments for interpretation of included terms.[19] Under civilian laws, on the contrary, the merger clause does not have an effect on the judge's ability to consider external circumstances when assessing the meaning and the scope of the contract, such as the purpose of the contract, the duty of good faith between the parties, or the parties' conduct after the contract was entered into.[20] The UPICC provision recognizes the clause, thus giving the impression that it embraces the English law approach. However, it specifies that prior statements or agreements may be used to interpret the contract. This is one of the applications of the general principle of good faith, a principle that is quite

---

[16] Discussion on the topic of the Common Frame of Reference (CFR) in the Council of the European Union, initiated by the Presidency on 28 July 2008, 8286/08JUSTCIV 68 CONSOM 39.

[17] H Eidenmüller, F Faust, HC Grigoleit, N Jansen, G Wagner, R Zimmermann, 'The Common Frame of Reference for European Private Law Policy Choices and Codification Problems' (2008) 28:4 *Oxford Journal of Legal Studies* 659–708.

[18] Green paper from the Commission on policy options for progress towards a European Contract Law for consumers and businesses, COM (2010) 348 final.

[19] Edwin Peel, 'The common law tradition: application of boilerplate clauses under English law' in G Cordero-Moss (ed) *Boilerplate Clauses, International Commercial Contracts and the Applicable Law* (CUP 2011) 136ff [hereinafter edited book cited as G Cordero-Moss (ed) *Boilerplate Clauses*].

[20] G Cordero-Moss, 'Conclusion: the self-sufficient contract, uniformly interpreted on the basis of its own terms: an illusion, but not fully useless', in G Cordero-Moss (ed), *Boilerplate Clauses*, 353 *et seq*.

central in the UPICC. The UPICC, as well as the PECL, contain a general clause on good faith in, respectively, Articles 1.7 and 1.201, requiring each party to act in accordance with good faith and fair dealing in international trade. They also contain numerous provisions[21] that apply the general principle of good faith to specific situations.

The general principle of good faith, in other words, is, in these restatements, an overriding principle that functions as a corrective action to the mechanisms regulated in the contract whenever a literal application leads to results that seem too harsh as applied to one of the parties. In order to apply this principle, the interpreter shall look beyond the wording of the contract. An accurate implementation of the contract may be considered to be against the principle of good faith if it amounts to an abuse of right. An abuse of right is defined by the official commentary to Article 1.7 of the UPICC as follows: 'It is characterized by a party's malicious behaviour which occurs for instance when a party exercises a right merely to damage the other party or for a purpose other than the one for which it had been granted, or when the exercise of a right is disproportionate to the originally intended result.'[22]

In respect of article 2.1.17 and the merger clause, it is unclear how far the principle of good faith goes in overriding the clause inserted by the parties. If prior statements and agreements may be used to interpret the contract, does this mean that more terms may be added to the contract because, for example, the parties have discussed certain specifications at length during the negotiations and this has created in one of the parties the reasonable expectation that they would be implied in the contract? This would run counter to the wording of the merger clause, but it would be a reasonable approach under a general principle of good faith. Article 1.8 of the UPICC would seem to indicate that this would be the preferred approach under the UPICC. According to this provision, a party may not

---

21 Comment No 1 to Article 1.7 in the 2nd edition of 2004, which at the moment of writing is the latest available comment (available at <http://www.unidroit.org/english/principles/contracts/principles2004/integralversionprinciples2004-e.pdf>, accessed 19 May 2011) mentions the following provisions: Articles 1.8, Arts 1.9(2); 2.1.4(2)(b), 2.1.15, 2.1.16, 2.1.18 and 2.1.20; 2.2.4(2), 2.2.5(2), 2.2.7 and 2.2.10; 3.5, 3.8 and 3.10; 4.1(2), 4.2(2), 4.6 and 4.8; 5.1.2 and 5.1.3; 5.2.5; 6.1.3, 6.1.5, 6.1.16(2) and 6.1.17(1); 6.2.3(3)(4); 7.1.2, 7.1.6 and 7.1.7; 7.2.2(b)(c); 7.4.8 and 7.4.13; 9.1.3, 9.1.4 and 9.1.10(1). Also the PECL have numerous specific rules applying the principle of good faith, for example, in Articles 1: 202, 2:102, 2: 104, 2:105, 2:106, 2:202, 2:301, 4:103, 4:106, 4:109, 4:110, 5:102, 6:102, 8: 109, 9:101, 9:102, 9:509.

22 Comment No 2 to Article 1.7, above n 21 (accessed 19 May 2011).

act in a way inconsistent with reasonable expectations that it has created in the other party. According to this logic, the detailed discussion during the phase of negotiations of certain characteristics for the products at issue under the contract may create the reasonable expectation that those specifications have become part of the agreement even if they were not written in the contract; their subsequent exclusion on the basis of the merger clause may be deemed to be against good faith.

In the commentary to Article 1.7, the UPICC affirm that the standard of good faith always must be understood as 'good faith in international trade,' and that no reference has to be made to any standard that has been developed under any state law.[23] This approach is in line with the requirement of autonomous interpretation of the UPICC contained in Article 1.6 thereof: the UPICC are an instrument with an international character, and it would not serve the purpose of becoming a uniform law if the courts of every state interpreted them each in a different way, in light of their own legal culture. While the requirement of autonomous interpretation of the UPICC and the corresponding requirement in Article 1:106 of the PECL are understandable in light of the ambitions of harmonizing the law of contracts, they do not contribute to creating clarity in respect of the content of good faith as a standard, as will be seen below.[24]

Legal standards, or general clauses, are, per definition, in need of a specification of their content that depends to a large extent on the interpreter's discretion. When the general clause belongs to a state system, the interpreter's discretion is restricted or guided by principles and values underlying that particular system – for example, in the constitution, in other legislation or in the society at large.[25] How would the interpreter evaluate the wording of the contract which seems to provide for and permit the very conduct prohibited by the principle of good faith? An interpreter belonging to a tradition where there is no general principle of good faith might tend to consider that the clear wording of the contract

---

[23] Comment No 3 to Article 1.7, above n 21 (last visited 19 May 2011).

[24] See G Cordero-Moss, 'Does the use of common law contract models give rise to a tacit choice of law or to a harmonised, transnational interpretation?' in G Cordero-Moss (ed) *Boilerplate Clauses,* 52ff (discussing the lack of a recognised standard of good faith in international contract law) [hereinafter Cordero-Moss, 'Does the use of common law contract models'].

[25] See P Schlechtriem, 'The Functions of General Clauses, Exemplified by Regarding Germanic Laws and Dutch Law' in S Grundmann, D Mazeaud (eds), *General Clauses and Standards in European Contract Law*, (Kluwer Law International 2005) 41–55, 49 *et seq*. (analysing the application of general clauses, with particular but not exclusive reference to the German system).

indicates that the parties had considered all eventualities, made provision for them and accepted the consequences, and that therefore the articles of the UPICC and the PECL are not applicable. An interpreter belonging to a legal tradition with a strong general principle of good faith, on the other hand, may consider that consequences of a literal application of the contract must be mitigated if they disrupt the balance of interests between the parties. To the former interpreter, fairness or good faith interpretation consists in an accurate interpretation of the contract. To the latter, it consists in intervening and reinstating a balance between the parties. There do not seem to be any uniform transnational principles or values that are sufficiently precise to permit choosing between these two approaches.[26]

To assess how the UPICC are applied in practice, thus, it is not sufficient to read their text: it is necessary to examine case law. The UNIDROIT has taken a commendable measure to contribute to the development of a body of case law that may enhance a harmonized interpretation and thus predictability of the UPICC; following the example of CLOUT, a system established by the UNCITRAL for the collection and dissemination of court decisions and arbitral awards relating to UNCITRAL instruments, the UNIDROIT has established Unilex,[27] a database collecting case law and bibliography on the UPICC and the CISG. In 1992, Unilex started collecting and publishing, *inter alia*, arbitral awards that contain references to the UPICC. Making available the case law that otherwise would be scattered among the publications issued by different arbitral institutions all over the world (if published at all) is a valuable step promoting the development of a uniform body of law. When the number of the collected decisions becomes significant and their level of detail is such that they can be used to determine the specific scope of general clauses such as the principle of good faith, the UPICC will be in a position to contribute to the harmonization of the general contract law.

The Unilex database contains four decisions on Article 2.1.17 of the UPICC. In the first decision, ICC award No 9117 of 1998, the arbitral tribunal emphasized that a merger clause is to be considered as typical in a commercial contract, and said that 'there can be no doubt for any party engaged in international trade that the clauses mean, and must mean, what

---

26 See, for more details, G Cordero-Moss, 'Does the use of common law contract models', above n 24, in G Cordero-Moss (ed), *Boilerplate Clauses*, 52ff. More extensively, see also G Cordero Moss, 'Consumer protection except for good commercial practice: a satisfactory regime for commercial contracts?' in R Schulze (ed), *CFR and Existing EC Contract Law* (Sellier 2009) 78–94.

27 <http://www.unilex.info/>.

they say'.[28] The contract also contained a No Oral Amendments clause, which is recognized in Article 2.1.18 of the UPICC, a provision containing the same restrictions as Article 2.1.17 regarding conduct that has created expectations in the other party. The arbitral tribunal said that 'the explicit integration clause and the written modification clause, as contained in the Contract, operate as a bar against the assumption that a certain behaviour or practice could reach the level of becoming legally binding between the Parties.' Thus, according to this award, the principle of good faith contained in Articles 1.7 and 1.8 of the UPICC, and specified in Articles 2.1.17 and 2.1.18, does not affect a literal application of the contract's language. This approach seems to be consistent with the ideology underlying the drafting style of international contracts, as described above.[29] Consequently, it considerably restricts the applicability of the principles underlying the UPICC.

Another decision mentioned in Unilex under Article 2.1.17 is by the English Court of Appeal.[30] There Lord Justice Mummery stated that, under English law, extrinsic evidence could be used to ascertain the meaning of a term contained in a written contract if the term was ambiguous or unclear. On the contrary, extrinsic evidence could not be used to ascertain the content of the contract.[31] Lady Justice Arden considered this distinction too conservative and argued for a broader use of extrinsic evidence, referring to the UPICC in support of her view.[32]

In addition, Unilex mentions another award,[33] without, however, reproducing its full text. According to the abstract, the tribunal held that a merger clause 'simply indicates that there are no binding agreements between the parties other than those contained in the contract but does in no way affect the rules of interpretation established under the applicable law (in the case at hand, Art. 1362 of the Italian Civil Code). In reaching this conclusion the Arbitral Tribunal expressly referred, along with legal

---

[28] The award may be found at <http://www.unilex.info/case.cfm?pid=2-do=case&id=661&step=FullText> accessed 19 May 2011. The paragraphs are not numbered.

[29] For a more extensive discussion of the rationale behind the drafting style of contracts, see G Cordero-Moss, 'Conclusion: the self-sufficient contract' in G Cordero-Moss (ed), *Boilerplate Clauses*, 346 *et seq*.

[30] *Proforce Recruit Limited v The Rugby Group Limited*, 2006 EWCA Civ 69.

[31] Ibid, at 41.

[32] Ibid, at 57.

[33] Rendered on 28.11 2002 at the Chamber of Arbitration of Milan <http://www.unilex.info/case.cfm?pid=2&do=case&id=995&step=FullText> accessed 19 May 2011.

writings, to Art. 2.17 [Article 2.1.17 of the 2004 edition] of the UNIDROIT Principles, as well as to the Comments which state "the effect of such a clause is not to deprive prior statements or agreements of any relevance: they may still be used as a means of interpreting the writing document".'[34]

Finally, Unilex refers to an ICSID award[35] in which the tribunal stated that article 2.1.17 requires that expectations raised during the negotiations must be reflected in the text of the agreement.[36]

The Unilex database, in summary, shows two approaches to Article 2.1.17 of the UPICC: one advocating the primacy of the contract's language, and the other assuming that the UPICC provide for the primacy of the real intention of the parties.

Evidently, this is not sufficient to give guidance as to which approach to choose when addressing the conflict between the contract's language and the principle of good faith.

As seen above, the same dilemma described in connection with article 2.1.17 of the UPICC will affect the interpretation of the corresponding provision in the PECL. Depending on the development of the ongoing process to develop a European contract law and the DCFR, however, the PECL may become the basis of a European body of rules that eventually may be subject to interpretation or application by the European Court of Justice. In such case, with time, a coherent body of case law would be formed, and the content of the principle of good faith would be easier to determine.

2.2.2 Contract clauses

The impact of the legal tradition on the legal effects of a text may be seen even in respect of specific language contained in contracts. Commercial contracts are often written using a style that is quite standardized and originally inspired by the way in which contracts tailored for English law are written. Notwithstanding the uniformity of appearance, using a standardized contract text will not necessarily ensure uniformity of legal effects across various jurisdictions, unless also the different applicable laws are uniform. Thus, contract clauses may be interpreted literally if they are subject to a governing law in which formalism prevails, whereas the exercise of rights and remedies regulated in the contract will be mitigated,

34 <http://www.unilex.info/case.cfm?pid=2&do=case&id=995&step=Abstract> accessed 19 May 2011.

35 *Joseph C Lemire v Ukraine*, ICSID Case No Arb/06/18.

36 <http://www.unilex.info/case.cfm?pid=2&do=case&id=1533&step=FullText> accessed 19 May 2011.

supplemented or corrected if the contract is subject to a law giving stronger influence to the principle of good faith and fair dealing.[37] Traditionally, English law is deemed to be formalistic, whereas systems belonging to the civil law tradition are held to give more room to considerations of material justice in the interpretation of contracts. The impact that the governing law has on the interpretation and performance of a contract may be seen, for example, in respect of termination clauses or clauses in pre-contractual documents excluding liability for the break-off of negotiations.

Termination clauses stipulate that the contract may be terminated prior to its planned expiry if certain events occur; for example, one party may be given the power to terminate the contract early upon breach by the other party of certain obligations. The purpose of this clause is to give one party the power to terminate the contract early upon breach by the other party of specific obligations, irrespective of the consequences of the breach or of the early termination. By this clause, the parties attempt to avoid the uncertainty connected with the evaluation of how serious the breach is and what impact it has on the contract. This evaluation is due to the requirement, to be found in most applicable laws, that a breach must be fundamental if the innocent party shall be entitled to terminate the contract. By defining in the contract certain terms as essential, or by spelling out that certain breaches give the innocent party the power to terminate the contract, the parties attempt to create an automatism instead of allowing an evaluation that takes all circumstances into consideration.

It falls within the parties' contractual freedom to regulate their respective interests and to allocate risk and liability. Among other things, this means that the parties are free to determine on which conditions the contract may be terminated early. However, a literal interpretation of the clause may lead to unfair results, such as when the breach under the circumstances does not have any consequences for the innocent party, but this party uses the breach as a basis to terminate a contract that it no longer considered profitable on other grounds – for example, after the market has changed.

If the contract is interpreted in accordance with English law, the contract's language will prevail over considerations of fairness. If it is not possible to avoid unfair results on the basis of the contract language, English courts are inclined to give effect to the clause according to its terms, even though the result under the circumstances may be deemed to be unfair.

---

[37] Extensively on this subject see above n 19, G Cordero-Moss (ed), *Boilerplate Clauses*.

English courts do so, even if with evident reluctance, to ensure consistency in the law underlying the repudiation and termination of the contract.[38] In this context, therefore, properly drafted language achieves the effects that follow from a literal application of the clause even if these effects are unfair. Other legal systems, on the contrary, would not allow a literal application of the clause if this had consequences that may be deemed to be unfair, because of the general principle of good faith and loyalty[39] or on the assumption that parties cannot have intended to achieve such unfair results.[40]

Another example of contract language that may have different legal effects depending on the law according to which it is interpreted is the clause excluding liability for the break-off of negotiations. The purpose of this clause is to free the negotiating parties from any liability in case they do not reach a final agreement. This clause protects important interests in international commerce: it must be possible for the parties to wait until they have completed all negotiations before they make a decision on whether to enter into the contract. Often negotiations are complicated and are carried out in various phases covering different areas of the prospective transaction, whereby partial agreements on the respective area are recorded and made 'subject to contract'. When all partial negotiations are concluded, the parties will be able to have a full evaluation and only then will they be in a position to finally accept the terms of the deal.

The parties may freely agree when and under what circumstances they will be bound. However, a literal application of the clause may lead to abusive conduct, such as when one of the parties never really intended to enter into a final agreement and used the negotiations only to prevent the other party from entering into a contract with a third party.

In this case, as in respect of the clause on termination of the contract,

---

38 See Peel, above n 19, 148 et seq.

39 See, for Germany, the principle on good faith in the performance contained in §242 of the BGB; for France, X Lagarde, D Méheut and J-M Reversac, 'The Romanistic tradition: application of boilerplate clauses under French law' in G Cordero-Moss (ed), *Boilerplate Clauses*, 217 *et seq*; for Denmark, P Møgelvang-Hansen, 'The Nordic tradition: application of boilerplate clauses under Danish law' in G Cordero-Moss (ed), *Boilerplate Clauses*, 239 *et seq*; for Finland, G Möller, 'The Nordic tradition: application of boilerplate clauses under Finnish law' in G Cordero-Moss (ed), *Boilerplate Clauses*, 258 *et seq*. The same would be obtained under Russian law, based on the principle prohibiting abuse of rights: see Ivan S Zykin, 'The East European tradition: application of boilerplate clauses under Russian law' in G Cordero-Moss (ed), *Boilerplate Clauses*, 335 *et seq*.

40 See, for Norway, V Hagstrøm, 'The Nordic tradition: application of boilerplate clauses under Norwegian law' in G Cordero-Moss (ed), *Boilerplate Clauses*, 270 *et seq*.

there is a dichotomy between the common law approach and the civil law approach. English law seems to permit the parties to negate the intention to be bound, without being concerned with the circumstances under which the clause will be applied. A certain sense of unease may be detected in the English courts at permitting parties to go back on a deal, but it seems that a very strong and exceptional context is needed to override the clause.[41] Civil law, on the contrary, like the UPICC and the PECL, is concerned with the possibility that such a clause may be abused by a party to enter into or continue negotiations without having a serious intention to finalize the deal. Therefore, such conduct is prevented either by defining the clause as a potestative condition and therefore null[42] or by assuming a duty to act in good faith during the negotiations.[43]

Parties, therefore, may generally rely on the possibility of negating the intention to be bound if the relationship is subject to English law. If the applicable law belongs to a civilian system, however, the parties will be subject to the principle of good faith under the negotiations irrespective of what language they have used to avoid it.

Even standard terms of contract, to the extent that they at all can be elevated to the status of some binding practice,[44] do not have an autonomous existence but must necessarily be interpreted in the light of the

---

[41] See Peel above n 19, 154 *et seq.*

[42] See above n 34, for France, X Lagarde *et al.*, 'The Romanistic tradition' in G Cordero-Moss (ed), *Boilerplate Clauses*, 220 *et seq.* Potestative conditions are null also under Italian law, see Article 1355 of the Civil Code.

[43] See above n 19, for France, X Lagarde *et al.*, 'The Romanistic tradition' in G Cordero-Moss (ed), *Boilerplate Clauses*, 220 *et seq.*; for Denmark, P Møgelvang-Hansen, 'The Nordic tradition', above n 40, in G Cordero-Moss (ed), *Boilerplate Clauses*, 242 *et seq.*; for Finland, G Möller, 'The Nordic tradition', above n 39, in G Cordero-Moss (ed), *Boilerplate Clauses*, 259 *et seq.*; for Norway, V Hagstrøm, 'The Nordic tradition', above n 40, in G Cordero-Moss (ed), *Boilerplate Clauses*, 271 *et seq*; for Russia, I Zykin, 'The East European tradition', above n 39, in G Cordero-Moss (ed), *Boilerplate Clauses*, 338 *et seq.* The duty to act in good faith during the negotiations is spelled out also in §311 of the German BGB and in Article 1337 of the Italian Civil Code. See, for the UPICC and the PECL, Chapter 3, Section 2.4. For Hungarian law, see A Menyhárd, 'The East European tradition: application of boilerplate clauses under Hungarian law' in G Cordero-Moss (ed), *Boilerplate Clauses*, 314 *et seq.*

[44] See R Goode, H Kronke and E McKendrick, *Transnational Commercial Law Texts, Cases and Materials* (Oxford 2007) 33 and S Symeonides, *Party Autonomy and Private-Law Making: The Lex Mercatoria that Isn't* (19 November 2006), available at SSRN <http://ssrn.com/abstract=946007> 24 (convincingly criticizing the 'rather extravagant claims' that standard contract terms represent a legal norm in spite of the large variety of such terms).

governing law. Clauses that have a clear linguistic meaning do not necessarily have the same legal effects once they are read against the background of the interpretation doctrine and the general principles of the governing law. In addition to the influence that can be exercised by the presence or absence of the principle of good faith, as seen immediately above, it may suffice here to refer to another area of contract law where legal systems may have different approaches: the question of liability for non-performance of a contractual obligation. According to the civilian tradition, liability is a consequence of lack of diligence; according to the common law tradition, it is a consequence of an objective allocation of risk between the parties and does not depend on diligence or negligence. Hence, a clause excluding liability for non-performance because of impediments beyond the control of the non-performing party may be interpreted differently according to the legal tradition of the judge: a civilian judge may evaluate whether the impediment was under the actual control of the party, whereas an English judge may determine the sphere of control on the basis of objective allocation of risk without considering whether there was an actual possibility to influence the circumstances or not.[45]

Therefore, even if the language of the contract is the same, the effect of the contractual regulation varies as a consequence of the interplay between the contract and its governing law.

2.3 Summing Up

Rules regulating specific aspects of a legal relationship are a useful complement to the governing law and are enforceable if they are incorporated into the contract by the parties and do not violate mandatory rules of the governing law. If these rules represent trade usages, they will be applicable even without incorporation by the parties, since most of the legal systems refer to trade usages. If these rules are enacted in binding instruments, such as national laws or international conventions, they also may have the ability to prevail over mandatory rules. These specific rules may achieve uniformity within their scope of application.

To the contrary, uniformity is not always achievable if the rules are so general that they need to be interpreted – because the interpreter's legal

---

[45] See G Cordero-Moss, *International Commercial Law*, in Publications Series of the Department of Private Law, University of Oslo, 185/2010, 96 *et seq* (analysing how differently the formulation 'beyond the control' may be interpreted, in respect of the incorporation into Norwegian law of the formula of Art. 79 of the Vienna Convention on the Contract for International Sale of Goods).

tradition will impact on the effects of the rules. Also, if application of the rules implies the necessity to coordinate with other areas of the applicable legal system, the different legal traditions may affect the result of application of rules even when they are precisely formulated.

2.4 Need for Precise Scope in Investment Law

It seems equally true in commercial and in investment law that a source must be precise and its interpretation must not depend on rules or principles that vary in different legal traditions if the source is to be applied in a predictable and uniform manner.

We saw that the harmonization of general contract law is difficult to achieve through soft law because of the influence of the various legal traditions on the principles of good faith, fair dealing and similar notions affecting the interpretation and application of regulation. Similarly, it seems that it could be difficult to achieve full harmonization in investment law of general standards such as fair and equitable treatment. Admittedly, it is relatively easy to reach an agreement on the general principle that a host country shall grant foreign investors fair and equitable treatment, and certain more specific criteria seem to be emerging to render the standard more precise.[46] However, even the more precise criteria are so broad that their application will heavily depend on interpretation.[47] A harmonized application of the principle to specific cases is therefore likely to require the development of a unitary system of law that goes beyond what can be achieved with soft codification.

To the contrary, the rule on expropriation seems to have a scope that is sufficiently precise to permit harmonizing the criteria developed, among other things, in investment case law. A soft codification of that rule could contribute to the clarification of an autonomous standard of international law.[48]

---

[46] Such as, for example, the protection of the investor's legitimate expectations, see C Schreuer, 'Fair and equitable treatment in arbitral practice' (2005) 6:3 *Journal of World Investment and Trade* 357–86.

[47] Kaufmann-Kohler, 'Arbitral Precedent', above n 2, 372.

[48] See A Reinisch, Chapter 10 in this volume (discussing the various aspects of a soft codification of the rule on expropriation); see also Kaufmann-Kohler, 'Arbitral Precedent', above n 2, 370.

3. ENFORCEABILITY OF THE RESULTS

Soft law instruments support enforceable results when they lead to contracts or decisions that do not conflict with mandatory rules of the governing law. In many situations, as described in section 2.1 above, transnational sources will be applied as a supplement to the governing law – either because they regulate details not regulated by the governing law, or because they regulate matters not regulated by mandatory rules of the governing law. In some situations, however, transnational sources might conflict with mandatory rules of the applicable law. The relationship between contractual terms and transnational law on one side, and state law on the other side, becomes then apparent.

As seen above, the UCP 600 are a successful source of soft law regulating letters of credit. In some cases the mechanism of the letter of credit has been considered to conflict with rules of the governing law, and has been overridden by state law. The principle of autonomy of the payment obligation, for example, was deemed by the Swiss Supreme Court to conflict with the principle against abuse of right.[49] The Bank had refused payment under a letter of credit because not all the documents listed in the instructions had been presented. In particular, a 'receipt signed and proving delivery of the goods' was listed as one of the documents to be presented, and was not presented. The beneficiary claimed that payment was due in spite of the lack of these documents, because the delivery could be proven by other means. According to the principles that rule documentary credits, as seen above, the obligation of the bank to pay is strictly dependent upon the instructions that it has received. If the instructions provide for payment upon presentation of specific documents, then payment has to be effected upon presentation of those documents (irrespective of any supervening circumstance), and only upon presentation of exactly those documents. Payment on presentation of documents different from those listed in the instructions can expose the bank to liability towards the applicant. In the case described here, one of the listed documents was a receipt, and this was not presented. An application of the principles governing documentary credits, therefore, should lead to the conclusion that payment was not to be effected by the bank. The creditor maintains its claims towards the debtor, but the bank cannot effect a payment in violation of the instructions. The creditor will

---

49 *Société de Banque Suisse v Société Generale Alsacienne de Banque*, BGE 105 II 67 (1989).

have to satisfy its claim directly with the debtor. However, the Swiss Supreme Court decided that the bank had to effect payment. Invoking the instructions to refuse payment, in spite of the presence of other documentation showing that payment was due, would be an abuse of right in contrast with Article 2 of the Swiss Code of Obligations, which is mandatory. The Swiss Supreme Court, therefore, found that the principle on abuse of right prevailed over the soft rule on payment upon presentation of the listed documents.

Generally, two techniques are adopted to avoid conflicts between soft codifications and mandatory rules of the applicable law: (i) the soft law instrument contains open references to the governing law, or (ii) the instrument reflects the lowest common denominator among the legal systems where it will be applied. The former leads to harmonization only to the extent corresponding to the scope of the freedom of contract (thus reinforcing the observation made above that soft law is effective when it has a restricted scope of application); the latter brings all regulation in line with the strictest among the laws that may be applicable.

3.1 References to the Applicable Law

The UNCITRAL Arbitration Rules are an example of the first-mentioned technique to ensure enforceability. These Rules are an instrument that the parties to an arbitration dispute may decide to adopt to regulate the procedural aspects of the arbitral proceeding. Once they are adopted, they have the status of a contract between the parties. The arbitral proceeding will be subject to the Rules and to the applicable arbitration legislation of the country where the arbitral tribunal has its venue. In addition to a general principle confirming that mandatory rules of the applicable law prevail in case of conflict with the Rules (Article 1.3), various provisions refer to the applicable law: Article 16 on exclusion of arbitrators' liability, Article 17.4 on the arbitral tribunal's power to authorize non-simultaneous communication between the parties, Article 22 on the scope of the arbitral tribunal's jurisdiction, Article 34.5 on legal duties to make the award public, and finally the note contained in the annex on the possible waiver statement excluding recourse against in the award.

3.2 Lowest Common Denominator

Standard contracts are an example of the second-mentioned technique to ensure enforceability.

The European Commission seemed to encourage, albeit for a short period, standard contracts as a tool towards harmonization of the various state contract laws.[50] It was soon realized, however, that contracts, even if they are standardized, are subject to a governing law and cannot derogate from this law's mandatory rules.[51] Therefore, a standard contract, to be effective in the whole territory of the European Union, would necessarily have to comply with the strictest of the criteria set by the various member states. This, in turn, would have prevented the standard contracts from adopting any more flexible criteria offered in other member states, thereby preventing progress in contract practice. This would not have led to a harmonization that seems desirable.

That a contract, even a standard contract, is subject to a governing law – and that the governing law, even for an international contract, is a national law – has impact even beyond that law's mandatory rules. As shown in this chapter, national laws differ from one another in respect of how contracts are to be interpreted, and this may lead to standard contracts being interpreted differently and having different legal effects depending on the governing law.[52] Standard contracts, therefore, do not seem to be the appropriate tool to harmonize commercial contract laws. Moreover, there is an abundance of standard terms issued by a large number of organizations such as the ICC, branch associations such as ISDA, FIDIC or Orgalime, or even by commercial companies. Standard contracts prepared by FIDIC and Orgalime compete to regulate similar contractual relationships within the same branch of construction; the very fact of this competition speaks against their ability to reflect a harmonized transnational law.

The wealth of documents issued by a disparity of sources creates an additional uncertainty, since it creates the risk of attaching normative value to terms written by organizations or institutions that do not act impartially.[53]

---

[50] See the Action Plan on a More Coherent European Contract Law, COM(2003) 68 final and European Contract Law and the Revision of the Acquis: The Way Forward, COM(2004) 651 final.

[51] First Annual Progress Report on European Contract Law and the Acquis Review, COM(2005) 456 final.

[52] See also H Collins, *The Freedom to Circulate Documents: Regulating Contracts in Europe*; S Whittaker, *On the Development of European Standard Contract Terms*; G Cordero-Moss, 'Anglo-American Contract Models and Norwegian or other Civilian Governing Law: Introduction and Method', in *Anglo-American Contract Models*, Vol I, in Publications Series of the Department of Private Law, 169/2007, University of Oslo, 1–112.

[53] See above n 44, R Goode, H Kronke and E McKendrick, *Transnational Commercial Law*, and S Symeonides, *Party Autonomy and Private-Law Making*, 6,

3.3 Compliance with the Applicable Law and Arbitration

The necessity to comply with the applicable legal framework applies not only to contracts that will be subject to court decisions, but also to contracts containing an arbitration clause, as well as to arbitral awards. This is because the validity and enforceability of arbitral awards, although to a large extent unified by the 1958 New York Convention and harmonized by the UNCITRAL Model Law on Arbitration (a soft law instrument), are limited by certain rules of national law – mainly regarding legal capacity, public policy, arbitrability and procedural principles. Thus, in these areas soft law instruments must refer to or comply with principles of the various legal systems, if the contract or arbitral award based on them is to be effective.[54]

Admittedly, parties whose disputes are submitted to arbitration often enjoy a wide flexibility when it comes to choosing the applicable law. The UNCITRAL Model Law on International Commercial Arbitration, for example, which has been adopted more or less literally in over 50 countries, provides in Article 28(1) that the arbitral tribunal shall apply the 'rules of law' chosen by the parties. This terminology, as opposed to the word 'law' used in Article 28(2) for the eventuality that the parties have not made a choice, is often interpreted to be an opening to non-national and non-authoritative sources of soft law.[55]

That the parties, in the frame of arbitration, may choose to replace the governing law with soft sources, however, is not sufficient to ensure a harmonization of the general contract law. First of all, there may be gaps in the soft sources, so that ultimately the application of a state law may be necessary.[56] Furthermore, as was demonstrated above, certain principles

---

who wishes a 'check to the unbounded euphoria that seems to permeate much of the literature on the subject' of non-state norms as a source of the new *lex mercatoria*.

[54] For a more extensive discussion and references see G Cordero Moss, 'International arbitration and the quest for the applicable law', 8:3 *Global Jurist: (Advances)*, Article 2 1–42 (2008). A research project that I run at the Oslo University studies the impact of national law on the enforceability and validity of international awards: Arbitration and Party autonomy <http://www.jus.uio.no/ifp/english/research/projects/choice-of-law/>.

[55] See the 'Explanatory Note' to the UNCITRAL Model Law on International Commercial Arbitration 1985 with amendments as adopted in 2006, UNCITRAL, 2008, para 39 (available at <http://www.uncitral.org/pdf/english/texts/arbitration/ml-arb/07-86998_Ebook.pdf>, accessed on 19 May 2011).

[56] Both the UPICC and the PECL shall be interpreted autonomously, see,

of general contract law are deeply rooted in the legal tradition of the interpreter and harmonization will not be achieved in full until there is a centralized court that establishes a uniform legal tradition. An instrument with the task of harmonizing different legal traditions must be precise and leave little to the judge's discretion; otherwise, the harmonized rules will be applied differently by the different countries' courts.[57]

3.4 Need for Enforceability of Investment Awards

The criteria for enforceability of commercial awards are applicable also to investment awards whenever the arbitral proceeding is based on commercial arbitration rules such as those of the UNCITRAL, the Stockholm Arbitration Institute, the ICC or the LCIA. This means that the provisions of the 1958 New York Convention on Recognition and Enforcement of Foreign Arbitral Awards (in particular, its Article V) and of the applicable domestic arbitration law (for the arbitration acts that are based on the Model Law, the provisions corresponding to Articles 34 and 36 of the Model Law) will set certain limits on the validity and the enforceability of investment awards. In turn, this restricts the scope within which soft codification may be effective.

The risk of annulment or refusal to enforce by state courts is confined to areas that fall within the rather restricted scope of the mentioned provisions on validity and enforceability of the awards. Broadly summarizing, an award may be set aside or refused enforcement if the

---

respectively, Articles 1.5 and 1:106. However, should it still be impossible to fill a gap, the governing law shall be applied. This is expressly provided for in Article 1:106, second paragraph of the PECL. The UPICC do not state it expressly in their provisions, but they imply it, see the official commentary to the UPICC, published by the UNIDROIT in 2004 at <http://www.unidroit.org/english/principles/contracts/principles2004/integra/versionprinciples2004-e.pdf>, comment No. 4 to Article 1.6, accessed 19 May 2011. Also the Model clause permits the parties to choose the state law to be used as a supplement, see the footnote to the preamble, both in the 2004 and in the 2010 version of the UPICC. If the parties do not choose the law that will supplement the UPICC, this law will be identified on the basis of the applicable choice of law rules.

[57] H Eidenmüller, F Faust, H C Grigoleit, N Jansen, G Wagner and R Zimmermann, 'The Common Frame of Reference for European Private Law Policy Choices and Codification Problems', (2008) 28:4 *Oxford Journal of Legal Studies* 659–708 (criticizing the Draft Common Frame of Reference presented by two academic groups in the framework of the work on a European contract law, and largely based on the PECL, for not being sufficiently precise). See also R Schulze (ed), *CFR and Existing EC Contract Law*, 2nd rev edn, (Sellier 2009).

arbitral tribunal did not have jurisdiction (*inter alia*, because the arbitral agreement was not valid), if it exceeded the scope of its power, if it was not constituted properly, if fundamental rules of procedure were disregarded, if the dispute was not arbitrable or if the award conflicts with public policy. As this summary shows, state courts do not have the possibility of reviewing the merits of an award, whether on questions of fact or of law. Court control reaches primarily the existence and scope of the arbitral tribunal's power and the compliance by the arbitral tribunal with the principle of due process.

Thus, soft codification of matters that do not affect the tribunal's power or fundamental procedural principles, such as codification of substantive standards of investment protection or of specific procedural matters not touching on the areas listed above, does not seem likely to conflict with domestic rules on validity and enforceability of awards (unless it is deemed to violate the court's public policy). On the contrary, soft codification affecting the scope of the arbitral agreement or the tribunal's jurisdiction may fall within the scope of these rules; an award rendered on the basis of these codifications may thus run the risk of being set aside or refused enforcement if the soft codification does not take into proper account the relevant domestic rules.

This may, for example, affect soft codification clarifying the effect on jurisdiction of most favoured nation clauses contained in treaties.[58]

In investment arbitration, the validity of the arbitration agreement and the scope of the tribunal's power are regulated primarily in the treaty upon which the claim is based. If the treaty contains a narrow arbitration clause that apparently does not cover the subject matter of the dispute (for example, the treaty has a dispute resolution clause that restricts arbitration to questions regarding the measurement of compensation, whereas the claimant requests the arbitral tribunal to decide also on whether there has been an expropriation without compensation), the arbitral tribunal apparently does not have jurisdiction and any award may be set aside or refused enforcement.

Some tribunals have applied extensively the most-favoured-nation principle included in the treaty in order to extend the scope of their jurisdiction.[59] It is well known that the application of this provision to

---

[58] More extensively on these instruments see A Bjorklund, Chapter 4, this volume.

[59] *Maffezini v Spain* (25.12000), ICSID Case No ARB/97/7, award on jurisdiction, 25.1.2000; *Siemens v Argentina*, ICSID Case No ARB/02/8, decision on jurisdiction, 3.8.2004; *Gas Natural SDG, S.A. v The Argentine Republic*, ICSID

questions of jurisdiction is quite controversial;[60] therefore, it could *prima facie* seem useful to clarify the matter by developing soft rules specifying to what extent and under what circumstances a treaty's narrow consent to arbitration may be extended by application of the most-favoured-nation rule.

However, a legitimate question is whether a soft codification would be really effective in the matter of jurisdiction. The existence of the arbitral tribunal's power depends on the consent of the parties to the dispute; usually, the parties' consent is contained in the arbitration agreement. In investment arbitration, the consent is usually deemed to be represented by an offer made by the state in treaties or in its foreign investment legislation, which offer is then accepted by the investor when it initiates arbitration.[61] The question is whether a soft codification determining the effects of a most-favoured-nation clause has the power to extend the scope of the offer that the state made in the treaty or in its investment legislation. Should a court in the place of arbitration or in the place of enforcement find that soft law does not have such power, the award made on reliance of the soft law might be set aside or refused enforcement.

In this light, it may be questioned whether the question of jurisdiction (including the effectiveness of a most-favoured-nation provision, and also the purpose and meaning of umbrella clauses) is appropriate for soft codification.

Case No ARB/03/10, decision on jurisdiction, 17.6.2005; *Suez, Sociedad General de Aguas de Barcelona S.A., and InterAguas Servicios Integrales del Agua S.A. v The Argentine Republic,* ICSID Case No ARB/03/17, decision on jurisdiction, 16.5.2006; *RosInvestCo UK Ltd v The Russian Federation,* SCC Case No Arb V079/2005, award on jurisdiction, October 2007.

[60] The District Court of Stockholm decision T24891-07 of 9 November 2011 denied that the arbitral in the case of RosinvestCo UK Ltd v The Russian Federation referred to in the previous footnote had jurisdiction. More extensively on this matter see A Ziegler, Chapter 9, this volume. Against the applicability of the MFN provision to dispute resolution, see *Salini Costruttori S.p.A. and Italstrade S.p.A. v Jordan,* ICSID Case No ARB/02/13, decision on jurisdiction, 29.11.2004; *Plama Consortium Limited v. Bulgaria*, ICSID Case No ARB/03/24, decision on jurisdiction, 8.2.2005; *Telenor Mobile Communications A.S. v Republic of Hungary*, ICSID Case No ARB/04/15, award on jurisdiction, 13.9.2006; *Wintershall Aktiengesellschaft v Argentine Republic*, ICSID Case No ARB/04/14, award, 8.12.2008. See also, for more references, J A Maupin, 'MFN-based jurisdiction in investor-state arbitration: is there any hope for a consistent approach?', (2011) *J Int Econ L* 1–34.

[61] Jan Paulsson, 'Arbitration Without Privity', 10(2) *ICSID Review* (1995) 232.

This does not exclude, however, the possibility that other procedural matters not affecting the validity or enforceability of an award may successfully be regulated by soft law instruments. The IBA Rules on the Taking of Evidence are an example of successful soft codification of a procedural matter.

4. OTHER CRITERIA

4.1 Intended User and Effectiveness

Soft law instruments may take different forms, depending on to whom they are addressed: standard contracts, guidelines, definitions, best practice collections, etc. are addressed to the contract parties; codes, digests of principles and opinions are addressed to judges or arbitrators; model legislation, model conventions and legislative guides are addressed to legislators. Some instruments are intended to be used by all these groups – for example, the UPICC and the PECL affirm in their respective preambles that they are intended for all of these purposes.

Sometimes, the enforceability of arrangements based on the soft instruments may be affected if these are not used by the intended user. Certain rules may need the authority of a statute in order to be enforceable. For example, certain rules may become effective if they are included in the UNCITRAL Model Law on International Commercial Arbitration, which is meant to be used as a basis for legislation. If the same rules are adopted by arbitration institutions or by parties in their arbitration agreements, they may violate mandatory arbitration law or they may assume the existence of powers that are not supported by the applicable legislation.

Whether the instrument is going to be used by entities having legislative, judicial or simply contracting power is important not only for the effective use of these sources, but also for drafting the soft law codification. The instruments should not exceed the scope within which they are enforceable.

This became clear, for example, in the debate within the Working Group II during modernization of the UNCITRAL Arbitration Rules. The work on modernization of the Arbitration Rules started after the UNCITRAL Model Law on International Commercial Arbitration had been revised in 2006.[62] The Arbitration Rules are meant as a suggested

---

[62] The work started in the 45th session of the UNCITRAL Working Group II of September 2006, see the session's report A/CN.9/614.

complement to the arbitration agreement between the parties, and they are supposed to be compatible with the Model Law, which in turn is meant as a suggested arbitration act for legislators. After the Model Law was revised, it was only natural also to revise the Arbitration Rules, in order to reflect the modifications that had been made to the Model Law. However, after some discussion within the UNCITRAL Working Group II it became clear that some of the new provisions that the Working Group had inserted into the Model Law in 2006 could not be reflected in the revised version of the Arbitration Rules that the same Working Group finalized in 2010.[63] This is because some provisions are effective if they are supported by an instrument intended to have the force of law (such as the Model Law), but run the risk of violating fundamental principles of the applicable law and thus being ineffective if they only are based on a contractual instrument (such as the Arbitration Rules). In particular, the Model Law introduced some provisions on so-called preliminary orders (articles 17B and 17C): these provisions give the arbitral tribunal the power to issue orders without having heard the other party. This is a mechanism that may conflict with one of the fundamental principles of arbitration, namely the principle that each of the parties must be heard: an arbitral tribunal does not have this power, unless the arbitration law applicable to it expressly grants this power. The Model Law, after it was revised in 2006, proposes that arbitration acts grant this power to arbitral tribunals. In the revision of the Arbitration Rules made in 2010, however, this power is not mentioned. This is because the Arbitration Rules are an instrument intended to have the force of contract, and a contract may not grant such a power that may infringe the principle of due process present in the applicable arbitration law. The proper instrument of soft law to introduce such power, in short, must be an instrument addressed to the legislator, and not to the parties.

4.2 Description, Prescription and Effectiveness

Soft codifications may have various functions: some instruments of soft law have a descriptive function and systematize and restate rules and principles scattered in various binding sources – such as, for example, the Restatements of the American Law Institute. Other instruments are meant not to simply describe existing rules, but to prescribe new rules, improving existing ones or filling gaps. Below I will offer some considerations on

---

[63] See the report of the 50th session of the UNCITRAL Working Group of February 2009, A/CN.9/669, paras 100–12.

some challenges that may be encountered in connection with these techniques.

4.2.1 Descriptive instruments

Descriptive instruments, in order to be effective, should be written with accuracy. To preserve credibility, they should refrain from the temptation to improve the rules that need improvement or to fill gaps.

The European Research Group on Existing EC Private Law, for example, compiled an instrument known as the Acquis Principles, originally intended to ascertain the existing European law on contracts.[64] The Acquis Principles, however, do not seem to have resisted the temptation to go beyond the existing rules. Rather, they have written the law as the authors deem that it should be. For example, they state that parties must negotiate according to good faith and fair dealing, they impose liability for having negotiated contrary to good faith and they have included a duty of disclosure of information during the pre-contractual phase (Articles 2:101, 2:103 and 2:201). These rules do not represent existing European law, first because there are no rules stemming from European sources on commercial contracts, and second because there is no such general principle common to all legal systems within Europe. In particular, these rules are not fully compatible with the English law of commercial contracts. In the phase of negotiations prior to the conclusion of the contract, expecting that a party also take into consideration the needs and expectations of the other party runs counter to the very essence of a negotiation, where each of the parties positions itself, opens alternative possibilities, and plays the various possibilities against each other to achieve the best economic result for itself. In an often-quoted House of Lords decision, Lord Ackner states that '[...] the concept of a duty to carry on negotiations in good faith is inherently repugnant to the adversarial position of the parties when involved in negotiations'.[65] Restrictions on a party's liberty to organize the negotiations as is most profitable for itself would have to be founded on an ideal of solidarity and loyalty between the parties which is unknown in a system that privileges the economic aspects of the transaction.[66]

---

64 Research group on the Existing EC Private Law (Acquis Group), Principles of the Existing EC Contract Law (Acquis Principles) Contract II: General Provisions, Delivery of Goods, Package Travel and Payment Services, (Sellier 2009).

65 Ackner LJ in *Walford v Miles* [1992] 2 WLR 174, 182.

66 See, among others, S van Erp, 'The Pre-contractual Stage' in A Hartkamp *et al.* (eds), *Towards a European Civil Code* (Kluwer Law International 1998) 201, 215 *et seq.*

The lack of a duty to act in good faith during the negotiations permits a party to conduct negotiations even without having the intention to conclude an agreement with the other party (for example, for the sole reason of preventing the other party from negotiating with a third party, or for obtaining business information, etc.). Even the doctrine of restitution, which could, at first sight, be deemed to be equivalent to a duty to enter into negotiations in good faith, does not ensure the same results. Restitution aims not at compensating the losses suffered by the other party, but at recovering a benefit gained by the party breaking off the negotiations.[67] If the unjustified break-off has caused losses for the other party, but has not resulted in a gain for the party breaking off, therefore, the party suffering losses is not necessarily entitled to compensation under the doctrine of restitution.[68]

Thus, the Acquis rule on good faith in the pre-contractual phase may not be generalized as a matter of status quo,[69] and the Acquis Principles lost their quality as a descriptive instrument when they codified it.

4.2.2 Prescriptive instruments directed at the parties

Prescriptive instruments, in order to be effective, depend on such a widespread use that they can be deemed as trade usage or, if the regulation is within the scope of contractual freedom, on the parties' decision to adopt them in their specific transaction.

For example, as seen above, the UPICC and PECL contain rules that enhance the role of good faith, both in the phase of negotiations and in the phase of performance of the contract, as well as in its interpretation. As opposed to the Acquis Principles, these instruments do not purport to describe existing law. Therefore, these rules may be taken as a suggestion of a regulation that is deemed to be a 'best rule'.

---

67 H Beale (ed), *Chitty on Contracts*, (29th edn, Sweet & Maxwell 2004), Vol 1, 1632.

68 In some cases, however, restitution was given even if no benefit had been gained: ibid, 1638, 1645. In these cases, the losses incurred by the other party consisted of services rendered at the request of the party breaking off the negotiations. It remains to be seen whether the lack of benefit can be disregarded as a prerequisite for restitution in cases where the losses were not incurred at the request of the party breaking off.

69 That a generalization of the consumer rule to general contract law may raise political issues is admitted even in the comments to these articles made in the Acquis Principles, see Part A, Section 3 ('Political Issues') in the comments on each of Arts 2:101 and 2:103. On the difficulty of finding a general duty to disclose in European law see also G Howells, 'Consumer Concepts for a European Code?' in R Schulze (ed), *New Features in Contract Law*, above n 4, 119, 122 *et seq*.

However, the central role given in these instruments to good faith does not seem to reflect commercial contract practice. Recurrent clauses in commercial contracts attempt to exclude the discretion of the interpreter and to create a self-contained regime for the contract based simply on an objective application of the contract's wording and excluding any role for external considerations such as good faith.[70]

Therefore, the UPICC and the PECL are not likely to be extensively adopted by contracting parties in commercial contracts and their success as soft instruments may be affected.

4.2.3 Prescriptive instruments directed at the legislator

When directed at the legislator, soft law instruments may go beyond recognition by the parties and may propose innovative regulation that requires a statutory basis to be enforceable. Successful harmonization measures, however, show that it is sometimes difficult for states to commit to rules or principles that may interfere with the states' own traditions or principles.

Binding instruments such as the CISG and the New York Convention refer often to national law instead of creating a common regulation. As an illustration, it suffices here to mention that the CISG refers in Article 28 to national law to determine whether the remedy of specific performance is applicable, and the New York Convention refers in Article V to national law to determine whether an arbitration agreement and even an arbitral award are valid. This is a price that needs to be paid in order to obtain the states' consent to participate in uniform legislation with binding effects: a balance must be found between the desired harmonization and the states' wish to maintain their sovereignty in areas where their interests or traditions prevent full uniformity.

Even the flexibility of soft codifications, however, may not be sufficient to persuade states to insert regulations that do not fully reflect their own legislation or tradition. The UNCITRAL Model Law on Arbitration, thus, contains numerous references to national legislation instead of proposing a new regulation common to all states that will adopt it: Article 1(5) on arbitrability; Article 8(1) on the courts' jurisdiction on the validity of the arbitration agreement; Article 9 on the courts' jurisdiction on interim measures; Articles 17 I(1)(a)(1)(i) and 17 I(1)(b)(ii) on the grounds to refuse recognition or enforcement of interim measures issued by the arbitral tribunal; Article 17J on the courts' jurisdiction to issue interim

---

70 For a more extensive discussion see G Cordero-Moss, 'Does the use of common law contract models' in G Cordero-Moss (ed), *Boilerplate Clauses*, above n 24, 48 *et seq*.

measures; Article 27 on court assistance in taking evidence; Article 28(2) on the choice of the applicable law; Articles 34(2)(a)(i) and 36(2)(a)(i) on incapacity and validity of the arbitration agreement in connection with, respectively, the validity and enforceability of the award; Articles 34(2)(b)(i) and 36(2)(b)(i) on arbitrability in connection with, respectively, the validity and enforceability of the award; and Articles 34(2)(b)(ii) and 36(2)(b)(ii) on public policy in connection with, respectively, the validity and enforceability of the award.

Thus, the interaction with authoritative state law sources needs to be carefully regulated even when the soft instrument is directed at the legislator.

4.3 The Drafting Process and Effectiveness

Soft law instruments that provide predictable and enforceable solutions are also based on a realistic prospect that the intended users will be interested in committing to the proposed solution.

During the negotiations of a soft law instrument, it may be tempting to propose rather progressive solutions that might be accepted with more difficulty if the drafted instrument was destined to become binding. Consensus is more easily reached when the soft instrument is not binding, because of the mental or even expressed reservation that mandatory law will anyway prevail in case of conflict. It is, however, questionable to what extent it may be considered a success of the soft codification that consensus is achieved thanks to the possibility of avoiding its application.

A prominent example is the already mentioned UPICC. These are non-binding restatements of principles; they are partially a codification of generally adopted principles of international contracts, and partially original regulations resulting from the work of a large group of scholars from various parts of the world. Because the outcome of the work is not binding, and conflicting mandatory rules or principles of the governing law prevail, the working group could agree to rules and formulations more easily than if it were drafting a convention destined to become binding. Moreover, the work did not require unanimity, and controversial matters could be regulated more easily than would be the case if a large consensus were needed – as happens when drafting a convention. These two aspects rendered it easier to codify 'best rules' in a restatement rather than in binding instruments; however, these same aspects render such a restatement less representative than an instrument based on a larger consensus and to which most members are committed.[71]

Thus, the UPICC include, as already seen, extensive references to the principle of good faith and regulate a duty of good faith between the parties in numerous specific situations. By comparison, the binding CISG convention does not contain any rule on the duty of good faith between the parties, notwithstanding discussion of the matter during the negotiations.[72] The inclusion of a duty of good faith in the soft instrument does not seem to have influenced contract or arbitration practice, as seen above in respect of the merger clause.

4.4 Room for Progressive Development in Investment Law

In light of the different interests involved in commercial and investment disputes, it may be questioned whether predictability and enforceability play as central a role in investment law as they do in commercial law.

Admittedly, even within commercial law uncertain arrangements under circumstances may be of value: for example, uncertainty about the interpretation of a contract term may induce the parties to find an out-of-court solution and so avoid time-consuming and costly proceedings; an arbitral award that is not enforceable may still be complied with by the

---

[71] See above n 44, extensively, R Goode, H Kronke and E McKendrick, *Transnational Commercial Law*, 509 and 528 *et seq* (explaining, in this light, why the principle of good faith and fair dealing was given such a central role in the UNIDROIT Principles but not in the CISG).

[72] During legislative work, specific proposals were presented on good faith in the pre-contractual phase, as well as general proposals dealing with the requirement of good faith. The specific proposals relating to pre-contractual liability were rejected, and the generic proposals on good faith were incorporated into Art 7, in such a way that the principle of good faith is not directed to regulate the parties' conduct in the contract, but rather is directed to the contracting state's interpretation of the convention. For an extensive evaluation of this matter, as well as references to literature and to the legislative history in this respect, see A Kritzer, 'Pre-Contract Formation', editorial remark on the internet database of the Institute of International Commercial Law of the Pace University School of Law, <www.cig.law.pace.edu/cisg/biblio/kritzer1.html> 2 *et seq*, with extensive references also to the Minority Opinion of M Bonell (Italy's delegate to the UNCITRAL Working Group that drafted the convention), M Bonell, 'Formation of Contracts and Precontractual Liability Under the Vienna Convention on International Sale of Goods', in ICC (ed), *Formation of Contracts and Precontractual Liability* (Paris 1990) 157–78. According to Bonell, an extensive interpretation of the CISG would justify application of both concepts of pre-contractual liability and of good faith. See also R Goode, H Kronke and E McKendrick, *Transnational Commercial Law*, above n 44, 279 *et seq*.

losing party if it is interested in preserving its commercial reputation. Apart from these marginal situations, however, commercial parties usually desire to rely on the predictability and enforceability of the instruments that they use, without having to count on the voluntary cooperation of the other party.

In many investment disputes, the involved interests may have a character different from the mere commercial and economic value of the transaction in dispute. This may mean that other policies should be given due attention, in addition to (or instead of) predictability and enforceability. However, as long as a soft codification in investment law is intended to be used in the resolution of a specific dispute, it seems that at least the criterion of predictability remains central.

Should a soft codification be intended not as a basis for dispute resolution, but as a phase in the shaping of investment law, for example instrumental to the development of future treaty regulation, it may be less relevant to focus on precise regulation that may be applied uniformly in a predictable manner. Precise regulation that is crucial in the context of deciding disputes may prevent compromises between states with diverging interests and not willing to limit their respective sovereignty. The experience of soft law in the commercial sector may be relevant in the former context of resolution of specific disputes, but not in the latter of progressive development of rules.

Also, the requirement that soft sources should not provide for solutions that run the risk of not being enforceable is less relevant if soft codification is seen as a stage in the process of norm creation.

The UNCITRAL Working Group on Arbitration's current discussions on developing a legal standard for transparency in treaty-based arbitration[73] may be looked upon as an example of the greater flexibility that soft codification enjoys when its purpose is to contribute to norm creation rather then to provide a set of rules to be applied in the solution of specific disputes.

Transparency and arbitration are traditionally considered to be antinomic, as confidentiality is generally held to be one of the important features of arbitration. This is based mainly on the observation that arbitration is an out-of-court mechanism for the solution of disputes between two parties, and that it does not have any relevance to the interests of third parties. While this observation may be correct if it refers

---

[73] The work started in the 53rd session of the UNCITRAL Working Group II of October 2010 see the session's report A/CN.9/712.

to commercial arbitration, it is not when it regards investment arbitration which, as seen above, involves public interests of various kinds. Various investment treaties, most notably the NAFTA, permit a significant degree of transparency in that the parties' submissions may be made public, the tribunal may be in a position to allow third parties to present submissions, etc.[74] Also the ICSID recognized the need to adapt arbitration's traditional preference for confidentiality to the relevance of public interest in investment arbitration, and in 2006 it introduced into its Arbitration Rules provisions ensuring a certain transparency.[75] Investment arbitration based on UNCITRAL Arbitration Rules, however, is not subject to any rules on transparency unless any such rules are contained in the treaty on which the claim is based. This is why the UNCITRAL Commission requested its Working Group II to develop a legal standard for transparency in treaty-based arbitration.[76]

When developing a legal standard for transparency in investment arbitration, the UNCITRAL Working Group needs to consider what kind of instrument would be the most appropriate. An amendment to the Arbitration Rules, or an annex thereto, would ensure that the transparency provisions become binding on the parties if the parties have agreed that the dispute shall be subject to the UNCITRAL Arbitration Rules. Apart from doubts about the applicability of these amendments or annexes to proceedings based on already existing treaties,[77] the distance between the approaches to confidentiality and transparency in arbitration seems to indicate that it may be difficult to reach an agreement on specific provisions, if the provisions are meant to be

[74] For example, NAFTA Articles 1127 and 1129(1) provide for disclosure of the pleadings and the produced evidence to the non-disputing parties; Article 1128 provides for participation of the non-disputing party on matters of treaty interpretation; Article 1137(4) provides for publication of the award. To strengthen the degree of transparency based on these Articles, the NAFTA Free Trade Commission issued on 31 July 2001 a Note of Interpretation of Certain Chapter 11 Provisions, confirming the absence of a duty of confidentiality, available at < <http://www.international.gc.ca/trade-agreements-accords-commerciaux/disp-diff/nafta-interpr.aspx?lang=en&view=d>.

[75] Rule 48(4) on public access to documentation and Rule 32(2) on open hearings. See also Regulation 22 of the ICSID Administrative and Financial Regulations, on publication of the requests for arbitration.

[76] At its 43rd session, June–July 2010 A/65/17, para 190.

[77] Some delegations in the Working Group have expressed doubts about the applicability of such an amendment or annex in case the treaty containing the offer to arbitrate predates the amendment or the annex: A/CN.9/712, paras 27–8 as well as A/CN.9/717 paras 33–41.

binding. Therefore, the Working Group is exploring alternative possibilities, such as non-binding guidelines or model arbitration clauses to be inserted into future treaties. These instruments may exercise considerable influence if they are applied by tribunals or adopted by states in new treaties. However, they do not have the ambition of becoming directly binding. On the one hand, this reduces the effectiveness of the instruments; on the other hand, it may be easier to reach an agreement on their content without fearing for their compatibility with existing principles or policies.

CONCLUSION

The criteria for success that have been identified above in respect of soft codification of contract law seem to be relevant also to investment law particularly if the soft codification is intended to be used as a basis for resolution of specific disputes. Soft codification with this purpose within investment law should also use precise terms rather than vague formulations resulting out of compromises between various interests, it should have a specific subject matter rather than address general principles and it should be compatible with the international and domestic instruments that regulate enforceability of the awards.

If soft codification is intended as a tool in the progressive development of law, however, these criteria are less relevant.

7. GATT/WTO law and international standards: an example of soft law instruments hardening up?

Melaku Geboye Desta*

I. INTRODUCTION

The World Trade Organization (WTO) has its roots in the General Agreement on Tariffs and Trade (GATT), an international agreement that was designed to facilitate international trade in goods by progressively reducing and, in many cases, eliminating national governmental measures that are restrictive of trade, which traditionally almost always meant import-restrictive measures. The GATT/WTO system has succeeded in reducing import tariffs in particular to such low levels that non-tariff measures have now become the major remaining obstacles to international trade.[1] This is a result of two interrelated developments: (1) with the reduction of tariffs, governments tend to resort to *new* non-tariff barriers in order to keep a certain level of protection in place,[2] while (2) the successful tariff reductions also have the effect of exposing *old* non-tariff barriers, appropriately compared by Kahler to the 'draining of a lake that

* I wish to thank the editors of this volume, Andrea Bjorklund and August Reinisch, for their patience, understanding and encouragement throughout. I am also grateful to my colleagues in Dundee in general for taking an active part at a staff seminar where I presented the paper, and Abba Kolo, Alistair Rieu-Clarke, Moshe Hirsch, Aloysius Gng and Vitaliy Pogoretskyy for helpful comments and suggestions on the draft. All errors of course remain my own.

1 Technical barriers have long been recognized as 'the largest category of non-tariff measures faced by exporters'. WTO, *Technical Barriers to Trade: Technical Explanation*, at <http://www.wto.org/english/tratop_e/tbt_e/tbt_info_e.htm> accessed 8 October 2011.

2 See D G Victor, 'The Sanitary and Phytosanitary Agreement of the World Trade Organization: An Assessment After Five Years' (2000) 32 *New York University Journal of International Law and Politics* 865 (describing it as a case of 'simply shifting from tariff to non-tariff measures').

reveals the mountain peaks formerly concealed'.[3] National measures to enforce product standards constitute a significant component of these non-tariff barriers to trade. When we refer to standards in the context of the WTO, we often mean the detailed specifications or characteristics required of a product and, in some cases, the process by which it is made, before it is placed on the market.

Standards are developed to meet trade and non-trade objectives, which could be related to consumer protection (e.g. product quality, safety, etc.), the environment (e.g. fuel consumption standards for cars), communication between producers and consumers (e.g. labelling requirements), and the like. Whatever their purpose, standards can be established by national public bodies, private associations or a combination of both, who set and enforce them within their jurisdictions insofar as their means permit. Traditionally governments issue mandatory standards to address health- and safety-related concerns, while private operators, often through their associations, develop voluntary standards mainly focused on matters that go beyond health and safety or set detailed production and processing methods that are designed to ensure that the minimum regulatory standards are complied with throughout the supply chain.[4]

Standards can achieve acceptance and prominence simply as indicators of quality, but they can also become mandatory once a government (*de jure*) or a chain of retailers (*de facto*)[5] makes them a condition for

---

[3] See M Kahler, 'Trade and Domestic Differences' (1996), quoted in M J Trebilcock and R Howse, *The Regulation of International Trade* (3rd edn, Routledge 2005) 202.

[4] See T Josling, 'Private Standards and Trade' in J A McMahon and M G Desta (eds), *Research Handbook on the WTO Agriculture Agreement: New and Emerging Issues in International Agricultural Trade Law* (Edward Elgar 2012 forthcoming). See also T Havinga, 'Private Regulation of Food Safety by Supermarkets' (2006) 28:4 *Law and Policy* 515.

[5] Private-sector operators, such as supermarket chains, are increasingly introducing their own standards, a good example being GLOBALGAP (Good Agricultural Practices) for agricultural products. While these standards generally do not have the force of law in any country, their effectiveness is beyond doubt. See e.g. N Hachez and J Wouters, 'A Glimpse at the Democratic Legitimacy of Private Standards - Assessing The Public Accountability of Global G.A.P.' (2011) 14:3 *Journal of International Economic Law* 677. These authors note that GLOBALGAP standards are formally voluntary but they are meant to become 'a harmonized and single benchmark for Good Agricultural Practices, and in practice, they indeed have gained great prominence, as certification is now required by numerous retailers all across the globe. Without such certification the chances of a producer accessing the retailing market in many countries are severely compromised. In this

marketing the relevant products to the consumer (albeit limited to the consumer's access to products from within the premises of particular supermarkets or establishments in the case of private standards). Once standards become a condition for marketing a product to consumers in a particular country, all foreign producers and suppliers will also need to adapt their products to meet them and acquire the necessary certification. Potentially, that could mean as many different public standards for a single product as the number of jurisdictions in the world, or indeed potentially as many private standards as the number of retailers. In this area, the traditional distinction between soft law[6] and hard law does not matter much; when voluntary standards are adopted by market participants, the market provides the incentives to enforce them effectively, blindly and unsympathetically. A good example is the practice of wholesalers and retailers in the US who sometimes refuse to sell non-standard products because 'they do not wish to bear the responsibility in cases where such products create problems'.[7] In such cases, whether standards are soft or hard in origin is of little practical significance; even those that have soft roots can have equally hard ends.[8] It is also worth

---

regard GLOBALGAP standards have become a "norm", the significance of which extends throughout the supply chain and effectively "governs" the wholesale and consumer markets in respect of food safety, but also of social and environmental issues, well beyond the individual contractual relationship in which a retailer requires GLOBALGAP certification from a producer.' Ibid, 700. Also, a number of voluntary schemes are emerging with varying agenda – poverty alleviation in developing countries (e.g. fair trade labels, see Fairtrade International, at <http://www.fairtrade.net/>), environmental protection (e.g. conservation programmes: see e.g. Forestry Stewardship Council, which describes itself as a 'non-governmental, not-for-profit organization established to promote the responsible management of the world's forests' <http://www.fsc.org/about-fsc.html> accessed 8 October 2011), and so on.

6 For a discussion of soft law, see Desta, Chapter 3, this volume.

7 See WTO, *World Trade Report 2005*, 90. Likewise, Uganda reported that the US made importation of Nile perch, a major export item for Uganda, conditional on the existence of approved hazard analysis and critical control point (HACCP) systems of risk management in Uganda's fish factories. Uganda then ensured that all fish processing enterprises were certified to ISO 9001:2000 and implemented ISO 9000 Quality Management Systems and the principles of HACCP. According to Uganda, the implementation of HACCP made it possible to export fish to the US market. See WTO, *Fish Export from Lake Victoria – from Import Ban to Cash Earner: Communication from Uganda* (G/SPS/GEN/685, 6 April 2006).

8 See e.g. Hachez and Wouters, above n 5, 678 (noting that private food standards end up governing the food market and become *de facto* mandatory).

noting that sometimes governments also adopt new laws and regulations that incorporate norms that started life as part of private standards.[9] A good example in this respect would be organic food standards in the EU; although these standards originated on a voluntary basis, the EU has now introduced detailed regulations governing organic farming.[10]

The trade restrictive impact of such a complex system of standards, which can be public or private in origin and vary by country, is self-evident – leaving standard setting to every country makes it overly expensive and inefficient for producers, which will also be reflected in the prices on the market, thus damaging the interests of everyone involved in the value chain from the producer to the consumer. As a result, given the right conditions, product and process standards can play a significant facilitative role in international trade. Standards are thus known as the other language of international trade; just as we need a shared language to communicate, we need shared standards to effectuate trade.[11] However, in the absence of a degree of harmonization, it is also true that just as languages can be tools or barriers to communication, product and process standards can also serve to facilitate or hinder trade. It is out of this need that private and public international standard-setting institutions emerged mainly in the twentieth century with the objective of harmonizing standards across nations.[12]

The real challenges for the WTO in the area of standards are two-fold. First is the issue of balancing – i.e. while these standards serve a number of public-good functions and need to be encouraged, there is also the need to ensure that they do not serve as a cover for otherwise protectionist motives. Second, as noted above, the demand for standards has traditionally been met in a variety of ways and forms, including mandatory government regulations and voluntary private sector standards operating at the national level and those created through regional and international associations of standard-setting public and private institutions. As a purely intergovern-

---

9 See UNCTAD, *World Investment Report 2011*, 118.

10 For further information on EU law and policy relating to organic farming, see < http://ec.europa.eu/agriculture/organic/eu-policy/legislation_en >.

11 Nathan Koenig, one of the architects of the Codex Alimentarius Commission (Codex), wrote in 1964 that standards are 'especially important in providing buyers and sellers with a common language for local and long distance trading'. See N Koenig, 'A New Vital Influence in International Food Standards' (1964) 19 *Food Drug Cosmetic Law Journal* 335. He added that standards also serve as 'a yardstick for determining value.' Ibid. See also N Koenig, 'Developments in International Food Standards' (1965) 20:6 *Food Drug Cosmetic Law Journal* 317.

12 See Josling, above n 4.

mental body, the GATT/WTO system has found it difficult to deal with the multiplicity of actors and sources involved in this area. However, given the ever-growing role of standards as trade restrictive devices, the trading system could not ignore them for ever. The Uruguay Round of trade negotiations thus introduced two specific agreements dealing particularly with product standards – the Agreement on Sanitary and Phytosanitary Measures (SPS Agreement) and the Agreement on Technical Barriers to Trade (the TBT Agreement).[13]

These agreements do not create detailed and product-specific standards for WTO members to follow as a matter of legal obligation; they only establish a framework that sets the general conditions under which standards should be established and maintained, including through a statement of preference for standards established elsewhere by international technical institutions that do not necessarily have the mandate to make binding rules of international law. The SPS Agreement refers to three named international standard-setting institutions: the World Organization for Animal Health (OIE), the Codex Alimentarius Commission (Codex) on food safety and the International Plant Protection Convention (IPPC) for plant health; the TBT Agreement on the other hand is more open-ended, referring simply to international standardizing bodies that meet certain requirements. Both agreements give legal recognition for the standards set by these external bodies, an approach that is now recognized as revolutionary. Through them, the WTO has effectively created an avenue for the transformation of voluntary international standards into binding international norms. The two agreements, more than any in the WTO, have since become a fast-track route for the transformation of international soft law instruments into hard law international economic regulation. We shall see that the provisions in the two agreements that cross-refer to external international standards serve as a hard law bridge to link up the WTO system with soft law instruments and facilitate their steady flow into the world of binding international regulation. In the words of Horn and Weiler, the two Agreements represent 'as big a paradigm shift to international economic law as, say, the prohibition on the use of force and the introduction of the

---

[13] Note that before the entry into force of the Uruguay Round Agreements in 1995, the only standards-related agreement we had was the Tokyo Round Agreement on Technical Barriers to Trade, also known as the Standards Code, which was plurilateral in character (i.e. it applied only to some, and not to all, GATT contracting parties) and accepted by only 46 countries. The Standards Code has since been replaced by the multilateral TBT Agreement.

Security Council with binding resolution and police powers represented within the classical world of international law'.[14]

This chapter aims to examine two issues: the role of international soft law instruments in international trade regulation as enshrined in the SPS and TBT Agreements, and whether there are any lessons that can be learnt from the WTO approach about the actual or potential role of similar international soft law instruments in international investment law. To do that, section II discusses the WTO approach to the regulation of standards broadly; sections III and IV examine how the hard law instruments of the SPS and TBT Agreements, respectively, interact with and give legal effect to traditionally non-binding international standards in their respective areas of operation. Section V then assesses the implications of the WTO jurisprudence for international soft law standards in the WTO system. Section VI reflects on the question of what, if any, international investment law can learn from this WTO approach towards international soft law standards.

II. THE WTO AND INTERNATIONAL STANDARDS

A. General

WTO law applying to product characteristics distinguishes between standards and technical regulations. Both refer to documents which lay down 'product characteristics or their related processes and production methods'. However, under WTO law, while a standard is 'approved by a recognized body, that provides, for common and repeated use, rules [or] guidelines [...] with which compliance is not mandatory', a technical regulation is by definition a governmental document similar to a standard but 'with which compliance is mandatory'.[15] The term 'standard' is understood differently in the field of international investment law; indeed, the term lacks any official or authoritative definition and is used to mean

---

[14] See H Horn and J H H Weiler, 'European Communities – Trade Description of Sardines: Textualism and its Discontent', *The WTO Case Law of 2002* (2004) 5, available at <http://www.ali.org/doc/wto/wto2002/Sardines.pdf>. Horn and Weiler add that a 'central facet of this shift is the move towards an internationally determined normativity [...] whereby international standards achieve a prominent role as a basis for Members' individual technical regulations.' Ibid.

[15] See WTO Agreement on Technical Barriers to Trade, Annex 1, paras 1 and 2. For more on this see *infra* section IV on *US Tuna/Dolphin*.

different things in different contexts. In most cases, the term is used as a shorthand to refer to a diversity of substantive principles relating to the treatment of foreign investors in and by the host state – i.e. in the sense of 'standards of treatment'.[16] This use of the term is also common in GATT/WTO law, but here I use the term standard as a set of rules and guidelines, mandatory or voluntary, that lay down detailed characteristics, terminology, quality and safety requirements and other features for particular products or activities.[17]

B. Standards and International Trade

Trade liberalization is the principal mission of the GATT/WTO system, but it also recognizes that trade is only a means to an end, that end being welfare maximization. In pursuing trade liberalization, the multilateral trading system has always been sensitive to other public policy objectives such as food safety, animal and plant health, national security and the environment. Realizing the twin goals of promoting international trade on the one hand, and protecting such overriding public policy interests on the other, has been one of the most daunting challenges for the trading system.[18] As a result, the application of SPS and technical regulations to imports has been subject to the disciplines of GATT since 1947 and two specialized agreements since 1995: the WTO Agreement on Sanitary and Phytosanitary Measures (SPS Agreement) and the Agreement on

---

16 See e.g. A Reinisch (ed), *Standards of Investment Protection* (OUP 2008) in which he and his contributors understand a standard to mean such substantive principles of investment law as national treatment, MFN, fair and equitable treatment, and so on.

17 Note that the term 'international standard' is not defined in Annex 1 of the TBT Agreement; in such situations the TBT Agreement adopts the meaning given to the term under the ISO/IEC Guide 2:1991. This document defines an international standard as a 'standard that is adopted by an international standardizing/standards organization and made available to the public'. See *United States – Measures concerning the importation, marketing and sale of tuna and tuna products* (panel report, WT/DS381/R, 15 September 2011), para 7.663 [hereinafter *US Tuna/Dolphin*].

18 Indeed, the trade-restrictive impact of sanitary measures and other technical regulations has been a constant source of tension between developed countries and the poorest developing countries. The traditional propensity of most developed countries to keep their agricultural markets closed for competition often exacerbates the fear that health and safety standards could be used to disguise measures with purely protectionist motives. For more on this, see M G Desta and M Hirsch, 'African Countries in the World Trading System: International Trade, Domestic Institutions and the Role of International Law' (2012 forthcoming) *ICLQ*.

Technical Barriers to Trade (the TBT Agreement).[19]

The roots of both agreements lie in the GATT text, which set its own balance between the twin goals of promoting international trade on the one hand and protecting human, animal or plant life or health or other legitimate policy interests on the other. This balance is subject to a constant process of shifts and adjustments in response to several factors, such as the emergence of new pathogens, advances in science and technology, popular risk perception and tolerance levels, the invention of new products and services as well as pressure exerted by interest groups. The process of fine-tuning the balance between competing interests is discernible within the evolution of the GATT/WTO system over the past six decades, embodied particularly in GATT Article XX(b) and the two specialized WTO Agreements. At the same time, these two Agreements also represent a significant shift in the international regulation of national standards. For example, unlike in general GATT/WTO law where trade measures are designed to ensure a level playing field between imported and domestic products (e.g. through the principle of non-discrimination, the prohibition of certain types of anti-competitive practices, etc.), the two agreements make it clear that a national measure may fall foul of WTO requirements even when it affects equally both domestic and foreign products. This, coupled with their transformative role for non-binding international standards into binding legal norms, is what makes them particularly relevant for the discussion here.

C. GATT Article XX(b)

Under Article XX(b) of the GATT, countries are allowed to adopt measures 'necessary to protect human, animal or plant life or health', provided that such measures do not serve as means of arbitrary or unjustifiable discrimination between countries or as disguised restriction on international trade. Under this system, as long as countries are able to demonstrate that a certain measure is 'necessary' to achieve the specified health objectives, and the implementation of such measures passes the discrimination and disguised trade restriction tests, they can develop their measures with considerable discretion.[20] GATT Article XX(b) is thus an

---

[19] For a useful summary of the similarities and differences between the two agreements, see WTO, *World Trade Report 2005*, 158.

[20] As Sykes says, under the GATT, regulators were 'free to adopt whatever regulations they wished, even if the regulations raised the costs of foreign suppliers disproportionately and thus had the effect of insulating domestic firms from foreign competition'. A Sykes, 'Domestic Regulation, Sovereignty, and Scientific Evidence

exception that 'clearly allowed contracting parties to give priority to human health over trade liberalization'.[21]

In practice, many countries have tried to justify SPS and similar other measures on the basis of GATT Article XX(b) but have failed on the necessity requirement. An often-quoted paragraph from the WTO Appellate Body (AB) ruling in *Korea – Measures Affecting Imports of Beef* summarizes the current understanding of the term 'necessary' as used in GATT Article XX(d), which also applies to the use of the same term under Article XX(b):

> Measures which are indispensable or of absolute necessity or inevitable to secure compliance certainly fulfil the requirements of Article XX(d). But other measures, too, may fall within the ambit of this exception. As used in Article XX(d), the term 'necessary' refers, in our view, to a range of degrees of necessity. At one end of this continuum lies 'necessary' understood as 'indispensable'; at the other end, is 'necessary' taken to mean as 'making a contribution to.' We consider that a 'necessary' measure is, in this continuum, located significantly closer to the pole of 'indispensable' than to the opposite pole of simply 'making a contribution to'.[22]

The AB further explained that determination of whether a measure is 'necessary' 'involves in every case a process of weighing and balancing a series of factors which prominently include the contribution made by the [...] measure to the enforcement of the law or regulation at issue, the importance of the common interests or values protected by that law or regulation, and the accompanying impact of the law or regulation on imports or exports.'[23] According to the AB, to be characterized as necessary, a measure 'does not have to be indispensable' but 'its contribution to the achievement of the objective must be material, not merely marginal or insignificant'.[24] Furthermore, a measure qualifies as 'necessary' only if it is the least-trade-restrictive option available to a

---

Requirements: a Pessimistic View' (2002) 3 *CJIL* 353, 355.

21 See GATT, *Thailand–Restrictions on Importation of and Internal Taxes on Cigarettes*, Panel Report (DS10/R *BISD* 37S/200, adopted November 1990) para 73.

22 *Korea – Measures Affecting Imports of Fresh, Chilled and Frozen Beef* (2000) WT/DS161, WT/DS169, AB Report, para 161.

23 Ibid, para 164. The AB also observed in the context of Article XVI of the GATS that the weighing and balancing process in a necessity analysis 'begins with an assessment of the "relative importance" of the interests or values furthered by the challenged measure'. See *US – Gambling*, AB Report para 306.

24 See *Brazil – Measures Affecting Imports of Retreaded Tyres*, AB Report (WT/DS332/AB/R, 3 December 2007) para 210.

country to achieve its policy goals.[25] To determine whether this is the case, the AB said that the preliminary conclusion that a measure is necessary 'must be confirmed by comparing [it] with its possible alternatives, which may be less trade restrictive while providing an equivalent contribution to the achievement of the objective pursued'.[26]

In cases where respondents have passed the necessity test, their defences often failed on the requirements of the *chapeau* of GATT Article XX – i.e. that the application of such measures must not cause arbitrary or unjustifiable discrimination between countries or a disguised restriction on international trade.[27] As the AB said in *Brazil Retreaded Tyres,* the requirements in the *chapeau* serve 'to ensure that Members' rights to avail themselves of exceptions are exercised in good faith to protect interests considered legitimate under Article XX, not as a means to circumvent one Member's obligations towards other WTO Members'.[28]

The history of GATT/WTO dispute settlement shows that it has never been easy to successfully invoke GATT Article XX(b) as a justification for an otherwise illegal trade-restrictive measure. In the food sector in particular, however, this did not prevent GATT contracting parties from using SPS measures, including to achieve protectionist ends. It is thus hardly surprising that one aim of the Uruguay Round was to minimize the adverse effects of sanitary and phytosanitary regulations on agricultural trade.[29] The resulting SPS Agreement supplemented and clarified GATT Article XX(b) but also went further and imposed a 'new and comprehensive set of rules'.[30] Moreover, we shall see that, unlike GATT Article XX(b), the SPS Agreement (and also the TBT Agreement) sets harmonization of standards as one of its major objectives. It is in the effort to meet this objective that both agreements resort to international soft law

---

[25] See also *United States – Section 337 of the Tariff Act of 1930* (*BISD* 36S/345, panel report adopted 7 November 1989) para 5.26, and *Thailand – Cigarettes*, above n 21, paras 74–75.

[26] See *Brazil Retreaded Tyres*, AB Report, para 156.

[27] *Brazil Retreaded Tyres* is one good example where a respondent passed the necessity test under Art XX(b) but failed on the *chapeau*. See ibid, para 228.

[28] See ibid, para 215. The only case in which a GATT/WTO member successfully defended a measure on the basis of GATT Article XX(b) was *EC Asbestos*. See WTO, *European Communities – Measures Affecting Asbestos and Asbestos-Containing Products* (WT/DS135), AB Report adopted 5 April 2001, para 175.

[29] See GATT, *Ministerial Declaration on the Uruguay Round* (MIN.DEC) 20 September 1986, reproduced in GATT, *Focus Newsletter*, No 41 (October 1986).

[30] See P van den Bossche, *The Law and Policy of the World Trade Organization: Text, Cases and Materials* (2nd edn, CUP 2008) 841.

standards, a key distinguishing feature from the approaches followed under the GATT thitherto.

III. THE WTO SPS AGREEMENT

The SPS Agreement deals with SPS measures which may affect international trade. Annex A to the SPS Agreement defines an SPS measure to mean:

> 'any measure applied: (a) to protect animal or plant life or health within the territory of the Member from risks arising from the entry, establishment or spread of pests, diseases, disease-carrying organisms or disease-causing organisms; (b) to protect human or animal life or health within the territory of the Member from risks arising from additives, contaminants, toxins or disease-causing organisms in foods, beverages or feedstuffs; (c) to protect human life or health within the territory of the Member from risks arising from diseases carried by animals, plants or products thereof, or from the entry, establishment or spread of pests; or (d) to prevent or limit other damage within the territory of the Member from the entry, establishment or spread of pests.

SPS measures thus include:

> all relevant laws, decrees, regulations, requirements and procedures including, *inter alia*, end product criteria; processes and production methods; testing, inspection, certification and approval procedures; quarantine treatments including relevant requirements associated with the transport of animals or plants, or with the materials necessary for their survival during transport; provisions on relevant statistical methods, sampling procedures and methods of risk assessment; and packaging and labelling requirements directly related to food safety.[31]

Like GATT, the SPS Agreement also reaffirms that 'no Member should be prevented from adopting or enforcing measures necessary to protect human, animal or plant life or health'.[32] This is, however, subject to a series of conditions intended to reduce the likelihood of such rights being used for protectionist purposes.[33] It does this by recognizing scientific evidence as the final test.[34] The Agreement also encourages harmonization

---

31 See SPS Agreement, Annex A, para 1.

32 See WTO SPS Agreement preamble, para 1.

33 See e.g. ibid, preamble 1st para and Articles 2 and 5.

34 See DA Motaal, 'The "Multilateral Scientific Consensus" and the World Trade Organization' (2004) 38 *Journal of World Trade* 855 (noting that the Tokyo Round Agreement on Technical Barriers to Trade first explicitly introduced the

of SPS measures around international standards, but again it recognizes the right of countries to set their standards at whatever level they deem appropriate, even higher than the level of corresponding international standards. In such cases, however, members must ensure that measures are, *inter alia*, based on a risk assessment, scientific principles and a scientific justification.[35] The resulting balance is generally perceived as a reasonable compromise between food safety and trade interests, but the latitude it affords to the WTO members is also susceptible to abuse.

The WTO approach accepts the prospect that each country can have its own standards. Differing standards in different importing countries inevitably mean higher compliance cost for exporters. In recognition of these challenges, during the Uruguay Round negotiations, developing countries sought to minimize the risk of SPS measures being used 'as an alternative form of protection'[36] by pushing for 'the widest possible use of international standards'.[37] But the EC and others successfully argued against binding harmonization. They contended that 'countries which had achieved high health standards would find it difficult to accept moving to lower standards'.[38] The resulting compromise is contained in Article 3 of the SPS Agreement, which (in para 1) sets harmonization as a goal for the future,[39] encourages members to harmonize their national standards around international standards set by three technical intergovernmental institutions (Codex, OIE and IPPC), rewards them for conforming to international standards with a virtually irrefutable legal presumption of consistency with WTO law (para 2), and recognizes their right to exceed those international standards (para 3), in some cases including a right to take measures on the basis of the precautionary principle, i.e. where there are legitimate concerns but conclusive scientific evidence is lacking.[40] Our

---

concept of 'science' into the law of international trade, while the Uruguay Round further refined this instrument and broke it down into two separate agreements – the TBT Agreement and the SPS Agreement).

35 See Arts 2 and 5 of the WTO SPS Agreement.

36 See J Croome, *Reshaping the World Trading System: A History of the Uruguay Round* (WTO 1995) 236.

37 See ibid, 237.

38 Ibid.

39 See *European Communities – Measures Concerning Meat and Meat Products (Hormones)* (WT/DS26) AB report adopted 13 February 1998, para 165.

40 On the precautionary principle, see ibid, paras 123-124, and European Communities – Measures Affecting the Approval and Marketing of Biotech Products (WT/DS291) panel report adopted 21 November 2006, paras 7.88–7.89. This has led to the widely shared conclusion that the SPS Agreement largely reflects

primary interest in this chapter lies with the function of the SPS Agreement in giving binding legal effect to otherwise voluntary international standards. It does this through the requirement that members 'shall base their sanitary or phytosanitary measures on international standards, guidelines or recommendations, where they exist, except as otherwise provided for in this Agreement, and in particular in paragraph 3'.[41] We thus turn to the question of where these international standards, guidelines and recommendations come from and how they relate to WTO law.

(i) The SPS Agreement and International Standard-setting Institutions

As noted earlier, the WTO does not set its own product and process standards. As Motaal put it, 'countries did not want to turn what was a trade organization into a standard setting institution; the WTO would have neither the competence nor the mandate to itself set international norms'.[42] Consequently, the WTO only sets limits to what countries may do in the establishment and enforcement of their own SPS regulations. On the other hand, WTO law gives certain legal effect to otherwise voluntary international standards set by three named international standard-setting institutions: Codex, OIE and IPPC.[43] The SPS Agreement leaves an opening for the use of international standards, guidelines and recommendations promulgated by other relevant international organizations that work on matters not covered by the three named organizations.[44] In order to serve this purpose, such organizations have to be open for membership to all WTO members and, importantly, they will have to be identified as such by the SPS Committee. However, the Committee has not identified any such organization yet and the three named organizations remain the only institutions whose standards can be used for purposes of the SPS Agreement.

These three institutions serve a vital purpose in international trade by setting science-based standards on food safety and animal and plant health on the bases of which national standards could be developed and evaluated. The role of these technical institutions in international trade

---

the interests of developed countries. See RH Steinberg, 'Trade-Environment Negotiations in the EU, NAFTA, and WTO: Regional Trajectories of Rule Development' (1997) 91 *AJIL* 231, 241.

41 See SPS Agreement Article 3.1.

42 Motaal, above n 34, 855–6.

43 See SPS Agreement Article 3:4.

44 See SPS Agreement, Annex A, para 3(d).

has always been significant,[45] but by setting a requirement that WTO members base their SPS measures on the standards and recommendations of these international institutions, the SPS Agreement has effectively transformed those international standards into binding international law instruments.

In the famous *EC Hormones* case, the WTO AB had an opportunity to rule on the meaning and extent of the obligation to *base SPS measures on international standards*, which in this particular case related to Codex standards. The AB, however, limited itself largely to a discussion of what this requirement *is not* and the ways in which the panel interpreted and applied it wrongly, rather than what the requirement *is*; but we shall see that the AB used to the full its opportunity to interpret the similarly worded provisions of Article 2.4 of the TBT Agreement in *EC Sardines*.[46]

EC Hormones

In Council Directives issued between 1981 and 1988, the European Communities banned the use of six different growth-promoting hormones[47] in animals and prohibited the placing on the market of meat from such animals. The ban applied to both domestically produced and imported meat. The EC did this because of concerns that eating food containing hormone-treated meat would pose health hazards to humans. As such this is a matter of food safety, rather than animal health, and the relevant international standardization organization is the Codex Alimentarius Commission. Yet Codex did not have any standards on such hormones until much later – it was in June 1995 that the Codex Commission first adopted standards for five of the six hormones in dispute in this case.[48] Of

---

45 A look at their constituent documents shows facilitating international trade through the development of standards as a shared objective among these institutions. See Desta and Hirsch, above n 18.

46 For more on these two cases, see M M Du, 'Reducing Product Standards Heterogeneity Through International Standards in the WTO: How Far Across the River?' (2010) 44:2 *Journal of World Trade* 295.

47 These are called oestradiol-17ß, progesterone, testosterone, trenbolone acetate, zeranol and melengestrol acetate ('MGA'). The first three are naturally occurring hormones produced by humans and animals while the other three are synthetic or artificially produced hormones. See *EC Hormones*, Panel Report (circulated 18 August 1997) paras II.6–II.10.

48 The absence of a Codex standard for the sixth hormone, MGA, means that the issue of relationship between WTO law and international standards does not arise in connection with it. As a result, the panel and AB rulings relating to this particular hormone are not discussed in this chapter.

the five hormones, three are naturally occurring in meat and other foodstuffs; for these, Codex found it unnecessary to establish an acceptable daily intake (ADI) level or maximum residue limits (MRL). This meant that Codex was convinced that it was safe to eat meat from animals treated with these natural hormones.[49] But Codex considered it necessary to set ADI and MRL levels for the two artificial hormones, which means that, according to Codex, it is safe to eat meat treated with the two artificial hormones provided the limits are respected.[50] It is also worth noting that while the Codex Commission normally decides by consensus, this time it had to decide by majority vote because, *inter alia*, the EC was against it. Indeed, the standards were adopted by a very tight margin: 33 votes in favour, 29 votes against and 7 abstentions.[51]

In 1996 the US and Canada complained against the EC import prohibitions on hormone-treated meat and meat products alleging, *inter alia*, that the measures contravened Article 3.1 of the SPS Agreement because 'they were not based on the relevant international standards, guidelines or recommendations and that this departure from international standards was not justified by Article 3.3'.[52] The EC argued, *inter alia*, that the challenged measures met the requirements of the SPS Agreement; they were based on scientific principles and a risk assessment and they aimed to achieve a level of protection which was higher than could be achieved if Codex standards were followed.[53]

The panel started the relevant part of its analysis by establishing whether there were any 'international standards, guidelines or recommendations' with respect to the use on animals of any of the six hormones in dispute for growth promotion purposes. The panel identified the underlying concern to be one of food safety and determined, based on Annex A, para 3(a) of the SPS Agreement, that Codex is the relevant international standardization body. The next question therefore was whether there existed any Codex standards, guidelines or recommendations with respect to the administration of any of the six hormones in dispute. The panel's argument here was fairly straightforward: if Codex

---

[49] In the language of the relevant Codex committee, eating such meat is 'incapable of exerting a hormonal effect, and therefore any toxic effect, in human subjects', and is thus 'unlikely to pose a hazard to human health'. *European Hormones*, Panel Report, para 8.122.

[50] See ibid, paras 4.17–4.24.

[51] See ibid, para 8.67.

[52] See *European Hormones*, Panel Report, para 6.3.

[53] See ibid, para 6.6.

had standards on these hormones, then the EC measures 'should either be based on these standards or be justified under Article 3.3 of the SPS Agreement'.[54] The panel then found that Codex standards existed for five of the six hormones and went into an examination of 'the definition and scope of application of these Codex standards and determine whether they apply to the EC measures in dispute'.[55] This is where the decision gets interesting for our purposes.

As if to emphasize this, the panel started with an acknowledgement that Codex standards are 'not binding upon Codex members. They are only of an advisory nature.'[56] Add to this the fact that these Codex standards were adopted against EC objections, and by majority vote rather than the usual consensus-based decision-making, the question of whether the EC should be subject to any such standards *as a matter of international law* becomes particularly important. Indeed, this is a typical case of what Robert Howse described as a situation in which a WTO member 'may be bound to apply an international standard that it even voted against as a voluntary norm!'[57] The EC also highlighted these points and, referring to the fact that Codex began considering the development of these standards long before the SPS Agreement was negotiated, also suggested that at the time the standards were discussed, Codex members were 'unaware of the fact that the Codex standards, which within the Codex system are only of an advisory nature, would in the future become "binding" by virtue of the SPS Agreement'.[58]

The panel dismissed all of these EC arguments and proceeded to the question of whether the EC measures in respect of the five hormones were 'based on' the relevant Codex standards. But the EC did not even claim that its measures were based on Codex standards, arguing instead that no relevant Codex standards existed at the time, and in any case, the EC was allowed by the SPS Agreement to set its own levels of protection beyond what could be achieved on the basis of the relevant international standard. The panel acknowledged that the SPS Agreement does not define the words 'based on' and interpreted them as follows: 'for a sanitary measure

---

54 See ibid, para 8.57.
55 See ibid, para 8.58.
56 See ibid, para 8.59.
57 R Howse, 'A New Device for Creating International Legal Normativity: the WTO Technical Barriers to Trade Agreement and "International Standards"' in C Joerges and EU Petersmann (eds), *Constitutionalism, Multilateral Trade Governance and Social Regulation* (OUP 2006) 383, 389.
58 See *European Hormones*, Panel Report, para 8.68.

to be based on an international standard in accordance with Article 3.1, that measure needs to reflect the same level of sanitary protection as the standard'.[59] In other words, the panel effectively concluded that for a national measure to be 'based on' an international standard, it must 'conform to' that international standard. From this, the panel proceeded to compare the level of protection reflected in the EC measures in dispute and what was reflected in the Codex standards for each of the five hormones at issue.

The conclusion from hereon was predictable. The EC had effectively set its ADI and MRL limits for all five hormones under dispute at zero. Codex, on the other hand, had set above-zero limits for the two synthetic hormones, while it did not find it necessary to set any limits whatsoever for the three naturally occurring hormones. The panel thus concluded that the EC measures in dispute were 'not based on existing international standards as specified in Article 3.1'.[60] Moreover, in its examination of whether the EC measures could be justified under SPS Agreement Article 3.3, the panel introduced a rule-exception relationship between the two paragraphs of Article 3 and concluded by shifting the burden of proof on to the EC.[61] The panel then carried out an extensive analysis of the different elements of Article 3.3 and found that the EC measure failed to meet its requirements, *inter alia*, because it was not based on risk assessment.[62]

The EC appealed each of the above, and other, legal findings of the panel. On the key question of the relationship between the challenged national measures and the relevant international standards, the AB strongly disagreed with the panel.[63] After rejecting the panel's equation of 'based on' with 'conform to', the AB said: 'A measure that "conforms to" and incorporates a Codex standard is, of course, "based on" that standard. A measure, however, based on the same standard might not conform to that standard, as where only some, not all, of the elements of the standard are incorporated into the measure.'[64] Importantly for us here,

---

59 See ibid, para 8.73.

60 See ibid, paras 8.75–8.77.

61 See ibid, para 8.87.

62 See ibid, para 8.155.

63 The AB said: 'We read the Panel's interpretation that Article 3.2 "equates" measures "based on" international standards with measures which "conform to" such standards, as signifying that "based on" and "conform to" are identical in meaning. The Panel is thus saying that, henceforth, SPS measures of Members must "conform to" Codex standards, guidelines and recommendations.' See *European Hormones*, AB Report, para 162.

64 See ibid, para 163.

the AB went further and stressed that:

> To read Article 3.1 as requiring Members to harmonize their SPS measures *by conforming those measures with international standards*, guidelines and recommendations, *in the here and now*, is, in effect, to vest such international standards, guidelines and recommendations (which are by the terms of the Codex *recommendatory* in form and nature) with *obligatory* force and effect. The Panel's interpretation of Article 3.1 would, in other words, transform those standards, guidelines and recommendations into binding *norms*. But, as already noted, the *SPS Agreement* itself sets out no indication of any intent on the part of the Members to do so. We cannot lightly assume that sovereign states intended to impose upon themselves the more onerous, rather than the less burdensome, obligation by mandating *conformity* or *compliance with* such standards, guidelines and recommendations. To sustain such an assumption and to warrant such a far-reaching interpretation, treaty language far more specific and compelling than that found in Article 3 of the *SPS Agreement* would be necessary.[65]

The question then is: does Article 3.1 not really 'transform those standards, guidelines and recommendations into binding *norms*'? The AB simply reiterated why the panel's interpretation of 'based on' in *EC Hormones* to mean 'conform to' was wrong:

> the ordinary meaning of 'based on' is quite different from the plain or natural import of 'conform to'. A thing is commonly said to be 'based on' another thing when the former 'stands' or is 'founded' or 'built' upon or 'is supported by' the latter. In contrast, much more is required before one thing may be regarded as 'conform[ing] to' another: the former must 'comply with', 'yield or show compliance' with the latter. [...] A measure that 'conforms to' and incorporates a Codex standard is, of course, 'based on' that standard. A measure, however, based on the same standard might not conform to that standard, as where only some, not all, of the elements of the standard are incorporated into the measure.[66]

The AB was indeed clearly 'reticent' here, focusing on what is wrong in the panel report rather than telling us what the right approach should be.[67] On the other hand, the AB clearly recognizes that there is an incentive for member countries to base their national measures on international standards. In cases where countries do not wish to base their national measures on relevant international standards, which they are entitled to

---

65 See ibid, para 165 (emphasis in original; footnotes omitted).
66 See ibid, para 163 (emphasis in original; footnotes omitted).
67 See J Scott, *The WTO Agreement on Sanitary and Phytosanitary Measures: A Commentary* (CUP 2007) 253.

do, they will be subjected to more cumbersome procedural (e.g. having to carry out a risk assessment) and substantive (e.g. having to provide scientific justification) requirements.[68] To the extent that countries are free to deviate from international standards, the SPS Agreement has not transformed international standards into binding norms. On the other hand, to the extent these international standards serve as a benchmark against which national measures have to be evaluated, their legal character remains significant. The AB brings this out more clearly and directly in *EC Sardines*, where it dealt with Article 2.4 of the TBT Agreement provision, which effectively mirrors Article 3.1 of the SPS Agreement.

IV. THE TBT AGREEMENT

The TBT Agreement deals only with standards that fall outside the scope of the SPS Agreement – the two Agreements are mutually exclusive in their scope. The TBT Agreement shares a lot in common with the SPS Agreement but it also has significant differences.[69] For example, while the SPS Agreement applies to risks arising out of a limited number of sources, the TBT Agreement has a much wider remit, applying to measures with a number of legitimate policy goals, including national security, health, environmental and other objectives. Furthermore, in line with the limited source or type of risks covered by the SPS Agreement, the international standards that members are required to base their national SPS regulations on come from a closed list of three international institutions – Codex, OIE and IPPC, while the international standards for purposes of the TBT Agreement can come from a potentially large number of international institutions; indeed, the TBT Agreement only describes what such international standardizing bodies should be rather than gives a list of who they are. Accordingly, an international body or system for purposes of the TBT Agreement is a '[b]ody or system whose membership is open to the relevant bodies of at least all Members'.[70] The number of international standardization organizations that can come in through this

---

[68] See SPS Agreement, Article 3.3; see also *European Hormones*, AB Report, paras 169–77.

[69] For more on this, see Motaal, above n 34 and Du, above n 46. See also J Pauwelyn, 'Non-Traditional Patterns of Global Regulation: Is the WTO "Missing the Boat"?' in Joerges and Petersmann, above n 57, 208–11.

[70] TBT Agreement, Annex 1, para 4. For a discussion of how this definition was interpreted by a WTO panel, see *infra* 174–76.

large window is potentially unlimited,[71] and we shall see how in a recent WTO case even a regional convention with barely a dozen parties ended up being recognized as an international body and the resolutions of its contracting parties as international standards.[72]

Despite the differences highlighted above, the SPS and TBT Agreements adopt a similar, if not identical, approach towards the role of relevant external international standards in the regulation of national standards. Like the SPS Agreement, the TBT Agreement also recognizes the potential contribution of international standards and conformity assessment systems to improve efficiency of production and facilitate the conduct of international trade. The Agreement further recognizes the right of a member to take measures necessary to achieve its legitimate objectives subject to several important conditions, including the obligation not to create unnecessary obstacles to international trade or apply them in a manner which would constitute a means of arbitrary or unjustifiable discrimination or a disguised restriction on international trade.[73]

(i) The TBT Agreement and International Standards

Article 2 of the TBT Agreement is the most important and relevant provision of the TBT Agreement for our purposes here. A key obligation in Article 2 is the need to ensure that technical regulations[74] do not create unnecessary obstacles to international trade or be more trade-restrictive than necessary to fulfil a legitimate objective (para 2), and most

---

[71] See also Motaal, above n 34 at 857 (suggesting that the TBT Agreement leaves the list of potential international standardization bodies open 'probably due to its much broader coverage. Since the Agreement covers everything from a light bulb to an aeroplane, it would have been very difficult to list all the international standardizing bodies whose work would have been relevant').

[72] *US Tuna/Dolphin* panel report, above n 17.

[73] See TBT Agreement, preamble, para 6.

[74] A technical regulation is defined as a 'document which lays down product characteristics or their related processes and production methods, including the applicable administrative provisions, with which compliance is mandatory. It may also include or deal exclusively with terminology, symbols, packaging, marking or labelling requirements as they apply to a product, process or production method.' See TBT Agreement, Annex 1, para 1. As opposed to a technical regulation, which is mandatory, a standard is defined as a 'document approved by a recognized body, that provides, for common and repeated use, rules, guidelines or characteristics for products or related processes and production methods, with which compliance is not mandatory. It may also include or deal exclusively with terminology, symbols, packaging, marking or labelling requirements as they apply to a product, process or production method.' See TBT Agreement, Annex 1, para 2.

importantly, to use relevant international standards, where they exist, 'as a basis for their technical regulations except when such international standards or relevant parts would be an ineffective or inappropriate means for the fulfilment of the legitimate objectives pursued, for instance because of fundamental climatic or geographical factors or fundamental technological problems' (para 4). The AB itself calls Article 2.4 a 'central provision of the TBT Agreement'.[75] Just as does Article 3.1 of the SPS Agreement, this TBT Agreement requirement to use international standards as a basis for technical regulations plays a central role in the transformation of otherwise voluntary codes into binding norms of international law. The AB provided a lengthy comment on the similarities between the SPS and TBT Agreements particularly on this point:

> there are strong conceptual similarities between, on the one hand, Article 2.4 of the TBT Agreement and, on the other hand, Articles 3.1 and 3.3 of the SPS Agreement [...] The heart of Article 3.1 of the SPS Agreement is a requirement that Members base their sanitary or phytosanitary measures on international standards, guidelines, or recommendations. Likewise, the heart of Article 2.4 of the TBT Agreement is a requirement that Members use international standards as a basis for their technical regulations.[76]

The TBT Agreement has an in-built incentive for those members who not only use international standards as the bases for their technical regulations but also go further and ensure the outcome is 'in accordance with relevant international standards', which creates a rebuttable presumption that the regulations do not create unnecessary obstacles to trade.[77] Just as is the case with the SPS Agreement,[78] the TBT Agreement

---

[75] *European Communities – Trade Description of Sardines* WT/DS231 (panel report 29 May 2002, and AB report 26 September 2002). AB Report, para 208.

[76] Ibid, para 274. The AB added: 'Neither of these requirements in these two agreements is absolute. Articles 3.1 and 3.3 of the SPS Agreement permit a Member to depart from an international standard if the Member seeks a level of protection higher than would be achieved by the international standard, the level of protection pursued is based on a proper risk assessment, and the international standard is not sufficient to achieve the level of protection pursued. Thus, under the SPS Agreement, departing from an international standard is permitted in circumstances where the international standard is ineffective to achieve the objective of the measure at issue. Likewise, under Article 2.4 of the TBT Agreement, a Member may depart from a relevant international standard when it would be an "ineffective or inappropriate means for the fulfilment of the legitimate objectives pursued" by that Member through the technical regulation.'

[77] See TBT Agreement Article 2.5.

[78] But see Du above n 46, 313 (arguing that the AB has interpreted the

requirement of a relationship between an international standard and a national regulation has created an avenue for the development of an otherwise voluntary and non-binding international standard into a binding international legal commitment. A look at the WTO AB decision in *EC Sardines* will be enlightening in this respect.

EC Sardines

This was a case brought by Peru against the European Communities challenging a 1989 EC regulation (Regulation (EEC) 2136/89) which provided that only products prepared from fish of the species *Sardina pilchardus* could be marketed as preserved sardines. Peru, which traditionally produced and exported a different species of sardines, *Sardinops sagax*, claimed that this EC regulation effectively prevented its right to market its exports as Peruvian sardines. Peru identified a relevant Codex standard which requires that the term 'sardines' be reserved exclusively for *Sardina pilchardus*, but also adds that other types of sardines can be called sardines provided they are qualified as '"X sardines" of a country, a geographic area, the species, or the common name of the species'.[79] Peru thus argued, *inter alia*, that the EC Regulation was inconsistent with Article 2.4 of the TBT Agreement because it did not use the naming standard set out by Codex as a basis for its Regulation.[80] The EC argued, *inter alia*, that Article 2.4 of the TBT Agreement did not apply to measures that were drawn up before its entry into force.[81] The question

---

relevant texts in the SPS and TBT Agreements which imply that 'a higher threshold may be required in the TBT to deviate from a relevant international standard').

[79] See Codex Stan 94, para 6.1.1(ii), in annex to *EC Sardines*, Panel Report. For a summary of the facts of the case, see ibid, paras 2.1–2.9.

[80] According to Peru, 'the EC Regulation, prohibiting the use of the term "sardines" combined with the name of the country of origin ("Peruvian Sardines"); the geographical area in which the species is found ("Pacific Sardines"); the species ("Sardines – *Sardinops sagax*"); or the common name of the species *Sardinops sagax* customarily used in the language of the member State of the European Communities in which the product is sold ("Peruvian Sardines" in English or "Südamerikanische Sardinen" in German), is inconsistent with Article 2.4 of the TBT Agreement because the European Communities did not use the naming standard set out in paragraph 6.1.1(ii) of Codex Stan 94 as a basis for its Regulation even though that standard would be an effective and appropriate means to fulfil the legitimate objectives pursued by the Regulation.' Ibid, para 3.1.

[81] According to the EC, 'the question is whether Members are under an obligation after the WTO Agreement entered into force to revise their existing technical regulations to ensure that they could be considered to have used international standards "as a basis". It is clear from the text of Article 2.4 of the

once again was therefore whether the EC was bound by a Codex standard that the EC very clearly did not want to adopt.

The panel started its analysis with the challenged measure's consistency with TBT Agreement Article 2.4, which creates the link between international standards on the one hand and national regulations on the other. The panel first determined that the challenged EU measure constituted a technical regulation in the sense of the TBT Agreement because the EC Regulation 'lays down product characteristics for preserved sardines and makes compliance with the provisions contained therein mandatory'.[82] Once it established the nature of the challenged measure, the panel allocated the burden of proof between the parties as follows: Peru would need to establish a *prima facie* case under TBT Agreement Article 2.4 that a relevant international standard exists and that this standard was not used as a basis for the technical regulation,[83] at which point the burden would shift to the EC to establish that the relevant Codex standard is ineffective or inappropriate to fulfil the legitimate objectives pursued by the EC Regulation.[84]

Accordingly, Peru argued that Codex Stan 94 was a relevant international standard for the case under dispute, *inter alia*, because 'it was adopted by the Codex Alimentarius Commission which is an internationally recognized standard setting body that develops standards for food products'.[85] The EC did not question the status of Codex as an internationally recognized standard-setting body but set out a number of arguments why Codex Stan 94 was not a relevant international standard for purposes of the challenged EC Regulation.[86] The EC argued, *inter alia*, that: (1) the requirement to use relevant international standards as a basis set out in Article 2.4 of the TBT Agreement did not apply to existing measures; (2) Codex Stan 94 was not a relevant international standard as it did not exist when the EC Regulation was adopted, nor was its adoption imminent at the time; (3) Codex Stan 94 was not adopted by consensus; and (4) paragraph 6.1.1(ii) of Codex Stan 94 was not the relevant provision

---

TBT Agreement, especially the words "where technical regulations are required", that such an obligation has not been created by Article 2.4.' *EC Sardines*, Panel Report, para 4.20.

82 Ibid, para 7.35.

83 Ibid, para 7.50.

84 Ibid, para 7.50. Note that the AB reversed the panel's ruling on burden of proof. See AB Report, para 282.

85 *EC Sardines*, Panel Report, para 7.61.

86 Ibid, para 7.62.

for the EC Regulation because the EC Regulation did not regulate products other than preserved *Sardina pilchardus*.[87] It was in the context of its temporal argument, i.e. its view that Article 2.4 of the TBT Agreement does not apply to existing measures, that the EC went into the heart of the issue for our purposes here: imposing an obligation to review and amend existing technical regulations whenever an international standard is adopted or amended, argued the EC, 'would turn standardisation bodies virtually into "world legislators"'.[88]

The panel rejected this EC argument. According to the panel, Article 2.4 of the TBT Agreement imposes 'an ongoing obligation on Members to reassess their existing technical regulations in light of the adoption of new international standards or the revision of existing international standards'.[89] The panel then specifically rejected the institutions-as-world-legislators claim of the EC as follows:

> the nature of the obligation agreed to by Members is circumscribed by four elements. First, the obligation applies only 'where technical regulations are required'. [...] Second, the obligation exists only to the extent that the international standard is relevant for the existing technical regulation. Third, if it is determined that a technical regulation is required and the international standard is relevant, Members are to use that international standard 'as a basis', which means that Members are to use a relevant international standard as 'the principal constituent [...] or fundamental principle' and does not mean that Members must conform to or comply with that relevant international standard. The requirement to use the relevant international standard as a basis does not impose a rigid requirement to bring the technical regulation into conformity with the relevant international standard. This provides Members with a certain amount of latitude in complying with the obligation set out in Article 2.4 of the TBT Agreement. In our view, the reference to the term 'use as a basis' in Article 2.4 of the TBT Agreement recognizes that there may be various ways in which Members can use the relevant international standard in the formulation of their technical regulations. Finally, Members are not obliged to use the relevant international standard if such international standard is ineffective or inappropriate to fulfil the legitimate objectives pursued by the technical regulation. Thus, a judicious application of the obligations contained in Article 2.4 provides assurances against the over-reaching implied by the European Communities.[90]

The panel thus interpreted the word 'basis' to mean 'the principal constituent of anything, the fundamental principle or theory, as of a

---

87 Adapted from ibid, para 7.62.
88 Ibid, para 7.77.
89 Ibid, para 7.78.
90 Ibid, para 7.78 (footnotes omitted).

system of knowledge',[91] and found that under the challenged EC Regulation, certain species of sardines could not be called 'sardines' and therefore Codex Stan 94 (the relevant international standard here) was not used 'as a basis for' the EC Regulation.[92] According to the panel, an international standard is used 'as a basis for' a technical regulation 'when it is used as the principal constituent or fundamental principle for the purpose of enacting the technical regulation'.[93] The panel further ruled that Codex Stan 94 was not an ineffective or inappropriate means for the fulfilment of the EC's legitimate objectives of consumer protection, market transparency and fair competition.[94] The panel thus concluded that the EC Regulation was inconsistent with Article 2.4 of the TBT Agreement.

On appeal, the EC argued that the panel's interpretation of the meaning of 'as a basis for' in TBT Agreement Article 2.4 was wrong. According to the EC,

> in order to determine whether a relevant international standard, or a part of it, is used 'as a basis for' a technical regulation, the criterion to apply is not, as the Panel suggested, whether the standard is the principal constituent or the fundamental principle of the technical regulation, but, rather, whether there is a 'rational relationship' between the standard and the technical regulation on the substantive aspects of the standard in question.[95]

The AB, however, agreed with the panel's interpretation, and arguably even went further to say, 'there must be a very strong and very close relationship between two things in order to be able to say that one is "the basis for" the other'.[96] In other words, when the TBT Agreement requires of members to use international standards as a 'basis' for their national regulations, the type of relationship between the international standard and the national regulation must be 'very strong and very close'. Perhaps even more importantly, the AB said: 'In our view, it can certainly be said – at a minimum – that something cannot be considered a "basis" for something else if the two are contradictory.'[97] Applying this test to the question whether the challenged EU technical regulation and the relevant Codex standard were contradictory, the AB concluded that the two are

---

91 Ibid, para 7.110.
92 Ibid, para 7.112.
93 *EC Sardines*, Panel Report, para 7.110.
94 Ibid, para 7.138.
95 *EC Sardines*, AB Report, para 241.
96 Ibid, para 245.
97 Ibid, para 248.

'manifestly contradictory' and, as a result, 'Codex Stan 94 was not used "as a basis for" the EC Regulation'.[98] The AB also agreed with the panel that Codex Stan 94 was not ineffective or inappropriate,[99] and the EC Regulation is inconsistent with Article 2.4 of the TBT Agreement.

US Tuna/Dolphin

US Tuna/Dolphin is the latest case in which the source, meaning and role of international standards in the regulation of national standards took centre stage. The case concerns a set of three US legal instruments (the 1990 Dolphin Protection Consumer Information Act, its implementing regulations, and a federal court decision) that together impose detailed and specific conditions on the use of a US government official 'dolphin-safe' label on tuna and tuna products marketed in the US. A threshold question in this respect was whether these US measures were mandatory technical regulations subject to Article 2 of the TBT Agreement or non-binding standards subject to Article 4 of the TBT Agreement. The Appellate Body had already established, in *EC Sardines*, three criteria for a document to be considered a 'technical regulation' – that it must: (1) apply to an identifiable product or group of products; (2) lay down one or more characteristics of the product; and (3) require compliance with those characteristics.[100] However, this apparently clear distinction between a technical regulation (mandatory) and a standard (voluntary) was controversial enough to split the panel in this most recent *US Tuna/Dolphin* panel report.

The majority agreed with Mexico that the US measures amounted to a mandatory technical regulation because 'they prescribe, in a binding and legally enforceable instrument, the manner in which a dolphin-safe label can be obtained in the United States, and disallow any other use of a dolphin-safe designation'.[101] Although it was not compulsory to meet these requirements and to bear the label, in order to sell tuna on the US

---

98 Ibid, para 257.

99 Although the AB reversed the panel ruling on burden of proof relating to the second part of TBT Agreement Article 2.4, which allows WTO members not to use relevant international standards as a basis for their technical regulations if those international standards are 'an ineffective or inappropriate means for the fulfilment of the legitimate objectives pursued', the AB agreed with the panel that Peru had adduced sufficient evidence to establish that Codex Stan 94 was not ineffective or inappropriate.

100 See ibid, para 176.

101 *US Tuna/Dolphin* panel report, para 7.131.

market, the panel held that the US measures 'prescribe "in a negative form" [. . .] that no tuna product may be labelled dolphin-safe [. . .] if it does not meet the conditions set out in the measures, and thus impose a prohibition on the offering for sale in the United States of tuna products bearing a label referring to dolphins and not meeting the requirements that they set out'.[102] One of the panellists disagreed with the majority view on this very question, suggesting that labelling schemes can be compulsory 'when the use of a certain label is compulsory to access the market, or they can be voluntary when products can be marketed with or without the label'.[103] From this, the panellist argued that since Mexican tuna could still be marketed in the US without the dolphin-safe label, the US measures were merely voluntary.[104] It is interesting to see how such apparently clear language as a distinction between mandatory and voluntary measures can lead to such genuine differences of views between such eminent experts, a division that was reflected among scholars and commentators soon after publication of the report.[105]

Be that as it may, the particular relevance of this case for our purposes here lies in its interpretation of the meaning, source and role of international standards in the regulation of national standards. Once the majority of the panel characterized the US measures as mandatory regulation, the next question was whether the US used relevant international standards as a basis for these regulations, begging the question whether there existed such international standards in the first place. It is worth recalling that the TBT Agreement does not define an 'international standard'. In such situations the TBT Agreement adopts the meaning given to the term under the ISO/IEC Guide 2:1991, which defines an international standard as a 'standard that is adopted by an international standardizing/standards organization and made available to the public'.[106] The institutional equivalent of the 'international standardizing/standards organization' under the TBT Agreement is the international body or system, which is defined as a '[b]ody or system whose

---

102 Ibid.

103 Ibid, para 7.150.

104 Ibid, para 7.150.

105 For a lively, insightful and still divided exchange of views among scholars, see 'Technical Regulations vs. Standards in the Tuna Panel Report', *International Economic Law and Policy Blog*, <http://worldtradelaw.typepad.com/ielpblog/2011/09/technical-regulations-vs-standards-in-the-tuna-panel-report.html> accessed 8 October 2011.

106 See *US Tuna/Dolphin* panel report, para 7.663.

membership is open to the relevant bodies of at least all Members'.[107] The next task was therefore to determine (1) whether there is such international body or system for this purpose, and if yes, (2) whether it has adopted any relevant international standards; and again if yes, (3) whether this standard would not be inappropriate or ineffective to achieve the US objectives. As we shall see below, the panel found that an international body and a relevant international standard existed, but concluded that this international standard would be inappropriate or ineffective to achieve the US's stated objectives for the challenged measures.[108]

Mexico submitted that the 1998 Agreement on International Dolphin Conservation Program (AIDCP) was a relevant international standardization body and its *Resolution to Adopt the Modified System for Tracking and Verification of Tuna* constituted a relevant international standard that the US should have used as a basis for its regulations, but failed to do so in breach of its obligations under Article 2.4 of TBT Agreement. The AIDCP is an international treaty that governs fishing activities in a geographically limited and defined 'Agreement Area', which covers the eastern part of the Pacific Ocean between the 40°N and 40°S parallels, and has only 13 contracting parties.[109] Although the AIDCP was initially open for signature until 14 May 1999 to states whose vessels fished for tuna in the Agreement Area, any accession afterwards is possible only by invitation of the contracting parties.[110] Not surprisingly, therefore, the US argued that

---

107 TBT Agreement, Annex 1, para 4.

108 See *US Tuna/Dolphin*, paras 7.726–7.740.

109 See Agreement on International Dolphin Conservation Program, Article III and Annex I (concluded 21 May 1998, entered into force in February 1999), available at <http://www.iattc.org/PDFFiles2/AIDCP-amended-Oct-2009.pdf>. The parties to the AIDCP are Costa Rica, Ecuador, El Salvador, the European Union, Guatemala, Honduras, Mexico, Nicaragua, Panama, Peru, the United States, Vanuatu and Venezuela. See <http://www.iattc.org/IDCPENG.htm> accessed 8 October 2011.

110 Articles XXIV provides that the Agreement was open for signature from 21 May 1998 until 14 May 1999 by 'States with a coastline bordering the Agreement Area and by States or regional economic integration organizations which are members of the IATTC [i.e. Belize, Canada, China, Chinese Taipei, Colombia, Costa Rica, Ecuador, El Salvador, European Union, France, Guatemala, Japan, Kiribati, Korea, Mexico, Nicaragua, Panama, Peru, United States, Vanuatu, Venezuela] or whose vessels fish for tuna in the Agreement Area while the Agreement is open for signature.' For those countries that do not meet the geographical or activity requirements set out in Article XXIV, Article XXVI provides that they may join if they are 'invited to accede to the Agreement on the basis of a decision by the Parties'. See <http://www.iattc.org/HomeENG.htm> accessed 8 October 2011.

the AIDCP is not an international body for the purposes of the TBT Agreement,[111] and the said resolution is not a relevant international standard because 'it is not (1) a standard; (2) international; or (3) relevant'.[112] This then became the first opportunity for the WTO dispute settlement system to clarify whether a *de facto* regional international treaty – the AIDCP – qualifies as an international body for purposes of the TBT Agreement, i.e. as a body whose membership is open to the relevant bodies of *at least all* WTO members – and whether a resolution passed by contracting parties to such treaty amounted to an international standard.[113]

The panel sided with Mexico on both issues – that the AIDCP was an international standardizing organization for the purpose of Article 2.4 of the TBT Agreement and the resolutions passed by the AIDCP contracting parties qualified as international standards.[114] The panel held that, despite limited actual participation by WTO members in the work of the AIDCP, membership was, and remains, open to states whose vessels fished for tuna in the Agreement Area, though even the panel admitted that future accessions are possible only by invitation. From this, the panel went into an investigation of whether the US used AIDCP resolutions as a basis for its technical regulations.

Remarkably, the panel observed that 'the US legislator has constructed the US dolphin-safe labelling scheme building on the AIDCP foundations',[115] an observation that appears to show that the panel was probably following a procedural approach to the interpretation of the phrase 'as a basis for' in which it was considering the process by which the US law-making authority put its technical regulations together.[116] The

---

[111] The US argued that 'neither the AIDCP nor the parties to it constitute a "body" (i.e. a "legal or administrative entity that has specific tasks and composition"). . . . [A]ssuming *arguendo* that the AIDCP was a "body" it does not have recognized activities in standardization and, therefore, would not constitute a "recognized" body.' See *US Tuna/Dolphin*, para 4.103.

[112] See ibid, para 4.102.

[113] The panel has issued its verdict; whether the AB will have the chance to review depends on whether an appeal will be lodged by either or both of the parties. At the time of writing this remains open.

[114] See *US Tuna/Dolphin*, para 7.692; more generally, see paras 7.666–7.697. Agreement on International Dolphin Conservation Program, Article III and Annex I (concluded 21 May 1998, entered into force in February 1999), available at <http://www.iattc.org/PDFFiles2/AIDCP-amended-Oct-2009.pdf>.

[115] *US Tuna/Dolphin* panel report, para 7.712.

[116] For the procedural and substantive approaches to interpretation of 'use as a basis of', see Horn and Weiler, above n 14.

panel also noted that there was a 'strong relationship between the two bodies of rules', i.e. between the relevant international standard and the challenged national measures. The 'strong relationship' test echoes the AB language of a 'very strong and very close' relationship in *EC Sardines*. However, the panel went further and added, in a language that sounds as if it was not convinced by what it itself was saying: 'However, the strong relationship between the two bodies of rules *appears to be* insufficient to infer that the AIDCP standard was used as a basis for the technical regulation.'[117] The panel then quoted the AB's ruling in *EC Sardines* where it introduced the contradiction test – i.e. that a member cannot have used a relevant international standard if its challenged technical regulation in any way contradicts that standard.[118] This is a substantive test which goes beyond the process of law-making and effectively compares the final outcomes, i.e. the actual requirements set by the challenged national measure against those contained in the relevant international standard. The hesitant language used by the panel in this respect is probably indicative of its discomfort with respect to the contradiction test that the AB introduced in *EC Sardines*. As noted above, the panel ultimately dismissed Mexico's claim of violation of Article 2.4 of the TBT Agreement on the grounds that the US would not have been able to achieve its stated objectives if it had based its measures on the relevant international standards, thereby declaring the relevant international standards inappropriate and ineffective.[119] That does not, however, alter the fact that the panel also agreed with the AB's contradiction test in the examination of the relationship between national measures and relevant international standards. We now look at the implication of the contradiction test for the role of international soft law standards in WTO law.

---

[117] *US Tuna/Dolphin* panel report, para 7.712 (emphasis added).

[118] *EC Sardines*, AB Report, para 248.

[119] The panel found that the use of the relevant international standard would be ineffective or inappropriate to fulfil the two US legitimate objectives pursued by the challenged measures – (1) ensuring that consumers are not misled or deceived about whether tuna products contain tuna that was caught in a manner that adversely affects dolphins; and (2) contributing to the protection of dolphins by ensuring that the US market is not used to encourage fishing fleets to catch tuna in a manner that adversely affects dolphins. *US Tuna/Dolphin*, panel report, paras 7.726–7.740.

V. IMPLICATIONS OF THE WTO JURISPRUDENCE FOR INTERNATIONAL SOFT LAW STANDARDS

The legal consequence of the two WTO Agreements as interpreted by panels and the AB is that standards established by qualifying international standardization bodies create, in principle,[120] an obligation for WTO members to ensure their existing or future standards do not contradict relevant international standards. There is no grandfather clause that protects national regulations that predate any relevant international standard, nor is there any consent clause that protects a WTO member country from the application of a particular international standard it never consented to, or it explicitly voted against, even when it was only a non-binding recommendation or a set of guidelines. Indeed, it is immaterial whether a WTO member is in fact a member of the international standardization body that established a particular standard; the fact that a country is a member of the WTO is enough to create the obligation not to contradict it.

Despite the remaining uncertainties about the relationship that needs to exist between national regulations and international standards under the SPS and TBT Agreements, it is now clear that the AB, by introducing the no-contradiction test, has opened wide enough a window for a large number of norms developed outside the WTO system to enter the world of binding international law that is endowed with a highly effective dispute settlement mechanism. While this opening exists in both the SPS and TBT Agreements, two important differences are notable here: (1) the international standards referred to in the SPS Agreement are developed by three named organizations,[121] while those referred to in the TBT Agreement are more open-ended; and (2) the three institutions named in the SPS Agreement are all intergovernmental organizations, while those contemplated by the TBT Agreement could include intergovernmental as well as semi-private international organizations such as the International Organization for Standardization (ISO). There is a qualitative difference

[120] Note that WTO members can of course 'contradict' international standards provided they meet additional requirements, such as having to conduct proper risk assessment and furnish scientific justification (see Article 3.3 SPS Agreement) or show that international standards would be inappropriate or ineffective to achieve the legitimate objectives of the measures at issue (see Article 2.4 (second part), TBT Agreement).

[121] See above notes 43–45 and accompanying text (discussing the three named institutions).

in the level of legitimacy concern[122] when the international standard is set by an intergovernmental organization as opposed to a semi-private international body. Using the WTO agreements to give hard law effect to non-binding instruments issued by intergovernmental organizations such as the Codex Commission is already innovative; using WTO agreements to give hard law effect to non-binding instruments issued by non-governmental or quasi-governmental transnational organizations such as the ISO is innovation of a different magnitude. But that is what the TBT Agreement in particular achieved.[123] The resulting anomalous situation of a sovereign state being subject to guidelines set by an international organization of which it might not even be a member thus becomes more pronounced within the TBT Agreement. After noting the open-ended nature of the international standardization bodies under this Agreement, Professor Joost Pauwelyn recently asked:

> Would it be enough, for example, for 20, 10 or even two WTO members to set up a standardising body, issue trade-restrictive standards on a product that they want to protect [...] and open this standardising body to all other WTO members [...] in order for the standard to offer a safe haven from WTO violation, even as against WTO members that decided *not* to join the body?[124]

On the surface, at least, it is difficult to see why such an approach would not work. Indeed, one might even go a step further and ask whether Pauwelyn's hypothetical countries could do exactly what he says but, in addition to – or in lieu of – using their standards to protect their own measures from challenge before the WTO, also challenge other WTO members for not using those standards 'as a basis for' their national regulations contrary to Article 2.4 of the TBT Agreement. To illustrate with the help of ideas from the *EC Sardines* dispute, what would happen if

---

[122] As per Hachez and Wouters, above n 5, 679, legitimacy here refers broadly to 'the sense that we are governed by the right institutions, the right people, and the right norms'.

[123] As David Wirth observed, by so doing, the TBT Agreement effectively '"hardens" ISO standards into binding law, at least under certain circumstances. [...] The result is that, through a trade agreement, the expectations of what, at least from the point of view of the United States, is a *private* standardizing organization are transformed into an outer limit of rigor – a ceiling – for *public* regulation to protect health and environment in the United States.' DA Wirth, 'Commentary: Compliance with Non-Binding Norms of Trade and Finance', in D Shelton (ed) *Commitment and Compliance: The Role of Non-Binding Norms in the International Legal System* (OUP 2000) 339–40.

[124] See Pauwelyn, above n 69, 212.

the EC and a few other countries had set up Pauwelyn's standardizing body (open to all WTO members for membership) and issued a standard that would restrict the use of the name 'sardines' to products that contained only *Sardina pilchardus*, and not any of the other species of sardines regardless of any geographical or other qualification that may be added? Pauwelyn's question would be whether the EC could successfully defend itself against any WTO challenge to its measures under Article 2.4 of the TBT Agreement. One might then add: what if the EC brings action against other countries that allow the use of the term 'sardines' for species of sardines other than *Sardina pilchardus*? Could the EC force them to change their regulations and effectively restrict the global market for sardines to a species that only the EC and a few others can supply?

The result could be the use of these international standards to ratchet up national measures so as to make them more trade-restrictive than otherwise,[125] but in a manner that serves the trade interests of the claimant member in this scenario. As Pauwelyn argues, it is indeed hard to imagine that this is what the drafters had in mind, but a textual reading of the language of these agreements could lead to such a result.[126] While these hypotheticals may be 'too hypothetical', the potential complications that can arise from the TBT Agreement's approach are very real. As Howse noted, the absence of any definition of international standards and a list of international organizations that can promulgate such standards, coupled with the AB interpretation of Article 2.4 of the TBT Agreement, could lead to the absurd conclusion that

> any combination of public and private actors from different countries with an interest in imposing a global regulatory approach in some issue area could come together, emit a self-declared 'international standard' and, with regard to WTO membership, the material in question would automatically acquire the force of international law, would be binding on states which did not participate in the process, as well as on those which did, but objected to the standard.[127]

Possibly in recognition of such risks, the WTO Committee on Technical Barriers to Trade adopted a *Decision on Principles for the Development of International Standards, Guides and Recommendations* in which it laid down principles and procedures that 'should be observed, when international standards, guides and recommendations [. . .] are elabo-

125 See ibid, 214.
126 See ibid, 213–14.
127 See Howse, above n 57, 391 (footnotes omitted).

rated [. . .]'.[128] However, an EU attempt to rely on this Decision in *EC Sardines*, so as to exclude the relevant Codex standard from the scope of 'international standards' under the TBT Agreement for lack of consensus during its adoption, was dismissed by the panel as a mere 'policy statement of preference and not the controlling provision in interpreting the expression "relevant international standard" as set out in Article 2.4 of the TBT Agreement'.[129] Most definitions of soft law could easily apply to such WTO committee Decisions, but the apparent dismissal by the panel is broadly representative of the textualist approach of the WTO AB in general.[130]

A number of scholars have suggested alternative interpretive approaches in order to minimize the risks emanating from the requirement to use international standards 'as a basis for' technical regulations. Horn and Weiler have suggested two possible ways of understanding the type of relationship that must exist between these two – one that is procedural in nature and the other that is substantive. Under the procedural interpretation, which they favour, a government that starts with an international standard, examines it, deliberates upon it, and reaches a decision will have used that international standard 'as a basis for' its technical regulation and therefore in full compliance with its obligations under Article 2.4 of the TBT Agreement. This would be the case regardless of the regulation's degree of substantive conformity or similarity to the international standard. The substantive interpretation, on the other hand, would focus on the outcome of the process rather than the process itself. In other words, under a substantive interpretation, whether a national measure is based on an international standard is determined by the extent to which that national measure conforms to the international standard.[131]

Professor Robert Howse has also suggested a reasonableness test for the interpretation of the relationship between the domestic regulation and the international standard. He has argued that such a standard would 'encompass both procedural and substantive elements' but also 'leaves a

---

[128] See WTO Committee on Technical Barriers to Trade, *Decision on Principles for the Development of International Standards, Guides and Recommendations* (G/TBT/9, 13 November 2000) para 20 and Annex 4.

[129] *EC Sardines* Panel Report, para 7.91.

[130] See e.g. Horn and Weiler, above n 14. Note, however, *US Tuna/Dolphin* panel's statement that Section C of this *Decision* 'may assist us in interpreting the term "international standardizing/standards organization"'. *United States – Measures Concerning the Importation, Marketing and Sale of Tuna and Tuna Products* (Panel Report, WT/DS381/R, 15 September 2011) para 7.691.

[131] See Horn and Weiler, above n 14.

great deal to context' and 'allows judgments to be made about the relative legitimacy of different kinds of standards'.[132] Howse has further argued that, by interpreting 'use [. . .] as a basis for' to imply a 'very strong and substantial relationship', the AB 'has clearly suggested that international standards have considerable, automatic legal force in the WTO'.[133] As a result, the TBT Agreement turns 'a mass of normative material that *never before* had the status of international law into international legal obligation'.[134] It remains, however, that the no-contradiction test applied by the AB, and followed by the panels (if only hesitantly as in *US Tuna/ Dolphin*) so far, is more substantive than procedural.[135]

VI. INTERNATIONAL STANDARDS AND INTERNATIONAL INVESTMENT LAW

Soft law is far from alien to international investment law. Indeed, soft law played a critical role in the development of international investment law. Bishop, Crawford and Reisman identify a number of examples of attempts from the middle of the twentieth century to conclude international investment treaties, such the Havana Charter for the establishment of the International Trade Organization (1948), the Agreement of Bogota (1948), the Convention on Investments Abroad (1959), and the draft OECD Convention on the Protection of Foreign Property, all of which were unsuccessful.[136] However, the authors also identify a number of international soft law instruments, such as the ICC Code of Fair Treatment of Foreign Investors (1949), the Sohn-Baxter Draft Convention on the International Responsibility of States for Injuries to Aliens (1961), and several UN General Assembly resolutions, which played a significant role in, or exercised a 'profound influence' on,[137] the development of international investment law. The issue this section attempts to address is, however, a much more limited one: are there any lessons that international investment law can learn from the WTO

[132] See Howse, above n 57, 386.
[133] Ibid, 387.
[134] See ibid, 384.
[135] But see ibid, 385 (arguing that the Panel in *EC Hormones* took a procedural approach).
[136] See R Doak Bishop, James Crawford and W Michael Reisman, *Foreign Investment Disputes* (Kluwer Law International 2005) 4–5.
[137] This is how the authors describe the role of particularly the Sohn-Baxter draft convention. See ibid, 5.

approach to the use of international soft law instruments developed by qualifying international technical institutions?

A. Lesson from the WTO Jurisprudence?

As currently understood by WTO panels and the Appellate Body, it is clear that the WTO has effectively created a channel through which non-binding international standards meeting certain requirements can automatically acquire legal significance within the WTO system independently of any positive action by the WTO itself or its members. It is equally clear that the source of this legal significance for the otherwise non-binding international standards has nothing to do with their inherent characteristics as soft law instruments or any of their other features; it comes only from the WTO members' explicit decision to give hard law effect to certain types of soft law instruments developed, or to be developed, by certain types of international institutions. Alvarez refers to the relationship between Codex standards and the two relevant WTO Agreements as an example of International Organizations' recommendations, 'otherwise non-binding under the organizations' charters, [which] acquire legally binding authority through express provision in another treaty'.[138] Using the WTO Agreements to give hard law effect to non-binding instruments issued by intergovernmental organizations such as the Codex Commission is already revolutionary; using WTO Agreements to give hard law effect to non-binding instruments issued by non-governmental or quasi-governmental transnational organizations such as the ISO is a revolution of a different magnitude. But that is what the TBT Agreement in particular has achieved.

Whatever hard law quality these international standards have acquired within the WTO system thus comes from specific hard law rules of the WTO itself. To put it differently, WTO panels refer to these international standards because these standards have been given legal status and effect by explicit reference in the WTO's own covered agreements; but for this explicit reference, panels and the Appellate Body would be unlikely to accord weight to these standards even as tools for the interpretation of relevant WTO rules.[139] Even when the WTO used international soft law

---

[138] J E Alvarez, *International Organizations as Law-Makers* (OUP 2005) 221.

[139] But see Footer, who argues that soft law is 'frequently used in the WTO legal order'. Footer, above n 15, 248. However, Footer adopts an expansive definition of soft law in the WTO context, covering anything from special and differential treatment provisions in WTO covered agreements to WTO ministerial declarations and even WTO Secretariat papers. Ibid, 248–51.

instruments explicitly, as in *Shrimp/Turtle* where it referred to, *inter alia*, Agenda 21 (the 300-page plan contained in the 1992 Rio Declaration 1992 for achieving sustainable development in the twenty-first century) to interpret the scope of the term 'exhaustible natural resources' so as to include living resources, the AB was careful to stress not only 'the recent acknowledgement by the international community of the importance of concerted bilateral or multilateral action to protect living natural resources', but also 'the explicit recognition by WTO Members of the objective of sustainable development in the preamble of the *WTO Agreement*'.[140]

This is not to say that WTO panels and the AB ignore international soft law completely; it is only to stress that, if they do, they either avoid an explicit reference to such instruments or go to extra lengths in order to find some form of textual basis for so doing within the WTO covered agreements. This approach of the WTO judicial organ does not only accord with the legal positivist view that only formally binding sources of international law (as enumerated in Article 38 of the ICJ Statute) can be a source of rights and obligations for purposes of adjudication, but is also recognized even by legal realists who are prepared to see beyond those formal sources.[141] As Shaffer and Pollack noted recently, while soft law provisions can 'indirectly inform the interpretation and application of existing WTO texts and thus shape the outcome of WTO panel and Appellate Body decisions', it is 'highly unlikely' that panels and the AB will 'formally declare that they are taking into account soft-law provisions and norms from a separate regime if they find that such provisions or norms are outside of their jurisdiction'.[142]

B. Implication for International Investment Law

The investment law lessons that can be learnt from the above analysis appear to be rather limited. International standards in the sense of the SPS and TBT Agreements of the WTO have only an indirect relevance to

---

[140] See *Shrimp-Turtle*, AB report, paras 130–1.

[141] Legal realists believe that judges are 'situated decision makers who respond to disputes in light of particular social, political, and historical contexts which shape their views of the facts of a particular case'; they do not decide 'simply in response to formal rules and legal doctrine'. G C Shaffer and M A Pollack, 'Hard vs. Soft Law: Alternatives, Complements, and Antagonists in International Governance', (2010) 94 *Minnesota Law Review*, 706–99, 749.

[142] Ibid, 749–50.

investment law. Many international investment disputes often revolve around the question of whether measures taken by a host government that adversely affect the interests of a foreign investor in its territory (short of direct expropriation) fall within the accepted police powers of the state (and hence are non-compensable) or amount to regulatory/indirect expropriation/taking (and hence are compensable).[143] In such cases, would the presence or absence of an international standard on which the said national measure is based make a difference in the determination of a case? For example, consider a government measure to destroy all animals in a farm owned and operated by a foreign investor (a rancher) in order to control a disease outbreak but without payment of compensation to the farmer-investor. Would the fact that the government carried out the measure in accordance with WHO/OIE guidelines (or not) matter in the determination of whether the damage is compensable? This is just a hypothetical example. In reality, it appears that there are no cases where such questions were directly at issue.[144]

The closest arbitration case I could find is a NAFTA dispute that involved animal-disease related measures, where Canadian cattle producers claimed that a US import ban on Canadian livestock and

---

143 For more on this, see H Mann, *International Investment Agreements, Business and Human Rights: Key Issues and Opportunities* (IISD, February 2008), available at <http://www.iisd.org/pdf/2008/iia_business_human_rights.pdf> accessed 11 November 2011.

144 An interesting example, albeit outside arbitration, is an ECJ case in which two Scottish aquaculture companies sued their government for compensation after the government took sanitary measures to control fish disease outbreak in their fish farms. See *Marine Harvest McConnell (C-20/00) and Hydro Seafood GSP Ltd (C-64/00)* joined cases, judgment issued 10 July 2003. Following the disease outbreak, the government ordered that some fish be killed and their carcasses destroyed, while others had to be slaughtered for marketing immediately. The companies requested compensation for their loss, which the government declined. As a result, the companies brought separate actions before Scottish courts against the government seeking judicial review of the decision and the relevant regulation on which the decision was based. At first instance, the Court of Session found that 'the Secretary of State had acted illegally by failing to provide either legislative or administrative means for payment of any compensation where slaughter orders were made under that regulation'. Ibid, paras 37 and 42. On appeal, the Court of Session referred the matter in both cases to the ECJ for preliminary ruling. The ECJ combined the two cases and ruled in favour of the government, arguing that the measures involved normal commercial risks inherent in the business of fish farming and the measures of immediate destruction and slaughter in order to control diseases 'do not constitute, in the absence of compensation for affected owners, a disproportionate and intolerable interference impairing the very substance of the right to property'. Ibid, para 86.

beef products, which followed the discovery in 2003 of mad cow disease in a cow in Canada, was in breach of their investment rights under NAFTA Chapter 11. But the arbitral tribunal dismissed the case for lack of jurisdiction on the grounds that claimants did not have investment in the United States and did not go to the substance of the dispute.[145]

The implication of the above analysis on the WTO approach to international soft law standards under the SPS and TBT Agreements is that in order for any soft law or other external non-hard law instrument or obligation to have direct legal effect in international investment dispute settlement, the said instrument must first be accorded some form of legal recognition through the accepted sources of legal obligation in international investment law, such as the bilateral or other international investment treaty, an investment contract, national law or any other accepted source of law. The need for some form of 'internalization' or 'incorporation', or at least explicit cross-reference, is well recognized in the investment law literature relating to the issue of whether, or to what extent, investment tribunals can, or should, give effect to non-investment international hard law, such as environmental law and human rights law.[146] As Bruno Simma argued in a recent piece, an investment arbitration tribunal can take human rights into account in the interpretation of an investment treaty only if the 'external' human rights rules are 'placed in a particular relationship with the investment treaty concerned'.[147] Simma identifies two such relationships: the principle of evolutionary or dynamic interpretation[148] and the interpretative presumption that 'treaties are intended to produce effects which accord with existing rules of international law'.[149]

---

[145] See *The Canadian Cattlemen for Fair Trade v the USA* (NAFTA/Uncitral arbitration), award on jurisdiction (28 January 2008), available at <http://www.state.gov/documents/organization/99954.pdf>.

[146] See B Simma and T Kill, 'Harmonizing Investment Protection and International Human Rights: First Steps Towards a Methodology', in C Binder, U Kriebaum, A Reinisch and S Wittich (eds) *International Investment Law for the 21st Century: Essays in Honour of Christoph Schreuer* (OUP 2009) 678–707; also Mann, above n 143.

[147] See B Simma, 'Foreign Investment Arbitration: a Place for Human Rights?' (2011), 60 *ICLQ* 573, 582–3.

[148] According to Simma, this principle means that 'where treaties use "known legal terms whose content the parties expected would change through time", the meaning of these terms will be determined by reference to international law as it has evolved and stands at present, rather than to the state of the law at the time of the conclusion of the treaty'. Ibid.

[149] Simma notes that this interpretative presumption is used 'to resolve issues

The approach adopted by the WTO *vis-à-vis* international soft law standards set by 'external' institutions is different from this. By explicitly referring to these standards and by setting them effectively as benchmarks against which national regulations are to be judged, WTO law has to an extent 'internalized' these international standards, thereby making them part of its hard law instruments. Indeed, given that these international standards are not hard law instruments in themselves, neither of Simma's particular forms of relationship would have been sufficient to bring them into the interpretative context. Likewise, in the absence of some form of 'internalization' into international investment law of non-binding international standards, giving effect to non-binding 'external' standards in international investment arbitration, for example, would have the anomalous effect of elevating them to a higher level than equally 'external' but binding rules of international law.

The question for us thus becomes one of whether international investment law has any clauses 'internalizing' international soft law standards in a manner similar to the WTO's approach in the SPS and TBT Agreements. At least in the first instance, this is an empirical question of whether or not such provisions exist at all in international investment agreements. And the answer is fairly clear that international investment treaties (IITs) generally do not have rules cross-referring to or internalizing such external soft law instruments.[150] Accordingly, the major avenue opened by the SPS/TBT Agreements for the transformation of non-binding international standards into binding international law norms does not really exist in international investment law. Besides, there is also a plausible reason behind that.

It is important to bear in mind that both the SPS and TBT Agreements resort to international soft law instruments as tools to advance a shared objective – the harmonization of product standards across the WTO membership.[151] International investment law, unlike WTO law, is

---

of interpretation relating to the broader normative content of a treaty rather than to the meaning of a specific term'. Ibid, 583.

[150] See UNCTAD, Investor–State Dispute Settlement and Impact on Investment Rulemaking (New York and Geneva 2007).

[151] See e.g. para 6 of the preamble to the SPS Agreement (which expresses the desires 'to further the use of harmonized sanitary and phytosanitary measures between Members, on the basis of international standards, guidelines and recommendations developed by the relevant international organizations [. . .]'); Article 3 of the SPS Agreement then contains detailed rules on how to advance the goal of harmonization of standards on the basis of international soft law instruments. Likewise, Article 2.6 of TBT Agreement (which provides that '[w]ith a view to harmonizing technical regulations on as wide a basis as possible, Members

contained in a collection of nearly 3,000 independent bilateral investment treaties (BITs),[132] bilateral and regional free trade agreements with investment content (e.g. NAFTA), and a small number of 'multilateral' investment agreements such as the Energy Charter Treaty (ECT). A global framework for investment, similar to the WTO for trade, is still lacking, further complicating the question of whether international investment law could come up with a similar avenue to that of the WTO. As a collection of stand-alone and largely bilateral treaties, international investment law does not have the means to pursue harmonization of standards as a systemic goal. In the circumstances, it is unlikely that any particular investment treaty would have the ambition to pursue significant harmonization of standards. To this extent, it appears that there is no investment parallel to the WTO's approach of giving legal effect to non-binding international standards.

At the same time, it is notable that the approach of international investment law in respect of non-trade concerns is much closer to the approach of GATT prior to 1995. GATT had mechanisms with which to give priority for overriding public policy interests related to human, animal and plant life or health or the environment over those of trade.[153] But GATT did not have any harmonization objectives, nor did it explicitly refer to any international soft law instruments to achieve any of its more modest objectives. Historically the bilateral investment treaties that make up the lion's share of the corpus of international investment law today did not make any references to non-investment policy issues of the type covered in GATT Article XX.[154] On the other hand, the more recent bilateral investment treaties, as well as the FTAs and the ECT, increasingly contain GATT Article XX-like exceptions to allow the use of otherwise illegal local content requirements when this is found necessary to achieve genuine national health, environmental or similar other objectives.[155] The similarity with the GATT approach in this area extends

---

shall play a full part, within the limits of their resources, in the preparation by appropriate international standardizing bodies of international standards for products for which they either have adopted, or expect to adopt, technical regulations.')

[152] See UNCTAD, *World Investment Report 2011*, 100 (reporting that, at the end of 2010, there were 2,807 BITs).

[153] See particularly GATT Article XX.

[154] As Howard Mann noted, the early generations of international investment agreements 'were focused solely and exclusively on investor rights. It was not until the 1990s that any references to social issues, such as labour and the environment, materialized in any such agreements.' Mann, above n 143, 9–10.

[155] See e.g. Articles 1106:6 and 1114 of NAFTA; Articles 10.5.3(c) and 10.12 of

beyond the languages of the exceptions; a number of investment treaty arbitration awards, especially those issued in the early days of investment arbitration, have explicitly referred to GATT jurisprudence for the interpretation of relevant investment treaty provisions.[156]

Indeed, further reflecting contemporary societal concerns, some of the most modern BITs and FTAs are taking tentative steps towards giving a degree of legal recognition to soft international, mainly private, norms. UNCTAD, in its latest investment report, refers to a small but growing number of agreements that include corporate social responsibility-specific clauses and mentions three Canadian FTAs (with Colombia in 2008, Peru in 2009, and Panama in 2010) as examples.[157] Article 816 of the Canada-Colombia FTA, which is entitled Corporate Social Responsibility, states that:

> Each Party should encourage enterprises operating within its territory or subject to its jurisdiction to voluntarily incorporate internationally recognized standards of corporate social responsibility in their internal policies, such as statements of principle that have been endorsed or are supported by the Parties. These principles address issues such as labour, the environment, human rights, community relations and anti-corruption. The Parties remind those enterprises of the importance of incorporating such corporate social responsibility standards in their internal policies.[158]

Innovative as this approach is, it is also clear that even this hard law *instrumentum* has chosen a soft *negotium*[159] to give effect to the relevant soft law instruments, thus sending a signal that, while the states party to the convention recognize the normative significance of corporate social

---

the US-Chile FTA; Articles 15.8.3(c) and 15.10 of the US-Singapore FTA; and more generally Articles 8.3(c) and 12 of the US Model BIT 2004 from which the above and many other investment treaty provisions emanated. Note, however, that NAFTA Article 21.01 has a replica of Article XX that explicitly does not apply to Chapter 11.

156 See e.g. *S.D. Myers v Canada*, Partial Award, 13 November 2000 (the tribunal noted that 'where a state can achieve its chosen level of environmental protection through a variety of equally effective and reasonable means, it is obliged to adopt the alternative that is most consistent with open trade. This corollary also is consistent with the language and the case law arising out of the WTO family of agreements.' Ibid, para 221).

157 See UNCTAD, *World Investment Report 2011*, 119–20.

158 Text of the agreement available at <http://www.international.gc.ca/trade-agreements-accords-commerciaux/assets/pdfs/En%2008%20Colombia%20FTA.pdf>.

159 See Jean d'Aspremont, 'Softness in International Law: A Self-Serving Quest for New Legal Materials' (2008) 9:5 *EJIL* 1075–93.

responsibility standards, they are not yet ready to give them binding force through a convention. It is thus hardly surprising that, as UNCTAD put it, 'the implementation of CSR provisions in "real" IIAs remains to be seen'.[160]

C. Conclusion

The evidence so far leads me to the preliminary conclusion that while international soft law instruments do play a significant role in international investment law, just as in any other area of international economic law, the lesson that investment law can learn from trade law in the field of international standards remains minimal. In order for international investment law to learn from the WTO experience with respect to the use of international soft law standards, international investment law will have to reach a position where it will seek to advance a policy of harmonization of national standards among a large number of contracting parties. The current patchwork of investment treaties is ill suited for such a legislative policy to have a place.

It is worth stressing at the same time that, even if we were to accept the above conclusion as correct, it does not follow from this that soft law lacks any role in international investment arbitration. Indeed, there have been a number of investment cases where international soft law has been resorted to.[161] All we are saying is that international standards or other soft law instruments do not have direct legal force until and unless they are somehow incorporated into the legal basis of the investment relationship by some explicit reference thereto. Just as a WTO panel is unlikely to explicitly refer to international soft law instruments outside the SPS/TBT or similar context discussed above, it is also unlikely that an international investment arbitration tribunal would explicitly base its ruling on such external instrument. At the same time, an investment tribunal is unlikely to be totally immune from the influence of such widely recognized international soft law instruments as Agenda 21. The main difference is that while a WTO Appellate Body was able to invoke Agenda 21 and justify its action on the basis of concepts contained in the text of a WTO covered agreement, an investment tribunal dealing with a BIT that does not make such reference would struggle to justify any explicit reliance on such an instrument. In such circumstances, judicial practice within the

---

160 See UNCTAD, *World Investment Report 2011*, 120.

161 For examples on this, see the chapters by Bjorklund, Hirsch, Miles, Reinisch, and Ziegler, this volume.

WTO appears to support the legal realist view that an investment tribunal may reach a decision informed by, or because of, a soft law instrument but it is likely to present its legal reasoning in exclusively hard law terms to the complete exclusion of any reference to soft law.

Finally, the influence of international soft law on the development of international investment law is of course much wider than the *ex post* enforcement stage which has occupied us in this chapter; it plays an even more prominent, and less controversial, role at the *ex ante* or negotiation and development stage of international investment law.[162] The immense potential of soft law to contribute to the development of general international law in this respect also applies fully to international investment law.

---

[162] See Desta (Chapter 3, this volume).

8. The evolution of investment protection based on public international law treaties: lessons to be learned

Christian Tietje and Emily Sipiorski

INTRODUCTION

This chapter examines the historical development of investment protection instruments – a development that has led to the current network of bilateral investment treaties (BITs) and free trade agreement (FTA) investment chapters. The examination provides a broad picture of investment protection and indicates the development of a coherent set of values that establish the architecture of the current system. An international constant has developed within the regime despite the variations in past protection instruments. This consistency indicates the ripeness for the development of a soft law instrument, while also providing structure for such an instrument. At the same time, attention must be paid to the distinctions within the BIT network that indicate a preservation of negotiating power and autonomy of states, a level of state control that certainly contributes to the success of the system. Understanding that multi-layered architecture serves an important structural purpose in the larger context of a possible soft law codification.

In order to gain a full picture of this investment protection structure, the analysis considers the development of these protections over time. This begins with consideration of the agreements, including concessions and treaties that preceded the current BIT form, foreshadowing the more specific protections currently included in the investment protection instruments. The overview begins with merchant concessions from as early as the tenth century, trade association concessions from a middle period, and finally Treaties of Friendship, Commerce and Navigation (FCNs) from the late eighteenth century to the mid-twentieth century. Logically, as the treaties develop over time, the protections provided relate more closely to current investment protection. Nonetheless, the early concessions similarly provide insight into the development of the modern protections. These developments are important to consider carefully while examining the possibility of creating a functional soft law instrument in an economically dynamic world.

Turning to the post-1959 world and the first BITs, in the second section of the chapter four stages of development are generally identified. The chapter explores language choices and the scope of protection throughout these development stages. Despite following the FCNs, the earliest BITs proved to begin a trend towards more precise investment protections.

These four historical periods of BIT development, more specifically, are 1) early BITs with basic investment protection provisions and state-state dispute settlement clauses, from 1959 until the end of the 1960s; 2) second generation BITs with investor-state arbitration clauses limited to assessing the amount of compensation due in cases of expropriation (1970s and 1980s); 3) third generation BITs with comprehensive arbitration clauses and substantive protection (1990s); and 4) fourth generation BITs, as illustrated by the most recent treaties which contain modifications of certain treatment and procedural standards. This analysis will also take recent FTAs with investment chapters into consideration. Although early FTAs did not include an investment chapter, at present many FTAs include an investment chapter that can be seen as the equivalent of a BIT and replaces the need for a BIT between the countries.[1] The North American Free Trade Agreement (NAFTA), the Energy Charter Treaty, the US-Australia FTA, and the Common Market for Eastern and Southern Africa Treaty (COMESA) will all be considered from this perspective.

The changes that have developed in the later treaties as well as their similarities with the earlier treaties will be examined. Length and language changes can be largely attributed to regional developments – both in relation to the European Union and the NAFTA. Notwithstanding these marked differences, however, a commonality in the scope of protections emerges. In fact, the core protections – those written in the first 1959 BIT – have largely endured despite 50 years of other changes. Most BITs and investment chapters ensure that those same basic protections are respected. These are the standards that have carefully evolved since the earliest protective agreements were concluded.

These changes offer lessons that can be learned while considering the

---

[1] Chang-fa Lo, 'A Comparison of BIT and the Investment Chapter of Free Trade Agreement from Policy Perspective' (2008) 3 *Asian Journal of WTO & International Health Law and Policy* 147, 153.

development of a soft law instrument. This chapter is intended as a general overview to the historical transformation of the most essential BIT language, and examines whether these core, most essential provisions form the basis for codifying a soft law instrument. This analysis of background development and structure of investment protection cannot be exhaustive. Of the over 2,800 BITs currently in existence, this chapter only explores a representative number. To provide a reasonably broad scope, however, the treaties and agreements are generally taken from selected jurisdictions: China, the Czech Republic, Germany, the United States and Uruguay. This choice is intended to provide a sampling of agreements between countries situated in different continents as well as countries with different levels of development status.

I. PRE-1959

The beginning of investment protection instruments started much earlier than 25 November 1959 when the first BIT was signed. This first section examines these precursors to bilateral investment treaties and investment chapters. Some of the earliest protections that form the historical skeleton of modern investment protection emerged from trade concessions. A party's interest in trading in a region can be associated with the modern activity of in fact entering a country by making an investment.

This general period forming the forerunners of BITs can be broadly separated into three historical periods. As economic interchange increased during these three periods, the associated need for protection of economic interests simultaneously resulted in the creation of more clearly demarcated protections. Thus, as economic connections increased and grew, the protections evolved towards the protections currently included in BITs. For the purposes of this historical overview, the consideration of the other protections ends shortly after World War II. This moment was characterized by an increase in investments abroad in addition to the expansion of international political instability. These two factors, of course, created the need for a more reliable and complete form of protection and thus marked the historic turning point in the development of protections.

Some of the first appearances of investment protection are generally considered to have emerged in the tenth century.[2] At this time, Venetian merchants were granted concessions to enter Byzantine Ports without

---

2 Jeswald W Salacuse, *The Law of Investment Treaties* (OUP 2010) 80.

paying duties.[3] Genoese traders similarly negotiated concessions at the Byzantine Ports.[4] These same types of concessions were later used by English kings in the twelfth century.[5] These concessions often allowed for the traders to operate within the trading cities under the laws of their home jurisdiction.[6] Although these instruments were not investment protection agreements as such but were more accurately trade concessions, they provide an indication of the manner by which protection occurred in its earliest form. The earliest investment protection instruments were concessions granted by a sovereign to foreign traders, rather than a negotiation for reciprocal treatment between two sovereigns.[7] Nonetheless, these agreements contained reciprocal benefits for the sovereign and the merchants, including – on a basic level – promoting trade as well as improving relations with foreign territories.[8] These early agreements served the dual purpose of establishing economic relationships as well as creating an umbrella for economic domination.[9] Many of these protections were procedurally limited even where substantive protections existed: an aggrieved party would need to petition his own sovereign when his interests had been injured in a foreign state.[10]

Another historical example of organization and control of trade is the Hanseatic League which united trading cities on the Baltic Sea from the thirteenth through seventeenth centuries.[11] The League provided certain commercial privileges as well as monopolies, and thus a form of protection for the traders investing in commercial transactions within the League. Trading partners were granted a certain minimum right of protection.

The structure and value of interstate investment and trade protection agreements changed significantly during the seventeenth and eighteenth centuries. With the emergence of the nation-state, commercial and trading rights were then negotiated between two sovereigns, modernizing in

---

3 See generally Richard B Lillich, *The Human Rights of Aliens in Contemporary International Law* (Manchester University Press 1984) 7.

4 Ibid.

5 Salacuse, above n 2, 80; see also Peter Fischer, *A Collection of International Concessions and Related Instruments* (Oceana Publications 1976).

6 Lillich, above n 3, 7.

7 Salacuse, above n 2, 80.

8 Ibid.

9 Ibid, 81.

10 Lillich, above n 3, 9.

11 Johannes Schildhauer, *Die Hanse: Geschichte und Kultur* (Kohlhammer 1984); see also Stephan Leibfried and Dieter Wolf, 'Europeanization and the Unravelling European Nation State: Dynamics and Feedback Effects' (2005) 10 *European Foreign Affairs Review* 479–99.

response to a world quickly developing into defined states.[12] These agreements were usually finalized in writing and acted as a way for the sovereign to control and regulate the state's economic activity.[13] This period of treaty drafting resulted in many bilateral agreements in Europe that recognized protections for foreign-owned property in a state – thus, the early emergence of investment protection.[14]

When considering these treaties as a forerunner of modern investment protection instruments, the similarity of the basic protections is notable. Some of the specific areas protected by these international agreements include '(1) protection and security of aliens and their property; (2) special means of protection for asset recovery and monetary transfers; (3) most-favoured-nation treatment[...](4) national treatment[...]; and (5) guarantees of access to justice and safeguards against its denial.'[15]

By the end of this period, as the development of colonial holdings deepened, the need for treaties significantly decreased. Fewer treaties were required for the advancement of commercial and economic interests as the domination of the regions through political and military power did not necessitate any mutually recognized agreements.[16] During the mid-seventeenth century, for example, England was enacting laws that regulated the trade to and from colonial holdings, ensuring England the economic benefits and thus withholding concessions to other potential trading partners.[17]

With the changes during the end of the eighteenth century in the international context, states without colonial holdings began to develop a new instrument to protect their economic interests abroad. In particular, in the early days of the United States, while Thomas Jefferson was working on the Declaration of Independence, John Adams was drafting a model treaty of alliance and commerce.[18] The first such treaty was signed between the United States and France in 1778, the Treaty of Amity and Commerce.[19] Later referred to as Treaties of Friendship, Commerce and

---

12 Salacuse, above n 2, 81.

13 Ibid.

14 Ibid.

15 Ibid.

16 Ibid, 82.

17 See *An Act for Increase in Shipping, and Encouragement of Navigation for this Nation*, England, 9 October 1651.

18 Kenneth J Vandevelde, *Bilateral Investment Treaties: History, Policy and Interpretation* (OUP 2009) 19.

19 Salacuse, above n 2, 84; Treaty of Amity and Commerce between the United States and France, 6 February 1778, available at <http://avalon.law.yale.edu/18th_century/fr1788-1.asp>.

Navigation (FCNs), these treaties included the idea of most-favoured-nation standard of treatment between two state parties and further developed the idea in a way that closely resembles modern BIT language.[20] The United States developed these legal instruments both to form stronger relationships with the European powers for the promotion of national security and commerce and to 'create new commercial relations with other emerging nations'.[21]

By 1784, the US Congress had created a committee to negotiate further FCNs – the value of the treaties being apparent to the early government as well as to the countries entering into the agreements. Treaties with Prussia, Morocco, England and Spain resulted from these efforts.[22] Although the earliest of these treaties were with European powers as a means to establish commercial relations, the United States began negotiating with Latin American, Asian and African states as the economies of these countries opened to commercial exchange.[23]

Other states also began negotiating these agreements for the purpose of fostering trade. One characteristic of these treaties in contrast to the earlier concession agreements was a greater balance in power between the two signatory states.[24] The treaties had a more reciprocal nature. FCN treaties are considered the true precursor to the modern bilateral investment treaties, providing relatively balanced protections to both parties to the

---

[20] Andreas R Ziegler, 'Most-Favoured-Nation (MFN) Treatment' in August Reinisch (ed) *Standards of Investment Protection* (OUP 2008) 59–86, 62; Vandevelde, above n 18, 19.

[21] Salacuse, above n 2, 84.

[22] A Treaty of Amity and Commerce between His Majesty the King of Prussia, and the United States of America, 10 September 1785, available at <http://avalon.law.yale.edu/18th_century/prus1785.asp>; Treaty of Peace and Friendship, Treaty with Morocco, 28 June and 15 July 1786, available at <http://avalon.law.yale.edu/18th_century/bar1786t.asp>; Treaty of Amity Commerce and Navigation, between His Britannick Majesty and The United States of America, by Their President, with the advice and consent of Their Senate, The Jay Treaty, 19 November 1794, available at <http://avalon.law.yale.edu/18th_century/jay.asp>; Treaty of Friendship, Limits, and Navigation Between Spain and The United States, 27 October 1795, available at <http://avalon.law.yale.edu/18th_century/sp1795.asp>.

[23] See generally Kenneth J Vandevelde, 'U.S. Bilateral Investment Treaties: The Second Wave' (1993) 14 *Mich J Int'l L* 621, 623.

[24] Salacuse, above n 2, 82; see for example Treaty of Friendship, Commerce and Navigation Between Argentina and the United States, 27 July 1853, available at <http://avalon.law.yale.edu/19th_century/argen02.asp>; Brazil-US, Treaty of Amity, Commerce, and Navigation, 12 December 1828, available at <http://avalon.law.yale.edu/19th_century/brazil01.asp>.

agreement: national treatment was provided for the treaty parties and the foreign traders had the right to use domestic courts to protect their interests and in defence of their rights.[25] The combination of procedural and substantive benefits was essential to ensuring the equality between the parties, most notably demonstrated by the principle of 'fair and equitable treatment' which later became an element of these FCNs.[26] The standard of treatment provisions later included 'most-favoured nation' and 'national treatment'.[27]

The FCN treaties were drafted in a simple form and were relatively short in length. The early treaties were typically composed of around 30 articles, while the trend in the nineteenth century was to shorten the length and number of articles depending on the purpose of the treaty. The 1829 Austro-Hungarian Treaty[28] contained only 13 and the 1853 treaty with Argentina[29] was composed of 14 articles. This shortening, however, was not universal: the 1858 treaty concluded by the United States with Bolivia[30] contained 34 articles. Although longer, this treaty also had the express purpose of promoting peace between the two countries a common feature of FCNs.

The preamble and title of the treaties often expressly reaffirmed the parties' commitment to their friendship. In the earlier treaties, this idea of friendship or amity was in the substance of the first article. The 1778 treaty between the US and France notes in the first Article that '[t]here shall be a firm, inviolable and universal Peace, and a true and sincere Friendship' between the parties.[31] The FCN between the US and Argentina similarly

---

[25] Dieter Blumenwitz, 'Treaties of Friendship, Commerce and Navigation' in Rudolf Bernhardt (ed), *EPIL* (vol IV, 2000) 954–5.

[26] Blumenwitz, above n 25, 955; Andrea K Bjorklund, 'National Treatment' in August Reinisch (ed) *Standards of Investment Protection* (OUP 2008) 29–58, 31.

[27] Salacuse, above n 2, 85.

[28] The Austro-Hungarian treaty is for the purposes of commerce and navigation, thereby naturally excluding all language of 'friendship' as included in the other treaties. This exclusion may also justify the shorter length of the document as the first article begins directly with the 'liberty to enter ports'.

[29] Treaty of Friendship, Commerce and Navigation Between Argentina and the United States, 27 July 1853, above n 24.

[30] Bolivian-American Diplomacy – Treaty of Peace, Friendship, Commerce, and Navigation, 13 May 1858, available at <http://avalon.law.yale.edu/19th_century/bolivia01.asp>.

[31] Treaty of Amity and Commerce Between The United States and France, 6 February 1778, above n 19.

indicated in the first Article that commitment to 'sincere friendship', with only slight modification from an even earlier treaty.[32]

The second Article of the Treaty of Amity between the US and France includes most-favoured-nation protections:

> [...] engage mutually not to grant any particular Favor to other Nations in respect of Commerce and Navigation, which shall not immediately become common to the other Party, who shall enjoy the same Favor freely, if the Concession was freer made, or on allowing the same Compensation, if the Concession was Conditional.[33]

Similar protection was provided in the 1832 treaty concluded with Chile,[34] among other treaties.

From the procedural perspective, the Jay Treaty of 1794,[35] concluded between the United States and Britain following the Revolutionary War, demonstrates important developments in dispute resolution. This treaty was the first of its kind to provide for mixed commissions for the resolution of disputes. The commission's awards were final and binding in regard to both the dispute and the amount to be paid. The treaty provided for this dispute resolution for both British citizens and citizens of the United States.

> For the purpose of ascertaining the amount of any such losses and damages, Five Commissioners shall be appointed and authorized to meet and act in manner following-viz-Two of them shall be appointed by His Majesty, Two of them by the President of the United States by and with the advice and consent of the Senate thereof, and the fifth, by the unanimous voice of the other Four; and if they should not agree in such Choice, then the Commissioners named by the two parties shall respectively propose one person, and of the two names so proposed, one shall be drawn by Lot in the presence of the Four Original Commissioners.[36]

Following World War I, the United States concluded FCN treaties intended to protect US nationals and businesses abroad from arbitrary

---

[32] Treaty of Friendship, Commerce and Navigation Between Argentina and the United States, 27 July 1853, above n 24.

[33] Treaty of Amity and Commerce Between The United States and France, 6 February 1778, above n 19.

[34] Chile-US, Convention of Peace, Amity, Commerce, and Navigation, 16 May 1832, available at <http://avalon.law.yale.edu/19th_century/chile01.asp>.

[35] Treaty of Amity Commerce and Navigation, between His Britannick Majesty; and The United States of America, 'Jay Treaty', Art 6, 19 November 1794, above n 22.

[36] Treaty of Amity Commerce and Navigation, between His Britannick Majesty; and The United States of America, 'Jay Treaty', above n 22.

and discriminatory governmental actions.[37] These treaties also included procedural protections in regard to expropriation and demonstrated agreements on processes for settling disputes. The FCN Treaty between the United States and Siam,[38] signed in 1937, provided that US citizens shall have full access to the courts of Siam, protection equivalent to a national or a national of the most-favoured nation:

> The nationals of each of the High Contracting Parties shall have free access to the Courts of Justice of the other in pursuit and defense of their rights; they shall be at liberty, equally with nationals of the State of residence and with the nationals of the most-favored nation, to choose and employ lawyers, advocates and representatives to pursue and defend their rights before such Courts. There shall be imposed upon the nationals of either of the High Contracting Parties no conditions or requirements in connection with such access to the Courts of Justice of the other which do not apply to nationals of the State of residence or to the nationals of the most-favored nation.[39]

The 1937 US-Siam FCN Treaty further provided provisions on expropriation: 'property shall not be taken without due process of law or without payment of just compensation'.[40] National treatment and most-favoured-nation treatment were included as well as 'protection and security' for companies of one party conducting business in the other country:

> The nationals of each of the High Contracting Parties shall receive, in the territories of the other, the most constant protection and security for their persons and property, and shall enjoy in this respect the same rights and privileges as are or may be granted to nationals of the State of residence on their submitting themselves to the conditions imposed upon nationals of the State of residence. . . .
>
> Parties shall throughout the whole extent of the territories of the other on condition of reciprocity be placed in all respects on the same footing as the nationals of the most-favored nation.[41]

---

[37] Salacuse, above n 2, 86.

[38] Treaty of Friendship, Navigation, and Commerce, between the U.S. and Siam, 13 November 1937, available at <http://untreaty.un.org/unts/60001_120000/19/24/00037188.pdf>. This treaty was later replaced by the Treaty of Amity and Economic Relations between the Kingdom of Thailand and the United States of America, signed 29 May 1966, available at <http://www.thailawforum.com/database1/amity.html>. The 1966 Treaty of Amity provides similar standards of treatment and protection regarding expropriation.

[39] Treaty of Friendship, Navigation, and Commerce, between the U.S. and Siam, above n 38, Art 4.

[40] Treaty of Friendship, Navigation, and Commerce, between the U.S. and Siam, above n 38, Art 1.

[41] Treaty of Friendship, Navigation, and Commerce, between the U.S. and Siam, above n 38.

Despite the signing of these FCN treaties, the actual level of US investment abroad was relatively small and Europe was not investing outside of former colonial holdings to a great enough extent to warrant negotiation of further investment protection instruments. Despite the limited benefits to be gained, both the United States and various European countries expanded their FCN treaty programmes during the post-war period. In particular, the United States drafted a model FCN treaty, which included a uniform clause on the protection of investments. Property taken by expropriation was to be protected by 'due process of law' and 'just compensation',[42] an expansion from the 'full and perfect protection' of the early nineteenth century.[43]

Changes, however, were beginning to occur. Classical rules of international law were becoming less applicable and useful in the way that they had once been for the purpose of protection of property.[44] Domestic government measures were beginning to impact on foreign property holdings in certain countries.[45] Land reforms resulting from the Mexican revolution and the end of World War I in Europe added to the changing landscape.[46]

This incongruence between the international political atmosphere and FCN treaties only grew following the end of World War II. The treaties concluded for commercial interests no longer fit the global economic environment. Specifically in regard to the US FCN programme, countries were not as willing to conclude FCNs where the goal of the agreements was the protection of property owned by US parties with specific provisions on how those investments would be treated by the other government.[47]

With the creation of global monetary institutions after the war, namely the International Bank for Reconstruction and Development, the International Monetary Fund, and the General Agreement on Tariffs and Trade (GATT), other institutions also served the goal of promoting trade and tariff reduction.[48] GATT in particular largely eliminated the need for

---

42 Kenneth J Vandevelde, *United States Investment Treaties: Policy and Practice* (Kluwer 1992) 50–1.

43 Kenneth J Vandevelde, *U.S. International Investment Agreements* (OUP 2009) 11.

44 Rafael Leal-Arcas, *International Trade and Investment Law: Multilateral, Regional and Bilateral Governance* (Edward Elgar 2010) 182; see also Vandevelde, above n 42, 31–2.

45 Leal-Arcas, above n 44, 182–3.

46 Ibid.

47 Vandevelde, above n 23, 623–4; Salacuse, above n 2, 88–9.

48 Salacuse, above n 2, 86–7.

bilateral FCNs; thus, investment protection became the primary goal of bilateral treaty negotiations.[49]

The investment climate, however, was also changing. The Socialist bloc was nationalizing properties. Nationalization was also occurring, albeit on a much more limited scale, in France and the United Kingdom. Hostility to foreign investment was growing in the Middle East.[50] Decolonization also resulted in newly independent countries seeking control of foreign-owned property: their 'main political and economic goal [was] to regain control over natural wealth and economy'.[51] In 1959 two notable events occurred. These may have impacted on the US perspective on investments abroad, but also mark the moment when European countries began re-evaluating the way in which their investments abroad were protected. Regarding US foreign investments, first, Fidel Castro came to power to Cuba and expropriated US investments in the country. Second, in May of 1959, a US electric company in Brazil was seized.[52] There were no modern FCNs in place in either Cuba or Brazil at the time of the expropriations.[53] These two events were decisive in demonstrating that there was a global need for a different type of investment protection. Thus, investment protections were necessarily reformulated.

These pre-1959 treaties provide the architecture for what follows in the next 50 years. From the earliest treaties where foreign concessions were first offered to the FCNs where additional specific protections were offered for foreign investors, the protections provided became more detailed and developed in a way to facilitate changing economic relationships, providing more efficient means for resolution of disputes and treatment protections in line with global needs. This evolution not only marks the increasing economic integration of a world ever becoming more global, but also demonstrates an evolving view towards the advantages of investment protection. In the FCN programmes, the treaties served broader purposes and allowed the countries to maintain friendly relations. The protections after 1959 serve similar purposes yet more fully developed the specific area of investor-state relationships. A wide range of protections, substantive and procedural, were incorporated into the treaties.

---

[49] Vandevelde, above n 43, 22.

[50] Vandevelde, above n 42, 43.

[51] Leal-Arcas, above n 44, 184.

[52] Vandevelde, above n 43, at 16; see also Keith S Rosenn, 'Note: Expropriation in Argentina and Brazil: Theory and Practice' (1975) 15 *Va J Int'l L* 277, 304–5.

[53] Vandevelde, above n 43, 16.

This evolution also demonstrates the direction that the protections may take in the future. Of course, the investment protections provided in BITs and investment chapters are not static. As will be discussed in the following section, these protections have also transformed over the course of the 50 years of their existence. Examination of these much earlier protections provides a level of insight into the general direction that may be taken in the future. Thus, these early treaties are a rough roadmap to the ways protections change as the world becomes more economically connected. In the same light, these treaties could provide clues as to how treaties can develop in the future in a world fearful of outside engagement, specifically in regard to limiting access to certain dispute resolution procedures. This evolution is particularly apparent in the BITs and FTAs between two developed countries. More caution is applied in regard to procedural as well as substantive protections. States are less apt to give sovereignty over matters to international tribunals and at times less eager to allow foreign investors into the market with the same protections as local companies. This trend may be indicative of BITs and investment protection instruments in the future.

II. POST-1959 BITS AND FTA INVESTMENT CHAPTERS

A. Overview

This section follows with an examination of the development of BITs over the last 50 years, regarding both style and substance. By beginning with the first treaty concluded in 1959 and examining that language and substance compared to both the most recently negotiated treaties and the treaties concluded over the course of the 50-year period, this approach sheds some light on the values and substance that have endured over time as well as on essential changes that have occurred. In such an examination, difficulties arise because of both the large number of BITs that have been concluded and the variety of legal systems involved. There is a clear difference between the BITs concluded by the United States and Canada, influenced by the investment chapter in NAFTA, and those of other states. Development status, however, appears to have very limited impact on the language and substance of the BITs. Although there is no way to prevent overlooking certain issues, the BITs and investment chapters chosen are intended to provide an overview of the treaties.

The development of substantive protections cannot be described at length and in detail in this study. Instead, the chapter considers the development of the protections from a broader perspective. Notably, the issues of most-favoured-nation treatment[54] and expropriation[55] are dealt with in detail elsewhere in this volume. The following section also examines several of the more recent additions to BITs and investment chapters, in particular the inclusion of related non-investment issues.

The development of BITs over these 50 years will be broken down into four general stages. The first stage considers the BITs signed between 1959 and the mid-1970s – generally at the point of the rejection of the Hull Doctrine by the New International Economic Order (NIEO). The second stage runs through the mid-1980s. The third stage is divided by the entry of the United States into the development of a BIT programme and active treaty negotiation with foreign states. The final stage, representing the latest BITs concluded and several updates of earlier BITs, reveals a movement away from reliance on traditional procedural dispute resolution mechanisms. This section examines each phase in regard to style and both procedural and substantive issues. The section also considers the investment and non-investment issues that have been incorporated into the language of the BITs, from specific provisions on the extent of protections to the use of human-rights-based exceptions.

As noted above, with the transforming international economic environment in regard to investment in the late 1950s, the Federal Republic of Germany began negotiating treaties with the specific goal of investment protection. Other Western European countries followed the Federal Republic's lead. The treaties came with different titles but all achieved investment and capital protection goals. The first treaty, concluded between Germany and Pakistan in 1959, was titled: 'Treaty for the Promotion and Protection of Investments'.[56] Later German treaties were for 'the promotion and reciprocal protection of investments'.[57] The treaties concluded by the Belgium-Luxembourg Economic Union during the 1960s were titled 'Convention[s] concerning the encouragement of capital investment and the protection of property'.[58]

---

54 See Andreas R Ziegler, Chapter 9, this volume.

55 See August Reinisch, Chapter 10, this volume.

56 Germany-Pakistan, Treaty for the Promotion and Protection of Investments, 25 November 1959, available at <http://www.iisd.org/pdf/2006/investment_pakistan_germany.pdf>.

57 See for example Treaty between the Federal Republic of Germany and the Republic of Liberia for the promotion and reciprocal protection of investments, 12 December 1961, available at <http://www.unctad.org/sections/dite/iia/docs/bits/germany_liberia_gr_eng.pdf>.

58 See for example Belgo-Luxembourg Economic Union and Tunisia

There were advantages to the use of BITs over the use of FCNs. These documents more successfully achieved the goal of specific investment protections than the broader FCN treaties that had previously offered protections in this area among others. The specificity of the BITs was advantageous for ensuring protection. The earliest BITs were characterized by their short form and broad definitions of terms. These BITs demonstrate marked similarities to the most recently negotiated BITs in some countries, while appearing as only a shadow of the post-NAFTA US and Canadian BITs. The protections focused on expropriation of investments and dispute settlement was limited to state-to-state resolution, as discussed further below. Compensation was not reliant on a freely transferable currency but rather on the currency of the expropriated investor. Moreover, the procedural elements of these early treaties limited the bringing of claims.[59] Without international mechanisms for dispute resolution in place, the treaties required a more detailed explanation of procedural aspects of dispute resolution.

The push for the early BITs was centralized in European states. Between 1959 and 1972, Germany concluded 46 BITs and Switzerland concluded 27. During the same period, the United States concluded two modern FCNs. Despite its earlier widespread FCN treaty programme, the United States was relatively slow in following the strong European lead in developing bilateral treaties.

A later development during this early stage was the creation of the International Centre for the Settlement of Investment Disputes (ICSID) under the World Bank. Although created in 1966, the first disputes were not taken to ICSID until the 1970s. Nonetheless, it served an essential role as a neutral mechanism for the settlement of disputes – an alternative to the ICJ – and negotiators had an option of incorporating arbitration under ICSID as one of the available dispute settlement mechanisms.[60] The creation of this dispute resolution system opened the door for disputes to be submitted directly by the investor, thus enabling the BIT system to evolve from its earlier form as a state-to-state dispute resolution mechanism.[61]

Convention concerning the encouragement and capital investment and the protection of property (with exchange of letters), 15 July 1964, available at <http://untreaty.un.org/unts/1_60000/16/30/00031499.pdf>.

[59] See for example Germany-Pakistan, Treaty for the Promotion and Protection of Investments, above n 56.

[60] Salacuse, above n 2, 93–5.

[61] See generally Christian Tietje, Karsten Nowrot and Clemens Wackernagel, *Once and Forever? The Legal Effects of a Denunciation of ICSID* (March 2008), available at <http://www.wirtschaftsrecht.uni-halle.de/sites/default/files/altbestand/Heft74.pdf>; Salacuse, above n 2, 92–3.

The shift to the second stage of BIT development largely emerged in the early 1970s. This procedural advance inevitably meant fewer conflicts of interests between a state acting in its diplomatic role and its desire to protect the economic interests of its own citizens. Thus, moving away from the issues the United States had during the expropriations in Latin America in the 1960s and 1970s, this provision enabled more autonomy for the investors and inevitably better, more secure protection for their foreign interests.

During this period, there was an increased use of model treaties as countries were beginning to use the system more widely and enter more frequently into the treaties, thus creating a need for convenient templates for initiating negotiations. The language of these model BITs was kept broad, providing for relatively general standards of protection. In addition, the categories of countries negotiating the treaties with one another were expanding beyond the limited number of Western European countries that had initiated the investment protection instruments. Specifically, non-Western European countries began entering into treaties with one another. There was an effort by Egypt, in particular, to conclude treaties with its trading partners.[62] Some of the first non-European partnerships included Korea-Tunisia (1975)[63] and Egypt-Japan (1978).[64]

The United States also began developing its BIT programme during this stage, specifically beginning the programme in 1977, nearly a decade after the investment protection mechanism had advanced in Europe.[65] The first US BITs, however, were not signed until 1982, namely with Egypt[66] and Panama,[67] and the earliest did not enter into force until 1989.

---

62 See for example Egypt-Romania Agreement on the promotion and mutual guarantee of capital investments (with protocol), signed 10 May 1976, available at <http://www.unctad.org/sections/dite/iia/docs/bits/romania_egypt.pdf>.

63 Accord Entre Le Gouvernement de La République de Corée et Le Gouvernement de La République Tunisienne Relatif a l'Encouragement et La Protection Réciproque des Investissements, 28 November 1975, available at <http://www.unctad.org/sections/dite/iia/docs/bits/korea_tunisia_fr.pdf>.

64 Agreement Between Japan and the Arab Republic of Egypt Concerning the Encouragement and Reciprocal Protection of Investment, available at <http://www.unctad.org/sections/dite/iia/docs/bits/Egypt_Japan.pdf>.

65 Vandevelde, above n 23, 623.

66 Treaty Between the United States of America and the Arab Republic of Egypt Concerning the Reciprocal Encouragement and Protection of Investments, signed 11 March 1986 (modified), entered into force 27 June 1992, available at <http://www.unctad.org/sections/dite/iia/docs/bits/us_egypt.pdf>.

67 Treaty Between the Government of the United States of America and the Government of the Republic of Panama Concerning the Treatment and Protection

The third stage of BITs, beginning in the early 1990s, included more comprehensive arbitration clauses and growing conformity in the substantive protections offered to investors, including fair and equitable treatment, national treatment as well as most-favoured-nation treatment and expropriation protections.[68] The 1992 Australia-Hungary BIT[69] exemplifies the level of specificity that was included in the dispute settlement clauses during this stage. The BIT provides for a detailed analysis of the procedure for resolving a dispute, including time limits and procedures for those instances when parties cannot agree on the method of resolution.[70]

---

of Investments, 27 October 1982, available at <http://www.unctad.org/sections/dite/iia/docs/bits/us_panama_1982.pdf>.

[68] UNCTAD 2007, Bilateral Investment Treaties 1995–2006: Trends in Investment Rulemaking, available at <http://www.unctad.org/en/docs/iteiia20065_en.pdf>.

[69] Agreement between Australia and the Republic of Hungary on the Reciprocal Promotion and Protection of Investments, 15 August 1991, available at <http://www.unctad.org/sections/dite/iia/docs/bits/australia_hungary.pdf>.

[70] Agreement between Australia and the Republic of Hungary on the Reciprocal Promotion and Protection of Investments, Art 12, providing:

> (1) In the event of a dispute between a Contracting Party and a national of the other Contracting Party relating to an investment, the parties to the dispute shall initially seek to resolve the dispute by consultations and negotiations.
>
> (2) If the dispute in question cannot be resolved through consultations and negotiations either party to the dispute may, in accordance with the law of the Contracting Party which has admitted the investment, initiate proceedings before its competent judicial or administrative bodies.
>
> (3) Where the dispute arises under Article 7 of this Agreement, either party to the dispute may take the following action irrespective of whether any local remedies available pursuant to action under paragraph (2) of this Article have already been pursued or exhausted:
>
> (a) if both Contracting Parties are at that time party to the 1965 Convention on the Settlement of Investment Disputes between States and Nationals of Other States ('the Convention'), refer the dispute to the International Centre for Settlement of Investment Disputes ('the Centre') for conciliation or arbitration pursuant to Article 28 or 36 of the Convention. Where this action is taken by a national of one Contracting Party the other Contracting Party shall consent in writing to the submission of the dispute to the Centre within thirty (30) days of receiving such a request from the national;
>
> (b) if both Contracting Parties are not at that time party to the Convention, refer the dispute to an Arbitral Tribunal constituted in accordance with Annex B of this Agreement.
>
> (4) Where the dispute in question arises otherwise than under Article 7 of

There was also a limiting of the scope of application of the treaties during this period. Exception clauses, addressing issues such as the environment, national security, as well as taxes, were more frequently used. This period marks the emergence of non-investment issues being incorporated in the BITs, as further discussed below. The BITs also provided that their scope was limited to investor-state disputes.[71]

This period further marks the proliferation of treaties between developed economies and the former communist countries of Eastern Europe. Treaties were concluded in particularly high numbers with Hungary, Poland, the Czech Republic and the Slovak Republic. Poland, for example, signed 62 BITs, the first in 1987 and the last during this

---

this Agreement, action pursuant to paragraph (3) of this Article may be taken where local remedies available pursuant to paragraph (2) of this Article have been exhausted. Where action in accordance with this paragraph is taken by a national of one Contracting Party the other Contracting Party shall consent in writing to the submission of the dispute to the Centre within thirty (30) days of receiving such a request from the national.
(5) Where a dispute is referred to the Centre in accordance with paragraphs (3) or (4) of this Article:
(a) if the parties to the dispute cannot agree whether conciliation or arbitration is the more appropriate procedure, the national affected shall have the right to choose, and
(b) a company which is constituted or incorporated under the law in force in the territory of one Contracting Party and in which before the dispute arises the majority of shares are owned by nationals of the other Contracting Party shall in accordance with Article 25(2)(b) of the Convention be treated as a company of the other Contracting Party.
(6) Once an action referred to in paragraphs (2), (3) or (4) of this Article has been taken, neither Contracting Party shall pursue the dispute through diplomatic channels unless:
(a) the relevant judicial or administrative body, the Secretary-General of the Centre, the Arbitral Authority or Tribunal or the Conciliation Commission, as the case may be, has decided that it has no jurisdiction in relation to the dispute in question; or
(b) the other Contracting Party has failed to abide by or comply with any judgment, award, order or other determination made by the body in question.
(7) In any proceeding involving a dispute relating to an investment, a Contracting Party shall not assert, as a defence, counter-claim, right of set-off or otherwise, that the national concerned has received or will receive, pursuant to an insurance or guarantee contract, indemnification or other compensation for all or part of any alleged loss.

71 UNCTAD (2007) 99.

period in 1998.[72] Similarly, the 79 Czech treaties were mostly signed during this decade. This proliferation of treaties by the former communist countries in Europe may largely explain the general surge in the number of BITs worldwide.[73]

The fourth stage of investment protection has emerged relatively recently. There is a continued use of Model BITs by parties entering into negotiations to conclude the treaties, but the most notable change is the inclusion of investment chapters in FTAs. This period can be particularly characterized by changes in the use of arbitration to resolve disputes between parties. Thus, the procedural mechanisms are being reformed in these most recent treaties and agreements as exemplified by the recent Australian investment chapters that do not include investor-state dispute resolution, discussed below.

B. Language and Style

Although there are significant similarities in the style and structure of investment agreements, there has been an evolution over the historical course of BIT development. Some of the main areas where this evolution has occurred include length, use of preambles, and authenticity issues. The approach taken by states to the language and style issues during the negotiation process indicates a growth in country-specific styles of drafting the treaties, but as will be addressed in the following section, this state-specific dimension of negotiation and style does not inherently lead to highly different results in content and protection.

1. Length

The length of treaties has generally increased over the 50 years of BIT negotiations – a general indication of increased specificity of language and breadth of provisions. These changes are not, however, a clear indication of broader protections. The first BITs were relatively short. Specifically the

---

[72] An earlier treaty was signed in 1979 but never went into force. The most recent treaty was signed in 2006. See for example Agreement between the Government of the United Kingdom of Great Britain and Northern Ireland and the Government of the Polish People's Republic for the Promotion and Reciprocal Protection of Investments, 8 December 1987, available at <http://www.unctad.org/sections/dite/iia/docs/bits/uk_poland.pdf>; Agreement between the Government of the Hashemite Kingdom of Jordan and the Republic of Poland on the Reciprocal Promotion and Protection of Investments, 4 October 1997, available at <http://www.unctad.org/sections/dite/iia/docs/bits/jordan_poland.pdf>.

[73] See generally UNCTAD 2006, International Investment Arrangements: Trends and Emerging Issues, 8.

1959 Germany-Pakistan BIT contained 14 articles.[74] This was characteristic of the BITs negotiated during these early phases. Changes in length began to particularly emerge towards the end of the second phase, and most notably by the late 1990s. The most significant moment for an increase in the length of treaties was the period following the NAFTA negotiations.

The treaties from Canada and the United States in the 1980s and 1990s were typically no longer than contemporary German or French treaties. Nonetheless, since 2000 the provisions in these treaties have increased in word count as well as specificity. The careful negotiation of the NAFTA by the three countries involved clarified the language necessary to ensure certain protections were met and drafted in such a way to respect the domestic jurisprudence on such issues. Both Canada and the United States base the language of their post-1994 BITs mostly on the Investment Chapter of NAFTA. The 2009 Canada-Jordan BIT with 52 articles and four annexes is a particularly noteworthy example regarding length.[75]

The BITs arising out of the NAFTA model from the third and most recent phase also typically have longer definitions in addition to more provisions generally. This naturally arises from drafters hoping to anticipate unknown situations rather than leaving those uncertainties to the law to resolve. This specific aspect of length will be discussed in more detail below. The same length issues hold true for the investment chapters in FTAs in the United States and Canada, in comparison to other countries, and also in contrast to the investment chapters that are being negotiated into EU FTAs. The consideration of the use of terms by the US Subcommittee for the Recommendation of the Model BIT provides insight into some of the reasons why these provisions may be so long. In one section of the Report, the subcommittee urges against use of certain terms that may be abused because of their general nature:

> 6. Recognizing that words such as 'to the extent possible' in Article 11(2), 'wherever possible' from Article 11(4)(a) and words 'when time, the nature of the proceeding, and the public interest permit' from Article 11(4)(b) could be abused in order to prevent the transparency that is important for investment, we recommend that the Administration consider the creation of a Transparency

---

[74] Germany-Pakistan, Treaty for the Promotion and Protection of Investments, 25 November 1959, above n 56.

[75] Agreement between Canada and the Hashemite Republic of Jordan for the Promotion and Protection of Investments, 28 June 2008, available at <http://www.unctad.org/sections/dite/iia/docs/bits/Canada-JordanFIPA-eng.pdf>.

Council that could help the Parties to a BIT make continuing progress in this area.[76]

Another difference in length emerges because of difference in legal systems. It has been noted that common law countries have 'better legal protection for property rights [and] are much less likely to sign [BITs] than are civil law countries'.[77] This suggestion is difficult to prove as there are substantially more civil law countries in the world and common law countries were simply later at developing BIT programmes. Nonetheless, the language of the treaties can be directly influenced by these property rights protections, and specifically the language developed in the courts. Negotiators in these jurisdictions may be hesitant to remove language seen as vital to protecting specific interests or ensure certain outcomes.

It should be noted, however, that certain provisions in NAFTA-influenced BITs in comparison to civil law BITs are no different in length. Moreover, other common law countries, namely the United Kingdom and Australia, do not have similarly detailed or numerous articles. Treaties between two less developed countries, even where one country is a common law jurisdiction, have retained a relatively short length.

In civil law jurisdictions with highly developed BIT programmes, similar increases in length are not as apparent. For example, German treaties have generally not increased in length over this same period of time. When comparing the 1959 Germany-Pakistan BIT to the recently negotiated 2009 Germany-Pakistan BIT,[78] one notes that although several substantive changes have been implemented into the new treaty, the number of provisions has in fact decreased by one.[79] Certain provisions have even been simplified; notably the provisions detailing dispute resolution procedures have been simplified as international dispute

---

[76] Report of the Subcommittee on Investment of the Advisory Committee on International Economic Policy Regarding the Model Bilateral Investment Treaty, 30 September 2009, Presented to: The Department of State, available at <http://www.state.gov/r/pa/prs/ps/2009/sept/130097.htm>.

[77] Zachary Elkins, Andrew T Guzman and Beth Simmons, 'Competing for Capital: The Diffusion of Bilateral Investment Treaties' (2006) 60 *Int'l Org* 811, 843.

[78] German-Pakistan Agreement on the Encouragement and Reciprocal Protection of Investments, 1 December 2009, available at <http://dipbt.bundestag.de/dip21/btd/17/052/1705264.pdf>.

[79] The changes in the new treaty specifically include a clause allowing investors to directly bring suit against the host government, payment of interest in cases of expropriation, and inclusion of a deadline for transfer of capital and revenues.

resolution rules provide the rules of procedure – rules that were previously included in detail in the article of the agreement.

Longer treaties also mean, of course, that the treaties provide more detail about the protections they contain. The treaties that provide the greatest specificity thus also provide investment tribunals with the most direction in deciding disputes. Increasing specificity in newer treaties then provides a greater assurance that if certain circumstances arise, the decision will more likely be decided in a certain manner. The pivotal point in this regard, however, is consideration of why not all states have added more specific provisions to the negotiated BITs if there is concern regarding tribunal interpretations of current provisions. This difference in length marks one of the key existing variations in treaty writing style, and therefore suggests a certain lack of consistency in protections from one state to another as provisions regarding frivolous claims, limits on standards of protections, and expropriation provisions develop in different detail. However, when considering soft law codification, it must be kept in mind that the increase in length is generally only in Canadian and US BITs – thus direct response to intricacies in domestic jurisprudence and to their experience in cases brought under NAFTA Chapter 11.

2. Preambles

BITs have preambles to serve the general purpose of providing the goal for the treaty that follows but offering no binding commitments.[80] In nearly all of those preambles three common elements are noted: 1) creation of favourable conditions for investment; 2) reciprocal encouragement or cooperation; and 3) stimulating business or economic development. This basic language logically follows the most basic goals for concluding a BIT: promotion and protection of investments.[81] Although some BITs have maintained a short preamble that incorporates these elements, some treaties have included additional detail. This detail may acknowledge non-investment issues, such as protection of environment or human rights, as will be discussed later in this chapter.

The most recent US Model BIT includes a clause that states: 'Desiring to achieve these objectives in a manner consistent with the protection of health, safety, and the environment, and the promotion of internationally

---

[80] Our research has not uncovered any exceptions to this statement – albeit exceptions may exist.

[81] Salacuse, above n 2, 109–11.

recognized labor rights.'[82] Some of the additional preamble language was introduced at key historical moments. Language regarding labour rights, for example, was included in some treaties during the rapid expansion of BITs in Central and Eastern Europe in the early 1990s as will be discussed more specifically below. The US-Czechoslovakia BIT – later continued as two separate BITs with the Czech Republic and the Slovak Republic respectively – provides in the preamble:

> Convinced that private enterprise operating within free and open markets offers the best opportunities for raising living standards and the quality of life for the inhabitants of the Parties, improving the well-being of workers, and promoting overall respect for internationally recognized worker rights [. . .][83]

Other treaties, most often when the parties have a historic relationship, include language that notes a desire to strengthen ties of friendship. The Dutch-South Africa BIT expressly refers to the 'traditional ties of friendship'.[84] The Netherlands-Indonesia BIT includes similar language: 'Bearing in mind the friendly and cooperative relations existing between the two countries and their peoples'. This express reference to 'friendship' in these treaties alludes to the earlier FCNs. The FCN preambles consistently pointed to the goal of 'strengthening the bonds of friendship', as stated in the US-German FCN which entered into force in 1956.[85] In contrast, however, the much earlier 1855 FCN signed between Argentina and the United States only refers to friendship in reference to the treaty itself, not as a special goal in the preamble.[86]

---

[82] 2004 US Model Treaty, Treaty Between the Government of the United States of America and the Government of [Country] Concerning the Encouragement and Reciprocal Protection of Investment, available at <http://ustraderep.gov/assets/Trade_Sectors/Investment/Model_BIT/asset_upload_file847_6897.pdf>.

[83] Treaty with the Czech and Slovak Federal Republic Concerning the Reciprocal Encouragement and Protection of Investment, 22 October 1991, available at <http://www.unctad.org/sections/dite/iia/docs/bits/czech_us.pdf>.

[84] Agreement between the Government of the Kingdom of the Netherlands and the Government of the Republic of Indonesia on Promotion and Protection of Investment, 1 July 1995, avaliable at <http://www.unctad.org/sections/dite/iia/docs/bits/netherlands_indonesia.pdf>.

[85] Treaty of Friendship, Commerce and Navigation Between the United States of America and the Federal Republic of Germany, signed 29 October 1954, available at <http://usa.usembassy.de/etexts/friendtreaty4555.htm>.

[86] Treaty of Friendship, Commerce and Navigation Between Argentina and the United States, 27 July 1853, available at <http://avalon.law.yale.edu/19th_century/argen02.asp>.

In the treaties concluded in the past two decades, this specific type of diplomatic language has been largely excised. Nonetheless, the free trade agreements signed between the United States and Latin American parties often refer back to this idea of friendship. Notably, the recent Dominican Republic – Central America – United States FTA states in the first line of the preamble that the parties resolve to '[s]trengthen the special bonds of friendship and cooperation among their nations [. . .]'.[87]

Sovereignty is another term used to promote a certain ideal in the treaty. The 1989 Canada-USSR BIT expressly notes the principle of 'sovereignty' in the preamble.[88] The BIT states that 'investment relations should be promoted and economic cooperation strengthened in accordance with the internationally accepted principles of mutual respect for sovereignty, [. . .] and mutual confidence'. The 1989 Ghana-China BIT similarly states in the preamble that the agreement is based on 'principles of mutual respect for sovereignty, equality, and mutual benefit and for the purpose of the development of economic cooperation'.[89]

Although some changes and additions have occurred over the past 50 years, these changes appear more country-specific than indicative of a trend in investment law in general. The 2009 Germany-Pakistan BIT Preamble has changed little from the original 1959 version, only adding the phrase 'Recognizing that an understanding reached between the two States is likely to promote investment, encourage private industrial and financial enterprise and increase the prosperity of both Contracting States'.[90]

As preambles provide no legally binding force, the variation in preambles from one treaty to another often points only to the broader

---

[87] The Dominican Republic – Central America – United States Free Trade Agreement, 5 August 2004, available at <http://www.ustr.gov/trade-agreements/free-trade-agreements/cafta-dr-dominican-republic-central-america-fta/final-text>.

[88] Agreement Between the Government of Canada and the Government of the Union of Soviet Socialist Republics for the Promotion and Reciprocal Protection of Investments, 20 November 1989, available at <http://www.unctad.org/sections/dite/iia/docs/bits/canada_ussr.pdf>.

[89] Agreement Between the Government of the People's Republic of China and the Government of the Republic of Ghana Concerning the Encouragement and Reciprocal Protection of Investments, 12 October 1989, available at <http://www.unctad.org/sections/dite/iia/docs/bits/china_ghana.pdf>.

[90] German-Pakistan Agreement on the Encouragement and Reciprocal Protection of Investments, 1 December 2009; see generally 'Bilateral treaty on the protection and promotion of investments', available at <http://www.pakistan.diplo.de/Vertretung/islamabad/en/05_Business_Economy/1_ExternalEconomicPromotion/Invest_Schutz_Abk_Seite.html>.

political relationship between the countries rather than a real effort by the drafters to include essential values, which would instead be included in substantive articles. However, by defining the object and purpose of the treaty, the preamble serves an important role in interpretation issues.[91] This area has a place in a soft law instrument. Such an instrument would be well served by establishing the impact that the key preamble language plays on treaty interpretation.[92]

3. Authenticity

The next language issue is of a more technical nature, namely situations where an agreement is authentic in more than one language. Based on the international nature of BITs, there is a significant chance that the language spoken by the two parties is different. Thus, provisions must be included to indicate which text is binding in the event of a disagreement. The 1959 Germany-Pakistan BIT provided that the text was equally authentic in both English and German. In the early German generation of BITs, where the agreement was with a country where the official language was not English, the treaty was drafted in German, the language of the contracting party, and English. All texts were considered equally authentic, but if a conflict arose, the English, thus the neutral language, would prevail.[93] Where a common language is spoken in the two countries, the BIT will likely be drafted in that language, provided that it is a recognized treaty language. The official language of the 1965 Belgo-Luxembourg Economic

---

91 See generally *Tokios Tokelės v Ukraine*, ICSID Case No ARB/02/18, available at <http://italaw.com/documents/TokiosAward.pdf>; *SGS Société Générale de Surveillance S.A. v Republic of the Philippines*, Decision on Jurisdiction of 29 January 2004, ICSID Case No ARB/02/6, available at <http://icsid.worldbank.org/ICSID/FrontServlet?requestType=CasesRH&actionVal=-showDoc&docId=DC657_En&caseId=C6>.

92 On the functions and importance of preambles see generally the *Asylum Case (Colombia v Peru)*, Judgment of 20 November 1950, ICJ Rep 1950, 282; *Case Concerning Rights of Nationals of the United States of America in Morocco (France v USA)*, Judgment of 27 August 1952, ICJ Rep 1952, 196; *Golder v United Kingdom*, Judgment of 25 February 1975, ECHR Appl No 4451/70, para 34; Richard Gardiner, *Treaty Interpretation* (OUP 2008) 186 *et seq*., at 192 with further references. Specifically on the content of preambles to investment agreements, see, eg, UNCTAD, *Bilateral Investment Treaties 1995–2006: Trends and Investment Rulemaking* (2007) 3 *et seq*.; Andrew Newcombe and Lluís Paradell, *Law and Practice of Investment Treaties* (Kluwer 2009) 122 *et seq*.

93 See for example Treaty between the Republic of Korea and the Federal Republic of Germany Concerning the Promotion and Reciprocal Protection of Investments, 4 February 1964, available at <http://www.unctad.org/sections/dite/iia/docs/bits/germany_korea.pdf>.

Union and Morocco BIT is French, a language widely spoken by citizens of all three countries, although the national language of Morocco is Arabic and French is only one of three national languages in both Belgium and Luxembourg.[94] Convenience, of course, plays a decisive role in language choice – the more negotiators fluent in a given language, the more likely such a treaty will be authentic in that language.

For example, the Finland-Guatemala BIT exemplifies the technique of using the two official languages and then a third 'international' language in case of dispute.[95] The agreement is equally authentic in Finnish, Spanish and English. Where a conflict arises, the English text prevails. The general pattern for authenticity of text is in both languages of the contracting parties plus English or French. Unless the official language of one of the parties is English, the English text is used to resolve any conflicts in interpretation. Some treaties, however, fail to provide one text that prevails where a conflict arises between two equally authentic texts. The Australia-Uruguay BIT, for example, simply provides for equal authenticity in both English and Spanish.[96] This leaves a dangerous gap as the legal interpretation of the treaty may vary from one language to another.

In order for the BIT to be fairly applied, it is important for a neutral language to be used for the final interpretation of the agreement. Without this neutral language, one party may be intentionally or unintentionally placed in a more favourable situation than the other party in the agreement. This result would undermine the system of bilateral protection at its very core by allowing for imbalanced application. When considering this from the perspective of a soft law instrument, the language considered in such an instrument should similarly reflect this neutrality. It also implies that a soft law instrument would necessarily need to take the many languages of BITs and investment chapters into account when providing bases for investment protection.

---

94 Accord Entre le Gouvernement du Royaume du Maroc et l'Union Economique Belgo-Luxembourgeoise Concernant l'Encouragement et la Protection Réciproques des Investissements, 13 April 1999, available at <http://www.unctad.org/sections/dite/iia/docs/bits/Morocco_Belgo_Luxembourg_fr.pdf>.

95 Agreement Between the Government of the Republic of Finland and the Government of the Republic of Guatemala on the Promotion and Protection of Investments, 12 April 2005, available at <http://www.unctad.org/sections/dite/iia/docs/bits/finland_guatemala.PDF>.

96 Agreement between Australia and Uruguay on the Promotion and Protection of Investments, 3 September 2001, available at <http://www.unctad.org/sections/dite/iia/docs/bits/australia_uruguay.pdf>.

C. Procedural Provisions

The current study of procedural provisions will be limited specifically to dispute resolution. Such issues as, *inter alia*, amicable settlement procedures, frivolous claims provisions, provisional measures, consolidation of claims, counterclaims, and transparency of proceedings are all important and relevant procedural provisions currently incorporated into BIT articles and investment chapters. The length of the current study unfortunately requires a limit to the relevant issues considered. In this context, the focus of the study will be the dispute resolution provisions, as the greatest consistency and value for a soft law instrument may be developed in this regard. Certainly over the course of the 50 years of modern investment protection instruments, the system has not been uniform. Even now, procedures vary from one treaty to another. This presents certain complications in considering the development of a soft law instrument. The variation in the scope of procedure may lead to unclear results. However, beneath all the variation, there exists a general preference for arbitration under ICSID, ICSID Additional Facility or UNCITRAL Rules. The development of these sets of rules has been the key turning point in the development of the procedural provisions in investment treaties.

1. Basic dispute resolution procedures

The dispute resolution provisions have advanced and – at times – again retracted over the course of the past 50 years of investment protection. Emerging from the FCNs which provided for resolution between the state parties, the new instruments of investment protection required recognition of the inherently private nature of an investment. Arbitration has been considered the most favourable dispute resolution technique for much of the recent life of investment protection instruments. By providing a forum outside the home courts, issues of lack of impartiality or immunity could generally be avoided.

The early treaties, enacted prior to the establishment of ICSID, utilized the ICJ in the process of settling disputes. The first generation of treaties, for example the Germany-Pakistan treaty, provided that when disputes arose concerning the interpretation or application of the treaty, such disputes would be taken to the ICJ for settlement if agreed by both parties. The process, however, was to begin with consultation between the state parties in order to find a solution 'in the spirit of friendship'.[97] Where the

---

[97] Germany-Pakistan, Treaty for the Promotion and Protection of Investments, 25 November 1959, above n 56.

parties could not agree on a settlement at the ICJ, the treaty provided that disputes could be resolved by arbitration. This arbitration would be resolved by three arbitrators; the arbitrators would be chosen in the usual mixed commission manner. If the parties failed to appoint an arbitrator, then the President of the ICJ, or Vice President, if a conflict arose, would appoint instead. If the dispute was to be settled by an arbitral tribunal, the tribunal could determine its own rules of procedure. This allowance of choosing procedure filled the gap as no widely accepted investment arbitration rules were yet in place.

There is now, however, a general conformity regarding the binding arbitration mechanisms for investor-state dispute resolution. ICSID as well as ICSID Additional Facility Rules have become common in BITs because of the ICSID Convention's well-developed system designed specifically for the resolution of investment disputes.[98] The UNCITRAL Rules are also often incorporated into BIT language, or may be incorporated as an alternative to dispute resolution at ICSID, as in the 2004 US Model BIT.[99] Other arbitral institutions, such as the International Chamber of Commerce, the London Court of International Arbitration and the American Arbitration Association, provide rules that are capable of administering investment arbitration.[100] Likewise, the Stockholm Chamber of Commerce rules are integrated into the Energy Charter Treaty and are popular in BITs signed with former Soviet countries.[101]

Recent dispute settlement chapters in FTAs also provide alternatives to binding arbitration. Australia has traditionally been hesitant to engage in investment protection generally and binding investor-state arbitration specifically. In April 2011, the Australian government issued a Trade Policy Statement in which it indicated that it would no longer include investor-state dispute resolution provisions in its BITs or FTAs.[102]

---

[98] August Reinisch and Loretta Malintoppi, 'Methods of Dispute Resolution' in Peter Muchlinski, Federico Ortino and Christoph Schreuer (eds), (OUP 2008) *The Oxford Handbook of International Investment Law*, 691–720, 692.

[99] See generally, ibid, 693; Treaty between the Government of the US and the Government of [country] Concerning the Encouragement and Reciprocal Protection of Investment, 2004 US Model BIT, available at <http://www.state.gov/documents/organization/117601.pdf>.

[100] Reinisch and Malintoppi, above n 98, 708.

[101] Ibid, 709.

[102] Gillard Government Trade Policy Statement: Trading our way to more jobs and prosperity, April 2011, available at <http://www.dfat.gov.au/publications/trade/trading-our-way-to-more-jobs-and-prosperity.html#investor-state>.

Limitations on dispute resolution, however, applied in the agreements even before this new policy was issued. The investment chapter of the 2005 Australia-US FTA[103] exemplifies the caution in its investment protection instrument. This agreement does not include the right of an investor to bring a dispute directly against the state; instead it permits the state to bring a dispute to the other state on behalf of the investor. This type of caution, however, could be considered as a compromise where parties have an equal interest in not being taken to an arbitral tribunal by an investor and protecting the investor in the foreign state. This also could be a compromise procedure for two countries with highly developed legal systems.

A cautious approach to dispute resolution has been similarly incorporated into the Japan-Philippines Economic Partnership Agreement.[104] Japan has negotiated only 14 BITs. Although the substantive protections in the Agreement are expansive 'it confines itself with regard to potential international remedies available to foreign investors to stipulate in Article 107 (1) that the contracting parties "shall enter into negotiations after the date of entry into force of this Agreement to establish a mechanism for the settlement of an investment dispute between a Party and an investor of the other Party"'.[105] When parties fail to agree on a mechanism for resolving the dispute, arbitration or conciliation can only be used upon mutual consent of both parties, 'adding in a so far quite unusually explicit manner that "[t]his means that the disputing Party may, at its option or discretion, grant or deny its consent in respect of each particular investment dispute and that, in the absence of the express written consent of the disputing party, an international conciliation or arbitration tribunal shall have no jurisdiction over the investment dispute involved"'.[106]

---

103 Australia-United States Free Trade Agreement, 1 January 2005, available at <http://www.dfat.gov.au/fta/ausfta/final-text/index.html>.

104 Agreement between Japan and the Republic of the Philippines for an Economic Partnership, 9 September 2006, available at <http://www.mofa.go.jp/region/asia-paci/philippine/epa0609/index.html>; see also Luke Nottage, 'The Rise and Possible Fall of Investor-State Arbitration in Asia: A Skeptic's View of Australia's "Gaillard Government Trade Policy Statement"' in Sydney Law School, Legal Studies Research Paper No 11/32, June 2011.

105 Karsten Nowrot, 'International Investment Law and the Republic of Ecuador: From Arbitral Bilateralism to Judicial Regionalism' (May 2010) 22, available at <http://www.wirtschaftsrecht.uni-halle.de/sites/default/files/altbestand/Heft_96.pdf>.

106 Nowrot, above n 105, 22.

This resistance to arbitration is not universal among countries, and the resistance is not even consistent within countries. In this regard, the 2004 Japan-Mexico FTA does not contain similar reservations to the process of arbitration.[107] Section 2 of the agreement, which covers investment disputes, provides for settlement of disputes by arbitration in the standard typically provided for in BITs. In this agreement, Article 79 provides that following a written request for consultations, disputes may be submitted under ICSID, the ICSID Additional Facility, UNCITRAL, or any other arbitration rules agreed upon by the parties.

In addition to these recent exceptions regarding treaty provisions, the choice of Bolivia and Venezuela to withdraw from the ICSID Convention presents an additional question as to whether future instruments will be as reliant on ICSID resolution methods.[108]

Despite the significance of the above-noted exceptions in the recent conclusion of several investment protection instruments, there is a general uniformity in choice of dispute resolution, in particular investor-state dispute resolution in ICSID, under the UNCITRAL Rules or administered by another arbitration institution. The development of this type of dispute resolution also demonstrates the importance of the development of external soft law instruments, namely arbitration rules, as a means for supporting the various aspects of investor-state dispute settlement.

D. Substantive Issues

This section on substance is divided into two areas, first dealing with investment-related substantive issues, including definitions, and second turning to non-investment issues that have begun to be incorporated into the agreements. Notably, expropriation is dealt with in detail elsewhere in this volume.[109] The development of these issues over time indicates both regularity and differences in the substantive protections of the agreements. A line, however, runs through all agreements. This line of protections closely reflects the protections of the first BITs. Thus, even where the treaties have significantly expanded or where additional detail informs the provisions, these core protections often remain intact.

---

[107] Agreement between Japan and the United Mexican States for the Strengthening of the Economic Partnership, 17 September 2004, available at <http://www.mofa.go.jp/region/latin/mexico/agreement/agreement.pdf>.

[108] See generally Tietje, Nowrot and Wackernagel, above n 61.

[109] See August Reinisch, Chapter 10, this volume.

1. Definitions

On a basic level, the most common terms to be defined in the agreement are a) 'investor', b) 'investment', c) 'territory' and d) 'returns'. These four definitions are included in the majority of BITs drafted. Some BITs certainly include more, typically BITs drafted by NAFTA countries. Notably, the US Model[110] and the current Canadian treaties[111] include a much more extensive list of definitions, adding specificity and detail as well as defining terms that are often subject to further clarification in specific articles.

The reliability of the four basic definitions and general uniformity in the way that these four terms have been defined, even when additional definitions are present, ensure a solid basis for consideration in a soft law instrument.

a. 'Investor'

The definition for investor typically provides details of who is a juridical person under the laws of each state. The German-Jordan BIT provides a basic example of this style:

> (3) The term 'investors' shall mean
> a) in respect of the Federal Republic of Germany:
> – Germans within the meaning of the Basic Law of the Federal Republic of Germany,
> – any juridical person as well as any commercial or other company or association with or without legal personality having its seat in the territory of the Federal Republic of Germany, irrespective of whether or not its activities are directed at profit;
> b) in respect of the Hashemite Kingdom of Jordan:
> – a natural person who is a national of the Hashemite Kingdom of Jordan in accordance with its legislation;
> – legal persons or other entities, including companies, corporations, business associations and partnerships which are constituted or otherwise duly

---

[110] Notably, the 2004 US Model Treaty also includes definitions for central level of government, claimant, covered investment, enterprise as well as enterprise of a Party, existing, freely usable currency, government procurement, investment agreement, investment authorization, measure, national, non-disputing Party, person, person of a Party, protected information, regional level of government, respondent, and state enterprise.

[111] Canada's Foreign Investment Protection and Promotion Agreement (FIPAs) Negotiating Programme, available at <http://www.international.gc.ca/trade-agreements-accords-commerciaux/agr-acc/fipa-apie/what_fipa.aspx?lang=en#structure&menu_id=45>; see generally Andrew Newcombe, 'Canada's New Model Foreign Investment Protection Agreement (August 2004)', available at <http://ita.law.uvic.ca/documents/CanadianFIPA.pdf>.

organized under the legislation of the Hashemite Kingdom of Jordan and have their effective economic activities in its territory.[112]

The definition often expressly includes natural persons as well as businesses or other associations that have incorporated under the laws of a particular state thus covering both natural and legal persons.[113] The treaty establishing COMESA, for example, provides definitions of both 'natural persons' and 'juridical persons'.[114] The ASEAN-Australia-New Zealand FTA defines investor simply as 'a natural person of a Party or a juridical person of a Party that seeks to make, is making, or has made an investment in the territory of another Party'.[115] The definition includes a footnote that clarifies the terms:

> For greater certainty, the Parties understand that an investor that 'seeks to make' an investment refers to an investor of another Party that has taken active steps to make an investment. Where a notification or approval process is required for making an investment, an investor that 'seeks to make' an investment refers to an investor of another Party that has initiated such notification or approval process.[116]

The US Model BIT makes an express distinction between an investor of a Party and an investor of a non-Party.[117] Where Parties have expressly excluded third party protection under the definition of investment, they may choose to similarly reaffirm this exclusion under the definition section. The Australia-China BIT provides that the Agreement 'shall not apply to a company organised under the law of a third country . . . [or] to a person who is a permanent resident but not a citizen of the Contracting Party', if the protection provisions have been elsewhere invoked or the person is a citizen of the other Contracting Party.[118]

---

[112] Agreement between the Federal Republic of Germany and the Hashemite Kingdom of Jordan concerning the Encouragement and Reciprocal Protection of Investment, 13 November 2007, available at <http://www.unctad.org/sections/dite/iia/docs/bits/germany_jordan.pdf>.

[113] UNCTAD (2007) 13.

[114] The Common Market for Eastern and Southern Africa Treaty, 5 November 1993, available at <http://about.comesa.int/attachments/comesa_treaty_en.pdf>.

[115] Agreement Establishing the ASEAN-Australia-New Zealand Free Trade Area, 27 February 2009, available at <http://dfat.gov.au/fta/aanzfta/aanzfta.PDF>.

[116] ASEAN-Australia-New Zealand FTA, Chapter 11, Article 2.

[117] US Model BIT, 2004.

[118] Agreement between the Government of Australia and the Government of

It should be noted that some tribunals have incorporated additional requirements based on customary international law into the definition of investment, beyond what is expressly noted by the definition. In this regard, the *Phoenix* tribunal found an obligation for the parties to invest in accordance with the host state's laws, citing obligations of good faith.[119] Although this exemplifies the close relationship between customary international law and investment law, other tribunals have not found a similar requirement.[120]

b. 'Investment'

Most treaties provide a brief definition of investment before listing several examples of what could include an investment – with most treaties also noting that the list is not exhaustive. The 2003 Canadian Model BIT provides a finite list of covered investments and then provides examples of what is not covered under the definition of investment. This style for defining 'investment' is a well-accepted way to reduce the scope of investment in BITs.[121]

A typical definition states that the 'term "investment" means every kind of asset invested directly or indirectly by investors of one Contracting Party in the territory of the other Contracting Party', as stated in the Germany-China BIT.[122] Decisions about whether to include language noting both direct and indirect investments varies between treaties. The 2005 Czech Republic-China BIT[123] offers of an example of a treaty that does not expressly address direct and indirect investments, but provides a simple definition similar to other treaties.

> The term 'investment' means every kind of asset invested in connection with

---

the People's Republic of China on the Reciprocal Encouragement and Protection of Investments, 11 July 1988, available at <http://www.unctad.org/sections/dite/iia/docs/bits/australia_china.pdf>.

119 *Phoenix Action Ltd v the Czech Republic*, Award of 15 April 2009, ICSID Case No ARB/06/5, paras 100–1.

120 *Saba Fakes v Republic of Turkey*, Award of 14 July 2010, ICSID Case No ARB/07/20, para 110.

121 UNCTAD (2007) 11.

122 Agreement between the People's Republic of China and the Federal Republic of Germany on the Encouragement and Reciprocal Protection of Investments, 1 December 2003, available at <http://www.unctad.org/sections/dite/iia/docs/bits/china_germany.pdf>.

123 Agreement between the Czech Republic and the People's Republic of China on the Promotion and Protection of Investments, 8 December 2005, available at <http://www.unctad.org/sections/dite/iia/docs/bits/China_czechrep.PDF>.

economic activities by investors of one Contracting Party in accordance with the laws and regulations of the other Contracting Party in the territory of the latter, and in particularly [sic], though not exclusively, includes:

(a) movable and immovable property and other property rights such as mortgages, pledges and liens;

(b) shares, debentures, stocks or any other form of participation in a company;

(c) claims to money or to any other performance having an economic value associated with an investment;

(d) intellectual property rights which mean trade-marks, patents, industry designs, technical processes, know-how, trade secrets, trade names and goodwill associated with an investment;

(e) business concessions conferred by law or under contract permitted by law, including concessions to search for, cultivate, extract or exploit natural resources.

Any change in the form in which assets are invested does not affect their character as investments.[124]

c. 'Territory'

The definition of territory usually follows the general international law definition and thus includes the territorial sea, the exclusive economic zone and continental shelf, and anywhere else the country exercises sovereignty. Indeed contracting parties consistently refer to the idea of 'sovereignty' to establish what area is within a Party's territory.

Some of the earliest treaties contain no definition, instead fully relying on the accepted definitions in international law. The 1964 German-Korea BIT,[125] for example, relies heavily on the concept of territory, but does not define it. Similarly, the 1991 Czech-US BIT does not provide a separate definition of territory, but references the legal concept of territory in several provisions, including the most-favoured-nation provision.[126]

The issue of defining 'territory' is mixed in some of the more recent treaties. German treaties generally limit definitions to investment, investor

---

[124] Agreement between the Czech Republic and the People's Republic of China on the Promotion and Protection of Investments, above n 123, Art 1.

[125] Treaty between the Republic of Korea and the Federal Republic of Germany concerning the Promotion and Reciprocal Protection of Investments, 4 February 1964, available at <http://www.unctad.org/sections/dite/iia/docs/bits/germany_korea.pdf>.

[126] Article II (3) provides 'Subject to the laws relating to the entry and sojourn of aliens, nationals of either Party shall be permitted to enter and to remain in the territory of the other Party for the purpose of establishing, developing, administering or advising on the operation of an investment to which they, or a company of the first Party that employs them, have committed or are in the process of committing a substantial amount of capital or other resources.'

and returns, offering no definition for territory.[127] The Czech Republic-China BIT provides an example of a definition similar to other treaties. In reference to the Czech Republic, it notes that the territory includes the 'territory of the Czech Republic over which it exercises sovereignty, sovereign rights and jurisdiction in accordance with international law'.[128] The definition maintains that territory is determined by sovereignty.

d. 'Returns'

The 1959 Germany-Pakistan BIT provided a bare definition for returns to include: 'the amounts derived from investments as profits or interest for a specified period'.[129] By 1974, the language of the German BITs had been modified an insignificant degree: 'The term "returns" shall mean the amounts yielded by an investment for a definite period as profit or interest.'[130]

By the 1988 Australia-China treaty, the definition gained a form much more similar to its current definition in many treaties: '"Returns" means an amount derived from or associated with an investment, including profits, dividends, interest, capital gains, royalty payments, management or technical assistance feeds, payment in kind and all other lawful income.'[131] The 1993 Argentina-Finland Treaty defines the concept as '[...] the amount yielded by an investment, and in particular, though not exclusively, shall include capital gains, profits, interests, dividends, royalties, fees or other current incomes'.[132] Now the German BITs often provide the definition of 'returns' as 'amounts yielded by an investment for

---

[127] See for example the 2007 Germany-Jordan treaty. Agreement between the Federal Republic of Germany and the Hashemite Kingdom of Jordan concerning the Encouragement and Reciprocal Protection of Investment, 13 November 2007, above n 112.

[128] Agreement between the Czech Republic and the People's Republic of China on the Promotion and Protection of Investments, above n 123.

[129] Germany-Pakistan, Treaty for the Promotion and Protection of Investments, 25 November 1959, above n 56.

[130] Treaty between Malta and the Federal Republic of Germany Concerning the Encouragement and Reciprocal Protection of Investments, Art 8, 17 September 1974, available at <http://www.unctad.org/sections/dite/iia/docs/bits/germany_-malta.pdf>.

[131] Agreement between the Government of Australia and the Government of the People's Republic of China on the Reciprocal Encouragement and Protection of Investments, above n 118.

[132] Agreement between the Government of the Republic of Finland and the Government of the Republic of Argentina on the Promotion and Reciprocal Protection of Investments, 5 November 1993, available at <http://www.unctad.org/sections/dite/iia/docs/bits/argentina_finland.pdf>.

a definite period, such as profit, dividends, interest, royalties or fees'.[133] Generally, the definition states that returns are 'amounts yielded by an investment' and then includes a list of amounts. This list is typically not exhaustive. The 2004 US Model BIT does not include a definition of returns, but includes the concept of returns in Article 7 on Transfers.[134]

2. Standards of treatment

Standards of treatment include the 'rights and privileges granted and the obligations and burdens imposed'.[135] General standards of treatment include all facets of the investment's activities in the host country.[136] Absolute standards included in this category include 'fair and equitable treatment' as well as 'full protection and security' and 'treatment in accordance with international law'.[137]

a. Fair and equitable treatment

Fair and equitable treatment is a common standard of treatment included in BITs and investment chapters.[138] The fair and equitable treatment standard had already been used in the Havana Charter of 1948; namely Article 11(2) of the Charter provided that the International Trade Organization would have power to promote agreements designed to 'assure just and equitable treatment for the enterprise, skills, capital, arts and technology brought from one Member country to another'.[139] This Charter, of course, never went into force. In fact, none of the early multilateral treaties that attempted to incorporate the term was ever actually enacted. Nonetheless, the term has become embedded in

[133] See for example, Treaty between the Federal Republic of Germany and the Kingdom of Bahrain concerning the Encouragement and Reciprocal Protection of Investments, 5 February 2007, available at <http://www.unctad.org/sections/dite/iia/docs/bits/germany_bahrain.pdf>.

[134] US Model BIT, 2004.

[135] *Anglian Water Group (AWG) PLC v Argentina*, Award of 3 August 2006, UNCITRAL, para 55.

[136] Salacuse, above n 2, 205.

[137] Salacuse, above n 2, 206.

[138] Katia Yannaca-Small, 'Fair and Equitable Treatment Standard: Recent Developments' in August Reinisch (ed), *Standards of Investment Protection* (OUP 2008) 111–30, 113.

[139] UNCTAD, *International Investment Instruments: A Compendium* (vol I, 1996) 4, as cited in Salacuse, above n 2, 218; Final Act of the United Nations Conference on Trade and Employment: Havana Charter for an International Trade Organization, 24 March 1948, available at <http://www.worldtradelaw.net/misc/havana.pdf>.

customary international law.[140] There is a debate, however, on the extent of coverage arising out of this provision.[141] One argument is that it is merely a subset of the minimum standard of treatment in customary international law (the approach favoured by NAFTA and by the United States and Canada in their model BITs); the other is that 'fair and equitable' treatment is a stand-alone provision that might accord a higher level of attention. A third interpretation incorporates the standard from customary international law as a minimum, providing that the protection should not go below that standard.

As early as the post-WWII FCNs, the United States began incorporating the principle of fair and equitable treatment into the language of the agreements.[142] The inclusion of this principle has continued. This provision has different names and appearances in different BITs. The BIT between the Czech Republic and China of 8 December 2005, for example, calls this provision the 'Promotion and Protection of Investment'.[143] Naturally this provision connects to the preamble and the intention of the investment.

> 1. Each Contracting Party shall encourage and create favourable conditions for investors of the other Contracting Party to make investments in its territory and shall admit such investments in accordance with its laws and regulations.
> 2. Investments of the investors of either Contracting Party shall at all times be accorded fair and equitable treatment and shall enjoy full protection and security in the territory of the other Contracting Party.[144]

The Germany-Jordan BIT includes a similar provision in Article 2, entitled 'Promotion and Admission'. This article details that promotion of the investment should include fair and equitable treatment of the investments, and that investments shall not be 'impair[ed] by arbitrary or discriminatory measures'.

---

140 Salacuse, above n 2, 219.

141 For further information on the extensive debate on the coverage of fair and equitable treatment, see Christoph Schreuer, 'Fair and Equitable Treatment in Arbitral Practice' (2005) *Journal of World Investment & Trade* 360; Ioana Tudor, *The Fair and Equitable Treatment Standard in the International Law of Foreign Investment* (OUP 2008) 33.

142 Robert R Wilson, *United States Commercial Treaties and International Law* (Hauser 1960) 120 as cited in Salacuse, above n 2, 219.

143 Agreement between the Czech Republic and the People's Republic of China on the Promotion and Protection of Investments, 8 December 2005, available at <http://www.unctad.org/sections/dite/iia/docs/bits/China_czechrep.PDF>.

144 Ibid.

The provision can also be minimalistic, as in the Argentina-Australia BIT, which simply provides: 'Each contracting Party shall at all times ensure fair and equitable treatment to investments.'[145] This simplistic model is followed also in the recent Chinese BITs, including the 2004 China-Latvia BIT: 'Investments of investors of each Contracting Party shall all the time be accorded fair and equitable treatment in the territory of the other Contracting Party.'[146]

The provision lacks a certain level of specificity that is found in other provisions, instead providing a provision that is subject to interpretation by tribunals. '[I]ts very vagueness and generality endow it with a flexibility that will permit it to evolve in light of experience by investors, host countries, and international arbitration tribunals.'[147] Thus the specific facts of the case allow for this fair and equitable treatment standard to be interpreted on a case-by-case basis.

There is a reliance placed on the interpretation of the principle in customary international law, even where there is no express reference to customary international law in the treaty provisions.[148] Certain treaties, including NAFTA, make an express reference to international law, but it is arguable that this protection may also extend beyond what is provided in customary international law.[149] Some states have carefully constructed the provision in order to better anticipate such modified interpretations.

Several early cases under NAFTA raised the question of the meaning of fair and equitable treatment under that treaty. NAFTA Article 1105

---

[145] Tudor, above n 141, 24; Agreement between the Government of Australia and the Government of the Argentine Republic on the Promotion and Protection of Investments, and Protocol, Art 4, 23 August 1995, available at <http://www.unctad.org/sections/dite/iia/docs/bits/argentina_australia.pdf>.

[146] Agreement Between the Government of the People's Republic of China and the Government of the Republic of Latvia on the Promotion and Protection of Investments, 15 April 2004, Art 3, available at <http://www.unctad.org/sections/dite/iia/docs/bits/China_Latvia.pdf>.

[147] Salacuse, above n 2, 228.

[148] Todd Grierson-Weiler and Ian A Laird, 'Standards of Treatment' in Peter Muchlinski, Federico Ortino and Christoph Schreuer (eds), *The Oxford Handbook of International Investment Law* (OUP 2008) 259–304, 264.

[149] Katia Yannaca-Small, 'Fair and Equitable Treatment Standard: Recent Developments', in August Reinisch (ed), *Standards of Investment Protection* (OUP 2008) 113; see also Salacuse, above n 2, 226. Professor Wälde noted the growth of the fair and equitable treatment standard in the *International Thunderbird Gaming Corporation* Decision. See *International Thunderbird Gaming Corporation v Mexico*, Award of 26 January 2006, UNCITRAL (NAFTA), Separate Opinion, para 37, as cited in Yannaca-Small.

requires 'treatment in accordance with international law, including fair and equitable treatment and full protection and security', and the provision is entitled 'Minimum Standard of Treatment'. It follows that the standard has been interpreted in NAFTA in accordance with international law.[150] In order to be sure that the 'fair and equitable treatment' standard in NAFTA was interpreted as a subset of the international minimum standard of treatment at customary international law, the NAFTA Free Trade Commission adopted an interpretation providing that 'The concepts of "fair and equitable treatment" and "full protection and security" do not require treatment in addition to or beyond that which is required by the customary international law minimum standard of treatment of aliens.'[151] Several US BITs include a provision in the preamble that states 'agreeing [...] that fair and equitable treatment of investment is desirable in order to maintain a stable framework for investment and maximum effective use of economic resources'.[152]

The lack of clarity about the precise definition of fair and equitable treatment led to cautious conclusions by the US subcommittee on recommendations for a future model BIT: 'A common concern was that, though the term "customary international law" is used frequently in the international legal community, there was little agreement in the international legal community as to its precise scope with respect to the minimum standard of treatment.'[153] In addition, the definition has been

---

[150] Rudolf Dolzer, 'Fair and Equitable Treatment: A Key Standard in Investment Treaties' (2005) 39 *International Lawyer* 87, 92: see also Patrick Dumberry, 'The Quest to Define "Fair and Equitable Treatment" for Investors under International Law: The Case of the NAFTA Chapter 11 Pope & Talbot Awards' (4/2002) 3 *The Journal of World Investment* 657, 665.

[151] Notes of Interpretation of Certain Chapter 11 Provisions (NAFTA Free Trade Commission, 31 July 2001) <http://www.international.gc.ca/trade-agreements-accords-commerciaux/disp-diff/NAFTA-Interpr.aspx?lang=en&view=d> accessed 28 October 2011.

[152] See generally Tudor, above n 141, Appendix I.

[153] Report of the Subcommittee on Investment of the Advisory Committee on International Economic Policy Regarding the Model Bilateral Investment Treaty, 30 September 2009, Presented to: The Department of State, available at <http://www.state.gov/r/pa/prs/ps/2009/sept/130097.htm>: 'Various members of the Subcommittee expressed different views on what the minimum standard of treatment obligation should entail as well as how that obligation should be defined. Some Subcommittee members believe the Administration should consider codifying the position taken by the State Department in a recent arbitral proceeding, Glamis Gold Ltd. v. United States. Regarding the content of the minimum standard of treatment under customary international law, the State Department argued that state practice and opinio juris had established minimum standards of treatment in only a 'few areas' and provided examples of those areas.'

refined further in the US Model and the recent FTAs to specify which obligations are included, namely justice in 'criminal, civil, or administrative adjudicatory proceedings' relying on principles of due process. In BITs where the interpretation could extend beyond the standard set by customary international law, this only provides the foundation from where the standard can be derived.[154] Depending on the preamble and the interpretation of that language by the tribunal, such increased protection may in fact be common usage outside of NAFTA and through BIT practice represent the development of a higher standard in general customary international law.

There is a distinction in this provision depending on the countries signing the agreement. When a BIT is signed between two developed countries, the provision is most often included in the treatment section; however, when the BIT is signed between one developed country and one developing, 'fair and equitable treatment' is often included in the provisions regarding promotion of investments.[155]

b. Full protection and security

The provisions for full protection and security are typically applied when civil unrest or violence interferes with the investment, but are in fact rarely used.[156] Moreover, the incorporation of full protection and security into BITs and investment chapters lacks consistency. There are several ways that such provisions are incorporated into the BITs and investment chapters,[157] often reflecting language differences. The following are several examples of differences in word choice as noted by Cordero-Moss: investments shall be accorded 1) fair and equitable treatment and shall enjoy full protection and security;[158] 2) full legal protection and full legal

[154] See generally Dolzer, above n 150, 97.

[155] Tudor, above n 141, 29.

[156] Giuditta Cordero-Moss, 'Full Protection and Security', in Reinisch (ed) *Standards of Investment Protection* (OUP 2008) 131–50, 131.

[157] Ibid, 133–4.

[158] Agreement between the Government of the United Kingdom of Great Britain and Northern Ireland and the Government of the Arab Republic of Egypt for the Promotion and Protection of Investments, 11 June 1975, available at <http://www.unctad.org/sections/dite/iia/docs/bits/egypt_uk.pdf>, Article 2(2); Agreement between the Government of the United Kingdom of Great Britain and Northern Ireland and the Government of the Democratic Socialist Republic of Sri Lanka for the Promotion and Protection of Investments, 13 February 1980, available at <http://www.unctad.org/sections/dite/iia/docs/bits/srilanka_uk.pdf> Article II 2(a).

security;[159] 3) fair and equitable treatment and shall not be impaired by unreasonable or discriminatory measures;[160] 4) full protection and security in accordance with the principle of fair and equitable treatment;[161] and 5) full protection and security and shall in no case be accorded treatment less than that required by international law.[162]

BITs have similarly included language providing for exceptions to the protection provided in the BIT for reasons of international security and peace.[163] The 2005 US-Uruguay BIT clarifies this provision, requiring in addition to 'full protection and security' that the parties to the treaty will provide 'the level of police protection required under customary international law'.[164]

Variations in wording, however, seem to make little difference in the interpretation of the protection by tribunals.[165] And importantly in

---

[159] Vertrag zwischen der Bundesrepublik Deutschland und der Argentinischen Republik über die Förderung und den gegenseitigen Schutz von Kapitalanlagen, 9 April 1991, available at <http://www.unctad.org/sections/dite/iia/docs/bits/germany_argentina_sp.pdf> Article 4(1).

[160] Agreement on Encouragement and Reciprocal Protection of Investments between the Kingdom of the Netherlands and the Argentine Republic, available at <http://www.unctad.org/sections/dite/iia/docs/bits/netherlands_argentina.pdf > Articles 3.1 and 3.2.

[161] Décret no 93-834 du 28 mai 1993 portant publication de l'accord entre le Gouvernement de la République Française et le Gouvernement de la République Argentine sur l'encouragement et la protection réciproques des investissements (ensemble une declaration), signé à Paris le 3 juillet 1991, available at <http://www.unctad.org/sections/dite/iia/docs/bits/france_argentina_fr.pdf> Article 5.1.

[162] Treaty with the Czech and Slovak Federal Republic Concerning the Reciprocal Encouragement and Protection of Investment, 22 October 1991, available at <http://www.unctad.org/sections/dite/iia/docs/bits/czech_us.pdf> Article II 2(a); Treaty between United States of America and the Argentine Republic Concerning the Reciprocal Encouragement and Protection of Investment, 14 November 1991, available at <http://www.unctad.org/sections/dite/iia/docs/bits/argentina_us.pdf> Article II.2(a); Treaty between the United States of America and the Republic of Turkey concerning the Reciprocal Encouragement and Protection of Investments, 3 December 1985, available at <http://www.unctad.org/sections/dite/iia/docs/bits/us_turkey.pdf> Article II (3).

[163] UNCTAD (2007) 99.

[164] Salacuse, above n 2, 207; Treaty between the United States of America and the Oriental Republic of Uruguay concerning the Encouragement and Reciprocal Protection of Investment, November 2005, available at <http://www.unctad.org/sections/dite/iia/docs/bits/US_Uruguay.pdf>.

[165] Cordero-Moss, above n 156, 135. See *Siemens A.G. v The Argentine Republic*, Award of 6 February 2007, ICSID Case No ARBB/02/8.

consideration of a soft law instrument, the standard that is applied by tribunals seems to be the equivalent of the protection under international law in general.[166]

c. National treatment

National treatment provisions, guaranteeing that the foreign investor will be treated no less favourably than a domestic investor, are included in nearly all BITs. The inclusion of this language is important as customary international law does not require a state to treat aliens in a particular manner.[167] An early example of a treaty that did not include this provision was the Germany-USSR BIT,[168] where arguably the German investors did not have an interest in being treated in the same manner as domestic Soviet investors in the Soviet market. Certainly where nationals are not being treated well, such provision has no benefit. Interestingly, however, the Canadian-USSR BIT from the same time period did include a national treatment provision[169] – perhaps a more forward-thinking treaty on the part of either the Soviets or the Canadians, or simply a copy of the other treaties that were being completed at the time. Regardless of the treatment of nationals, an international minimum standard of treatment exists, ensuring a certain level of protection.[170]

The specific protections – where provided – can vary from one treaty to another, particularly in regard to rights of establishment and protection of both investments and investors.[171]

The investment chapter, Part III, of the Energy Charter Treaty includes a provision providing for national treatment of investors:

> Each Contracting Party shall accord to Investments in its Area of Investors of other Contracting Parties, and their related activities including management,

---

[166] Cordero-Moss, above n 156, 137.

[167] Campbell McLachlan, Laurence Shore and Matthew Weiniger, *International Investment Arbitration: Substantive Principles* (OUP 2007) 7.38.

[168] Federal Republic of Germany and the Union of Soviet Socialist Republics Agreements concerning the promotion and reciprocal protection of investments (with protocol), 13 June 1989, available at <http://www.unctad.org/sections/dite/iia/docs/bits/germany_ussr.pdf>.

[169] Agreement between the Government of Canada and the Government of the Union of Soviet Socialist Republics for the Promotion and Reciprocal Protection of Investments, 20 November 1989, available at <http://www.unctad.org/sections/dite/iia/docs/bits/canada_ussr.pdf>.

[170] Andrea K Bjorklund, 'National Treatment', in August Reinisch (ed) *Standards of Investment Protection* (OUP 2008) 29, 31.

[171] Ibid, 32.

> maintenance, use, enjoyment or disposal, treatment no less favourable than that which it accords to Investments of its own Investors[...]and their related activities including management, maintenance, use, enjoyment or disposal, whichever is the most favourable.[172]

The recent US Model BIT has modified the language of the national treatment provision from protecting foreign investors in 'like situations' to stating that investors in 'like circumstances' will receive the benefits, a reflection of NAFTA language.[173] The recent US agreements concluded with Uruguay[174] and Australia[175] reflect this language. This slight change in language may in fact have no effect on the protections.

E. Non-investment Issues

The 2007 UNCTAD Report noted that one of the recent trends in the development of BIT protection is the extension of the protection from merely traditional investment protection to assurances in regards to health and safety, the environment, labour and security. Some of these additional protections are part of broader human rights standards now being incorporated into BITs, arising from concerns that these basic protections have been neglected for the broader goal of investment protection. Environmental protections, in particular, have gained widespread acceptance in BITs and FTAs in the past decade.[176]

The US Subcommittee on the development of BITs presented a concern for certain human rights values in its 2009 report on the modernizing of the 2004 Model BIT.

> In light of the enhanced effectiveness and considerably expanded scope of application of international investment law, the possibility of disputes increasingly arises which involve impairments of economic interests of foreign

---

172 Energy Charter Treaty, Part III, Art 10(7), available at <http://www.encharter.org/fileadmin/user_upload/document/EN.pdf>.

173 US Model BIT, 2004.

174 Treaty between the United States of America and the Oriental Republic of Uruguay concerning the Encouragement and Reciprocal Protection of Investment, November 2005, available at <http://www.unctad.org/sections/dite/iia/docs/bits/US_Uruguay.pdf>.

175 Australia-United States Free Trade Agreement, 1 January 2005, above n 103.

176 Kathryn Gordon and Joachim Pohl, 'Environmental concerns in international investment agreements: A Survey', OECD Working Papers on International Investment, No 2011/1, OECD Investment Division <www.oecd.org/daf/investment>.

> investors covered by respective protection standards of international investment agreements that are justified by the host state in question under recourse to public interest concerns like the protection of human rights.[177]

At times these additional issues are included in the preambles. The US-Uruguay BIT states in the preamble: 'Desiring to achieve these objectives in a manner consistent with the protection of health, safety, and the environment, and the promotion of consumer protection and internationally recognized labor rights [. . .]'.[178] Similarly, the preamble of the US-Colombia FTA investment chapter includes a provision in regard to the protections of the investors.[179] The language specifically provides that the intention of the investment protections is to 'promote sustainable development'.[180] There is a growing trend, however, to expressly include certain protections in independent articles.[181] Even where the provisions are not expressly included, through VCLT 31(3)(c) these public interests would be protected in the host states 'at least in case they have already found their manifestation in other norms of international law applicable to the parties'.[182]

The US Model BITs have included language on the protection of labour rights, evolving over the course of the BIT programme. Appropriately, the model developed in 1991, intended to be used in negotiations with the emerging free market economies in Eastern Europe, noted the importance of workers' rights. The then current US Model BIT specifically stated in the preamble that 'the development of economic and business ties can contribute to the well-being of workers in both Parties and promote respect for internationally-recognized worker rights'. Later US Model BITs have maintained these objectives while modifying the language.

The US Model BIT, beginning with the 1994 version, includes language

---

177 Nowrot, above n 105, 18.

178 Treaty between the United States of America and the Oriental Republic of Uruguay concerning the Encouragement and Reciprocal Protection of Investment, above n 164.

179 Warren H Maruyama and Charles B Rosenberg, 'The Investment Chapter of the U.S.-Colombia FTA: New Protections for U.S. Investors' (3/2010) 11 *The Journal of World Investment & Trade* 409–118.

180 US-Colombia Trade Promotion Agreement, 22 November 2006, available at <http://www.ustr.gov/trade-agreements/free-trade-agreements/colombia-fta/final-text>.

181 Gordon and Pohl note an increasing trend for environmental protections to be included in the body of the treaty; see Gordon and Pohl, above n 176, 14.

182 Nowrot, above n 105, 34.

in the preamble that directly addresses concerns for health as well as the environment: 'Agreeing that these objectives can be achieved without relaxing health, safety and environmental measures of general application'. The US 2004 Model BIT notes the 'effective utilization of economic resources' as well as the 'protection of health, safety, and the environment, and the promotion of internationally recognized labor rights'. These are concepts that are becoming more prevalent in BITs – certainly in part because of the increasingly recognized importance put on these factors as protections within public international law. The 2004 Model BIT has significantly condensed the labour rights language in the preamble. However, the Model includes a separate article on 'Investment and Labor'. This article explicitly states that 'it is inappropriate to encourage investment by weakening or reducing the protections afforded in domestic labor laws'.[183] 'Investment and the Environment' is also included as a separate article. This inclusion of the principles as a separate article ensures that parties have a greater opportunity to in fact use and promote those goals.

The Netherlands-Costa Rica BIT is another example of these additional human rights issues being addressed:

> The provisions of this Agreement shall, from the date of entry into force thereof, apply to all investments made, whether before or after its entry into force, by investors of one Contracting Party in the territory of the other Contracting Party in accordance with the laws and regulations of the latter Contracting Party, including its laws and regulations on labour and environment.[184]

The concepts have also become integrated into the agreement for the creation of the Common Market for Eastern and Southern Africa. The agreement

> establishes the COMESA Common Investment Area Committee, being entrusted, inter alia, with the task of making recommendations on the 'development of common standards relating to investment in areas such as: (i) environmental impact and social impact assessments; (ii) labour standards; (iii) respect for human rights; (iv) conduct in conflict zones' and on the issue of corruption (Article 7 (2) lit. d).[185]

---

[183] US Model BIT (2004), Art 13.

[184] Agreement on encouragement and reciprocal protection of investments between the Republic of Costa Rica and the Kingdom of the Netherlands, 1999, available at <http://www.unctad.org/sections/dite/iia/docs/bits/netherlands_costarica.pdf>, as cited in Gordon and Pohl, above n 176, 15.

[185] Nowrot, above n 105, 21–2.

This recent trend of incorporating human rights issues into investment agreements highlights an important aspect to be considered in the development of a soft law instrument. Although the core purpose of an investment protection agreement is the protection and promotion of investments, the interrelated nature of economics and human rights cannot be ignored. Of particular importance in this respect is the incorporation of environmental protection as an interrelated aspect of investment protection.[186] The close interconnection between these extra-investment protections suggests that these issues are beginning to be seen as essential elements of investment protection. Thus, the protection of investments cannot be separated from these additional issues, and certainly the trend leads more in the direction of such a relationship. This connection indicates that a soft law instrument should include consideration of such extra-investment issues and how they interact with and mould investment protection in general.

CONCLUSIONS

This historical development of the investment protection mechanisms, in earlier treaties as well as the evolution in the BIT process, opens ground for a more in-depth consideration of a multilateral soft law instrument in the form of a model treaty available to all states. The development identifies a structure that persists despite the varied investment goals reflected in different treaties. It is clear that such an instrument would need to take into account the variations that occur in both the language and the extent of protections. Investment treaties have been drafted based on the autonomy of state parties to enter into the agreements that best fit their distinct relationship, and in order to fully meet the goals of investment protection, such an instrument cannot be blind to the parties' own investment goals. Nonetheless, significant common ground exists, and it is from this common ground that a soft law instrument will succeed.

This chapter has set out a framework for the construction of a soft law instrument, identifying the essential provisions that currently form the architecture of investment protection. The common provisions which do offer general uniformity across BITs and investment chapters can offer a broad starting point for development of a soft law instrument, thus providing the basic outline for the specificity provided in the complementary chapters of this project.

---

[186] See Kate Miles, Chapter 5, this volume.

As the number of BITs increases and the general uniformity grows, the relevance of this soft law instrument becomes clearer and offers more benefit to the development of investment practice. Although this chapter provides architecture for the general uniformity of these developments, it also offers caution, particularly in regard to the development of investment protection language across various legal traditions and the need for levels of specificity in various provisions. Importantly, the study also identifies the newly emerging issues protected in investment treaties but going beyond basic investment protection, indicating a transformation in investment protection. Any successful soft law instrument must necessarily take these important complexities into account.

9. Is the MFN principle in international investment law ripe for multilateralization or codification?

Andreas R. Ziegler*

1. INTRODUCTION

The most-favoured-nation (MFN) principle, standard or treatment is a very traditional legal rule in international (economic) law. It has normally been included in treaties having an economic character for centuries. With regard to modern investment treaties and their predecessors (e.g. Treaties on Friendship, Commerce and Navigation or Establishment) this holds equally true. There is hardly a modern BIT that would not contain a reference to MFN and most multilateral or regional codification projects have included this principle.

At the same time, it must be noted that the formulations used to incorporate this principle are by no means uniform. A wide variety of models and specific formulations exist. While it was in the past generally thought that this was a purely linguistic problem – more due to different traditions and pragmatism of the negotiators rather than to deliberate choice – recent case law has shown that the scope of the MFN principle can be construed in very different ways. It is thus by no means clear that all parties involved in a codification project would necessarily agree on the exact scope and interpretation to be given to a provision on MFN treatment.

In addition, the experience with the observance of the MFN principle as contained in the most important multilateral treaty relating to economic activities – namely the WTO (and formerly the GATT of 1947) with regard to the multilateral trading system – is also far from encouraging. Here it is the desire to take part in a multilateral system without prejudicing one's power to enter into preferential agreements that has traditionally undermined the MFN principle and its guiding function. The need to guarantee a balance between an open, uniform and non-discriminatory system and preferential relations taking into account specific nuances in bilateral relations remains thus an important stumbling block for any multilateral system.

2. CONCEPT

Most-favoured-nation treatment is treatment accorded by the granting State to the beneficiary State, or to persons or things in a determined relationship with that State, not less favourable than treatment extended by the granting State to a third State or to persons or things in the same relationship with that third State.[1] A most-favoured-nation treatment clause *per se* entails international obligations and rights not only among the Contracting States of the international treaty incorporating it (often referred to as 'the basic treaty'), but also among these Contracting States and other States (often referred to as 'the third-party treaty') by virtue of different international treaties. Therefore, a most-favoured-nation treatment clause is not only a normal treaty clause, but also a source of international obligations other than those explicitly included in the basic treaty. It allows 'borrowing' treaty provisions from other treaties or possibly State practice regarding third States. The material scope of the MFN obligation is thus open as the contents of future treaties and state practice cannot be totally foreseen and identified when the basic treaty is concluded. Even with regard to existing treaty obligations in relation to third States, it may be that negotiators are not always completely aware of them.[2]

By its very nature the MFN clause is different from other international obligations that are usually agreed upon, as it seems at first view contrary to the general principle of treaty negotiations that normally a treaty does not create either obligations or rights for a third State without its consent as enshrined also in Article 34 of the United Nations (Vienna) Convention on the Law of Treaties.[3] However, a closer analysis shows that MFN

---

1 See Article 5 Draft Articles on Most-Favoured-Nation Clauses (1978), International Law Commission, available at <http://untreaty.un.org/ilc/texts/instruments/english/draft%20articles/1_3_1978.pdf> accessed 14 October 2011. This section draws heavily on Andreas R Ziegler, 'Most-Favoured Nation (MFN) Treatment' in August Reinisch (ed), *Standards of Investment Protection* (OUP 2008) 29–86.

2 See International Law Association, Report of the Committee on Foreign Direct Investment presented at the Biennial Meeting 2008, Section B4, London 2009.

3 1155 UNTS 331, reprinted also in 8 *ILM* (1969) 679; signed at Vienna 23 May 1969, entry into force: 27 January 1980.

treatment is in conformity with the principle that the consent of a State can lead to the creation of new rights as a consequence of a treaty between third States (Article 36 of the Vienna Convention) although it is not a requirement that the contracting States of the later treaty intended the provision to accord that right also to the third State. More importantly, one can say that with regard to MFN treatment the new right is not created by the new treaty but was already encompassed under the basic treaty and thus is not a case of the application of the rules covered by Part III Section 4 of the Vienna Convention on the Law of Treaties. As a matter of fact, the 1969 Vienna Convention left this issue basically untouched, thereby justifying the ongoing work of the ILC in this context.[4]

In the case of the MFN clause, the basic treaty becomes a dynamic source of law in so far as the practice of either party to the basic treaty, in particular with regard to later treaties, becomes of relevance to existing rights and duties under the basic treaty. The MFN clause thus constitutes a prior consent to extend favours granted to third States to the Contracting Parties of the basic treaty.

It is important to note that the MFN principle does not require identical treatment but 'treatment at least as favourable'. Often this will mean identical treatment as any other treatment would lead to new problems in relation to third States, but it may also lead to better treatment or different treatment that is considered to be qualitatively identical or at least as favourable as the treatment of third parties. This distinction may be of lesser importance in the area of investment but can be important when it comes to tariff concessions in the area of trade.

This very nature of the MFN principle is obviously also contrary to a strict application of the reciprocity principle so cherished by States in their traditional diplomatic relations.[5] While, normally, States will mutually grant each other MFN treatment, the material content of this provision may differ from the beginning or, especially, change over time. This is the main reason why some politicians and even lawyers have always been

---

[4] See Article 5 Draft Articles on Most-Favoured-Nation Clauses (1978), above n 1 and Pia Acconci, 'Most-Favoured Nation Treatment and International Law on Foreign Investment' in Peter Muchlinski, Federico Ortino and Christoph Schreuer (eds), *The Oxford Handbook of International Investment Law* (OUP 2008) 363–407 with reference to para 59 of the Rapport de la Commission à l'Assemblée générale sur les travaux de sa trentième session, 16.

[5] See for example Chang-fa Lo, *The Reciprocity Principle in the International Regulation of Economic Relations* (typescript photocopy), Thesis (SJD) Harvard Law School, 1989, available at <http://de.scientificcommons.org/4449832> accessed 14 October 2011.

critical of the MFN clause. They consider it to be a disincentive to negotiate mutually acceptable improvements of their relations, e.g. investment or trade, as one party may benefit from improvement made only by the other party without having to improve its own standards. It thus can lead to so-called free-rider effects. MFN clauses are only reciprocal in the sense that they are reciprocally granted but their content is open to divergences and dynamic developments and thus not subject to the reciprocal granting of identical treatment and market access rights.

One way to limit these effects of the MFN principle is to make it not automatic or unconditional but conditional (conditional MFN treatment). An alternative is to provide explicit (temporary) exceptions. This has been discussed[6] in particular with regard to tariff concessions before World War II, but also with regard to more recent negotiations such as under the GATS.[7] Conditional MFN treatment means normally that the application of new more favourable rules or preferences is only granted to existing treaty partners if they agree to apply the same rules; conditional MFN treatment therefore is basically a right to obtain the more favourable treatment upon condition to do the same (reciprocity) while unconditional MFN treatment requires no corresponding commitment by the beneficiary. Economic theory, especially in the field of trade, has shown that liberalization, even unilateral, is more likely to lead to increased welfare and hence often recommends unconditional MFN treatment.[8] Generally, MFN clauses found in modern BITs are unconditional[9] but they may be limited in scope and/or subject to exceptions. The basic problem in developing a coherent theory in view of the existing case law stems from the fact that the clauses at stake were often very differently phrased. While they all fall into the same category, their wording allows (at least) technically for a differentiation with regard to their scope.[10]

---

6 See for example Julius Wolf, 'Vorwort' in Lorenz Glier (ed), *Die Meistbegünstigungsklausel* (Reimer 1905) v.

7 Article II:2 GATS; see in this respect Andreas F Lowenfeld, *International Economic Law* (OUP 2002) 117.

8 See for an overview on recent economic studies in this field Carlos EJM Zarazaga, 'Measuring the benefits of unilateral trade liberalization; part 2: dynamic models' (Issue Q1, 2000) *Economic and Financial Policy Review* 29–39.

9 See also Acconci, above n 4, Section 3.

10 See the diverging case law as reported in the next section and, for details, ibid, Section 3.1, who rightly refers to Dionisio Anzilotti, *Cours de droit international* (1929), pointing out that '[...]juridiquement parlant, il n'existe pas *une clause* de la nation la plus favorisée; il existe autant de stipulations distinctes qu'il y a de traités qui la contiennent, de sorte que toute question relative à la nature et aux effets de la

3. MULTILATERAL CODIFICATION PROJECTS

3.1 Havana Charter (1948)

The negotiations after World War II for a comprehensive new trade and investment system took place in the framework of the United Nations Conference on Trade and Employment.[11] They led to the adoption of the so-called Havana Charter. This document included certain references to investment, mostly regarding negotiation of bilateral agreements and the establishment of foreign investors and investments.[12] They were, however, of a rather rudimentary and hortatory character which may have been one of the reasons for their failed ratification by the Unites States.[13] Article 12, entitled 'International Investment for Economic Development and Reconstruction,' contained a very general reference to non-discrimination in this respect:

> 2. Members therefore undertake: . . . (ii) to give due regard to the desirability of avoiding discrimination as between foreign investments; . . .

3.2 Abs-Shawcross Draft (1958)

In 1955 the German banker Hermann Josef Abs, who was to become the Chairman of Deutsche Bank, presented the idea to draft a Magna Carta

---

clause est avant tout une question d'interprétation d'une clause donnée dans un traité déterminé' (at 438). See also Rudolf Dolzer and Terry Myers, 'After TECMED: MFN Clauses in Investment Protection Agreements' (2004) 19 ICSID Review – *Foreign Investment Law Journal* 49, 50 et seq; Emmanuel Gaillard, 'Establishing Jurisdiction through a Most-Favored-Nation Clause', *New York Law Journal* (2 June 2005) 8. For an overview of existing examples see UNCTAD, Recent Developments in International Investment Agreements, UNCTAD/WEB/ITE/IIT/2005/1 (30 August 2005) and UNCTAD, International Investment Rule-Setting: Trends, Emerging Issues and Implications, TD/B/COM.2/68 (18 January 2006).

[11] Held at Havana, Cuba from 21 November 1947 to 24 March 1948. This section draws heavily on an article I have previously published in German: 'Multilateraler Investitionsschutz im Wirtschaftsrecht' (Multilateral Investment Protection and International Economic Law) in Dirk Ehlers, Hans-Michael Wolffgang and Ulrich J Schröder (eds), *Rechtsfragen Internationaler Investitionen* (Verlag Recht und Wirtschaft 2009) 63–80.

[12] See for example Edwin Borchard, 'Protection of Foreign Investments' (1946) 11 *Law and Contemporary Problems* 835–47.

[13] See in this respect Franziska Tschofen, 'Multilateral Approaches to the Treatment of Foreign Investment' in Ibrahim FI Shihata (ed), *Legal Treatment of Foreign Investment: The World Bank Guidelines* (1993) 267 *et seq.*, 270.

for the protection of foreign property.[14] In 1958 he presented, together with Sir Hartley Shawcross, a document entitled *Convention on Investments Abroad*,[15] usually referred to as Abs-Shawcross Draft. The German Government officially transmitted this document to the Organisation for European Economic Co-operation (OEEC).[16] It was intended to constitute a reference for the minimum protection to be granted to foreign property and thus did not contain an MFN principle, but to the contrary hinted in its Article VI at the idea that members would negotiate more favourable agreements.

> Article VI: The provisions of this Convention shall not prejudice the application of any present or future treaty or municipal law under which more favourable treatment is accorded to nationals of any of the Parties.

3.3 OECD Draft Convention (1967)

The OECD Council published a *Draft Convention on the Protection of Foreign Property* in 1967, but the draft was never formally adopted. Rather it was recommended for use as a model treaty by members. It contained in its very first article a provision relating to the treatment to be granted, which included the following language:

> Each Party [...] shall not in any way impair the management, maintenance, use enjoyment or disposal [...] [of the property of the national of the other Parties] by unreasonable or discriminatory measures.

In the absence of any consent regarding a comprehensive instrument regarding foreign direct investment, the OECD published from 1961 onwards a number of instruments in the area of capital movements, such as the *OECD Code of Liberalisation of Capital Movements* and the *OECD Code of Liberalisation of Current Invisible Operations*.[17] In their current

---

[14] See Lothar Gall, *Der Bankier Hermann Josef Abs* (2006) 491 (note 25).

[15] See Arthur S Miller, 'Protection of Private Foreign Investment by Multilateral Convention' (1959) 53 *AJIL* 371–8.

[16] See Ulf R Siebel, 'Bemerkungen zum Thema Schiedsverfahren und Investitionsschutz bei internationalen Anleihen' in Alain Plante (ed), *Festschrift für Ottoarndt Glossner zum 70. Geburtstag* (1994) 393, 410.

[17] The *Code of Liberalisation of Capital Movements* and the *Code of Liberalisation of Current Invisible Operations* constitute legally binding rules, stipulating progressive, non-discriminatory liberalization of capital movements, the right of establishment and current invisible transactions (mostly services). The most recent editions of 2011 are reprinted in *OECD Code of Liberalisation of*

form they put a lot of emphasis on non-discrimination without, however, using the MFN principle. In addition, the instruments normally provided for a broad exception for preferential arrangements in the framework of regional economic integration and the possibility of communicating specific exceptions for members. Good examples constitute Articles 9 and 10 of the OECD *Code of Liberalisation of Capital Movement:*[18]

> Article 9: Non-discrimination: A Member shall not discriminate as between other Members in authorising the conclusion and execution of transactions and transfers which are listed in Annex A and which are subject to any degree of liberalisation.
>
> Article 10: Exceptions to the principle of non-discrimination: special customs or monetary systems: Members forming part of a special customs or monetary system may apply to one another, in addition to measures of liberalisation taken in accordance with the provisions of Article 2(a), other measures of liberalisation without extending them to other Members. Members forming part of such a system shall inform the Organisation of its membership and those of its provisions which have a bearing on this Code.

3.4 Charter of Economic Rights and Duties of States (1974)

The Charter of Economic Rights and Duties of States, as adopted by the General Assembly of the United Nations in 1974,[19] refers also in very general terms to non-discrimination[20] in international economic relations. The MFN principle was explicitly mentioned but only with regard to trade.[21]

Capital Movements: 2011 Edition (OECD, Paris 2011), available at <http://dx.doi.org/10.1787/9789264110779-en>.

[18] Nevertheless, this general principle was always supplemented with an important list of exceptions that member States maintained (Annex E).

[19] Resolution 3281 (XXIX), Charter of Economic Rights and Duties of States, adopted on 12 December 1974.

[20] Article 19: 'With a view to accelerating the economic growth of developing countries and bridging the economic gap between developed and developing countries, developed countries should grant generalized preferential, non-reciprocal and non-discriminatory treatment to developing countries in those fields of international economic cooperation where it may be feasible.'

[21] Article 26: 'All States have the duty to coexist in tolerance and live together in peace, irrespective of differences in political, economic, social and cultural systems, and to facilitate trade between States having different economic and social systems. International trade should be conducted without prejudice to generalized non-discriminatory and non-reciprocal preferences in favour of developing countries, on the basis of mutual advantage, equitable benefits and the exchange of most-favoured-nation treatment.'

3.5 World Bank Guidelines (1992)

In its Part III dedicated to treatment, the World Bank Guidelines[22] mention in Section 3 (b) that '[a]s concerns such other matters as are not relevant to national investors, treatment under the State's legislation and regulations will not discriminate among foreign investors on grounds of nationality'.[23] Interestingly, there is a specific exception from the MFN principle in Part III with regard to certain preferential trade agreements:

> 4. Nothing in this Guideline will automatically entitle nationals of other States to the more favorable standards of treatment accorded to the nationals of certain States under any customs union or free trade area agreement.

3.6 Energy Charter Treaty (1994)

The Energy Charter Treaty (ECT) is probably the international instrument which comes closest to the concept of a multilateral binding agreement providing explicit rules on the protection of foreign investors and investment admittedly in a mostly regional setting for a specific sector. The agreement, as signed on 17 December 1994, is currently in force for 51 members. It contains as early as the preamble a strong affirmation of the MFN principle, which is then taken up in various Articles of the operative part. The most elaborate reference is made in Article 10:

> Preamble: [. . .] Affirming that Contracting Parties attach the utmost importance to the effective implementation of full national treatment and most favoured nation treatment, and that these commitments will be applied to the Making of Investments pursuant to a supplementary treaty; [. . .]
>
> Article 10 Promotion, Protection and Treatment of Investments:
> (1) Each Contracting Party shall, in accordance with the provisions of this Treaty, encourage and create stable, equitable, favourable and transparent conditions for Investors of other Contracting Parties to make Investments in its Area. Such conditions shall include a commitment to accord at all times to Investments of Investors of other Contracting Parties fair and equitable treatment. Such Investments shall also enjoy the most constant protection and security and no Contracting Party shall in any way impair by unreasonable or discriminatory measures their management, maintenance, use, enjoyment or disposal. In no case shall such Investments be accorded treatment less

---

[22] Reprinted e.g. in Ibrahim FI Shihata, *Legal Treatment of Foreign Investment: The World Bank Guidelines* (Martinus Nijhoff 1993) 401 *et seq.*

[23] Non-discrimination is also mentioned in the context of expropriation (IV.1) and more specifically with regard to comprehensive nationalizations (IV.10).

> favourable than that required by international law, including treaty obligations. Each Contracting Party shall observe any obligations it has entered into with an Investor or an Investment of an Investor of any other Contracting Party. [. . .]
>
> (7) Each Contracting Party shall accord to Investments in its Area of Investors of other Contracting Parties, and their related activities including management, maintenance, use, enjoyment or disposal, treatment no less favourable than that which it accords to Investments of its own Investors or of the Investors of any other Contracting Party or any third state and their related activities including management, maintenance, use, enjoyment or disposal, whichever is the most favourable.

Article 21 (3) contains an important exception regarding taxation measures and Articles 24 (4) and 25 provide important exceptions regarding free-trade areas or customs unions or other types of economic integration agreements (EIA).

3.7 MAI Negotiations (1998 draft)

From 1995 to 1998 the OECD hosted a series of negotiations designed to produce a multilateral agreement on investment (MAI). The negotiating group produced a draft text, but the negotiations stalled.[24] The text included in its Part III dedicated to the treatment of investors and investments an MFN clause which is impressively similar to the one used in the WTO. Under the heading 'National Treatment and Most Favoured Nation Treatment' the following text was included in the 1998 draft:

> 1. Each Contracting Party shall accord to investors of another Contracting Party and to their investments, treatment no less favourable than the treatment it accords [in like circumstances] to its own investors and their investments with respect to the establishment, acquisition, expansion, operation, management, maintenance, use, enjoyment and sale or other disposition of investments.
>
> 2. Each Contracting Party shall accord to investors of another Contracting Party and to their investments, treatment no less favourable than the treatment it accords [in like circumstances] to investors of any other Contracting Party or of a non-Contracting Party, and to the investments of investors of any other Contracting Party or of a non-Contracting Party, with respect to the establishment, acquisition, expansion, operation, management, maintenance, use, enjoyment, and sale or other disposition of investments.
>
> 3. Each Contracting Party shall accord to investors of another Contracting

[24] For a draft text, see The Multilateral Agreement on Investment: Draft Consolidated Text, DAFFE/MAI(98)7/REV1 (22 April 1998).

Party and to their investments the better of the treatment required by Articles 1.1 and 1.2, whichever is the more favourable to those investors or investments.

4. MFN IN BILATERAL TREATIES

4.1 Historic Development

In purely bilateral treaties the inclusion of the MFN principle was usually considered a specific safeguard to maintain privileged access for and treatment of one Party's nationals by the other, be it in relation to administrative practice or as a result of (subsequent) negotiations with third parties.

In general, the major problem in this context was to define the scope of the MFN principle. While it is not always difficult to demonstrate that nationals of another Party are treated more favourably in a specific case, the question as to whether that specific treatment is covered by an MFN treatment obligation is often disputed.[25] For example, in a decision of 1994 the Swiss authorities decided that the MFN clause in a treaty on establishment and legal protection of their citizens concluded between Greece and Switzerland in 1927 was not specific enough to allow Greek citizens to invoke the benefit of a multilateral treaty on the harmonization of civil procedure not ratified by Greece as the objectives of the two treaties were not identical.[26]

Despite early calls after World War II for a need to clarify the scope of MFN clauses in international treaties, this general debate has remained rather silent since the International Law Commission suspended its work on the issue in the mid-1970s.[27]

With regard to bilateral investment treaties (BITs), clauses relating to most-favoured-nation (MFN) treatment did not give rise to any particular questions until very recently.[28] These clauses were normally considered as

---

[25] See for famous examples Arbitral Commission, Award of 6 March (*Ambatielos*), in United Nations, Recueil des sentences arbitrales, vol XIII, 106 s, and International Court of Justice, Judgment of 11 July 1952 (*Anglo-Iranian Oil Co. (Preliminary Exceptions)*, Recueil 1952, 110.

[26] See VPB 59.155 (Direction du droit international public, 11 mars 1994) also published in: *Revue suisse de droit international et de droit européen* no 5, 1995, 25.

[27] It was recently suggested that this work should resume in the ILC. For a historic overview see Ziegler, above n 1.

[28] See on the MFN clause in the area of Foreign Direct Investment (FDI) in general: UNCTAD, Most-Favoured Nation Treatment, Series on Issues on

a relic of the traditional way to negotiate establishment and treatment rights for foreign investors in the nineteenth century.[29] Now the scope of the MFN treatment clauses has become of interest to arbitrators and legal writers.[30] It is especially the question whether the clause applies also to procedural rights (in particular dispute settlement) and definitions (e.g. the definition of a foreign direct investment or a foreign investor) that remains controversial, and has over recent years been addressed in several cases.

The MFN clause was rediscovered in the context of international investment arbitration following the decision of an arbitral tribunal in the

---

International Investment Agreement Series, Document UNCTAD/ITE/IIT/10 (Vol III), 1999, based on a manuscript prepared by Joachim Karl.

[29] At the same time it must be noted that one can trace back the concept as such back to the 11th and 12th century. See Endre Ustor, 'First Report on the Most-Favoured Nation Clause' (1969) 2 *YB Int'l L Comm'n* 157, 159, UN Doc A/CN.4/213; Organización para la Cooperación y el Desarrollo Económico [OCDE], Most-Favoured-Nation-Treatment in International Investment Law 3 (Directorado de Asuntos Financieros y Empresariales, Working Paper on International Investment No 2004/2, 2004) (preparado por Marie-France Houde), available at <http://www.oecd.org/dataoecd/21/37/33773085.pdf> accessed 14 October 2011.

[30] For very recent examples see Tony Cole and Madhu Agrawal, 'When is a Forum "More Favourable"? The Use of MFN Clauses to Found an Investment Arbitration Tribunal's Jurisdiction' (2010) SSRN, available at <http://ssrn.com/abstract=1674378> and Julie A Maupin, 'MFN-Based Jurisdiction in Investor-State Arbitration: Is There Any Hope for a Consistent Approach?' (paper presented at the Society of International Economic Law (SIEL), Second Biennial Global Conference, University of Barcelona, 8–10 July 2010), available at <http://ssrn.com/abstract=1633012>; Guido Santiago Tawil, 'Most Favoured Nation Clauses and Jurisdictional Clauses in Investment Treaty Arbitration' in Christina Binder, Ursula Kriebaum, August Reinisch and Stephen Wittich (eds), *International Investment Law for the 21st Century: Essays in Honour of Christoph Schreuer* (OUP 2009) 9–30; Kaj Hober, 'MFN Clauses and Dispute Resolution in Investment Treaties – Have We Reached the End of the Road?' in Christina Binder, Ursula Kriebaum, August Reinisch and Stephen Wittich (eds), *International Investment Law for the 21st Century: Essays in Honour of Christoph Schreuer* (OUP 2009) 31–41; Stephan W Schill, *The Multilateralization of International Investment Law* (CUP 2009) 121–96, 128; Jarrod Wong, 'The Application of Most-Favoured-Nation Clauses to Dispute Resolution Provisions in Bilateral Investment Treaties' (2008) 3 *Asian J WTO & Int Health L & Pol'y* 171, 174; Yas Banifatemi, 'The Emerging Jurisprudence on the Most-Favoured-Nation Treatment in Investment Arbitration' in Andrea K Bjorklund, Ian A Laird and Sergey Ripinsky (eds), *Investment Treaty Law: Current Issues III* (British Institute of International and Comparative Law 2008) Part 2, Chapter 7; Scott Vesel, 'Clearing a Path Through a Tangled Jurisprudence: Most-Favoured Nation Clauses and Dispute Settlement Provisions in Bilateral Investment Treaties' (2007) 32 *Yale J Int'l L* 125, 129;

case *Maffezini* v *Spain*[31] in 2000. Since then a number of tribunals have had to address the issue of the correct application and interpretation of the MFN clause.[32]

4.2 Issues Addressed in the MFN Clause

4.2.1 Like circumstances

The dynamic nature of the MFN clause is intended to operate only in situations that are comparable, i.e. a different treatment occurs and seems less favourable although the circumstances are comparable to those relating to the allegedly better treatment provided to another investment or investor. One can see this caveat as a normal limitation of any non-discrimination rule as it exists in most if not all legal systems. This is sometimes taken up in the respective language describing MFN with the

---

Gabriel Egli, 'Don't Get Bit: Addressing ICSID's Inconsistent Application of Most-Favored-Nation Clauses to Dispute Resolution Provisions' (2007) 34 *Pepperdine Law Review* 1045 *et seq.*; Okezie Chukwumerije, 'Interpreting Most-Favoured-Nations Clauses in Investment Treaty Arbitrations' (2007) 8 *The Journal of World Investment and Trade* 597 *et seq.*; see also earlier Dana H Freyer and David Herlihy, 'Most-Favored-Nation Treatment and Dispute Settlement in Investment Arbitration: Just How "Favored" is "Most-Favored"?' (2005) 20 ICSID Review – *Foreign Investment Law Journal* 58 *et seq.*; Locknie Hsu, 'MFN and Dispute Settlement – When the Twain Meet' (2006) 7 *The Journal of World Investment and Trade* 25 *et seq.*; and Francisco Orrego Vicuña, 'Bilateral Investment Treaties and the Most-Favored-Nation Clause: Implications for Arbitration in the Light of a Recent ICSID Case' in Gabrielle Kaufmann-Kohler (ed), *Investment Treaties and Arbitration: ASA Swiss Arbitration Association Conference in Zurich of January 25, 2002* (2002) 133 *et seq.*

[31] *Maffezini v Spain*, Decision on Jurisdiction of 24 January 2000, ICSID Case No ARB/97/7, paras 53 *et seq.*; this and all other awards mentioned in this chapter are available at <http://ita.law.uvic.ca/index.htm> accessed 14 October 2011. For comments see Stephen Fietta, 'Most Favoured Nation Treatment and Dispute Resolution under Bilateral Investment Treaties: a Turning Point?' (2005) *International Arbitration Law Review* 131–8; Lahra Liberti, 'Arbitrato ICSID, clausola della nazione più favorita e problemi di attribuzione' (2004) *Rivista dell'arbitrato* 580 *et seq.*

[32] For an overview on the case law see Marie-France Houde and Fabrizio Pagani, 'Most Favoured Nation Treatment in International Investment Law' in OECD (ed), *International Investment Law: A Changing Landscape – A Companion Volume to International Investment Perspectives* (2005) Chapter 4; Ruth Teitelbaum, 'Who's Afraid of Maffezini? Recent Developments in the Interpretation of Most Favored Nation Clauses' (2005) 22 *Journal of International Arbitration* 225–38; Acconci, above n 4, 363–407; August Reinisch, 'Maffezini v. Spain Case', in *Encyclopaedia of Public International Law* (2010).

terms 'in like situations' or 'in like circumstances', although some would say it is superfluous in view of the nature of MFN treatment.[33] The most famous example constitutes probably the wording used in the GATT 1947 which became standard in the framework of the WTO: the final draft of the MAI contained these terms in squared brackets.

When it comes to the application of the MFN clause in the basic treaty to invoke the applicability of a specific treatment provision in a third-party treaty, this principle is normally referred to as the '*ejusdem* (or *eiusdem*) *generis* principle'. It is normally understood to mean that the third-party treaty must, in principle, regulate the same subject matter as the basic treaty, otherwise the specific treatment standard would be taken out of its context and thus not be accorded in 'like circumstances' or in 'like situations'. No other rights can be claimed under a most-favoured-nation clause than those falling within the limits of the subject-matter of the clause. Furthermore, one can extend this principle to the 'persons and things' covered by the standard, which must be of the same category.[34] Even where the treaty does not specify that the MFN principle applies only to 'like circumstances' or in 'like situations', those limitations can be considered as an inherent principle underlying the MFN principle.[35] This concept has sometimes been invoked in investment disputes in discussing the scope of the MFN provision, at least when the MFN clause as such did not contain any (applicable) limitations.

So far, ascertaining the application of this principle has not given rise to controversial issues within investment cases. In reality, the *ejusdem generis* principle has been extensively discussed only by the ICSID Tribunals in the *Maffezini* and *Suez* cases.[36] More recently the *Wintershall* Tribunal

---

[33] For a typical example of the comparison of two situations see *Parkerings-Compagniet AS v Lithuania*, Award of 11 September 2007, ICSID Case No ARB/05/8 (Norway/Lithuania BIT).

[34] Endre Ustor, 'Most Favoured Nation Clause' in *Encyclopaedia of Public International Law* (1997) 472; see also *The Anglo-Iranian Oil Company (Jurisdiction) Case (United Kingdom v Iran)*, Judgment of 22 July 1952, ICJ Rep 1952, 109 and Articles 9 and 10 of the Draft Articles on Most-Favoured-Nation Clauses (1978), International Law Commission, as available at <http://untreaty.un.org/ilc/texts/instruments/english/draft%20articles/1_3_1978.pdf> accessed 14 October 2011.

[35] See also with regard to the specific case of Swiss BITs: Michael Schmid, *Swiss Investment Protection Agreements: Most-Favoured-Nation Treatment and Umbrella Clauses* (2007) 43.

[36] See Acconci, above n 4, 363–407; see on the application of this principle with regard to the *Maffezini* and *Plama* Cases also Campbell McLachlan, Laurence Shore and Matthew Weiniger, *International Investment Arbitration: Substantive Principles* (OUP 2007) 254–57.

also referred to it, and the *Renta4* Tribunal discussed whether access to jurisdiction falls in the same category as the substantive investment protections accorded other parties by a BIT.[37] This can be explained by the fact that investors have normally invoked rules contained in third-party BITs under the MFN clause of a BIT (basic treaty). Thus, the *ejusdem generis* principles would not foreclose use of the MFN clause given the nearly identical protections afforded by each of the treaties.

The use of the MFN Clause to invoke the applicability of treaty norms between one Party of the Treaty at stake and a third State is subject to the condition that the two treaties create *like circumstances*, i.e. they must regulate the same subject matter.[38] In the *Tecmed* arbitral award,[39] the arbitral tribunal held that the MFN clause could not be used to invoke those provisions of a Treaty with a third State that were clearly the result of a particular negotiating situation with this third State and thus constituted part of a 'package deal' made up of specific rights and obligations ('[...]*core matters that must be deemed to be specifically negotiated by the Contracting Parties*[...]').[40]

In the view of the *Tecmed* arbitral tribunal, the very nature of these provisions makes them unfit for being invoked by third States under an MFN clause.[41] The provision providing for retroactive application of a BIT to investments made before the entry into force of the BIT especially was considered to be such a clause that had only been granted to the respective treaty partner in view of the specific negotiating situation and

37 *Wintershall Aktiengesellschaft v Argentine Republic*, Award of 8 December 2008, ICSID Case No ARB/04/14 (Germany/Argentina BIT); they refer to historic examples at para 101: '[A]n interesting application of this principle has been mentioned by Prof. George Schwazenberger [*sic*] in an Article in the British Yearbook of International Law 1945 ("*The Most-Favoured-Nation Standard in British State Practice*", para 96 at p 108, footnote 6). It is the decision of the Umpire of the British-Venezuelan Mixed Claims Commission in the case of *The Aroa Mines* under the Protocol of February 13, 1903. The Umpire held that the relevant MFN Clause on which Great Britain relied and which extended to the *administration of Justice* only applied to rights before national courts but not, as Great Britain had maintained, to the proceedings of the International Mixed Claims Commission, a restricted interpretation of an MFN Clause.' [emphasis in original].

38 See also Matthias Herdegen, *Internationales Wirtschaftsrecht* (6th edn, Beck 2007) 221.

39 *Técnical Medioambientales Tecmed S.A. v Mexico*, Award of 29 May 2003, ICSID Case No ARB/AF/00/2.

40 Ibid, para 69.

41 See also Herdegen, above n 38, 221.

could thus not be invoked by an investor under another BIT.

Earlier the *Maffezini* Tribunal had held that 'the beneficiary of the [MFN] clause should not be able to override *public policy considerations* that the contracting parties might have envisaged as fundamental conditions for their acceptance of the agreement in question'.[42] According to the tribunal this would apply, for instance,

> 1. where a State has conditioned its consent to arbitration on the exhaustion of local remedies;
> 2. where a BIT contains a 'fork-in-the-road' clause according to which a choice between domestic or international courts or tribunals becomes irreversible once made;
> 3. where a particular forum, such as ICSID or NAFTA, has been chosen;
> 4. when the parties have agreed to a highly institutionalized system of arbitration that incorporates precise rules of procedure such as NAFTA.[43]

However, the *Maffezini* Tribunal held that a mere requirement of first resort to domestic courts during a period of 18 months did not reflect a fundamental question of public policy that would have limited the scope of the MFN clause.[44] This argument was also important in the most recent *Wintershall* arbitral award. Here the 18-month time limit was considered an important element of the consent to arbitration given by the State Parties.[45]

In *Renta4 S.V.S.A. et al. v The Russian Federation* (2009), a case settled in the framework of the Stockholm Chamber of Commerce, the Tribunal held that the Spain-Russia BIT precluded recourse to the arbitration provisions of the Denmark-Russia BIT. The reason for that was found in the unusually worded MFN clause in the Spain-Russia treaty only. The award contains a lengthy discussion over the MFN clause in the applicable BIT.[46] Elaborating on the scope of the MFN principle in investment agreements, all three arbitrators took the view that an MFN clause does not need to refer to arbitration explicitly in order for the clause to apply to dispute settlement. Further, the view was expressed that there was no significant distinction to be made between 'procedural' and 'substantive'

---

42 *Maffezini v Spain*, above n 31, para 62.

43 Ibid, para 63.

44 See August Reinisch, 'Maffezini v. Spain Case' in *Encyclopaedia of Public International Law* (2010).

45 *Wintershall Aktiengesellschaft v Argentine Republic*, above n 37.

46 Article 5.2 of the Treaty concluded between Spain and Russia on 26 October 1990 foresaw only an MFN obligation with regard to the fair and equitable treatment (FET) standard contained in Article 5.1.

investment protection, since both aspects generally fall under 'investment protection'. However, the majority held that the particular MFN clause of the Spain-Russia treaty precluded recourse to the arbitration provisions of another investment treaty, namely the Denmark-Russia BIT.[47]

4.2.2 Specific limitations

As a result, one can say that some MFN clauses contained in BITs are very general in scope[48] and therefore their limitations have been ascertained by relying on the principles described above and on inherent limitations. However, many MFN provisions are more specific. The latter go further in their explicitness and define the types of situations in which the treatment is subject to the MFN standard. Article 1103 (Most Favored Nation Treatment) of the North American Free Trade Agreement (NAFTA) (which resembles very much Article 4 of the 2004 US Model-BIT[49]) reads:

> 1. Each Party shall accord to investors of another Party treatment no less favorable than that it accords, in like circumstances, to investors of any other Party or of a non-Party *with respect to the establishment, acquisition, expansion, management, conduct, operation, and sale or other disposition of investments.*
>
> 2. Each Party shall accord to investments of investors of another Party treatment no less favourable than that it accords, in like circumstances, to investments of investors of any other Party or of a non-Party *with respect to the establishment, acquisition, expansion, management, conduct, operation, and sale or other disposition of investments.* [emphasis added]

This MFN treatment clause is particular – in comparison to those clauses concluded especially by most European States (at least until recently) – in so far as it includes besides the 'management, conduct, operation, and sale or other disposition of investments' also the 'establishment, acquisition, expansion' of them and thus extends MFN

---

47 *Renta4 S.V.S.A. et al. v The Russian Federation*, Award of 20 March 2009, Arbitration Institute of the Stockholm Chamber of Commerce, Case No 024/2007; see Luke Eric Peterson (No 7, 2009) 2 Investment Arbitration Reporter.

48 A typical example is the clause in the Agreement between Spain and Argentina that was at stake in the *Maffezini* decision. Article IV (2) of the Argentina-Spain BIT is relatively open or unspecific with regard to the exact scope of the MFN clause: In *all matters subject to this Agreement*, this *treatment* shall not be less favourable than that extended by each Party to the investments made in its territory by investors of a third country.

49 Text made available online by the US Secretary of State at <http://www.ustr.gov/assets/Trade_Sectors/Investment/Model_BIT/asset_upload_file847_6897.pdf> accessed 14 October 2011.

treatment to market access or establishment, i.e. rights normally related to the pre-establishment phase of foreign direct investment. While traditionally only the United States and Canada have regularly included such market access rights, it is now very common for many states to include them in the general scope of the treatment standards of an agreement.[50]

Similarly, Article 40 Paragraph 1 (National Treatment and Most-Favoured-Nation Treatment) of the Investment Chapter in the EFTA Singapore Free Trade Agreement reads:

> Each Party shall accord to investors and investments of investors of another Party, *in relation to the establishment, acquisition, expansion, management, conduct, operation and disposal of investments*, treatment that is no less favourable than that which it accords *in like situations* to its own investors and their investments or to investors and their investments of any other State, whichever is more favourable. [emphasis added]

Here again we see that the extension of the MFN clause is limited to certain operations (including pre-establishment rights) and that it only applies in 'like situations'. Similarly NAFTA speaks of 'like circumstances'. Other variations of the MFN clause may not specify at all to what kinds of treatment they apply, i.e. to specific standards, to treatment in general or to any provision of the treaty. Article 3 (first part) of the Treaty between the Federal Republic of Germany and the Co-operative Republic of Guyana concerning the Encouragement and Reciprocal Protection of Investments of 6 December 1989[51] reads:

---

[50] See for many examples from the Canadian and US practice Acconci, above n 4, Section 3.1 with reference e.g. to Canada-Latvia (1995), Article II (3); Canada-South Africa (1995), Article II (3); US-Nicaragua (1995), Article II (1); Canada-Egypt (1996), Article II (3); Canada-Panama (1996), Article II (3); Canada-Venezuela (1996), Article II (3); Canada-Thailand (1997), Article II (3); US-Azerbaijan (1997), Article II (1); US-Jordan (1997), Article II (1); US-Bahrain (1999), Article 2 (1); US-El Salvador (1999), Article II (1); see also the 2004 Canadian Model BIT, Article 4, and and the 2004 U.S. Model BIT, Article 4. All made available by UNCTAD on its 'Investment Instruments Online' site, available at <http://www.unctadxi.org/templates/DocSearch779.aspx> accessed 14 October 2011; see also Jeswald W Salacuse and Nicholas P Sullivan, 'Do BITs Really Work? An Evaluation of Bilateral Investment Treaties and Their Grand Bargain' (2005) 46 *Harvard International Law Journal* 67, 93–4.

[51] As made available by UNCTAD on its 'Investment Instruments Online' site <http://www.unctadxi.org/templates/DocSearch 779.aspx> accessed 14 October 2011.

> Neither Contracting Party shall subject investments in its territory owned or controlled by nationals or companies of the other Contracting Party to *treatment* less favourable than it accords to investments of its own nationals or companies of any third State.
>
> Neither Contracting Party shall subject nationals or companies of the other Contracting Party, as regards their *activity in connection with investments in its territory, to treatment less favourable* than it accords to its own nationals or companies of any third State.... [emphasis added]

More specifically, when it comes to the treatment of investors, Article 4 of the 1995 Swiss Model BIT[52] provides:

> (2) Each Contracting Party shall in its territory accord investments or returns of investors of the other Contracting Party *treatment not less favourable* than that which it accords to investments or returns of its own investors or to investments or returns of investors of any third State, whichever is more favourable to the investor concerned.
>
> (3) Each Contracting Party shall in its territory accord investors of the other Contracting Party, as regards the *management, maintenance, use, enjoyment or disposal of their investments, treatment* not less favourable than that which it accords to its own investors or investors of any third State, whichever is more favourable to the investor concerned. [emphasis added]

Here the scope of the protection of investors is limited to specific situations when it comes to the protection of *investors* but not when it comes to the treatment of *investments* as such, although the term 'treatment' appears in both instances.[53]

Furthermore it is possible to include an additional MFN standard in a specific treaty provision thereby limiting the scope of this particular provision to the specific standard.[54]

Finally, some BITs, such as certain treaties negotiated by the UK, clearly specify that their most-favoured-nation treatment clauses are to be applied also to dispute settlement. The ICSID Tribunal in *Maffezini v Spain* noted, however, that such a clear intention explicitly mentioned in

---

[52] Ibid.

[53] It should be noted that this MFN clause applies only to the post-establishment phase, contrary to the solution negotiated by Switzerland with its EFTA partners in the Agreement with Singapore as shown above.

[54] See Acconci, above n 4, Section 3.1 with reference to Germany-Barbados (1994), Article 4(4) as a specific MFN clause relating to Article 4 in addition to the more general clause contained in Article 3 of the same agreement. See also Bolivia-Peru (1993), Article 7.

the text was not very common, as far as investment treaties were concerned.[55] Yet, in 1978, the Commentaries by the ILC included the administration of justice in general among the possible subject matters of MFN clauses.[56] Whether the failure to specify means that all aspects relating to investor-State dispute settlement are considered to be part of the treatment to be accorded is an open question.[57] Certain writers state that all international arbitration must be based upon an agreement of the parties, which must be clear and unambiguous, even where reached by incorporation or by reference, and hence they deny the application of the MFN principle to the incorporation of another dispute settlement provision where this is not explicitly stated.[58] This opinion has been adopted also by certain arbitral tribunals.[59]

While some arbitral tribunals in investment disputes have tried to distinguish the application of MFN clauses in investment cases that do not specify in detail their applicability to specific areas from the application of more open-worded provisions, it seems overall that the resulting theory is rather weak and makes the outcome of a specific arbitration unpredictable.[60] Of course, one may try to elaborate a coherent theory

---

55 *Maffezini v Spain*, above n 31, para 42 *et seq.* and in this respect also Acconci, above n 4, Section 5.1 with reference to *The Ambatielos Case (Greece v United Kingdom)*, Award of 6 March 1956, UNRIAA, 1963, vol XII, at 107; she confirms that the Draft Articles prepared by the UN International Law Commission included also the 'administration of justice' among the possible subject-matters of a most-favoured- nation clause (para 24); see Draft Articles on Most-Favoured-Nation Clauses (1978), International Law Commission, available at <http://untreaty.un.org/ilc/texts/instruments/english/draft%20articles/1_3_1978.pdf> accessed 14 October 2011.

56 Ibid, para 16 (f).

57 See for example Rudolf Dolzer and Margrete Stevens, *Bilateral Investment Treaties* (Martinus Nijuhoff Publishers 1995) 58 or Jean-Pierre Laviec, *Protection et Promotion des Investissements: Etude de Droit International Economique* (Presses Universitaires de France 1985) 98, and the arbitral awards of *Plama Consortium v Bulgaria*, Decision on Jurisdiction of 8 February 2005, ICSID Case No ARB/03/24, para 189 or *Siemens A.G. v Argentina*, Decision on Jurisdiction of 3 August 2004, ICSID Case No ARB/02/8, para 106.

58 See McLachlan, Shore and Weiniger, above n 36, 256.

59 *Wintershall Aktiengesellschaft v Argentine Republic*, above n 37, para 167.

60 See also Gabriel Egli, 'Don't Get Bit: Addressing ICSID's Inconsistent Application of Most-Favored-Nation Clauses to Dispute Resolution Provisions' (2007) 34 *Pepperdine Law Review* 1045, 1075 who states correctly: 'It is important to note, however, that the Maffezini Tribunal did not base its decision on the breadth of the MFN clause in the Argentina-Spain BIT. Instead, it asserted that "there are good reasons to conclude that today dispute settlement arrangements are inextricably related to the protection of foreign investors."' (*Maffezini v Spain*,

regarding the fundamental differences in the text of various treaties in question and the circumstances in which the MFN question arose[61] – but such an approach has clear limits and may be difficult to maintain over time. As a consequence several States have started to prefer to clearly state in the negotiating history or in the agreements itself what should be exempted from the application of the MFN clause.[62]

Over all, the main question in the *Maffezini*[63] arbitral award and later similar decisions has remained whether the MFN clause applied only to substantive rules (treatment provisions) or also to procedural rules, such as the rules relating to dispute settlement or application *ratione temporis* (retrospective application) or *ratione materiae* (umbrella clauses) under a BIT.[64]

Those authors and arbitrators opposed to applying the MFN clause to procedural guarantees, in particular dispute settlement, mostly consider such an application contrary to the intention of the Contracting Parties.[65] In the *Plama v Bulgaria* case, the arbitral tribunal stated accordingly:

> [A]n MFN provision in a basic treaty does not incorporate by reference dispute settlement provisions in whole or in part set forth in another treaty, unless the MFN provision in the basic treaty leaves no doubt that the Contracting Parties intended to incorporate them.[66]

Also the recent steps by Canada, the US and the European Union to limit the scope of the MFN clauses included in their BITs seem to hint at this direction.[67] At the same time, many arbitrators and authors consider

---

above n 31, para 54).

[61] Such as attempted by Scott Vesel, 'Clearing a Path Through a Tangled Jurisprudence: Most-Favored-Nation Clauses and Dispute Settlement Provisions in Bilateral Investment Treaties' (2007) 32 *Yale Journal of International Law* 125, 127.

[62] See next section below.

[63] *Maffezini v Spain*, above n 31, paras 53 *et seq*.

[64] The question as to whether the MFN treatment obligation applied also to procedural standards besides substantive treatment provisions has also arisen in the framework or trade, more specifically in relation to the GATT of 1947 in the case *United States – Section No. 337 of the Tariff Act of 1930*, see below Section IV.

[65] See Herdegen, above n 38, 221 with reference to the arbitral awards in *Salini Costruttori S.p.A. and Italstrade S.p.A. v The Hashemite Kingdom of Jordan*, Decision on Jurisdiction of 29 November 2004, ICSID Case No ARB/02/13, paras 102 *et seq*. and *Plama Consortium Ltd. v Bulgaria*, above n 57, para 223; most recently also in *Wintershall Aktiengesellschaft v Argentine Republic*, above n 37.

[66] *Plama Consortium Ltd v Bulgaria*, above n 57, para 223.

[67] See Section immediately before this one.

such limitation unnecessary or at least not supported by the treaty language used in the past. The *Maffezini* tribunal openly rejected Spain's argument that 'matters' can only be understood to refer to substantive matters or material aspects of the treatment granted to investors and not to procedural or jurisdictional questions. Relying on international precedents and considering the broad wording of the MFN clause, which refers to 'all matters subject to this Agreement', the tribunal emphasized that dispute settlement provisions in BITs were 'essential to the protection of the rights envisaged under the pertinent treaties; they are also closely linked to the material aspects of the treatment accorded'.[68] Similarly Gaillard considers it logical to include dispute settlement provisions among the types of treatment subject to MFN.[69] Also several other authors seem favourably disposed to including procedural rules as long as this seems not expressly precluded by the wording of a treaty or is supported by the context when interpreting the treaty at stake.[70]

It is interesting to observe that generally arbitral tribunals have limited their openness to letting the claimant borrow more favourable dispute settlement provisions to cases involving BITs concluded by Argentina and the question of a mandatory waiting period. This approach developed in *Maffezini* was even expanded in *Siemens v Argentina* (2004), where again the waiting period of 18 months was equally avoided this way. Other cases affirming the possibility of getting rid of a waiting period through importation of a different dispute settlement provision not containing this requirement into a BIT are *Gas Natural v Argentina* (2005), *Camuzzi v*

---

[68] *Maffezini v Spain*, above n 31, para 55 as summarized by Reinisch, above n 44.

[69] See Emmanuel Gaillard, 'Chronique des sentences arbitrales' (2005) 128 *Journal du Droit International* 135, 163: 'Lorsque la clause est rédigée en des termes très généraux, tout laisse à penser que l'intention des rédacteurs du traité était bien de lui permettre de jouer à l'égard de tous les bénéfices que l'Etat d'accueil serait susceptible d'accorder aux ressortissants d'Etats tiers. Or force est de constater que l'accès à un mécanisme efficace et neutre de règlement des différends . . . est bien l'un des bénéfices les plus importants, sinon le plus important, susceptible de résulter du droit contemporain de la protection des investissements.' Gaillard, above n 10.

[70] See also Piero Bernardini, 'Investment Arbitration under the ICSID Convention and BITs' in Gerald Aksen *et al.* (eds), *Global Reflections on International Law, Commerce and Dispute Resolution: Liber Amicorum in Honour of Robert Briner* (ICC Pub 2005) 95 *et seq.*; Christoph Schreuer, *The Dynamic Evolution of the ICSID System* (2006) 9; see also Michael Schmid, *Swiss Investment Protection Agreements: Most-Favoured-Nation Treatment and Umbrella Clauses* (Schulthess 2007) 43 and 46.

Argentina (2005),[71] *National Grid plc v Argentina* (2006),[72] as well as in *Suez, Sociedad General de Aguas de Barcelona S.A., and Vivendi Universal S.A.* and *AWG Group Ltd.* v. *Argentina* (2006).[73] All of these cases involve non-compliance with the waiting periods provided in some of Argentina's BITs. Only in *Wintershall Aktiengesellschaft v Argentine Republic* (2008) did the ICSID tribunal deny the implicit waiver of the 18-month waiting period through reliance on the MFN clause.[74]

In *Salini v Jordan* (2004),[75] in *Plama v Bulgaria* (2005),[76] in *Telenor v Hungary* (2006),[77] and in *Berschader v Russia* (2006),[78] however, the respective ICSID tribunals came to the conclusion that the applicable MFN clauses did not lend themselves to widening the substantive scope of the dispute settlement method specifically chosen in a selected BIT.[79] Only in *RosInvestCo UK Ltd v The Russian Federation* (2007)[80] did the tribunal uphold jurisdiction by allowing a British investor to invoke a dispute settlement clause with a wider substantive scope. This allowed the tribunal to extend its own jurisdiction to issues of occurrence and validity of expropriation which were not covered by the more limited jurisdiction clause in the BIT between Russia and the investor's home State.[81] This seems so far the only existing decision where a tribunal accepted the import of a procedural aspect of a dispute settlement provision other than the waiting period.

---

[71] *Camuzzi International S.A. v Argentina*, Decision on Objections to Jurisdiction of 11 May 2005, ICSID Case No ARB/03/2, para 121; see for details Acconci, above n 4, Section 5.1.

[72] *National Grid plc v The Argentine Republic*, Decision on Jurisdiction of 20 June 2006, UNCITRAL, paras 53 *et seq.*

[73] *Suez, Sociedad General de Aguas de Barcelona S.A., and Vivendi Universal S.A. v The Argentine Republic*, ICSID Case No ARB/03/19 and *AWG Group Ltd v The Argentine Republic*, Decision on Jurisdiction of 3 August 2006, UNCITRAL.

[74] *Wintershall Aktiengesellschaft v Argentine Republic*, above n 37.

[75] *Salini Costruttori S.p.A. and Italstrade S.p.A. v The Hashemite Kingdom of Jordan*, Decision on Jurisdiction of 29 November 2004, ICSID Case No ARB/02/13.

[76] *Plama Consortium Ltd v Bulgaria*, above n 57.

[77] *Telenor Mobile Communications A.S. v Republic of Hungary*, Award of 13 September 2006, ICSID Case No ARB/04/15.

[78] *Berschader v Russia*, Award of 21 April 2006, SCC Case No 080/2004 (Belgium/Russia BIT).

[79] See Reinisch, above n 44.

[80] *RosInvestCo UK Ltd v The Russian Federation*, Award on Jurisdiction of 28 October 2007, SCC Case No Arb V079/2005.

[81] See UNCTAD, Latest developments in investor-state dispute settlement, Doc. UNCTAD/WEB/ITE/IIA/2008/3, IIA MONITOR No 1 (2008) International investment agreements, Geneva, 2008, 6.

In the recent past, the divide between arbitrators regarding the scope of the MFN clause surfaced again prominently in *Impregilo S.p.A. v Argentine Republic*.[82] The majority confirmed that in view of the fact that the MFN provision, according to the text of the agreement under review, applied 'to all matters' and thus that a waiting period before arbitration not contained in other agreements concluded by Argentina could be waived. However, Brigitte Stern, in a comprehensive dissenting opinion, expressed her criticism of this approach and the parallel decisions in e.g. *Maffezini* and supported the finding in *Plama*.[83]

4.2.3 (General) exceptions

On the whole a very divergent and sometimes puzzling case law has evolved regarding the proper scope of MFN clauses. As a reaction more and more States have started to explicitly limit the scope of MFN clauses by including general or sector-specific specific exceptions. These exceptions or carve-outs are similar to those that have traditionally been included by certain States with regard to, for example, tax issues and most importantly in recent years with regard to economic integration agreements including free trade areas and customs unions. The same may be true for specific sectors such as telecom, aviation, and other important industries where more specific treaty regimes exist.[84]

Like any treaty provision the guarantee of the MFN clause can be subject to general exceptions contained in the Treaty. While this is well known in respect to the GATT (Article XX) or the GATS (Article XIV) it is a more recent tendency in BITs. The 2003 Canadian Model BIT includes a modified GATT Article XX-like, general exceptions provision that applies to all obligations in the model treaty. The general exceptions cover measures to protect human, animal or plant life or health, to ensure compliance with law and for conservation purposes. This type of general exceptions provision, while common in trade treaties, has traditionally not been used extensively in BITs but more recent practice shows that this has changed. In particular, FTAs containing trade and investment chapters

---

[82] *Impregilo S.p.A. v Argentine Republic*, Award of 21 June 2011, ICSID Case No ARB/07/17, Concurring and Dissenting Opinion of Judge Charles N Brower, Concurring and Dissenting Opinion of Professor Brigitte Stern.

[83] See § 14 of her dissent (as attached to the award): 'To be clear, I am very strongly convinced that MFN clauses should not apply to dispute settlement mechanisms and I therefore disagree with the result arrived at in the *Maffezini* and *al.* cases and consequently concur with the result arrived at in the *Plama* and *al.* cases.'

[84] See, for example, the NAFTA Agreement and, in particular, its Annex IV.

now often include a general exception clause – often very similar if not identical to those found in the in the GATT/GATS.[85]

In view of the recent character of this solution, the meaning of these exceptions with regard to investments is less tested than in the field of trade; as a consequence some agreements provide for the application *mutatis mutandis* of the exceptions known from trade in goods and trade in services. For example, the Free Trade Agreement between the EFTA States and Singapore[86] contains a chapter on investment and in this chapter Article 49 provides:

> The following provisions shall apply, *mutatis mutandis*, to this Chapter: Articles 33 [General Exceptions in the area of trade in services], 34 [security exceptions in the area of trade in services] and 35 [Restrictions to Safeguard the Balance-of-Payments], as well as Article 19 (e) [General exceptions relating to the trade in goods and prison labour], (f) [General exceptions relating to the trade in goods and the protection of national treasures of artistic, historic or archaeological value] and (g) [General exceptions relating to the trade in goods and measures relating to the conservation of exhaustible natural resources if such measures are made effective in conjunction with restrictions on domestic production or consumption].

4.2.4 Regional Economic Integration Organization exception

It is also possible that the applicability of the MFN clause is explicitly excluded in relation to specific treaties concluded with third States that go further in their scope and nature than the treaty including the MFN clause.[87] Another possibility is to exclude certain regulatory areas in general, such as taxation.[88]

The exclusion of specific treaties is particularly common in relation to so-called economic integration agreements in relation to mere investment protection agreements or chapters. Often the respective exception is

---

[85] See also Andrew Newcombe, 'Canada's New Model Foreign Investment Protection Agreement' (2004) 30 *Canadian Council on International Law Bulletin* 14, available at <http://www.ccil-ccdi.ca/index.php? option=com_content&task=view&id=89&Itemid=86&lang=fr> accessed 14 October 2011.

[86] Agreement between the EFTA States and Singapore, signed on 26 June 2002, available at <http://www.efta.int/content/free-trade/fta-countries/singapore> accessed 14 October 2011.

[87] See also Dolzer and Stevens, above n 57, 221.

[88] See Acconci, above n 4, Section 3 with reference to Kenneth J Vandevelde, 'The Political Economy of a Bilateral Investment Treaty' (1998) 92 *American Journal of International Law* 621 *et seq* and Arghyrios A Fatouros, 'Towards an International Agreement on Foreign Direct Investment?' (1995) 10 ICSID Review – *Foreign Investment Law Journal* 188, 195–6.

referred to as the REIO (Regional Economic Integration Organization) exception.[89] This practice parallels the exception of Article XXIV GATT, later applied also under Article V GATS.[90]

Article 3 (second part) of the Treaty between Guyana and Germany of 1989 reads:

> Such treatment shall not relate, to privileges which either Contracting Party accords to nationals or companies of third States on account of its membership or association with:
> – a customs or economic union, a common market or free trade area;
> – or other regional economic cooperation Agreements which have similar objections. The treatment granted under this Article shall not relate to advantages which either Contracting Party accords to nationals or companies of third States by virtue of a *double taxation agreement or other agreements regarding matters of taxation.* [emphasis added]

Similarly Article 40 paragraph 2 of the EFTA – Singapore Agreements provides:

> 2. If a Party accords more favourable treatment to investors of any other State or their investments by virtue of a *free trade agreement, customs union or similar agreement that also provides for substantial liberalisation of investments*, it shall not be obliged to accord such treatment to investors of another Party or their investments. *However, upon request from another Party, it shall afford adequate opportunity to negotiate the benefits granted therein.* [Emphasis added]

Similarly the FTA between Switzerland and Japan of 19 February 2009[91] provides in the MFN provision of the investment chapter (Article 88):

> 3. If a Party accords more favourable treatment to investors of a non-Party and their investments by concluding or amending a free trade agreement, customs union or similar agreement that provides for substantial liberalisation of investment, it shall not be obliged to accord such treatment to investors of the other Party and their investments. Any such treatment accorded by a Party shall be notified to the other Party without delay and the former Party shall endeavour to accord to investors of the latter Party and their investments treatment no less favourable than that accorded under the concluded or

[89] United Nations Conference on Trade and Development (UNCTAD), *The REIO exception in MFN treatment clauses,* UNCTAD series on international investment policies for development, 2004.

[90] See below Part IV.

[91] Text available at <http://www.seco.admin.ch/themen/00513/02655/02731/02970/index.html?lang=en>.

> amended agreement. The former Party, upon request by the latter Party, shall enter into negotiations with a view to incorporating into this Agreement treatment no less favourable than that accorded under such concluded or amended agreement.

These last two examples are particularly interesting as they exclude even '*any agreement that also provides for substantial liberalisation of investments*', but also confer a right to negotiate the same benefits. Such negotiations shall be initiated only upon request and they are obviously without any guarantee of a positive outcome. The general good faith principle remains, however, applicable to such negotiations.

A particular problem may relate to the fact that one party to a BIT or an investment chapter in an FTA is not a party to the GATT or the GATS or has opted for very limited commitments (possibly including reservations) in the framework of the GATT. Such constellations may require exemptions from the scope of an MFN clause with regard to these commitments in order to avoid unwanted modifications of the respective commitments under the WTO.[92] The FTA EFTA – Singapore contains a rule to separate the scope of application of the guarantees contained in the investment chapter from those in the chapter on trade in services under mode 3 (commercial presence) to avoid undesirable consequences:

> Article 40 (1) [*National Treatment and Most-Favoured-Nation Treatment*] shall not apply to measures affecting trade in services whether or not a sector concerned is scheduled in Chapter III [Trade in Services] [. . .] Article 40 (1) shall also not apply to investors of a Party in services sectors and their investments in such sectors. This provision is subject to review after a period of ten years from the date of entry into force of this Agreement, with a view to examining its continued need.

In its already mentioned Communication on 30 May 2006, the European Commission (DG Trade) stated:

> It appears necessary to exclude from the benefit of this clause the most deep-integration agreements the EU concludes (i.e. to exclude granting to third countries the advantages resulting from – for instance – the EU/Balkans

---

92 See Acconci, above n 4, Section 3.1 in fine; she refers with regard to the GATT to the fact that the 1992 U.S.-Russia BIT provides for a specific exception which reads as follows: '[. . .] the exclusion from the most-favored-nation treatment obligations shall apply also to advantages accorded by the United States by virtue of its binding obligations under any multilateral international agreement concluded under the framework of the GATT after the signature of this Treaty'. The Russia – US BIT has never been ratified and has thus never entered into force.

> Stabilisation and Association Agreements that could lead at a later stage to EU accession). To that aim, the classical regional economic integration organisation (REIO) clause needs to be adjusted to avoid a carve-out from the scope of MFN treatment of any FTA, which would be counter-productive.
>
> Here again, this approach is fully consistent with WTO commitments of the EU under the GATS, since the latter contains an MFN provision of general application. It is also consistent with existing EU agreements with third countries that already contain an MFN provision (ex: Article 30 of the EU-Jordan Association Agreement; Article 48 of the Agreement EU-FYROM).[93]

4.2.5 Exclusion of dispute settlement

More recently, in view of the uncertainty relating to the scope of MFN clauses following *Maffezini*[94] several States have started to explicitly address the issue of the scope in their Model agreements or in actually concluded agreements. The 2003 Canadian Model BIT (Foreign Investment Protection Agreement = FIPA), *inter alia*, includes a specific provision eliminating the possibility of borrowing treaty provisions from treaties with third parties.[95] According to Annex III to the Canadian Model BIT, its Article 4 (MFN clause): 'shall not apply to treatment accorded under all bilateral and multilateral international agreements in force or signed prior to the date of entry into this Agreement'.

Under this mechanism MFN treatment does not extend to treatment accorded under existing treaties. 'The MFN guarantee is therefore prospective. This ensures that foreign investors under the new model cannot reach back and try to obtain the protection afforded by previous treaties. This provision seeks to avoid investment treaty shopping – the argument that MFN applies not only to the actual treatment of other foreign investors but also to the protection guaranteed to other foreign investors in other FIPAs.'[96]

In its recent FTA with Colombia, Canada included the following language in the MFN provision of the investment chapter (Article 804.3):

---

[93] The text was made available online at <http://www.iisd.org/pdf/2006/tas_upgrading_eu.pdf> accessed 14 October 2011; see on this issue also Damon Vis-Dunbar and Luke Eric Peterson, 'European Commission makes another play for power to negotiate investment pacts', *Investment Treaty News* (9 July 2006) para 6, available at <http://www.investmenttreatynews.org/content/archives. aspx> accessed 14 October 2011.

[94] *Maffezini v Spain*, above n 31, paras 53 *et seq*.

[95] See Acconci, above n 4, Section 6 and Newcombe, above n 85, 14.

[96] See ibid.

> For greater clarity, treatment 'with respect to establishment, acquisition, expansion, management, conduct, operation, and sale or other disposition of investments' referred to in paragraphs 1 and 2 does not encompass dispute resolution mechanisms, such as those in Section B of this Chapter, that are provided for in international treaties or trade agreements.

The 2003 Draft FTAA Agreement includes a footnote (no. 13) whose text is to be deemed 'as a reflection of the Parties' shared understanding of the most-favoured-nation Article and the *Maffezini* case'. It reads currently:

> One delegation proposes the following footnote to be included in the negotiating history as a reflection of the Parties' shared understanding of the Most-Favoured-Nation Article and the *Maffezini* case. This footnote would be deleted in the final text of the Agreement:
>
> The Parties note the recent decision of the arbitral tribunal in Maffezini (Arg.) v. Kingdom of Spain, which found an unusually broad most favored nation clause in an Argentina-Spain agreement to encompass international dispute resolution procedures. See Decision on Jurisdiction §§ 38-64 (January 25, 2000), reprinted in 16 ICSID Rev. F.I.L.J. 212 (2002). By contrast, the Most-Favored-Nation Article of this Agreement is expressly limited in its scope to matters 'with respect to the establishment, acquisition, expansion, management, conduct, operation, and sale or other disposition of investments.' The Parties share the understanding and intent that this clause does not encompass international dispute resolution mechanisms such as those contained in Section C.2.b. (Dispute Settlement between a Party and an Investor of Another Party) of this Chapter, and therefore could not reasonably lead to a conclusion similar to that of the Maffezini case.[97]

Similarly during the negotiations for a Central America-Dominican Republic-United States Free Trade Agreement (CAFTA), in 2004 the parties had included at some point a footnote in the draft text with the following text:

> [t]he Most-Favored-Nation Treatment Article of this Agreement is expressly limited in its scope to matters 'with respect to the establishment, acquisition, expansion, management, conduct operation and sale or other dispositions of investments.' The Parties share the understanding and intent that this clause does not encompass international dispute resolution mechanisms such as those contained in Section C of this chapter, and therefore could not reasonably lead to a conclusion similar to that of the *Maffezini* case.

---

[97] The text is available at <http://www.ftaa-alca.org/FTAADraft03/ChapterXVII_e.asp#note13> accessed 14 October 2011.

The footnote was to be eliminated before the conclusion of the negotiations but its insertion in 2004 was specifically intended to make it part of the negotiating history. To the United States this approach obviously seems to be a way to prevent a '*Maffezini*-like' interpretation of the MFN clauses contained in its agreements without leading to an unwanted watering-down of the provision.[98] Another example of US practice is the Agreement concluded with Peru (Peru Trade Promotion Agreement; PTPA) which also rejects the interpretations adopted by some recent tribunals (also in cases not involving the United States) that treaty clauses guaranteeing most-favoured-nation treatment reach and import provisions in other treaties relating to dispute settlement procedures. Again a footnote (to Article 10.4) provides that MFN obligations do not extend to dispute resolution mechanisms provided for in other investment treaties or trade agreements.[99]

Furthermore, on 30 May 2006 the European Commission (DG Trade) presented an Issue Paper to the attention of what used to be the European Community's so-called 133 Committee (now governed by Article 207 Treaty on the Functioning of the European Union) in view of its future competence to negotiate investment treaties on behalf of the European Community (now EU) and thus taking over this competence from the Member States, as envisaged at that time in the proposals for treaty reform and now entered into force as Article 207 of the Treaty on the Functioning of the European Union. In this paper the Commission suggested, with regard to the inclusion of an appropriate MFN clause in future agreements:

> The scope of application of the MFN clause is focused and limited to establishment, thus clearly signalling that it could not extend to BIT provisions on expropriation and dispute settlement.

Finally, Switzerland has very recently partly changed its practice regarding the language related to MFN treatments in its BITs in what seems a clear reaction to the *Maffezini* case law. In the agreement with

---

98 See also Luke Eric Peterson in *Investment Law and Policy Weekly News Bulletin* (6 February 2004) available at <http://www.iisd.org/pdf/2004/investment_investsd_feb6_2004.pdf> accessed 14 October 2011 and 'International Law in Brief', American Society of International Law (6 February 2004) available at <http://www.asil.org/ilib/ilib0703.htm> accessed 14 October 2011.

99 See also (2009) 104 *AJIL* 768–70, 769.

Colombia signed on 17 May 2006,[100] the parties included an Annex which reads:

> For greater certainty, it is further understood that the most favourable nation treatment [. . .] does not encompass mechanisms for the settlement of investment disputes provided for in other international agreements concluded by the Party concerned.[101]

Similarly the FTA between Switzerland and Japan of 19 February 2009[102] stipulates in the MFN provision of the Investment Chapter (Article 88):

> It is understood that the treatment referred to in paragraph 1 does not include treatment accorded to investors of a non-Party and their investments by provisions concerning the settlement of investment disputes between a Party and the non-Party that are provided for in other international agreements.

5. CONCLUSIONS

This chapter has tried to provide a contemporary view of the state of the emerging jurisprudence of international investment law in the field of MFN. The following observations may be arrived at by studying the current case law and treaty practice regarding the MFN principle in the field of investment. While it is difficult to speak of a 'jurisprudence constante' in this field, the current trends in treaty practice seem rather clear:

1. It seems fair to claim that the inclusion of the MFN provision into modern BITs is not questioned as modern treaty practice proves. This seems also true for any attempt to multilateralize investment protection, as evidenced by the MAI negotiations and the Energy Charter Treaty.

---

[100] Swiss Federal Council, Despatch to the Swiss Parliament regarding the Agreements on the Promotion and Protection of Investments with Serbia and Montenegro, Guyana, Azerbaijan, Saudi Arabia and Colombia, 22 September 2006, Official Gazette (Bundesblatt) (2006) 8455 *et seq.*, 8460 available online in German at <http://www.admin.ch/ch/d/ff/2006/8455.pdf> accessed 14 October 2011.

[101] Protocol to the BIT (note 17) with Colombia *ad* Article 4 para 2.

[102] Text available at <http://www.seco.admin.ch/themen/00513/02655/02731/02970/index.html?lang=en>.

2. However, in comparison to the broad MFN provisions sometimes included (in some BITs) in the past, it seems that the tendency in view of the case law of recent years is to reduce the scope of these provisions. This can be done either by limiting the scope of the generally applicable MFN clause or by carving out specific fields. The tendency in recent negotiations seems to be to make the clause much more precise than in the past.

3. Traditional carve-outs exist in the field of tax issues, particularly in view of the existence of double taxation agreements. This may become even more important in view of the conclusion of highly complex recent treaties that focus to a large extent on administrative assistance in tax matters and involve highly complex questions of due process and the protection of the individual in domestic administrative proceedings.[103]

4. Another common exception with regard to the applicability of the MFN principle in investment law now often relates to regional integration agreements. At the same time one should not forget, as the experience with the WTO has shown, that most States will want to maintain more favourable economic relations with specific partners. Such preferential treatment must remain possible. More and more often, a reference to free trade areas and customs unions as in the WTO is included also in investment treaties. This approach may become too broad in view of the abundance of FTAs and the fact that they now normally include investment chapters. Here an alternative can be to refer to Regional Economic Integration Organization Agreements (REIO), as done in the Energy Charter Treaty. While the latter clearly protected the European Union, the inclusion of a REIO exception in a multilateral agreement might still lead to important questions as to when an agreement qualifies as a REIO. A debate similar to the one known in the WTO – when it comes to the

---

[103] See for example the agreements recently concluded between financial centres like Switzerland, Luxembourg or Liechtenstein with major economic powers on tax-related isses, e.g. Agreement between the United States of America and the Swiss Confederation on the request for information from the Internal Revenue Service of the United States of America regarding UBS AG, a corporation established under the laws of the Swiss Confederation of 19 August 2009; available at <http://www.irs.gov/pub/irs-drop/us-swiss_government_agreement.pdf> accessed 14 October 2011.

compatibility with regional trade agreements under Articles XXIV GATT and V GATS – may ultimately result. Possibly this controversy is less fundamental when it comes to capital flows than in the case of trade, but existing REIO exceptions in bilateral agreements, as shown above, remain a reality. Interesting is certainly the extension of the free movement of capitals as contained in the Treaty on the Functioning of the European Union (TFEU) but its effect remains limited due to other limitations.[104]

5. The most controversial issue in recent years with regard to the MFN principle has been its use to incorporate specific standards or definitions from BITs with third parties in order to establish the jurisdiction of an arbitral tribunal. This development has clearly led to a tendency in bilateral negotiations to exclude the applicability of the MFN principle to the dispute settlement mechanism. A codified model for use in bilateral agreements would very likely have to incorporate this limitation as well, in order not to perpetuate the uncertainty created by arbitrators. In the multilateral context it might be very likely to oblige all members to use only the existing dispute settlement mechanism contained in the multilateral agreement (with regard to violations of that particular agreement). Here again, however, the experience within the only comparable multilateral reference system, the WTO, is somewhat puzzling. The WTO members have increasingly negotiated FTAs (including dispute settlement provisions) in recent years and thereby made such use of the exception from the MFN clause that it has almost lost all its meaning. Under these FTAs specific dispute settlement proceedings are available which normally do not preclude the parallel or subsequent use of the WTO system, as the WTO DSU does not clearly entitle a WTO panel to consider whether in a separate FTA WTO members have foreseen a specific dispute settlement mechanism and had the intention to avoid duplication in the context of the multilateral system that is the WTO. If one tries to draw a lesson regarding the future of multilateral instruments in the field of investment, it seems difficult to prevent parallel proceedings and prevent actors from forum-shopping as long as separate BITs between certain parties to a multilateral system exist. At the same time, the

104 See Articles 63 and 64 (ex Articles 56 and 57 Treaty establishing the European Community).

number of known cases in the area of trade is relatively small, which seems to indicate that the problem is not (yet) of a calibre to threaten the multilateral system.[105]

[105] See for one recent summary survey on the issue Gabrielle Marceau and Julian Wyatt, 'Dispute Settlement Regimes Intermingled: Regional Trade Agreements and the WTO' (No 1, 2010) 1 *Journal of International Dispute Settlement* 67–95.

10. Is expropriation ripe for codification? The example of the non-discrimination requirement for lawful expropriations

August Reinisch*

I. INTRODUCTION

Any attempt to 'codify' or to 'distill' principles concerning the rules on expropriation usually contained in International Investment Agreements (IIAs) faces a number of challenges. On the one hand, the exact wording of the rules on expropriation, in particular the scope of the notion of indirect expropriation, the legality requirements and the applicable standard of compensation, may differ from one investment agreement to the other. On the other hand, the specific interpretation given to such rules may depend upon the individual investment tribunal deciding a specific dispute. In recent investment arbitration a considerable number of tribunals have addressed expropriation claims,[1] though only a few have come to the conclusion that expropriation rules were actually infringed.

* The author wishes to thank Andrea K Bjorklund for her comments on an earlier draft of this contribution.

[1] *ADC Affiliate Limited and ADC & ADMC Management Limited v Republic of Hungary,* Award of 2 October 2006, ICSID Case No ARB/03/16, paras 368, 423–45; *Archer Daniels Midland Company and Tate & Lyle Ingredients Americas, Inc. v Mexico*, Award of 21 November 2007, ICSID Case No ARB(AF)/04/5, paras 228–52; *Azinian, Davitian, & Baca v Mexico*, Award of 1 November 1999, ICSID Case No ARB(AF)/97/2, paras 85–124; *Azurix v Argentine Republic*, Award of 14 July 2006, ICSID Case No ARB/01/12, paras 308–23; *Bayindir Insaat Turizm Ticaret Ve Sanayi A.S. v Islamic Republic of Pakistan*, Decision on Jurisdiction of 14 November 2005, ICSID Case No ARB/03/29, paras 253–62; Award of 27 August 2009, paras 424–86; *BG Group Plc v Argentina*, Award of 24 December 2007, UNCITRAL, paras 244–72; *Biwater Gauff (Tanzania) Ltd. v United Republic of Tanzania*, Award of 24 July 2008, ICSID Case No ARB/05/22, paras 393–521; *Bogdanov and ors v Moldova*, Award, Ad hoc–SCC Arbitration Rules; Stockholm International Arbitration Review (SIAR), No 2006:3, 22 September 2005, paras

78–80; *CME Czech Republic B.V. v Czech Republic*, Partial Award of 13 September 2001, UNCITRAL, paras 591–609; *CMS Gas Transmission Company v The Argentine Republic*, Award of 12 May 2005, ICSID Case No ARB/01/8, paras 252–65; *Compañía de Aguas del Aconquija S.A. and Vivendi Universal v Argentine Republic*, Award of 20 August 2007, ICSID Case No ARB/97/3, paras 7.5.1–7.5.34; *Compañía del Desarrollo de Santa Elena SA v Costa Rica*, Award of 17 February 2000, ICSID Case No ARB/96/1, paras 68–74; *Consortium R.F.C.C. v Kingdom of Morocco*, Award of 22 December 2003, ICSID Case No ARB/00/6, paras 58–68; *Continental Casualty Company v Argentine Republic*, Award of 5 September 2008, ICSID Case No ARB/03/9, paras 271–85; *Corn Products International, Inc. v Mexico*, Decision on Responsibility of 15 January 2008, ICSID Case No ARB(AF)/04/01, paras 81–94; *Eastern Sugar BV v Czech Republic*, Partial Award and Partial Dissenting Opinion of 27 March 2007, SCC Case No 088/2004, paras 208–10; *EDF (Services) Limited v Romania*, Award of 8 October 2009, ICSID Case No ARB/05/13, paras 307–13; *EnCana Corporation v Republic of Ecuador*, Award of 3 February 2006, LCIA Case No UN3481, UNCITRAL, paras 169–99; *Enron Corporation and Ponderosa Assets, L.P. v Argentine Republic*, Award of 22 May 2007, ICSID Case No ARB/01/3, paras 234–50; *Eudoro Armando Olguín v Paraguay*, Award of 26 July 2000, ICSID Case No ARB/98/5, paras 65, 83–4; *Eureko B.V. v Republic of Poland*, Partial Award of 19 August 2005, paras 238–43; *Feldman v Mexico*, Award of 16 December 2002, ICSID Case No ARB(AF)/99/1, 18 ICSID Rev–FILJ 488 (2003), 42 ILM 625 (2003), paras 89–153; *Fireman's Fund Insurance Company v Mexico*, Award of 17 July 2006, ICSID Case No ARB(AF)/02/01, paras 169–218; *Bernardus Henricus Funnekotter and others v Republic of Zimbabwe*, Award of 22 April 2009, ICSID Case No ARB/05/6, paras 96–124; *GAMI Investments, Inc. v United Mexican States*, Award of 15 November 2004, paras 116–33; *Generation Ukraine, Inc. v Ukraine*, Award of 16 September 2003, ICSID Case No ARB/00/9, paras 20.1–23.1; *Glamis Gold, Ltd. v United States of America*, Award of 8 June 2009, UNCITRAL (NAFTA), paras 353–6; *Goetz and others v Burundi*, Award (Embodying the Parties' Settlement Agreement) of 10 February 1999, ICSID Case No ARB/95/3, 6 ICSID Rep 3, 15 ICSID Rev–FILJ 457, paras 124–33; *Lauder v Czech Republic*, Final Award of 3 September 2001, UNCITRAL, paras 196–204; *Link-Trading Joint Stock Company v Moldova*, Award of 18 April 2002, UNCITRAL, paras 63–92; *LESI SpA and ASTALDI SpA v Algeria*, Award of 12 November 2008, ICSID Case No ARB/05/3, paras 119–39; *LG&E Energy Corp., LG&E Capital Corp. and LG&E International Inc. v Argentine Republic*, Decision on Liability of 3 October 2006, ICSID Case No ARB/02/1, 46 ILM 36 (2007), paras 176–200; *Link–Trading Joint Stock Company v Moldova*, Decision on Jurisdiction of 16 February 2001, UNCITRAL Arbitration Rules, paras 33–49, Final Award, paras 54–92; *M.C.I. Power Group L.C. and New Turbine, Inc. v Ecuador*, Award of 31 July 2007, ICSID Case No ARB/03/6, paras 247–51, 297-306; *Metalclad Corporation v Mexico*, Award of 30 August 2000, ICSID Case No ARB(AF)/97/1, 16 ICSID Rev–FILJ 168 (2001), 40 ILM 36 (2001), 119 ILR 618 (2002); 5 ICSID Rep 212, paras 102–12, Review by the supreme court of British Columbia, 2 May 2001, paras 31–6, 77–105; *Metalpar S.A. and Buen Aire S.A. v Argentine Republic*, Award of 6 June 2008, ICSID Case No ARB/03/5, paras 165–74; *Methanex v United States*, Award of 3 August 2005, UNCITRAL (NAFTA), Part IV, D; *Middle East Cement Shipping and Handling Co SA v Egypt*, Award of 12 April 2002, ICSID Case No ARB/99/6, paras 97–144; *MTD Equity Sdn. Bhd. and*

Scholarly treatment of expropriation issues tends to focus on general commonalities found in the practice of investment arbitration.[2] It seems

---

MTD Chile S.A. v Republic of Chile, Award of 25 May 2004, ICSID Case No ARB/01/7, paras 207–14; *National Grid PLC v Argentina*, Award of 3 November 2008, UNCITRAL Arbitration Rules, paras 135–55; *Noble Ventures, Inc. v Romania*, Award of 12 October 2005, ICSID Case No ARB/01/11, paras 203–16; *Nykomb Synergetics Technology Holding AB v Latvia*, Award of 16 December 2003, Stockholm Rules, paras 4.3.1; *Parkerings-Compagniet AS v Lithuania*, Award of 11 September 2007, ICSID Case No ARB/05/8, paras 431–56; *Plama Consortium Limited v Bulgaria*, Award of 27 August 2008, ICSID Case No ARB/03/24 (ECT), paras 188–93; *Pope & Talbot Inc. v The Government of Canada*, Interim Award of 26 June 2000, UNCITRAL (NAFTA), paras 81–105; *PSEG Global et al. v Republic of Turkey*, ICSID Case No ARB/02/5, Award of 19 January 2007, paras 272–80; *Rumeli Telekom AS and Telsim Mobil Telekomikasyon Hizmetleri AS v Kazakhstan*, Award of 29 July 2008, ICSID Case No ARB/05/16, paras 682–715; *Saipem SpA v Bangladesh*, Decision on jurisdiction and recommendation on provisional measures of 21 March 2007, ICSID Case No ARB/05/07, paras 129–35; Award of 30 June 2009, paras 120–91; *Saluka Investments BV (The Netherlands) v The Czech Republic*, Partial Award of 17 March 2006, UNCITRAL paras 254–75, 468–70; *S.D. Myers, Inc. v Canada*, Award (Merits) of 13 November 2000, UNCITRAL (NAFTA), paras 279–88; *Sedelmayer v Russian Federation*, Award of 7 July 1998, paras 260–86; *Sempra Energy International v Argentina*, Award of 28 September 2007, ICSID Case No ARB/02/16, paras 271–89; *Société Générale v Dominican Republic*, Preliminary Objections to Jurisdiction, 19 September 2008, UNCITRAL, LCIA Case No UN 7927, paras 53–66; *Waguih Elie George Siag & Clorinda Vecchi v The Arab Republic of Egypt*, Award of 1 June 2009, ICSID Case No ARB/05/15, paras 427–44; *Siemens A.G. v Argentina*, Award of 6 February 2007, ICSID Case No ARB/02/08, paras 245–73; *Técnicas Medioambientales Tecmed, S.A. v United Mexican States*, Award of 29 May 2003, ICSID Case No ARB (AF)/00/2, 10 ICSID Rep 130, paras 95–151; *Telenor Mobile Communications A.S. v Republic of Hungary*, Award of 13 September 2006, ICSID Case No ARB/04/15, paras 63–80; *Tokios Tokelés v Ukraine*, Award of 26 July 2007, ICSID Case No ARB/02/18, paras 117–22; *Toto Costruzioni Generali SpA v Lebanon*, Decision on Jurisdiction of 11 September 2009, ICSID Case No ARB/07/12, paras 176–186; *Tradex Hellas S.A. v Albania*, Award of 29 April 1999, ICSID Case No ARB/94/2, paras 91–9, 132–205; *Waste Management, Inc. v United Mexican States*, Award of 30 April 2004, ICSID Case No ARB(AF)/00/3, paras 141–78; *Wena Hotel Limited v Arab Republic of Egypt*, Award of 21 November 2000, ICSID Case No ARB/98/4, 41 ILM 896 (2002), paras 96–101, Decision on the Application by Wena Hotels Ltd for Interpretation of the Award of 31 October 2005, paras 108–33.

[2] See, among others, Maurizio Brunetti, 'Iran-United States Claims Tribunal, NAFTA Chapter 11, and the Doctrine of Indirect Expropriation' (2000) 2 CJIL 203; George C Christie, 'What Constitutes a Taking of Property under International Law' (1962) 33 *BYIL* 307; Daniel Clough, 'Regulatory Expropriations and Compensation under NAFTA' (2005) 6 *JWIT* 553; R Doak Bishop, James Crawford and W Michael Reisman, *Foreign Investment Disputes* (Kluwer Law International 2005) 837 *et seq*; Rudolf Dolzer, 'Indirect

Expropriation of Alien Property' (1986) 1 ICSID Review-*Foreign Investment Law Journal* 41; Rudolf Dolzer, 'Indirect Expropriations: New Developments?' (2002) 11 *NYU Environmental Law Journal* 64; Rudolf Dolzer, 'New Foundations of the Law of Expropriation of Alien Property' (1981) 75 *AJIL* 553; Rudolf Dolzer and Christoph Schreuer, *Principles of International Investment Law* (OUP 2008) 89; Rudolf Dolzer and Margrete Stevens, *Bilateral Investment Treaties* (Kluwer Law International 1995) 97 *et seq*; Christopher Dugan, Don Wallace Jr, Noah Rubins and Borzu Sabahi, *Investor-State Arbitration* (OUP 2008) 429 *et seq*; Yves L Fortier and Stephen L Drymer, 'Indirect Expropriation in the Law of International Investment: I know It When I See It, or *Caveat Investor*' (2004) 19 ICSID Review-*Foreign Investment Law Journal* 293; Veijo Heiskanen, 'The Doctrine of Indirect Expropriation in Light of the Practice of the Iran-United States Claims Tribunal' (2007) 8 *JWIT* 215; Rosalyn Higgins, 'The Taking of Foreign Property by the State' (1982-III) 176 *Recueil des Cours* 259; Kaj Hobér, *Investment Arbitration in Eastern Europe: In Search of a Definition of Expropriation* (Juris 2007); Anne K Hoffmann, 'Indirect Expropriation' in August Reinisch (ed), *Standards of Investment Protection* (OUP 2008) 151–170; Christina Knahr, 'Indirect Expropriation in Recent Investment Arbitration' (December 2007) *Transnational Dispute Management*; Ursula Kriebaum, 'Partial Expropriation' (2007) 8 *JWIT* 69; Ursula Kriebaum, 'Regulatory Takings: Balancing the Interests of the Investor and the State' (2007) 8 *JWIT* 717; Ursula Kriebaum and August Reinisch, 'Property, Right to, International Protection' in *Max Planck Encyclopedia of Public International Law*; Bjørn Kunoy, 'Developments in Indirect Expropriation Case Law in ICSID Transnational Arbitration' (2005) 6(3) *JWIT* 467; Vaughan Lowe, 'Regulation or Expropriation?' (2002) 55 *Current Legal Problems* 447; Andreas F Lowenfeld, *International Economic Law* (2nd edn, OUP 2008) 536 *et seq*; Campbell McLachlan, Laurence Shore and Matthew Weiniger *International Investment Arbitration: Substantive Principles* (OUP 2007); Peter T Muchlinski, *Multinational Enterprises and the Law* (2nd edn, OUP 2007) 588 *et seq*; Andrew Newcombe, 'The Boundaries of Regulatory Expropriation in International Law' (2005) 20 ICSID Review-*Foreign Investment Law Journal* 1; Andrew Newcombe and Lluís Paradell, *Law and Practice of Investment Treaties* (2009) 321 *et seq*; Yves Nouvel, 'Les mesures équivalentes à une expropriation dans la pratique récente des tribunaux arbitraux' (2002) 106 RGDIP 79; Jan Paulsson and Zachary Douglas, 'Indirect Expropriation in Investment Treaty Arbitrations' in Norbert Horn and Stefan Kröll (eds), *Arbitrating Foreign Investment Disputes – Procedural and Substantive Legal Aspects* (2004) 145; August Reinisch, 'Legality of Expropriations' in August Reinisch, *Standards of Investment Protection* (OUP 2008) 171; August Reinisch, 'Expropriation' in Peter Muchlinski, Federico Ortino and Christoph Schreuer (eds), *The Oxford Handbook of International Investment Law* (OUP 2008) 407–58; August Reinisch, *Recent Developments in International Investment Law* (Pedone 2009) 51 *et seq*; Noah Rubins and N Stephan Kinsella, *International Investment, Political Risk and Dispute Resolution. A Practitioner's Guide* (Oceana Publications 2005) 155 *et seq*; Jeswald W Salacuse, *The Law of Investment Treaties* (OUP 2010) 285 *et seq*; Gary H Sampliner, 'Arbitration of Expropriation Cases under US Investment Treaties – A Threat to Democracy or the Dog that didn't Bark?' (2003) 18 ICSID *Review-Foreign Investment Law Journal* 1; Thomas Waelde and Abba Kolo, 'Environmental Regulation, Investment Protection and "Regulatory Taking" in International Law' (2001) 50 *International and Comparative Law*

worthwhile, however, to consider whether a more specific emphasis on the difference between IIA standards to be applied in specific cases should be made. At the same time, it is undeniable that the textual discrepancies found in different IIAs usually cannot conceal the fact that there is a broad common understanding of the underlying, often customary international law-based, notions of expropriation, its legality and consequences.

It is this latter recognition which merits a closer analysis of the common aspects; in case and to the extent that the different textual variations found in different IIAs can be regarded as expressions of common notions it will make sense to consider a potential codification of investment law principles and rules. Otherwise, such an attempt may not prove very promising.

This chapter will briefly assess the common core of expropriation provisions in IIAs as well as the common and divergent interpretations given to such provisions by arbitration tribunals. It will then, with a view to a potential 'codification' of expropriation rules, discuss different codification types. A concluding section will try to 'codify' the present state of the non-discrimination requirement in expropriation law by relying on a so-called commentary style technique.

II. THE COMMON CORE OF EXPROPRIATION PROVISIONS IN IIAS

IIAs, both bilateral investment treaties (BITs) and multilateral investment agreements, contain certain variations when it comes to the specific wording regarding the notion of expropriation, the legality of expropriation and the standard of compensation. This fact necessitates a closer inquiry into the underlying concepts in order to find out whether the difference in wording is intended to reflect substantive differences or whether the underlying rules converge.

Quarterly 811; John A Westberg, 'Applicable Law, Expropriatory Takings and Compensation in Cases of Expropriation; ICSID and Iran United States Tribunal Case Law Compared' (1993) 8 ICSID Review-*FILJ* 1; Burns H Weston, 'Creeping Expropriation under International Law: A Modest Foray into the Problem of Creeping Expropriation' (1975) 16 *VJIL* 103; C. Yannaca-Small, '"Indirect Expropriation" and the "Right to Regulate" in International Investment Law' in OECD (ed), *International Investment Law: A Changing Landscape* (2005) 43; UNCTAD, *Taking of Property* (2000) 11 *et seq.*

1. The Notion of Expropriation – What Constitutes an Expropriation?

Under customary international law it is widely accepted that expropriation may take different forms: broad nationalizations which affect entire industries and sectors; socializations of private property which abolish the entire or most of an existing system of private ownership; property confiscations which involve a punitive element; creeping expropriations which are achieved by a series of measures; and various forms of indirect expropriations which involve acts or omissions falling short of a direct transfer of ownership. The latter forms of indirect expropriation are often referred to as *de facto*, disguised, creeping, constructive, or regulatory expropriations.[3]

Compared to this rich semantic variety of describing the fact that expropriation may not only occur in a direct transfer of ownership, the actual language used in IIAs is relatively coherent. Most treaties provide that contracting parties shall not expropriate 'directly or indirectly through measures equivalent to expropriation', 'measures having equivalent effect'[4] or 'measures tantamount to expropriations'.[5]

Only recently, some investment treaties have started to define the notion of indirect expropriation in a more detailed way. The 2004 Canadian Model BIT,[6] as well as the 2004 US Model BIT,[7] are prime

---

[3] See on the terminology, August Reinisch, 'Expropriation' in Peter Muchlinski, Federico Ortino and Christoph Schreuer (eds) *The Oxford Handbook of International Investment Law* (OUP 2008) 407; Andrew Newcombe and Lluís Paradell, above n 2, 325*;* Anne K Hoffmann, 'Indirect Expropriation' in August Reinisch (ed) *Standards of Investment Protection* (OUP 2008) 153; Rudolf Dolzer and Margrete Stevens, *Bilateral Investment Treaties* (Kluwer Law International 1995) 99.

[4] See e.g. Art 5 (1) Agreement between the United Mexican States and the Republic of Austria on the Promotion and Protection of Investments; Art 6 (1) US Model BIT; Art 10.6 (1) United States-Morocco Free Trade Agreement; Art 13 ECT.

[5] See e.g. Art 3 (1) Treaty with the Czech and Slovak Federal Republic concerning the Reciprocal Encouragement and Protection of Investment; Art 1110 NAFTA.

[6] Foreign Investment Protection and Promotion Agreement 2004 (Canadian Model BIT) <http://www.naftaclaims.com/files/Canada_Model_BIT.pdf>; see also James McIlroy, 'Canada's New Foreign Investment Protection and Promotion Agreement: Two Steps Forward, One Step Back?' (2004) 5 *Journal of World Trade and Investment* 621; Andrew Newcombe, 'Canada's New Model Foreign Investment Protection Agreement', *Canadian Council of Int'l Law Bulletin*, Fall 2004.

[7] Model Treaty Between the United States and [Country] Concerning the Encouragement and Reciprocal Protection of Investment (US Model BIT),

examples of such attempts to clarify and specify the meaning of indirect expropriation, gradually developed by case law, in a treaty text.[8] The two definitions contained in the annexes therein as expressions of 'shared understandings' both emphasize the gradual character of indirect expropriation by referring to 'a measure or series of measures' and their *de facto* nature by stressing that indirect expropriation may take place 'without formal transfer of title or outright seizure'. They further stress, among the major factors to determine whether an expropriation has occurred, the 'economic impact of the measure', the 'interfere[nce] with distinct, reasonable investment-backed expectations', and 'the character of the measure'. Finally, they add the somewhat cryptic formula:

> Except in rare circumstances, such as when a measure or series of measures are so severe in the light of their purpose that they cannot be reasonably viewed as having been adopted and applied in good faith, non-discriminatory measures of

---

November 2004 <http://www.naftaclaims.com/files/US_Model_BIT.pdf>; see also Stephen M Schwebel, 'The United States 2004 Model Bilateral Investment Treaty: an Exercise in the Regressive Development of International Law' (April 2006) 3:2 *Transnational Dispute Management*; Kenneth J Vandevelde, 'A Brief History of International Investment Agreements' (2005) 12 *UC Davis J Int'l Law & Poly* 157; Kenneth J Vandevelde, *U.S. International Investment Agreements* (OUP 2009).

[8] See 2004 Canadian Model BIT, above n 6, Annex B 13(1) on the clarification of indirect expropriation ('The Parties confirm their shared understanding that:

a) Indirect expropriation results from a measure or series of measures of a Party that have an effect equivalent to direct expropriation without formal transfer of title or outright seizure;
b) The determination of whether a measure or series of measures of a Party constitute an indirect expropriation requires a case-by-case, fact-based inquiry that considers, among other factors:
   i) the economic impact of the measure or series of measures, although the sole fact that a measure or series of measures of a Party has an adverse effect on the economic value of an investment does not establish that an indirect expropriation has occurred;
   ii) the extent to which the measure or series of measures interfere with distinct, reasonable investment-backed expectations; and
   iii) the character of the measure or series of measures;
c) Except in rare circumstances, such as when a measure or series of measures are so severe in the light of their purpose that they cannot be reasonably viewed as having been adopted and applied in good faith, non-discriminatory measures of a Party that are designed and applied to protect legitimate public welfare objectives, such as health, safety and the environment, do not constitute indirect expropriation.').

a Party that are designed and applied to protect legitimate public welfare objectives, such as health, safety and the environment, do not constitute indirect expropriation.

This language broadly reflects the idea that indirect expropriations (including regulatory expropriations) which trigger an obligation to compensate have to be distinguished from normal regulatory measures (within the 'regulatory' or 'police powers' of a state) which do not constitute an expropriation and thus do not entail an obligation to compensate. This so-called police powers exception, largely inspired by US practice,[9] has been reflected in investment arbitration awards such as *Methanex*[10] and *Saluka*[11] and was likely to have influenced the above-quoted formulations of the 2004 Canadian and US Model BITs. As the tribunal remarked in the *Saluka* case, 'drawing a bright and easily distinguishable line' between these two situations is a difficult task,[12] and a number of decisions have taken issue with the emphasis on public purpose in *Methanex* and *Saluka*. Instead, tribunals such as the one in *Azurix*[13]

---

[9] American Law Institute (ed), *Restatement (Third) of the Foreign Relations Law of the United States* § 712 (1987) 201 ('A state is not responsible for loss of property or for other economic disadvantage resulting from bona fide general taxation, regulation, forfeiture for crime, or other action of the kind that is commonly accepted as within the police power of states [...]').

[10] *Methanex Corporation v United States of America*, Final Award on Jurisdiction and Merits of 3 August 2005, NAFTA Arbitral Tribunal, IV D para7 ('[...] as a matter of general international law, a non-discriminatory regulation for a public purpose, which is enacted in accordance with due process and, which affects, inter alios, a foreign investor or investment is not deemed expropriatory and compensable unless specific commitments had been given by the regulating government to the then putative foreign investor contemplating investment that the government would refrain from such regulation.').

[11] *Saluka Investments BV (The Netherlands) v The Czech Republic*, Partial Award of 17 March 2006, UNCITRAL, para 262 (' [...] the principle that a State does not commit an expropriation and is thus not liable to pay compensation to a dispossessed alien investor when it adopts general regulations that are "commonly accepted as within the police power of States" forms part of customary international law today.').

[12] Ibid, para 263 ('[...] international law has yet to identify in a comprehensive and definitive fashion precisely what regulations are considered "permissible" and "commonly accepted" as falling within the police or regulatory power of States and, thus, non-compensable. In other words, it has yet to draw a bright and easily distinguishable line between non-compensable regulations on the one hand and, on the other, measures that have the effect of depriving foreign investors of their investment and are thus unlawful and compensable in international law.').

[13] *Azurix Corp. v Argentine Republic*, Award of 14 July 2006, ICSID Case No ARB/01/12.

have suggested that other criteria, such as proportionality and non-discrimination, be taken into consideration in order to provide 'useful guidance for purposes of determining whether regulatory actions would be expropriatory and give rise to compensation'.[14]

2. The Pre-conditions for Lawful Expropriation

There seems to be an equally broad consensus on the main legality criteria, developed in customary international law, as to the conditions under which an expropriation can be considered to be lawful. The criteria of public purpose, non-discrimination and compensation, as well as often due process, are regularly found in investment treaties[15] and are broadly considered to constitute customary law.[16] Nevertheless, language in different BITs and IIAs shows some variety.[17] The determination whether

---

14 Ibid, para 312.

15 See the overview in August Reinisch, 'Legality of Expropriations' in August Reinisch (ed) *Standards of Investment Protection* (OUP 2008) 171.

16 See GA Res 1803 (XVII), UN GAOR, 17th Session, Agenda Item 39, para 4, UN Doc A/RES/1803 (XVII) (1962) ('Nationalization, expropriation or requisitioning shall be based on grounds or reasons of public utility, security or the national interest which are recognized as overriding purely individual or private interests, both domestic and foreign. In such cases the owner shall be paid appropriate compensation, in accordance with the rules in force in the State taking such measures in the exercise of its sovereignty and in accordance with international law.'); *Restatement (Third) of the Foreign Relations Law of the United States*, above n 9, § 712 ('A state is responsible under international law for injury resulting from: (1) a taking by the state of the property of a national of another state that (a) is not for a public purpose, or (b) is discriminatory, or (c) not accompanied by provisions for just compensation.'); UNCTAD, *International Investment Agreements: Key Issues* (2004) 235 ('Under customary international law and typical international investment agreements, three principal requirements need to be satisfied before a taking can be considered to be lawful: it should be for a public purpose; it should not be discriminatory; and compensation should be paid.').

17 See e.g. Article 3(2) 1959 Germany-Pakistan BIT ('Nationals or companies of either party shall not be subjected to expropriation of their investments in the territory of the other party except for public benefit and against compensation, which shall represent the equivalent of the investments affected.'); Article 5 1991 Czechoslovakia-Netherlands BIT ('Neither Contracting Party shall take any measures depriving, directly or indirectly, investors of the other Contracting Party of their investments unless the following conditions are complied with: (a) the measures are taken in the public interest and under due process of law; (b) the measures are not discriminatory; (c) the measures are accompanied by provision for the payment of just compensation.'); Article 4(1) 1998 China-Poland BIT ('Either Contracting Party may for security reasons or a public purpose, nationalize, expropriate or take similar measures (hereinafter referred to as 'expropriatory measures') against investments investors of the other Contracting Party in its

an expropriation is lawful or not is crucial for determining its legal consequences. While lawful expropriation entails a duty to compensate, according to the standard usually provided for in the applicable IIA, an unlawful expropriation triggers the obligation to make reparation under the principles of state responsibility – which in effect may often lead to higher financial costs.[18]

3. Compensation – Amount and Mode of Payment

The amount of compensation due in cases of expropriation has been one of the most controversial topics in general international law. It constitutes a textbook example of the clash between traditional western views with the emergence of a 'Third World' outlook on expropriation problems supported by socialist theories of international law.[19] In the 1960s and 1970s this ideologically motivated debate was reinforced by the New International Economic Order (NIEO) debate and led to a series of very controversial resolutions in the UN General Assembly.[20]

---

territory. Such expropriatory measures shall be non-discriminatory and shall be taken under due process of national law and against compensation.'); Article 6(1) 2004 US Model BIT ('1. Neither Party may expropriate or nationalize a covered investment either directly or indirectly through measures equivalent to expropriation or nationalization ("expropriation"), except: (a) for a public purpose; (b) in a non-discriminatory manner; (c) on payment of prompt, adequate, and effective compensation; and (d) in accordance with due process of law and Article 5 [Minimum Standard of Treatment](1) through (3).').

[18] See *infra* at note 41.

[19] Lowenfeld, above n 2, 469 *et seq*; Newcombe and Paradell, above n 2, 377; UNCTAD, *Taking of Property* (2000) 5; Salacuse, above n 2, 62 *et seq*.

[20] See e.g. UNGA Res 3171 (XXVIII), UN GAOR, 287th Session, para 3, UN Doc A/RES/3171 (XXVIII) (1973) ('. . . that the application of the principle of nationalization carried out by States, as an expression of their sovereignty in order to safeguard their natural resources, implies that each State is entitled to determine the amount of possible compensation and the mode of payment, and that any disputes which might arise should be settled in accordance with the national legislation of each State carrying out such measures.'); Article 2(2) of the so-called Charter of Economic Rights and Duties of States, UNGA Res 3281 (XXIX), UN GAOR, 29th Session, UN Doc A/9631 (1974) ('Each State has the right [. . .] (c) To nationalize, expropriate or transfer ownership of foreign property, in which case appropriate compensation should be paid by the State adopting such measures, taking into account its relevant laws and regulations and all circumstances that the State considers pertinent. In any case where the question of compensation gives rise to a controversy, it shall be settled under the domestic law of the nationalizing State and by its tribunals, unless it is freely and mutually agreed by all States concerned that other peaceful means be sought on the basis of the sovereign equality of States and in accordance with the principle of free choice of means.').

Today, however, there is a relatively high level of conformity in IIAs with regard to the question of the amount and modalities of compensation due in case of expropriation. Almost all BITs and IIAs contain language closely resembling the traditional Hull formula requiring adequate, prompt and effective compensation.[21] The minor language variations found in some BITs do not appear to lead to any different meaning.[22] The World Bank Guidelines on the Treatment of Foreign Direct Investment provide a generally accepted interpretation of the meaning of the qualifications of 'adequate, prompt and effective'.[23] Further, many IIAs include language defining more clearly the calculation of an adequate amount of compensation by clarifying that 'adequate' compensation refers to 'fair market value'.[24]

III. THE INTERPRETATION OF EXPROPRIATION PROVISIONS BY ARBITRATION TRIBUNALS

The growing case law of investment tribunals displays a remarkable

---

[21] Green Haywood Hackworth, *Digest of International Law* (vol III, 1942) 658–9, § 288 ('[...] government is entitled to expropriate private property, for whatever purpose, without provision for prompt, adequate and effective payment therefore').

[22] The phrase 'prompt, adequate and effective compensation' is found in Article 13(1)(c) ECT; Article 6(1)(c) 2004 US Model BIT; Article 13(1) 2004 Canadian Model BIT. The term 'appropriate compensation' is used in Article 5(1) 1995 France-Hong Kong BIT. Other BITs provide for 'just compensation' like Article 4(1)(c) 1989 Cyprus-Hungary BIT or merely 'compensation' like Article 4(2) 2004 German Model BIT.

[23] See 1992 World Bank Guidelines on the Treatment of Foreign Direct Investment, IV, (3)–(8), reprinted in 31 *ILM* 1363 (1992). Pursuant to these guidelines, 'prompt' means within a reasonable time and with interest and 'effective' requires compensation in a convertible currency. These interpretations have been specifically relied upon the in Article 1110(2)–(6) NAFTA; similarly, Article 6(2)–(4) US Model BIT (2004); Article 13(2)–(3) Canadian Model BIT (2004).

[24] See e.g. Article 13(1) ECT ('Such compensation shall amount to the fair market value of the Investment expropriated at the time immediately before the Expropriation or impending Expropriation became known in such a way as to affect the value of the Investment [...]'); see also Article 5(1) 1995 France-Hong Kong BIT ('Compensation shall amount to the real value of the investment immediately before the deprivation or before the impending deprivation became public knowledge whichever is the earlier, shall include interest at a normal commercial rate until the date of payment, shall be made without delay, be effectively realizable and be freely convertible.'); in NAFTA Article 1110 the formulation is slightly different but adds up to prompt, adequate, effective.

convergence of interpretation of the expropriation rules discussed in the previous section. While it is clear that investment tribunals are not bound by the interpretations found by previous tribunals, they generally attempt to reach consistent outcomes.[25] Further, the awards rendered by tribunals help to clarify elements contained in IIAs which are often of a rather general and abstract character.

Arbitral tribunals generally uphold the (sovereign) right of states to expropriate foreign property/investments both as a matter of customary international law[26] and under IIAs.

Investment tribunals have considerably contributed to the notion of 'indirect expropriation' by developing a rather restrictive approach to ascertain at what stage state measures may be considered to amount to expropriation. Tribunals appear to converge as regards the requirement that 'measures affecting property interests' had to be of a certain intensity or 'magnitude or severity',[27] and 'not merely ephemeral',[28] in order to amount to indirect expropriation. There is a predominant view that it does not depend upon the intent of a state but rather on the actual effect of state measures whether an indirect expropriation occurs.[29]

---

[25] See Andrea K Bjorklund, 'Investment Treaty Arbitral Decisions as Jurisprudence Constante' in Colin Picker, Isabella Bunn and Douglas Arner (eds), *International Economic Law: The State and Future of the Discipline* (Hart 2008) 265; Gabrielle Kaufmann-Kohler, 'Arbitral Precedent: Dream, Necessity, or Excuse' (2007) 23 *Arbitration International* 357; August Reinisch, 'The Role of Precedent in ICSID Arbitration' in *Austrian Arbitration Yearbook* (2008) 495.

[26] *Texaco Overseas Petroleum Company (Topco)/California Asiatic (Calasiatic) Oil Company v Libya*, Award of 19 January 1977, 17 ILM 1 (1978), para 59 ('[...]the right to nationalize is unquestionable today. It results from international customary law, established as the result of general practices considered by the international community as being the law.').

[27] *Pope & Talbot, Inc. v Government of Canada*, Interim Award of 26 June 2000, UNCITRAL (NAPTA) para 96.

[28] *Tippetts, Abbett, McCarthy, Stratton v TAMS-AFFA Consulting Engineers of Iran*, 6 Iran-US C.T.R. 219, 225 (29 June 1984) ('While assumption of control over property by a government does not automatically and immediately justify a conclusion that the property has been taken by the government, thus requiring compensation under international law, such a conclusion is warranted whenever events demonstrate that the owner was deprived of fundamental rights of ownership and it appears that this deprivation is not merely ephemeral.').

[29] See *Tippetts*, above n 28, 225, 226 ('The intent of the government is less important than the effects of the measures on the owner, and the form of the measures of control or interference is less important than the reality of their impact.'); *Técnicas Medioambientales Tecmed S.A. v The United Mexican States*, Award of 29 May 2003, ICSID Case No ARB(AF)/00/2, 43 ILM 133 (2004), para 116 ('The government's intention is less important than the effects of the measures

Further, international tribunals have endorsed an expansive concept of what kinds of property can be taken, both under customary international law[30] and under often broad, asset-based investment definitions in IIAs.[31]

Also with regard to the legality requirements typically contained in IIAs, investment tribunals have contributed to their specification in practice. More recent relevant investment decisions demonstrate that tribunals are increasingly willing to engage in a genuine investigation of whether the legality requirements are fulfilled and do not broadly defer to host state discretion. Some older tribunals exercised considerable restraint in adjudicating public policy issues, inherent in the determination of 'public purpose', by either refusing to second-guess 'public purpose' invocations by states at all[32] or by leaving them broad discretion in determining what constitutes 'public purpose'.[33] Today, however,

---

on the owner of the assets or on the benefits arising from such assets affected by the measures; and the form of the deprivation measure is less important than its actual effects.').

30 See e.g. *Amoco International Finance Corp. v Iran*, 15 Iran-US CTR 189 (1987), para 108 ('Expropriation, which can be defined as a compulsory transfer of property rights, may extend to any right which can be the object of a commercial transaction [. . .]'); *SPP v Egypt*, Award of 20 May 1992, 3 ICSID Rep 189, at 228, para 164 ('[T]here is considerable authority for the proposition that contract rights are entitled to the protection of international law and that the taking of such rights involves an obligation to make compensation therefor.').

31 See e.g. *Pope & Talbot, Inc. v Government of Canada*, Interim Award of 26 June 2000, para 96 ('The Tribunal concludes that the Investment's access to the U.S. market is a property interest subject to protection under Article 1110[. . .]'); *Methanex Corporation v United States of America*, Final Award on Jurisdiction and Merits of 3 August 2005, UNCITRAL (NAFTA), at IV D para 17 ('[. . .]the restrictive notion of property as a material "thing" is obsolete and has ceded its place to a contemporary conception which includes managerial control over components of a process that is wealth producing.').

32 *Libyan American Oil Company (Liamco) v Libya*, Award of 12 April 1977, 62 *ILR* 140, 194 ('Motives are indifferent to international law, each State being free to judge for itself what it considers useful or necessary for the public good.').

33 See e.g. *Amoco International Finance Corp v Iran*, 15 Iran-US CTR (1987) 189, 233, para 145 ('A precise definition of the "public purpose" for which an expropriation may be lawfully decided has neither been agreed upon in international law nor even suggested. It is clear that, as a result of the modern acceptance of the right to nationalize, this term is broadly interpreted, and the States, in practice, are granted extensive discretion.'); in *American International Group Inc, et al. v Islamic Republic of Iran, et al.*, Award No. 93-2-3, 19 December 1983, 4 Iran-US CTR (1983) 96, 105, the tribunal found that there was '[. . .]not sufficient evidence before the tribunal to show that the nationalization was not carried out for a public purpose'.

tribunals reaffirm the public purpose requirement,[34] insist on their judicial review power[35] and will even disqualify expropriatory measures lacking a genuine 'public purpose'.[36]

Similarly, investment tribunals have demonstrated their resolve to regard as illegal discriminatory expropriations either because they were directed at foreigners as opposed to nationals of the expropriating state or because they singled out particular groups of foreign nationals often motivated by political considerations.[37]

Though there is little arbitration practice on the 'due process' requirement, probably because it is not always found in the applicable IIAs, tribunals seem to approximate this legality requirement to a fair trial right offering affected investors an opportunity to challenge expropriation decisions before an independent and impartial domestic body.[38] Since

---

[34] See e.g. *Amco Asia Corporation v Republic of Indonesia*, Award of 20 November 1984, ICSID Case No ARB/81/1, 1 ICSID Rep 413, 466 ('[. . .] the right to nationalize supposes that the act by which the State purports to have exercised it, is a true nationalization, namely a taking of property or contractual rights which aims to protect or to promote the public interest.'); *Compañía del Desarrollo de Santa Elena, S.A. v Republic of Costa Rica*, Award of 17 February 2000, ICSID Case No ARB/96/1, para 71 ('International law permits the Government of Costa Rica to expropriate foreign-owned property within its territory for a public purpose [. . .]'); *Southern Pacific Properties (Middle East) Limited v Arab Republic of Egypt*, Award of 20 May 1992, ICSID Case No ARB/84/3, para 158.

[35] *ADC Affiliate Limited and ADC & ADMC Management Limited v Republic of Hungary*, Award of 2 October 2006, ICSID Case No ARB/03/16, para 432 ('A treaty requirement for "*public interest*" requires some genuine interest of the public. If mere reference to "*public interest*" can magically put such interest into existence and therefore satisfy this requirement, then this requirement would be rendered meaningless since the Tribunal can imagine no situation where this requirement would not have been met.').

[36] See e.g. *Liberian Eastern Timber Corporation (LETCO) v Republic of Liberia*, ICSID Case No ARB/83/2, Award of 31 March 1986, 2 ICSID Rep 343, 367; *ADC Affiliate Limited and ADC & ADMC Management Limited v Republic of Hungary*, Award of 2 October 2006, ICSID Case No ARB/03/16, para 433; see also from the older case-law, *British Petroleum v Libya*, Award of 10 October 1973 and 1 August 1974, 53 ILR 297, 329.

[37] See in more detail *infra*, text at n 78.

[38] *ADC Affiliate Limited and ADC & ADMC Management Limited v Republic of Hungary*, Award of 2 October 2006, ICSID Case No ARB/03/16, para 435 ('Some basic legal mechanisms, such as reasonable advance notice, a fair hearing and an unbiased and impartial adjudicator to assess the actions in dispute, are expected to be readily available and accessible to the investor to make such legal procedure meaningful. In general, the legal procedure must be of a nature to grant an affected investor a reasonable chance within a reasonable time to claim its legitimate rights and have its claims heard. If no legal procedure of such nature

many IIA provisions on expropriation refer to the treaty standards of fair and equitable treatment and/or the freedom from arbitrary and discriminatory measures, those latter standards may also be relevant in the context of assessing the lawfulness of an expropriation.

Investment tribunals are rather consistent in requiring compensation, or at least an offer of compensation,[39] in order to regard an expropriation as lawful.[40] The precise amount of compensation will usually be guided by the express treaty provisions on expropriation.

Finally, tribunals have been consistent in permitting the application of these treaty provisions only in cases of lawful expropriations. They largely concur that damages for an internationally wrongful act are due where an expropriation was carried out either not for a 'public purpose', in a 'discriminatory' fashion, or not in accordance with 'due process'.[41]

---

exists at all, the argument that "*the actions are taken under due process of law*" rings hollow.').

[39] *Liberian Eastern Timber Corporation (LETCO) v Republic of Liberia*, Award of 31 March 1986, ICSID Case No ARB/83/2, 2 ICSID Rep 343, at 366 ('state action must be "accompanied by payment (or at least the offer of payment) of appropriate compensation.'); *Goetz and Others v Republic of Burundi*, Decision on Liability of 2 September 1998, ICSID Case No ARB/95/3, 6 ICSID Rep 5, 43, 44, para 130 ('The treaty requires an adequate and effective indemnity; unlike certain domestic rights as regards expropriation, it does not require prior compensation.').

[40] *Siemens A.G. v Argentina*, Award of 6 February 2007, ICSID Case No ARB/02/08, para 273 ('[C]ompensation has never been paid on grounds that, as already stated, the Tribunal finds that are lacking in justification. For these reasons, the expropriation [. . .] was unlawful.')

[41] *Southern Pacific Properties (Middle East) Limited v Arab Republic of Egypt*, Award of 20 May 1992, ICSID Case No ARB/84/3, 3 ICSID Rep 189, para 183 ('[T]he Claimants are seeking "compensation" for a lawful expropriation, and not "reparation" for an injury caused by an illegal act such as a breach of contract. The cardinal point [. . .] in determining the appropriate compensation is that [. . .] Claimants are entitled to receive fair compensation for what was expropriated rather than damages for breach of contract.'); *CMS Gas Transmission Company v The Argentine Republic*, Award of 12 May 2005, ICSID Case No ARB/01/8, para 400 ('Restitution is the standard used to re-establish the situation which existed before the wrongful act was committed, provided this is not materially impossible and does not result in a burden out of proportion as compared to compensation.'); *Siemens A.G. v Argentina*, Award of 6 February 2007, ICSID Case No ARB/02/08, para 349 ('The law applicable to the determination of compensation for a breach of such Treaty obligations is customary international law. The Treaty itself only provides for compensation for expropriation in accordance with the terms of the Treaty.')

IV. TYPES OF 'CODIFICATION'

Before debating the most appropriate form of a potential 'codification' of investment law principles it is useful to highlight the different 'codification' styles adopted in different projects. These range from the US Restatements to commentaries in the continental-European tradition and traditional scholarly treatises. An analysis of their approaches will help to discuss their suitability for the purpose of 'codifying' investment law.

1. The Scholarly Narrative Technique

Many scholarly treatises on international law in general, and on international investment law in particular, contain chapters on expropriation. While there is controversy whether fair and equitable treatment as well as full protection and security should be considered to reflect a customary international law minimum standard of treatment or are to be regarded as treaty standards,[42] it is fairly accepted that the usual non-discrimination standards in the form of national treatment and MFN treatment are treaty based.[43] The extent to which the rules on expropriation regularly contained in international investment agreements merely affirm already existing rules of customary international law or go beyond these is equally controversial, at least in some aspects. It appears to constitute a widely shared opinion that states are in principle entitled to expropriate property, including property owned by foreigners. However, in particular the extent to which they have to compensate such foreign owners for the expropriation has for a long time belonged to the most controversial aspects

---

42 *ADF Group Inc. v United States*, Award of 9 January 2003, ICSID Case No ARB(AF)/00/1, 18 ICSID Rev–FILJ 195 (2003); 6 ICSID Rep 470 (2004), paras 175 *et seq*; *Loewen v United States*, Award of 26 June 2003, ICSID Case No ARB(AF)/98/3, 42 ILM 811 (2003), 7 ICSID Rep 442 (2005), paras 124 *et seq*; *Mondev International Ltd. v United States of America*, Final Award of 11 October 2002, ICSID Case No ARB(AF)/99/2, 42 ILM 85 (2003), 6 ICSID Rep 192 (2004), paras 100 *et seq*; *Pope & Talbot Inc. v The Government of Canada*, Award on Damages of 31 May 2002, UNCITRAL (NAFTA), 41 ILM 1347 (2002), paras 17 *et seq*; *Waste Management, Inc. v United Mexican States*, Award of April 30 2004, ICSID Case No ARB(AF)/00/3, 43 ILM 967 (2004), paras 89 *et seq*; see also Christoph Schreuer, 'Fair and Equitable Treatment' (2005) 2 *Transnational Dispute Management* 5; Katia Yannaca-Small, 'Fair and Equitable Treatment Standard: Recent Developments' in August Reinisch (ed), *Standards of Investment Protection* (OUP 2008) 111; Dolzer and Schreuer, above n 2, 124.

43 Andreas Ziegler, 'Most-Favored-Nation (MFN) Treatment' in August Reinisch (ed), *Standards of Investment Protection* (OUP 2008) 60; Newcombe and Paradell, above n 2, 149.

of international economic law. Thus, any treaty-based solution is at least a clarification if not a separate determination of legal rules.

Many scholarly works addressing the question of expropriation contain a combination of a narrative account of the development of applicable customary international law principles, the basic content of IIA provisions on expropriation as well as the way investment tribunals have interpreted these principles and provisions.

For instance, *Principles of International Investment Law* starts with affirming the convergence between the customary international law and the treaty-based right of states to expropriate foreign property, which is refined in the context of IIAs to encompass 'investment'.[44] It then recounts the legality criteria of public purpose, non-discrimination, and due process as well as compensation, which it describes as 'contained in most treaties' and 'also seen to be part of customary international law'.[45] The authors caution, however, that the 'measure of compensation has been by far the most controversial one'.[46] Reflecting the development of international investment law, Dolzer and Schreuer devote most space to the issue of identifying indirect expropriation.[47] After an overview of the widespread recognition of the concept of indirect expropriation in IIAs, as well as its refinement in recent Model BITs such as those of the United States and Canada, they give a broadly chronological account of the case law from the Permanent Court of International Justice (PCIJ) in the *Oscar Chinn Case*,[48] the Overseas Private Investment Corporation (OPIC) insurance case of *Revere Copper*,[49] European Court of Human Rights (ECtHR) cases like *Sporrong and Lönnroth*,[50] to modern International Centre for Settlement of Investment Disputes (ICSID) and non-ICSID cases. Further, they analyse the following sub-issues explicitly addressed in the case law: whether, in addition to the effect of a measure, a state's intent should play a role; the significance of an investor's legitimate expectations; the possibility of partial expropriation; the distinction between general

44 Rudolf Dolzer and Christoph Schreuer, *Principles of International Investment Law* (OUP 2008) 89, 90.

45 Ibid, 91.

46 Ibid.

47 Ibid, 92–115.

48 *Oscar Chinn Case (UK v Belgium)*, Judgment of 12 December 1934, PCIJ Ser A/B, No 63 (1934).

49 *In the Matter of Revere Copper and Brass Inc. v Overseas Private Investment Corporation*, Award of 24 August 1978, 56 ILR 258.

50 *Sporrong and Lönnroth v Sweden*, Judgement of 23 September 1982, Ser A No 52.

regulatory measures and indirect expropriation; the duration of a measure and the concept of creeping expropriation. Finally, they devote a short section to the judicial and arbitration practice concerning expropriation of contractual rights.

Another example of scholarly treatment of expropriation can be found in *International Investment Arbitration*.[51] Expropriation is addressed in a separate section, of equal rank to a section on 'Treatment of Investors', discussing fair and equitable treatment and full protection and security, within a chapter on 'Substantive Rights'. The authors first provide a broad overview of the expropriation provisions in multilateral and bilateral treaties.[52] Next, they deal with the differentiation between direct and indirect expropriation, broadly relying on the practice of investment tribunals.[53] Finally, the case-by-case approach of tribunals is analysed in a way which groups arbitral decisions around certain expropriation topics like the degree of interference, the question of subjective intention, the expectation of the investor, the issues of state organs, of regulatory activity, and of a potential taking of contractual rights.[54]

The chapter on expropriation in the *Oxford Handbook of International Investment Law* focuses on indirect expropriation and does not address the criteria for a lawful expropriation.[55] This reflects the development of modern investment law which is confronted by a growing tendency of states to abstain from acts of direct expropriation. The Handbook's account of the law of indirect expropriation combines an analysis of treaty language and of pertinent case law: the scope of protected property rights and the notions of indirect and creeping expropriation are viewed from the perspective of treaty language and the case law of international arbitral and judicial tribunals. In its central part the expropriation chapter identifies crucial elements of indirect expropriation as found in arbitral practice: the intensity of interference with property rights; the fact that expropriatory measures need not benefit the state; the effect on the investor as main criterion – the 'sole effect' doctrine; legality (including obligations of transparency and consistency); the protection of legitimate

---

[51] Campbell McLachlan, Laurence Shore and Matthew Weiniger, *International Investment Arbitration: Substantive Principles* (OUP 2007).

[52] Ibid, 268–86.

[53] Ibid, 290–7.

[54] Ibid, 298–309.

[55] August Reinisch, 'Expropriation' in Peter Muchlinski, Federico Ortino and Christoph Schreuer (eds), *The Oxford Handbook of International Investment Law* (OUP 2008) 407–58.

investor expectations; proportionality; and discrimination. On the basis of these elements, it identifies the relatively few situations in which tribunals have actually found an indirect expropriation to have occurred.

In their treatise on *Law and Practice of Investment Treaties* Newcombe and Paradell devote broad scope to the question of what constitutes an expropriation.[56] On the basis of investment law and practice they seek to ascertain the main features of identifying indirect expropriation. They then shortly address the legality requirements under the title 'conditions for expropriation'[57] and continue to discuss compensation issues at length.[58]

2. The Restatement Technique

An interesting method of 'codifying' elements of investment law can be seen in the US Restatement-type of 'restating' the law in the field of international law. For the purpose of comparing this approach to others an analysis of the expropriation chapter is well suited. US Restatements are part of a broader enterprise undertaken by the American Law Institute, established in 1923[59] for the purpose of summarizing and defining, or restating, major legal doctrines. Since the 1920s Restatements of the law have been adopted in a number of domestic law fields such as Agency, Conflict of Laws, Contracts, Judgments, Property, Restitution, Security, Torts, and Trusts. In a second round of Restatements after World War II, a Restatement of the Foreign Relations Law of the United States was included. This project was updated and led to the publication of the *Restatement (Third) of the Foreign Relations Law of the United States* in 1986.[60] While the 1986 Foreign Relations Restatement does not contain a separate investment chapter, it addresses issues of expropriation of foreign property.

In the *Restatement (Third)*, expropriation is treated by a general black letter law rule to be followed by Reporters' notes and comments.

---

56 Andrew Newcombe and Lluís Paradell, *Law and Practice of Investment Treaties* (2009) 321–69.

57 Ibid, 369–77.

58 Ibid, 377–99.

59 See Mitchell Franklin, 'The Historic Function of the American Law Institute: Restatement as Transitional to Codification' (1934) 47 *Harvard Law Review* 1367–94; for more on the history and the purposes of the Institute, see the ALI website at <http://www.ali.org/index.cfm?fuseaction=about.overview>.

60 *Restatement (Third) of the Foreign Relations Law of the United States* (1987), above n 9.

In the case of the expropriation chapter, the black letter rule of § 712, entitled 'State Responsibility for Economic Injury to Nationals of Other States', provides as follows:

> A state is responsible under international law for injury resulting from:
> (1) a taking by the state of the property of a national of another state that
> (a) is not for a public purpose, or
> (b) is discriminatory, or
> (c) not accompanied by provisions for just compensation.[61]

§ 712 continues to define the standard of compensation required to meet the criterion of a 'just compensation'. It further lays down the conditions under which a breach of contract or other acts or omissions by a state impairing the economic interests of foreigners may lead to international responsibility.

In addition to the black letter rules of individual sections, the Restatement contains two additional layers of relevant information, first Comments, second Reporters' Notes. In the case of the expropriation section, the comments address in more detail, among others, the issues of 'just compensation', taking for a public purpose, discriminatory takings, and the difficulty of distinguishing between expropriation and regulation, while the reporters' notes deal with the status of international law on expropriation, the standard of compensation and the notion of just compensation, etc., in a more detailed fashion emphasizing the relevant case law and scholarly writings in the field.

A few aspects appear rather remarkable and at the same time typical for the time of the Restatement's drafting. The problem of indirect expropriation is not broadly assessed. Rather, it is found in one of the comments to the black letter rule.[62]

---

[61] Ibid, § 712.

[62] Ibid, § 712 comment g ('Subsection (1) applies not only to avowed expropriations in which the government formally takes title to property, but also to other actions of the government that have the effect of "taking" the property, in whole or in large part, outright or in stages ("creeping expropriation"). A state is responsible as for an expropriation of property under Subsection (1) when it subjects alien property to taxation, regulation, or other action that is confiscatory, or that prevents, unreasonably interferes with, or unduly delays, effective enjoyment of an alien's property or its removal from the state's territory.').

3. The Commentary Technique

Another approach that could be relied upon in the field of investment law is the comprehensive commentary, widely used in continental European scholarship and only gradually adopted in public international law. The UN Charter Commentary,[63] first published in German,[64] and Commentaries to the ICJ Statute[65] as well as to the International Criminal Court,[66] are examples of the growing popularity of this form of scholarly assessment in the area of international law.

In general, a commentary is a detailed analysis of the individual provisions of a statute, a constitution, a treaty or any other fixed, already 'codified' law. In the field of international investment law, the most prominent use of a classic commentary approach is the Commentary to the ICSID Convention,[67] now in its second edition.[68] Since the ICSID Convention is a single fixed text it lends itself to being commented upon in the traditional commentary style. Each article of the Convention is reproduced followed by a general introduction, giving an overview of the purpose, negotiating history, and main issues of an article. The main commentary is contained in a detailed and extensive interpretation of the elements of each article, sometimes down to individual words. This interpretation amply considers arbitration practice where the provisions of the ICSID Convention have been applied.

The ICSID Commentary is less a codification of the law than an interpretation of already 'codified' treaty law. A true codification would work the other way round. Instead of departing from black letter treaty provisions, which are then interpreted in detail, a codification would attempt to arrive at black letter rules from an interpretation of the existing practice. Since there is widespread overlap and similarity between 'fixed' BIT and other IIA provisions it could be possible to find a way by which treaty provisions are grouped according to their similarities/differences to

---

63 Bruno Simma *et al.* (eds), *The Charter of the United Nations: A Commentary* (2nd edn, OUP 2002).

64 Bruno Simma and Hermann Mosler (eds), *Charta der Vereinten Nationen: Kommentar* (Beck 1991).

65 Andreas Zimmermann, Christian Tomuschat, Karin Oellers-Frahm, Christian Tams and Tobias Thienel (eds), *The Statute of the International Court of Justice. A Commentary* (OUP 2006).

66 Otto Triffterer (ed), *Commentary on the Rome Statute of the International Criminal Court: Observers' Notes, Article by Article* (2nd edn, Beck/Hart 2008).

67 Christoph Schreuer, *The ICSID Convention: A Commentary* (CUP 2001).

68 Christoph Schreuer with Loretta Malintoppi, August Reinisch and Anthony Sinclair, *The ICSID Convention: A Commentary* (2nd edn, CUP 2009).

be followed by a commentary highlighting both those similarities and differences in the main text.

There are also other commentary-like examples in investment law. For instance, the short Report of the World Bank Executive Directors on the ICSID Convention[69] is often regarded as a quasi-authoritative interpretation of the ICSID Convention. Investment tribunals often refer to it as a document of a highly persuasive force. In particular, the Report's short paragraph on the lack of a definition of the term 'investment' used in Article 25(1) of the ICSID Convention[70] has been frequently cited by investment tribunals attempting to lay down the essential elements of an 'investment' giving rise to the jurisdiction of the Centre.[71]

In the case of IIAs proper, commentaries of a status similar to the ICSID Commentary are exceptional. One of these rare examples relevant in the context of expropriation is the commentary to the 1967 OECD Draft Convention on the Protection of Foreign Property.[72] While the 1967 OECD Convention never entered into force, the commentary to its provisions, in particular the interpretation given to the notion of indirect expropriation, is of quite some relevance. Article 3 of the OECD Draft Convention on the Protection of Foreign Property merely provided as follows:

> No Party shall take any measures depriving, directly or indirectly, of his property a national of another Party unless the following criteria are complied with:
> (i) The measures are taken in the public interest and under due process of law;
> (ii) The measures are not discriminatory or contrary to any undertaking which the former party may have given;

---

[69] Report of the Executive Directors of the International Bank for Reconstruction and Development on the ICSID Convention (1965), reprinted in 1 ICSID Rep 23–33.

[70] Article 25(1) Convention on the Settlement of Investment Disputes between States and Nationals of Other States, 18 March 1965, 575 UNTS 159; 4 ILM 532 (1965) ('The jurisdiction of the Centre shall extend to any legal dispute arising directly out of an investment, between a Contracting State (or any constituent subdivision or agency of a Contracting State designated to the Centre by that State) and a national of another Contracting State which the parties to the dispute consent in writing to submit to the Centre. When the parties have given their consent, no party may withdraw its consent unilaterally.').

[71] See e.g. *Malaysian Historical Salvors Sdn Bhd v Malaysia*, Decision on the Application for Annulment of 28 February 2008, ICSID Case No ARB/05/10, paras 63, 70.

[72] OECD Draft Convention on the Protection of Foreign Property, 12 October 1967, 7 ILM 117 (1968).

> (iii) The measures are accompanied by provision for the payment of just compensation. Such compensation shall represent the genuine value of the property affected, shall be paid without undue delay, and shall be transferable to the extent necessary to make it effective for the national entitled thereto.

The commentary, however, makes indirect expropriation much more precise. According to it, indirect expropriation results from measures applied in such a way

> as to deprive ultimately the alien of the enjoyment or value of his property, without any specific act being identifiable as outright deprivation. As instances may be quoted excessive or arbitrary taxation; prohibition of dividend distribution coupled with compulsory loans; imposition of administrators; prohibition of dismissal of staff; refusal of access to raw materials or of essential export or import licenses.[73]

The expropriation provision of the 1967 OECD Draft Convention was largely based on a private codification draft prepared by the Harvard law professors Louis Sohn and Richard Baxter. Their Draft Convention on the International Responsibility of States for Injuries to Aliens[74] contained a provision on 'Taking and Deprivation of Use or Enjoyment of Property' accompanied by an extensive explanatory note addressing the definition of a 'taking', the criterion of wrongfulness, and other aspects of expropriation law.

The examples of the 1961 Harvard Draft and the 1967 OECD Draft Convention demonstrate that a traditional commentary style of investment law principles such as those applying to expropriation is perfectly feasible. Where investment tribunals have to apply one single text, as in the case of NAFTA Chapter 11[75] or the ECT,[76] a commentary on the relevant provisions may be a useful way of 'codifying' the actual practice and thus the gradually developing law of expropriation (or other investment standards).

In fact, the *Annotated Guide to NAFTA Chapter 11* by Kinnear,

---

[73] Notes and Comments to Article 3 OECD Draft Convention on the Protection of Foreign Property, 7 ILM 117, at 126 (1968).

[74] Louis B Sohn and Richard R Baxter, 'Responsibility of States for Injuries to the Economic Interests of Aliens: II. Draft Convention on the International Responsibility of States for Injuries to Aliens' (1961) 55 *AJIL* 548–84.

[75] North American Free Trade Agreement between the Government of Canada, the Government of the United Mexican States, and the Government of the United States of America (NAFTA), 17 December 1992, 32 *ILM* 289 (1993).

[76] Energy Charter Treaty, Annex 1 to the Final Act of the European Energy Charter Treaty Conference, 17 December 1994, 34 ILM 381 (1995).

Bjorklund and Hannaford comes closest to a commentary.[77] It contains an article-by-article annotation of the substantive investment protection (Articles 1101–14 NAFTA) as well as the dispute settlement provisions (Articles 1115–38 NAFTA). First, each article of Chapter 11 is reproduced, followed by an extensive documentation of the negotiating texts. Then, a 'Commentary' on each article discusses the historical background of the respective provision, its main purpose, and broadly provides for an interpretation on the basis of other scholarly work as well as arbitration practice where available. In the case of Article 1110 NAFTA, entitled 'Expropriation and Compensation', the Commentary section starts with a historical overview of expropriation law. It continues to discuss the scope of the obligation under Article 1110 NAFTA, focusing on the issue of determining when 'indirect expropriations' or 'measures tantamount to expropriation' have taken place, extensively addressing the relevant NAFTA case law. Next, the Commentary addresses the legality requirements of a public purpose, non-discrimination, due process and compensation as provided for in Article 1110(1)(a)–(d) NAFTA. Finally, it deals with a number of general issues arising under NAFTA's expropriation article, such as the scope of interests subject to expropriation, the notions of 'investment in the territory' of a NAFTA party, whether expropriatory 'intent' needs to be established, the specific rules on compensation of Article 1110(2)–(6) NAFTA, the distinction between regulation and expropriation, and other matters.

V. 'CODIFICATION' IN ACTION – THE NON-DISCRIMINATION REQUIREMENT FOR LAWFUL EXPROPRIATIONS

This final section will provide an example of a potential 'codification' approach in practice which will be limited to the issue of non-discrimination as a legality requirement for expropriations. Based on the templates developed in the previous section, it intends to give an overview of how to reduce the vast corpus of treaty provisions and their interpretations by arbitral tribunals into simple, straightforward black-letter rules and interpretations of these rules.

It will thereby follow broadly the style adopted by commentaries, being mindful of the fact that there is no single textual version of expropriation

[77] Meg Kinnear, Andrea K Bjorklund and John FG Hannaford, *Investment Disputes Under NAFTA: An Annotated Guide to NAFTA Chapter 11* (Kluwer 2006; updated 2008, 2009).

rules in international investment law, but rather a number of textual variations. Still, a commentary style appears to be the best approach for 'codifying' the emerging rule on non-discrimination as a requirement for determining whether an expropriation was lawful or not, because it provides the required background to demonstrate how widely accepted the rule has become.

1. Basic Rule

Any measures of direct or indirect expropriation must be 'non-discriminatory'.

2. Textual Variations

Most IIAs provide that expropriations or expropriatory measures must not be discriminatory. There are only minor linguistic differences. IIAs provide, for instance, that expropriations must be 'not discriminatory',[78] 'non-discriminatory',[79] taken 'on a non-discriminatory basis',[80] 'in a non-discriminatory manner',[81] or use otherwise comparable language.

3. Relationship to Customary International Law

The non-discrimination requirement is not only a standard element contained in most treaty provisions addressing the legality of expropriations. It is also widely regarded as a prerequisite for a lawful expropriation in customary international law by scholarly writers.[82]

Equally, general statements that expropriations have to be made on a non-discriminatory basis are often found in arbitral practice. For instance, the sole arbitrator in the *LIAMCO* case[83] reaffirmed the principle that a

---

[78] Article 13(1)(b) 1994 Energy Charter Treaty, 2080 UNTS 100; Article III(1)(c) 1982 United States-Egypt BIT, 21 ILM 927 (1982); Article 6(b) 1992 Netherlands-Bolivia BIT, 2239 UNTS 505.

[79] Article 4(1) 1998 China-Poland BIT.

[80] Article 1110(1)(b) NAFTA; Article 5(1) 1995 France-Hong Kong BIT.

[81] Article 6(1) 2004 US Model BIT; Article 13(1) 2004 Canadian Model BIT.

[82] Abul FM Maniruzzaman, 'Expropriation of Alien Property and the Principle of Non-Discrimination in International Law of Foreign Investment: An Overview' (1998) 8 *Journal of Transnational Law and Policy* 57; Ian Brownlie, *System of the Law of Nations: State Responsibility* (OUP 1983) 81.

[83] *Libyan American Oil Company (Liamco) v Libya*, Award of 12 April 1977; 62 ILR 140.

discriminatory expropriation would be unlawful as such.[84] He held that it was

> clear and undisputed that non-discrimination is a requisite for the validity of a lawful nationalization. This is a rule well-established in international legal theory and practice [. . .] Therefore, a purely discriminatory nationalization is illegal and wrongful.[85]

He concluded, however, that there was no actual discrimination involved since, according to the arbitrator's findings,

> [. . .] LIAMCO was not the first company to be nationalized, nor was it the only oil company nor the only American company to be nationalized [. . .] Other companies were nationalized before it, other American and non-American companies were nationalized with it and after it, and other American companies are still operating in Libya. Thus, it may be concluded from the above that the political motive was not the predominant motive for nationalization, and that such motive *per se* does not constitute a sufficient proof of a purely discriminatory measure.[86]

A similar reasoning was adopted by the arbitral tribunal in the *Aminoil* case.[87] Instead of relying on the distinction between unlawful and lawful expropriation, the tribunal adopted the term 'nationalization' for a non-discriminatory expropriation and held that

> [. . .] in order to distinguish nationalisation from other comparable measures, it is also claimed that a nationalisation must apply to the totality of a given sector of the economy – that is to say, without discrimination, to an assemblage of undertakings.[88]

Since the *Aminoil* tribunal found that the Kuwaiti government had merely engaged in a series of expropriations instead of expropriating all foreign oil companies at the same time, it concluded that the expropriation was not discriminatory.[89]

---

84 Ibid, 62 ILR 140, 194.

85 Ibid.

86 Ibid, 195.

87 *Kuwait v American Independent Oil Company (Aminoil)*, Award of 24 March 1982, 21 ILM 976 (1982).

88 Ibid, para 84.

89 Ibid, para 86 ('The Tribunal does not see why a Government that was pursuing a coherent policy of nationalisation should not have been entitled to do so progressively. It is hardly necessary, additionally, to stress the reasonable character of a policy of nationalisation operating gradually by successive stages, in step with the development of the necessary administrative and technical availabilities [. . . .]').

Also the Iran-US Claims Tribunal broadly affirmed the general customary law validity of the non-discrimination requirement for lawful expropriation. In the *Amoco* case it stated that '[d]iscrimination is widely held as prohibited by customary international law in the field of expropriation'.[90]

Expressly relying on *LIAMCO*, the ICSID Additional Facility tribunal in *Fireman's Fund* held that 'discriminatory treatment is used to determine whether the expropriation was unlawful'.[91]

4. Main Issues and Purpose

The precise content of the non-discrimination requirement for expropriations is not wholly clear. While discrimination on the basis of nationality is most often addressed, it seems that – at least under customary international law – also racial, ethnic, religious and cultural discrimination may play a role in assessing the legality of expropriatory action.

A. Discrimination against foreigners

Under customary international law expropriatory action 'that singles out aliens generally, or aliens of a particular nationality, or particular aliens, would violate international law' even absent explicit treaty protections.[92]

In practice, it was often the singling out of particular nationals, frequently as a result of political retaliation, which was considered to constitute a discriminatory taking. For instance, US courts considered the initial wave of expropriations after the Cuban revolution which was exclusively directed against US nationals to be unlawful under international law.[93] Similarly, ICSID tribunals have found that the

---

[90] *Amoco International Finance Corp. v Iran*, 15 Iran-US CTR 189, 232 (1987), para 140.

[91] *Fireman's Fund Insurance Company v Mexico*, Award of 17 July 2006, ICSID Case No ARB(AF)/02/01, para 205.

[92] *Restatement (Third) of the Foreign Relations Law of the United States*, above n 9, § 712, Comment f.

[93] *Banco Nacional de Cuba v Sabbatino*, 307 F2d 845, at 868 (1962) ('Since the Cuban decree of expropriation not only failed to provide adequate compensation but also involved a retaliatory purpose and a discrimination against United States nationals, we hold that the decree was in violation of international law.'), reversed on act of state grounds 376 US 398 (1964); *Banco Nacional de Cuba v Farr*, 243 FSupp 957 (SDNY 1965), affirmed, 383 F2d 166 (2d Cir 1967), cert denied 390 US 956 (1968). See also *Restatement (Third) of the Foreign Relations Law of the United States*, above n 9, § 712, Reporters' Note 5.

singling out of nationals of one state versus those of another state may constitute unlawful discrimination.[94] Thus, arbitral tribunals have been content with a showing that expropriatory measures affect all foreigners even if in successive stages in order to deny a discriminatory character.[95]

While it seems widely accepted that discrimination against certain foreigners falls under the prohibited forms of discrimination in the context of expropriations, it is less clear whether discrimination between nationals and foreigners in general is equally unlawful. There is, however, some limited arbitral practice according to which expropriatory measures directed against foreigners as opposed to nationals is unlawful.[96]

B. Racial discrimination

Racially motivated expropriations are usually regarded as evident examples of illegal takings.[97] Thus, the so-called 'Aryanization' policy of Nazi-Germany involving the systematic taking of Jewish property is regarded as discriminatory expropriation.[98] The same applies to the taking

---

[94] See e.g. *Liberian Eastern Timber Corporation (LETCO) v Republic of Liberia*, Award of 31 March 1986, ICSID Case No ARB/83/2, 2 ICSID Rep 343, at 366, see also *infra* text at n 118.

[95] *Texaco Overseas Petroleum Company (Topco)/California Asiatic (Calasiatic) Oil Company v Libya*, Award of 19 January 1977, 17 ILM 1 (1978), para 74 ('[...]it seems difficult to examine here the discriminatory nature of the measures enacted against plaintiffs. While it seems that such measures were of such a nature at the time when they were imposed, in fact analogous measures were taken in respect of other companies, in successive stages, which is evidence that the measures taken against plaintiffs were part of what may have been regarded as a policy of nationalization.').

[96] *Eureko B.V. v Republic of Poland*, Partial Award of 19 August 2005, para 242. See also in more detail text *infra* at n 114. See also *Marvin Feldmann v Mexico*, Award of 16 December 2002, ICSID Case No ARB(AF)/99/1, para 137, note 26 ('Moreover, under international law, there is considerable doubt whether the discrimination provision of Article 1110 covers discrimination other than that between nationals and foreign investors, i.e., it is not applicable to discrimination among different classes of investors, such as between producers and resellers of tobacco products, at least unless all producers are nationals and all resellers are aliens. Thus, under the Restatement, the relevant comment states that "a program of taking that singles out aliens generally, or aliens of a) particular nationality, or particular aliens, would violate international law." The comment does not refer to discrimination between national producers and resellers (whether national or foreign) operating under somewhat different circumstances, particularly under the tax laws.').

[97] Muthucumaraswamy Sornarajah, *The International Law on Foreign Investment* (2nd edn, CUP 2004) 399; UNCTAD, *Taking of Property* (2000) 13.

[98] *Oppenheimer v Inland Revenue Commissioner* [1975] 1 All ER 538. See e.g.

of property belonging to ethnic Indians by the Idi Amin regime in Uganda.[99] These extreme forms of discrimination are usually also regarded as lacking a legitimate public purpose.

Recently, expropriatory measures adopted by the Mugabe regime of Zimbabwe have been challenged as discriminatory and thus unlawful. In the ICSID case of *Funnekotter v Zimbabwe*,[100] the tribunal managed to avoid the issue by relying solely on the lack of compensation making the expropriation unlawful.[101]

In the case of *Campbell and Others v Zimbabwe*[102] before the Southern African Development Community Tribunal, racial discrimination was ascertained by the tribunal. The tribunal found that while the controversial law did not explicitly refer to white farmers it, in effect, applied to white farmers only and thus constituted indirect expropriation.

> In examining the effects of Amendment 17 on the applicants, it is clear to us that those effects have had an unjustifiable and disproportionate impact upon a group of individuals distinguished by race such as the Applicants. We consider that the differentiation of treatment meted out to the Applicants also constitutes discrimination as the criteria for such differentiation are not reasonable and objective but arbitrary and are based primarily on considerations of race. The aim of the Respondent in adopting and implementing a land reform programme might be legitimate if and when all

---

Kurt Siehr, 'International Art Trade and the Law' (1993) 243 RdC 9, at 134: 'When, however, property is taken because the owner is a Jew or the institution is Jewish, such expropriation is clearly discriminatory [. . .].' See also Muthucumaraswamy Sornarajah, *The International Law on Foreign Investment* 399 (2nd edn, CUP 2004).

[99] United Nations Committee on the Elimination of Racial Discrimination, Reports submitted by States Parties under Article 9 of the Convention, UN Doc CERD/C/358/Add.1 (24 October 2001), para 42: 'In 1972, President Idi Amin's regime legalized the expropriation of assets of Ugandans of Asian origin. This was, to all intents and purposes, a manifestation of racial discrimination [. . .] .'; See also Muthucumaraswamy Sornarajah, *The International Law on Foreign Investment* 399 (2nd edn, CUP 2004); Frank Woolridge and Vishnu Sharma, 'The Expropriation of the Property of the Ugandan Asians' (1974) 14 *IJIL* 61.

[100] *Bernardus Henricus Funnekotter and Others v Republic of Zimbabwe*, Award of 22 April 2009, ICSID Case No ARB/05/6.

[101] Ibid, para 98 ('The Tribunal will first examine whether or not the subparagraph (c) relating to the provisions of a just compensation has been breached. If it arrives to the conclusion that it has, it will not be necessary for it to consider whether, as alleged by the Claimants, the other conditions provided for in that Article or the provisions of Article 3 have also been breached.').

[102] *Mike Campbell (Pvt) Ltd and Others v Zimbabwe*, Decision of 28 November 2008, SADC (T) Case No 2/2007.

> lands under the programme were indeed distributed to poor, landless and other disadvantaged and marginalized individuals or groups.[103]

C. DISCRIMINATION AS UNREASONABLE MEASURES – 'JUSTIFIED' DISCRIMINATION

It is sometimes more broadly asserted that a 'discriminatory taking is one that singles out a particular person or group of people without a reasonable basis'.[104]

Further, although discriminatory expropriations affecting only members of a certain national, ethnic or other group are in principle unlawful, practice acknowledges that there might be situations in which the singling out of individual targets of expropriation may be justified in case there were other reasons why a particular property or investment was taken. Since 'discrimination' is regarded as 'unreasonable distinction', expropriations of certain persons may be lawful if such distinction is 'rationally related to the state's security or economic policies'.[105]

In this vein, tribunals have held that even the fact that one foreign investor was expropriated while another one was not did not necessarily imply a discriminatory taking as long as there were 'adequate reasons' for distinguishing between these investors. For instance, the tribunal in the *Aminoil* case[106] did not arrive at a finding of an unlawful discrimination although the US claimant had been expropriated while a non-US oil company (Arabian Oil) had not. According to the tribunal, the

> nationalisation of Aminoil was not thereby tainted with discrimination [. . .]. First of all, it has never for a single moment been suggested that it was because of the American nationality of the Company that the Decree Law was applied to Aminoil's Concession. Next, and above all, there were adequate reasons for not nationalising Arabian Oil.[107]

The specific reasons accepted by the *Aminoil* tribunal were that the non-US oil company operated in a more sophisticated way and held a concession granted by Kuwait and Saudi Arabia jointly.[108]

---

[103] Ibid, 53.

[104] Rubins and Kinsella, above n 2, 177.

[105] *Restatement (Third) of the Foreign Relations Law of the United States* above n 9, § 712, Comment f.

[106] *Kuwait v American Independent Oil Company (Aminoil)*, Award of 24 March 1982, 21 ILM 976 (1982).

[107] Ibid, para 87.

[108] Ibid ('AOC's high-cost off-shore production operations are such as to give it

A similar reasoning was adopted by the Iran-US Claims Tribunal in the *Amoco* case. The tribunal said that

> [it] finds it difficult, in the absence of any other evidence, to draw the conclusion that the expropriation of a concern was discriminatory only from the fact that another concern in the same economic branch was not expropriated. Reasons specific to the non-expropriated enterprise, or to the expropriated one, or to both, may justify such a difference in treatment.[109]

Also the NAFTA tribunal in *GAMI v Mexico* addressed the issue that some owners were expropriated while others were not. The tribunal, however, was not persuaded that

> GAM's circumstances were demonstrably so 'like' those of non-expropriated mill owners that it was wrong to treat GAM differently. [...] Mexico perceived that mills operating in conditions of effective insolvency needed public participation in the interest of the national economy in a broad sense. [...] The arbitrators are satisfied that a reason exists for the measure which was not itself discriminatory. That measure was plausibly connected with a legitimate goal of policy (ensuring that the sugar industry was in the hands of solvent enterprises) and was applied neither in a discriminatory manner nor as a disguised barrier to equal opportunity.[110]

5. Actual Findings of Discrimination in the Case Law

While the case law of international tribunals has generally affirmed the existence of a non-discrimination requirement for expropriations and while this affirmation is frequently found in arbitral awards and judicial decisions, often as an *obiter dictum*,[111] cases where courts or tribunals have actually found breaches of the non-discrimination requirement are rare.

In some of the Libyan Oil Concession cases[112] the expropriatory acts

---

a special position which requires a high degree of expertise. At the same time, it is working within the framework of a concession granted by both Kuwait and Saudi Arabia, so its position is completely different. Any modification of the concession must be agreed to by both countries.').

[109] *Amoco International Finance Corp. v Iran*, 15 Iran-US CTR 189, 232 (1987), para 142.

[110] *GAMI Investments, Inc. v United Mexican States*, Award of 15 November 2004, para 114.

[111] See *supra* text at note 83.

[112] *British Petroleum v Libya*, Award of 10 October 1973 and 1 August 1974, 53 ILR 297; *Texaco Overseas Petroleum Company (Topco)/California Asiatic (Calasiatic) Oil Company v Libya*, Award of 19 January 1977, 17 ILM 1 (1978); *Libyan American Oil Company (Liamco) v Libya*, Award of 12 April 1977; 20 ILM

were found to have a discriminatory character. For instance, in *British Petroleum v Libya*, the sole arbitrator regarded the expropriation as unlawful because it was politically motivated. He found that 'the taking by the Respondent of the property, rights and of the Claimant clearly violates public international law as it was made for purely extraneous political reasons and was arbitrary and discriminatory in character'.[113]

A discriminatory expropriation was also found in *Eureko v Poland*,[114] where a UNCITRAL tribunal concluded that the challenged Polish measures were aimed at excluding foreign investors from the Polish insurance business and thus discriminatory. It found a violation of the expropriation provision of the applicable BIT.[115] According to the tribunal, the challenged measures, i.e. the refusal to conduct a public offering, 'proclaimed by successive Ministers of the State Treasury as being pursued in order to keep [an insurance business] under majority Polish control and to exclude foreign control such as Eureko', were 'clearly discriminatory'.[116] In this case the discrimination was not one between different groups of foreigners but rather one between foreigners and nationals of the host state.[117]

ICSID cases equally confirmed the relevance of the non-discrimination

---

1 (1981), 62 *ILR* 140; see also Robert B von Mehren and P Nicholas Kourides, 'International Arbitration Between States and Foreign Private Parties: The Libyan Oil Nationalization Cases' (1981) 75 *AJIL* 476; Christopher Greenwood, 'State Contracts in International Law – The Libyan Oil Arbitrations' (1982) 53 *BYIL* 27; Robin White, 'Expropriation of the Libyan Oil Concessions – Two Conflicting International Arbitrations' (1981) 30 *ICLQ* 1.

[113] *British Petroleum v Libya*, Award of 10 October 1973 and 1 August 1974; 53 ILR 297, at 329.

[114] *Eureko B.V. v Republic of Poland*, Partial Award of 19 August 2005.

[115] Article 5 of the 1992 Netherlands/Poland BIT (Agreement between the Kingdom of the Netherlands and the Republic of Poland on Encouragement and Reciprocal Protection of Investments, 7 September 1992) provided: 'Neither Contracting Party shall take any measures depriving, directly or indirectly, investors of the other Contracting Party of their investments unless the following conditions are complied with: (a) the measures are taken in the public interest and under due process of law; (b) the measures are not discriminatory or contrary to any undertaking which the former Contracting Party may have given; (c) the measures are accompanied by provision for the payment of just compensation.

Such compensation shall represent the real value of the investments affected and shall, in order to be effective for the claimants, be paid and made transferable, without undue delay, to the country designated by the claimants concerned in any freely convertible currency accepted by the claimants.'

[116] *Eureko B.V. v Republic of Poland*, Partial Award of 19 August 2005, para 242.

[117] See *supra* text at n 96.

requirement. In *LETCO v Liberia*, a case concerning the unilateral abrogation of a concession for the exploitation of timber reserves in Liberia, the tribunal stressed that 'even if the Government had sought to justify its action as an act of nationalization, it would have had to . . . show that its action [. . .] was non-discriminatory'.[118] Since the tribunal found evidence that 'areas of the concession taken away from LETCO were granted to other foreign-owned companies [. . .] run by people who were "good friends" of the Liberian authorities'[119] it concluded that 'the taking of LETCO's property was [. . .] discriminatory'.[120]

Also in the ICSID case of *ADC v Hungary*, actions taken by the host state against the investor were considered discriminatory.[121] The tribunal found 'that in order for a discrimination to exist, particularly in an expropriation scenario, there must be different treatments to different parties'.[122]

The investor had argued that the regulatory framework prohibiting the operation of the airport by any third party other than the Hungarian airport operator entity was specifically aimed at it since it was the only operator of the airport. Hungary had argued that the new framework applied to all persons and business entities other than the statutorily appointed operator and was thus not discriminatory. The tribunal expressly rejected 'the Respondent's argument that as the only foreign parties involved in the operation of the Airport, the Claimants [were] not in a position to raise any claims of being treated discriminately'.[123] In a short explanation the tribunal held that 'the comparison of different treatments is made here between that received by the Respondent-appointed operator and that received by foreign investors as a whole',[124] in order to add that it 'therefore reject[ed] the contentions made by the Respondent and conclud[ed] that the actions taken by the Respondent against the Claimants [were] discriminatory'.[125]

---

118 *Liberian Eastern Timber Corporation (LETCO) v Republic of Liberia*, Award of 31 March 1986, ICSID Case No ARB/83/2, 2 ICSID Rep 343, at 366.

119 Ibid, 366.

120 Ibid, 367.

121 *ADC Affiliate Limited and ADC & ADMC Management Limited v Republic of Hungary*, Award of 2 October 2006, ICSID Case No ARB/03/16, para 443.

122 Ibid, para 442.

123 Ibid, para 441.

124 Ibid, para 442.

125 Ibid, para 443.

6. Summary

The practice of international tribunals strongly supports the assumption that non-discrimination is a requirement for the legality of an expropriation both under customary international law and under specifically applicable IIAs. While tribunals tend to qualify politically motivated or other egregious forms of discrimination as unlawful, they do apply a more nuanced approach to expropriations which affect only some foreigners if such discrimination may be the result of legitimate government policies. A major factor for the assessment of discrimination issues in the course of expropriations is the burden of proof required by tribunals. While most tribunals require the complaining investors to demonstrate that they have been discriminated against, some appear to shift the burden of proof to the expropriating state. In addition, there is case law demonstrating that not only discrimination among foreign investors but also between foreigners and nationals of the expropriating state is relevant. Some of these cases actually indicate that protectionist purposes leading to the discriminatory treatment may be particularly prone to being held unlawful.

VI. CONCLUSION

The law of expropriation, traditionally prominent under customary international law, still forms one of the core aspects of modern investment law. Though the case law under BITs and other IIAs is growing at a pace that makes a comprehensive analysis almost impossible, this accumulated practice of international tribunals strongly supports the notion that common principles may be ascertained.

11. Soft codification of international investment law

August Reinisch and Andrea K. Bjorklund

INTRODUCTION

At present, codification has become a contested concept. For many observers the era of codification in customary international law is a bygone period since most major topics have been subjected to more or less successful codification attempts, primarily under the prominent aegis of the International Law Commission (ILC), including its work on diplomatic[1] and consular[2] law, on the law of treaties,[3] on state responsibility,[4] state succession,[5] and state immunity.[6]

If one looks at today's work plan of the ILC, mostly technical areas remain. The Commission is addressing some of the unresolved questions in the Vienna Convention on the Law of Treaties (VCLT), such as

---

1 Vienna Convention on Diplomatic Relations, 18 April 1961, 500 UNTS 95.

2 Vienna Convention on Consular Relations, 24 April 1963, 596 UNTS 261.

3 Vienna Convention on Law of Treaties, 23 May 1969, 1155 UNTS 331.

4 Draft articles on Responsibility of States for internationally wrongful acts, adopted by the International Law Commission at its Fifty-third session (2001), Report of the International Law Commission on the work of its Fifty-third session, Official Records of the General Assembly, Fifty-sixth session, Supplement No 10 (A/56/10), Chp IV.E.2.

5 Vienna Convention on Succession of States in respect of Treaties, 23 August 1978, 1946 UNTS 3; Vienna Convention on Succession of States in respect of State Property, Archives and Debts, 8 April 1983, UN Doc A/CONF.117/14 (not yet in force); Draft Articles on nationality of natural persons in relation to the succession of States adopted by the Commission at its Fifty-first Session (1999), Official Records of the General Assembly, Fifty-fourth Session, Supplement No 10 (A/54/10).

6 The ILC project on State Immunity has resulted in the adoption by the General Assembly of the United Nations Convention on Jurisdictional Immunities of States and Their Property, UN Doc A/RES/59/38 (16 December 2004). As of 11 October 2011, 28 States had ratified the Convention but it had not yet entered into force.

reservations,[7] interpretation, conflicts between treaties addressing similar or overlapping issues (which has resulted in the well-known study on fragmentation),[8] and the effectiveness of treaties over time,[9] as opposed to the more fundamental and comprehensive law of treaties in the VCLT. Many of these current issues, though more specific than previous topics, are equally important. But the end of the classical codification period appears to be also evident in the fact that the questions dealt with by the ILC today are unlikely to lead to the traditional codification instruments, i.e. treaties embodying the ultimate 'hard' codification. Rather, they will be summarized in guidelines, draft articles or other softer forms of codification. As the example of the important Articles on State Responsibility[10] shows, even draft articles, by definition a non-binding instrument, can exert strong normative force, in particular where they are widely regarded as reflecting customary international law.[11] Investment arbitration is in fact full of examples where the ILC's State Responsibility Articles are invoked as evidence of such customary principles.[12]

NEW AREAS: TRADE AND INVESTMENT LAW

Recent years have shown growing interest in areas 'where the action is',

---

[7] Guide to Practice on Reservations to Treaties adopted by the ILC at its Sixty-third Session (2011), Official Records of the General Assembly Sixty-sixth Session, Supplement No 10 (A/66/10) para 75.

[8] Report of the ILC Fifty-seventh session (2005), Official Records of the General Assembly, Sixtieth Session, Supplement No 10 (A/60/10), Chp XI, para 444.

[9] Report of the ILC Sixty-third session (2011), Official Records of the General Assembly Sixty-sixth Session, Supplement No 10 (A/66/10), Chp XI, para 333.

[10] Draft articles on Responsibility of States for internationally wrongful acts, above n 4.

[11] David Caron, 'The ILC Articles on State Responsibility: The Paradoxical Relationship between Form and Authority' (2002) 96 *AJIL* 857; Kaj Hobér, 'State Responsibility and Attribution' in Peter Muchlinski *et al.* (eds) *The Oxford Handbook of International Investment Law* (2008) 533; Michael Feit, 'Responsibility of the State under International Law for the Breach of Contract Committed by a State-Owned Entity' (2009) 28 *BJIL* 146.

[12] *Noble Venture, Inc. v Romania*, Award of 12 October 2005, ICSID Case No ARB/01/11, paras 69–70; *Eureko B.V. v Republic of Poland*, Partial Award and Dissenting Opinion of 19 August 2005, paras 33–4 (ad hoc arbitration seated in Brussels); *SGS v Pakistan*, Decision of the Tribunal on Objections to Jurisdiction of 16 August 2003, ICSID Case No ARB/701/13, para 166; *L.E.S.I-DIPENTA v Algeria*, Award of 10 January 2005, ICSID Case No ARB/03/8, para 19.

such as trade and investment law. Both fields have been booming mostly as a result of the sharp increase in dispute settlement. In the case of trade law, this was institutionally anticipated through the 'legalization' of trade disputes, or the turn from trade diplomacy to trade law as a result of the Uruguay Round and the ensuing Dispute Settlement Understanding of the World Trade Organization (WTO DSU), which brought not only a quasi-right to have a WTO panel hear a complaint, but also a much more contentious procedure resulting in a binding report. In parallel, investment disputes came of age as a result of the growing number of BITs and other IIAs which provided for investor/state dispute settlement and the crucial jurisprudential development of regarding these treaty provisions as offers that could be accepted at any time by the protected investors of the other contracting parties. Thus, treaty arbitration has grown exponentially.

The treatification of international trade and investment law, combined with the availability of dispute settlement resulting in usually publicized awards, offers a rich and complex variety of sources that could influence a codification effort. Such an effort would not be a classic identification and codification of customary international law. Rather, we are faced with a multitude of interpretations given to multilateral (NAFTA/GATT/ECT) and bilateral (BITs) treaties providing a conventional core of rights and obligations sometimes supplemented by general international law. In addition, and particularly in investment law, there is probably underlying customary international law that has to be addressed. For instance, the typical expropriation clause in an investment treaty often resembles very closely the so-called Hull formula,[13] which arguably represents (or has represented) customary international law at least at some stage.[14] Similarly, there is a view held by many and reinforced by the actual formulation found in some IIAs that the fair and equitable treatment

---

[13] Green Hackworth, 3 *Digest of International Law* (1942) 658–9 ('[. . .] no government is entitled to expropriate private property, for whatever purpose, without provision for prompt, adequate and effective payment therefore.'); Muthucumaraswamy Sornarajah, *The International Law on Foreign Investment* (CUP 2010) 210.

[14] Patrick Norton, 'A Law of the Future or a Law of the Past? Modern Tribunals and the International Law of Expropriation' (1991) 85 *AJIL* 488, 495; Davis R Robinson, 'Expropriation in the Restatement' (1984)78 *AJIL* 176, 177; K Scott Gudgeon, 'Valuation of Nationalized Property under United States and other Bilateral Investment Treaties' in Richard B Lillich (ed), *IV The Valuation of Nationalized Property in International Law* (University of Virginia Press 1987) 113–14.

standard reflects the (customary) international minimum standard of treatment of aliens.[15]

While technically the treaty provisions which reflect the refinement of trade and investment law must have primacy, general international law remains highly relevant as contextual background. In both areas, the issue of systemic integration as a specific interpretation tool under Article 31(3)(c) of the VCLT plays an increasingly important role.[16] The heightened interest in the two fields of trade and investment is also evidenced by the ILC's current work on MFN.[17]

HARD CODIFICATION IN TRADE AND INVESTMENT LAW

In the fields of trade and investment law, 'hard' codification has been only partly successful. With regard to trade law, it is difficult to speak of a 'codification' of customary rules in general since most trade rules

---

[15] Stephen M Schwebel, *The Influence of Bilateral Investment Treaties on Customary International Law* (2007), Proceedings of the 98th Annual Meeting of the American Society of International Law (31 March–3 April 2004) 29–30; Andrew Newcombe and Lluís Paradell, *Law and Practice of Investment Treaties, Standard of Treatment* (Kluwer Law International 2009) 270; Ian Brownlie, *Principles of Public International Law* (OUP 2003) 520; Bernard Kishoiyian, 'The Utility of Bilateral Investment Treaties in the Formulation of Customary International Law' (1994) 14 *NJILB* 327; Steffen Hindelang, 'Bilateral Investment Treaties, Custom and a Healthy Investment Climate? The Question of Whether BITs Influence Customary International Law Revisited' (2004) 5 *JWIT* 767; Ioana Tudor, *The Fair and Equitable Treatment Standard in the International Law of Foreign Investment* (OUP 2008) 53–84.

[16] Brigitte Stern, 'Interpretation in International Trade Law' in Malgosia Fitzmaurice, Olufemi Elias and Panos Merkouris (eds), *Treaty Interpretation and the Vienna Convention on the Law of Treaties: 30 Years On* (Koninkliijke Brill NV 2010) 48, 111; Campbell McLachlan, 'The Principle of Systemic Integration and Article 31(3)(c) of the Vienna Convention' (2005) 54 *ICLQ*; *United States – Import Prohibition of Certain Shrimp and Shrimp Products*, WTO Dispute Settlement Body WT/DS58/AB/R (Report of the Appellate Body of 12 October 1998) at 158; *Pope & Talbot Inc v Canada*, NAFTA, Award on the merits of 10 April 2001, Award in respect of damages of 31 May 2002; *EC measures concerning meat and meat products (hormones)*, WTO Dispute Settlement Body WT/DS-26/AB/R – (Report of the Appellate Body of 16 January 1998); Campbell McLachlan, Laurence Shore and Matthew Weininger, *International Investment Arbitration: Substantive Principles* (OUP 2007) 66.

[17] Report of the International Law Commission, Sixty-third Session (2011) General Assembly Official Records Supplement No 10 (A/66/10) Chp XII, para 345.

embodied in bilateral as well as multilateral trade agreements like the GATT contain specifically extended trade benefits or privileges, such as better access to domestic markets for goods originating in other contracting states, that are typically specifically negotiated between parties and do not arise under customary international law.[18]

Nevertheless, the Uruguay Round, like the Tokyo Round before, led to some extent to the codification of earlier institutional practices, e.g. of dispute settlement under Article XXIII GATT, coupled with a number of rather innovative elements of progressive development, such as reverse consensus[19] and cross-retaliation.[20] Also in other fields of trade law, past practice was codified, such as in the Antidumping[21] and Subsidies[22] Agreements, the Agreement on Technical Barriers to Trade,[23] and the Agreement on the Application of Sanitary and Phytosanitary Measures.[24] WTO law does provide examples for a potential hardening of soft codification, such as the importation of non-binding standards set by various institutions, like the International Organization for Standardization (ISO), into the hard law TBT and SPS Agreements.[25] As Melaku

---

18 Stephen Zamora, 'Is there Customary International Economic Law?' (1990) 32 *GYIL* 9-42; Ignaz Seidl-Hohenveldern, *International Economic Law* (Kluwer Law International 1999) 29 *et seq.*

19 Article 16 of the Dispute Settlement Understanding (DSU).

20 Article 22 of the DSU.

21 Agreement on Implementation of Article VI of the General Agreement on Tariffs and Trade 1994 (Anti-dumping Agreement), 15 April 1994, entered into force 1 January 1995, Marrakesh Agreement Establishing the World Trade Organization, Annex 1A, 1868 UNTS 201.

22 Agreement on Subsidies and Countervailing Measures, 15 April 1994, entered into force 1 January 1995, Marrakesh Agreement Establishing the World Trade Organization, Annex 1A, 1869 UNTS 14.

23 Agreement on Technical Barriers to Trade, 15 April 1994, entered into force 1 January 1995, Marrakesh Agreement Establishing the World Trade Organization, Annex 1A, 1868 UNTS 120.

24 Agreement on the Application of Sanitary and Phytosanitary Measures, 15 April 1994, Marrakesh Agreement Establishing the World Trade Organization, Annex 1A, 1867 UNTS 493.

25 The Agreement on Technical Barriers to Trade encourages State Parties to comply with a Code of Good Practice; local government, non-governmental and other standardizing bodies, including the ISO, can also accept the Code of Good Practice. This cooperative approach contributes to a uniformity of technical regulations that facilitates, rather than impedes, trade. The Agreement on the Application of Sanitary and Phytosanitary Measures encourages members to use international standards, guidelines, and recommendations, such as those set out by the ISO.

Desta shows in his contribution,[26] WTO panels and the Appellate Body have struggled to explain this phenomenon in a number of cases, most prominently in *EC Sardines*.[27]

In investment law, hard codification has been rather unsuccessful. Attempts to agree on a multilateral investment agreement – such as the OECD projects of the 1960s, ending with a Draft Convention on the Protection of Foreign Property,[28] and the 1990s, leading to the aborted MAI negotiations[29] – led nowhere; though there are currently some signs on the horizon of a renewed interest in this matter. This, too, is likely a result of a lack of consensus on the nature of the customary international law that might be codified; the failure of the codification attempts of the 1960s can be traced to the post-colonial dissatisfaction with international law that culminated in the New International Economic Order of the 1970s; the failure of codification attempts of the 1990s had perhaps more to do with generalized distrust of 'globalization' than with specific objections to many of the core international investment law norms which by then were included in most BITs.

Indeed, starting in the 1960s, states began to conclude investment protection treaties on a bilateral basis leading to a dense web of almost 3,000 BITs. To some extent this decentralized BIT codification may be regarded as a substitute for the failed multilateral approach.

This is not to say that all BITs are identical; some contain different formulations of similar ideas (*viz* different formulations of umbrella clauses and MFN clauses), while others do not contain those obligations at all. One of the most contentious issues in investment law is the extent to which these differences in treaty language should lead to divergent outcomes, or whether treaties should be harmonized by use of various interpretive techniques. Although technically speaking, each BIT is an 'island to itself', it is obvious that the striking similarity between BITs

---

[26] Desta, Chapter 7, this volume.

[27] *European Communities – Trade Description of Sardines*, Report of the Panel, WT/DS231/R; *European Communities – Trade Description of Sardines*, Report of the Appellate Body, WT/DS231/AB/R (2002).

[28] The OECD Council published a Draft Convention on the Protection of Foreign Property in 1967, but the draft was never formally adopted. Resolution of the OECD Council, 12 October 1967, 7 ILM 117.

[29] From 1995 to 1998 the OECD hosted a series of negotiations designed to produce a multilateral agreement on investment (MAI). The negotiating group produced a draft text, but the negotiations stalled. For a draft text, see *The Multilateral Agreement on Investment: Draft Consolidated Text*, DAFFE/MAI(98)7/REV1 (22 April 1998).

suggests that they are regulating common problems in a common fashion. This justifies reliance on BIT arbitral decisions – not as binding precedent – but as part of a *de facto* case law or *jurisprudence constante*.[30]

This search for consistency may be viewed as the collective professional deformation of lawyers, but it is probably more than that. With the growth of an investment 'case law', the question becomes more and more acute whether a common law of investment can be ascertained and, if so, whether and to what extent it may be identified and described.

Traditionally, this would call for a hard law codification, but in the field of investment law, it seems that currently such a solution would be hard to achieve; thus a soft codification attempt is likely to prove more effective. We discuss various options below.

SOFT CODIFICATION IN INTERNATIONAL LAW

Soft codification, i.e. the formulation of legal rules on the basis of already established or at least emerging custom but in non-binding form, has become more widespread in mainstream public international law. The recent efforts of the ILC to 'codify' international law by means other than through conventions provide a good example.[31] The ILC Articles on State Responsibility is a pertinent example.

In addition, the ILA has a long-standing tradition of formulating different forms of 'soft' codifications, ranging from 'Draft Articles',[32] to

---

[30] See Andrea K Bjorklund, 'Investment Treaty Arbitral Decisions as Jurisprudence Constante' in Colin Picker, Isabella Bunn and Douglas Arner (eds), *International Economic Law: The State and Future of the Discipline* (Hart Publishing 2008) 265; Gabrielle Kaufmann-Kohler, 'Arbitral Precedent: Dream, Necessity, or Excuse' (No 4, 2007) 23 *Arbitration International* 357; August Reinisch, 'The Role of Precedent in ICSID Arbitration', in *Austrian Arbitration Yearbook* (2008) 495; Ian A Laird, 'The Emerging Jurisprudence of International Investment Law: Introduction to Conference' in Andrea K Bjorklund, Ian A Laird and Sergey Ripinsky (eds) *Investment Treaty Law, Current Issues III* (British Institute of International and Comparative Law 2009); Paolo Vargiu, 'Beyond Hallmarks and Formal Requirements: A "Jurisprudence Constante" on the Notion of Investment in the ICSID Convention' (2009) 10 *J World Inv & Trade* 753.

[31] See *supra* text starting at n 7.

[32] International Law Association, Montreal Draft Articles for a Convention on State Immunity 1982 (ILA Draft Convention), 22 *ILM* (1983) 287; The Buenos Aires Revised Draft Articles for a Convention on State Immunity, ILA Report (1994) 21, did not change the provisions on enforcement immunity.

'Rules', to 'Recommended Practices',[33] or the like in an attempt to contribute to the codification and development of various fields of international law.

Scholarly commentaries, such as the UN Charter Commentary,[34] the Commentary on the Statute of the ICJ,[35] and the ICSID Commentary,[36] offer useful techniques for a gradual codification effort. The way that the relevant users, including international courts and tribunals, rely on such sources demonstrates that an effective indirect codification may take place through heavily relied upon scholarly works. Andrea K Bjorklund demonstrated in her introductory chapter that different forms of both domestic and international soft law instruments can influence legal decision-makers and thus play a significant role in developing law notwithstanding their 'soft' nature. Some soft law instruments, such as OECD Model Tax Treaties,[37] Uniform Laws, and Draft Conventions, are specifically designed to serve as models for 'hard' law instruments but must be adopted by States in order to achieve that status. Others are not created as models for legislation or treaties, but are nonetheless faithful attempts to catalogue existing practice and potentially to influence future action, whether by states or by judicial or arbitral decision-makers, or both. Some may encapsulate existing practices, while others might seek to fill *lacunae* in the laws. Examples of such instruments include US Restatements,[38] Dicey and Morris on Conflict of Laws,[39] the UNIDROIT

---

[33] E.g. ILA Recommended Rules and Practices on the Accountability of International Organisations. Report of the Seventy-first Conference (ILA – Berlin Conference – 2004) 164.

[34] Bruno Simma (ed),The Charter of the United Nations: A Commentary (OUP 1994).

[35] Andreas Zimmermann, Christian Tomuschat and Karin Oellers-Frahm (eds), *The Statute of the International Court of Justice: A Commentary* (OUP 2006).

[36] Christoph Schreuer, *The ICSID Convention: A Commentary* (CUP 2001).

[37] The latest version is the *Articles of the Model Convention with Respect to Taxes on Income and Capital* (17 July 2008), available at <http://www.oecd.org/dataoecd/43/57/42219418.pdf>.

[38] For a complete list of US Restatements of the Law, see <http://tinyurl.com/24vm7rr>. A current Restatement project of interest for the Study Group project is the proposed Restatement on the US Law of International Commercial Arbitration. Chapter 6 of that Restatement will address investor-state dispute settlement as it interacts with US courts.

[39] Lawrence Collins, *Dicey, Morris and Collins on the Conflict of Laws* (Sweet & Maxwell 2006).

Principles,[40] the OECD Guidelines for Multinational Enterprises,[41] ILA resolutions,[42] Institut de Droit International resolutions,[43] and the Ruggie-commissioned study on stabilization clauses.[44] Still others will attempt to regulate behaviour by incorporating 'best practices' in negotiations between two or several entities. Examples include the Association of International Petroleum Negotiators standardized oil and gas contracts[45] and Energy Charter Treaty Secretariat model agreements.[46] If sufficient numbers adopt the same approach they may create soft-norms with respect to contract drafting.

SOFT CODIFICATION IN INVESTMENT LAW

This book is the product of a collective effort of members of the ILA Study Group on the Role of Soft Law Instruments in International Investment Law, established by the ILA Executive Council in November 2008. It aims to fulfil the express mandate 'to study the development of soft law instruments in international investment law and the feasibility of a "codification" of the present state of this field of international economic law'.[47]

The ILA Study Group has thus focused on identifying the main issues surrounding a potential 'codification' of investment law and investigating whether and in which form investment law may be 'codified.' This

---

40 *UNIDROIT Principles of International Commercial Contracts 2004*, endorsed by the UN Commission on International Trade Law, UN Doc A/62/17 (Part I) (23 July 2007) 52–4.

41 OECD, *OECD Guidelines for Multinational Enterprises*, DAFFE/IME/WPG(2000)15/FINAL (31 October 2001).

42 Reports of all ILA Conferences, including the text of the Resolutions adopted by the Association, are available on HeinOnline.

43 A chronological index of the resolutions adopted by the Institut de Droit International is available at <http://www.idi-iil.org/idiE/navig_res_chon.html>.

44 Andrea Shemberg, *Stabilization Clauses and Human Rights: A research project conducted for IFC and the United Nations Special Representative to the Secretary General on Business and Human Rights* (11 March 2008), available at <http://tinyurl.com/2excemo>.

45 For a list of model contracts available from the AIPN, see <http://www.aipn.org/modelagreements>.

46 Energy Charter Secretariat, *Model Intergovernmental and Host Government Agreements for Cross-Border Pipelines* (2nd edn, Energy Charter Secretariat 2007).

47 Andrea K Bjorklund and August Reinisch, *The Role of Soft-Law Instruments in International Investment Law, Report of the Seventy-fourth Conference* (ILA Conference – the Hague – 2010) 961.

'feasibility study' has led to a nuanced outcome. While it has identified a number of areas which embody relatively robust and coherent practical application of investment rules, evidenced by a homogeneous case law, which may thus be regarded as 'codifiable', it has also demonstrated that there is a growing number of fields where investment tribunals have given diverging interpretations to identical or similar BIT provisions. Examples go beyond the well-known divergent approaches by individual tribunals to the most-favoured-nation clause, the 'umbrella' clause, the notion of investment, or the nature and prerequisites of the necessity defence. In addition, they now include the question of how to interpret so-called narrow dispute settlement clauses referring to the amount and modalities of compensation in the case of expropriation[48] or the nature of so-called waiting periods.[49]

This does not mean that a soft codification is impossible, but that any codification attempt must take into account the variations in treaty language that might result in different interpretations. It also must faithfully represent the strands of thought in areas in which agreement on the correct interpretation has yet to coalesce. These considerations will require careful handling if the goal of the soft law instrument is to induce harmonization rather than divergence.

---

[48] Contrast the narrow interpretation of such clauses by the tribunals in *Vladimir and Moise Berschader v The Russian Federation*, SCC Case No 080/2004, Award of 21 April 2006; *RosInvestCo UK Ltd. v The Russian Federation*, Award on Jurisdiction 2007, SCC Case No ARB/V079/2005; *Austrian Airlines AG v The Slovak Republic*, UNCITRAL Final Award of 9 October 2009, with the wide interpretation given in *Saipem S.p.A. v The People's Republic of Bangladesh*, ICSID Case No ARB/05/07, Decision on Jurisdiction and Recommendation on Provisional Measures of 21 March 2007; *European Media Ventures SA v Czech Republic*, Judgment of the High Court of England and Wales of 5 December 2007 (2007) EWHC 2851 (Comm); *Tza Yap Shum v Republic of Peru*, ICSID Case No ARB/07/6 (China/Peru BIT), Decision on Jurisdiction and Competence of 19 June 2009.

[49] Most investment tribunals have treated 'consultation periods as directory and procedural rather than as mandatory and jurisdictional in nature'. *SGS Société Générale de Surveillance S.A. v Islamic Republic of Pakistan*, ICSID Case No ARB/01/13, Decision on Jurisdiction of 6 August 2003) para 184; *Ronald S. Lauder v The Czech Republic*, UNCITRAL, Final Award of 3 September 2001) para 190; *Bayindir Insaat Turizm Ticaret Ve Sanayi AS v Pakistan*, ICSID Case No ARB/03/29, Decision on Jurisdiction of 14 November 2005) para 100. More recently, however, a number of tribunals have insisted on the jurisdictional character of such requirements. *Burlington Resources Inc. v Republic of Ecuador and Empresa Estatal Petróleos del Ecuador (PetroEcuador)*, ICSID Case No ARB/08/5, Decision on Jurisdiction of 2 June 2010); *Murphy Exploration and Prod. Co. Int'l v Republic of Ecuador*, ICSID Case No ARB/08/4, Award on Jurisdiction of 15 December 2010).

DANGERS OF SOFT CODIFICATION

This study has also addressed a number of practical problems of 'codification'. The fact that there is an exponentially growing law (both in terms of treaties and in terms of cases decided under them) and that there are increasing instances of inconsistencies has already been mentioned. From a practical drafting perspective, in the case of conflicting approaches, choices made at the drafting stage might result in wording that would not necessarily be representative of any leading approach. These areas may thus require a more nuanced 'soft codification' approach that provides interpretative options instead of black letter law. Of potential use would be convergence around a single interpretation of identical or functionally identical treaty language, while still allowing for differences in interpretation of evidently different treaty language, thereby honouring the intention of the treaty drafters.

Moreover, in situations where there is no established case law a soft law instrument may have a gap or would have to state a principle by endorsing an approach that had not earned consistent or near-universal support.

Finally, a soft law instrument might have to be formulated so generally to be representative of all various approaches that it could not provide guidance when specific questions have to be decided. It would thus fail to induce harmonization of interpretation and might thus be considered practically ineffective.

GUIDANCE TAKEN FROM OTHER FIELDS

The Study Group decided early on to be guided by experiences with soft law instruments in other fields. Giuditta Cordero-Moss discussed soft codifications in the area of commercial law, addressing the scope of the relevant instruments (e.g. the specificity of INCOTERMS[50] vs the generalized nature of the UNIDROIT Principles of International Commercial Contracts[51]), language problems that may arise in the course of such 'codification' exercises, as well as the difficulties involved when ascertaining whether there was true or merely apparent consensus. In commercial law, soft law instruments have been very successful in practice

---

[50] ICC, *Incoterms 2000* (ICC Pub 1999).

[51] *UNIDROIT Principles of International Commercial Contracts 2004*, endorsed by the UN Commission on International Trade Law, UN Doc A/62/17 (Part I) (23 July 2007) 52–4.

when their use leads to predictable results, in particular where they are sufficiently precise so that they can be interpreted without being influenced by the legal tradition of the interpreter.

Melaku Desta focused on a particular field of GATT/WTO codification, the SPS and TBT Agreements and their 'incorporation' of soft law, non-binding standards set by various institutions, like the ISO or the Codex Alimentarius Commission. He demonstrated a field where soft law may be hardening as a result of a combination of hard law references to the soft law instruments (in GATT/WTO side agreements) and the binding case law under the WTO DSU.

Finally, Kate Miles scrutinized the potential model character of soft law instruments in environmental law for international investment law. Her conclusions are that soft law in the environmental arena has developed largely due to *lacunae* left by the relatively few hard law documents extant in the environmental realm; differences in the law-making processes in investment law might mean there is less space available for soft law to occupy. But a lesson that can be drawn from the international environmental experience is the flexibility and creativity of soft law, as well as its influence in shaping practice and eventual regulation. Investment law might benefit from a traditional Restatement-type soft law instrument, and could also be well served by innovative approaches to soft law that could contribute to the development of legal norms.

FORMER INVESTMENT LAW CODIFICATIONS

As already mentioned, the field of international investment law is not devoid of previous attempts to 'codify' the law. In order to identify the main stumbling blocks on the road to a 'hard' or 'soft' law codification of investment rules it is necessary to be aware of the history of such attempts. With a view to identifying the salient characteristics of different generations of BITs and other IIAs, Christian Tietje and Emily Sipiorski looked at the main strands of the last 50 years of BITs as well as their predecessors, such as FCN treaties. They concluded that the underlying structure of BITs is sufficiently similar to open ground for considering a multilateral agreement in the field. Andrea Bjorklund reviewed briefly those multilateral investment treaties that were unsuccessful in the past, including the Abs-Shawcross Convention, the German-initiated OECD Draft Convention on the Protection of Foreign Property, and the well-known multilateral agreement on investment (MAI), an OECD-led initiative that failed in the late 1900s.

POTENTIAL RIPENESS OF INVESTMENT LAW FOR CODIFICATION

One of the functions of a soft law instrument could be to provide a contemporary view of the state of the emerging and in several areas already settled jurisprudence of international investment law. While the ILA Study Group and this book could not exhaustively identify those areas in which one can speak already of a *jurisprudence constante* or settled 'soft' case law, it undertook to look at specific fields of the law in order to test their 'ripeness' for codification.

Describing the current state of international investment law in such fields contributes to the identification of customary international law as well as the lack of such hardened rules. Before it directly addressed two fields within investment law, MFN treatment and expropriations, to assess the ripeness of those areas for codification, a more general introductory chapter to this section dealt with the interrelationship of various sources of international investment law. Moshe Hirsch particularly emphasized that different sources of international law, ranging from the dominant treaties in the field, to custom and general principles of law, and also including a prominent role for the subsidiary sources of judicial and arbitral precedent, as well as scholarly writings, have all played an important role in the formation of a body of investment law as it is actually applied by investment tribunals.

EXAMPLES OF AREAS THAT MAY BE MORE OR LESS RIPE FOR CODIFICATION

Two specific studies in this book tested to what extent substantive standards are ripe for codification; one of them ventured into providing a sample codification approach. One of the typical BIT non-discrimination standards – most-favoured-nation treatment – was further explored, while the other sample addressed an aspect of the legality of expropriation.

The chapter on MFN by Andreas Ziegler gave an overview of treaty-makers' practice in this field, outlining in detail the various forms of MFN clauses found in bilateral and multilateral investment agreements. He demonstrated that there is probably a common understanding on the inclusion of an MFN clause in principle but that there appear to be diverging views as to the scope of MFN clauses as evidenced in the carve-outs for taxation issues, regional economic integration organizations, and the like. On the basis of current arbitration developments Ziegler also showed that the question whether an MFN clause also encompasses procedural/jurisdictional issues has been and still is the most controversial aspect of MFN clauses.

Another chapter addressed a particular issue of expropriation, a topic that has already formed the basis for a substantial amount of case law based on customary international law principles and on treaty provisions. By way of a 'sample codification', August Reinisch assessed a specific aspect of expropriation, the legality requirement of non-discrimination. International investment tribunal practice affirms that non-discrimination is a requirement for an expropriation to be considered lawful both under customary international law and under specifically applicable IIAs. While tribunals tend to qualify politically motivated or other egregious forms of discrimination as unlawful, they apply a more nuanced approach to expropriations which affect only some foreigners if such discrimination is the result of legitimate government policies. The chapter concluded that these fairly uniform interpretations of the non-discrimination requirement suggest that it is a standard ripe for codification.

CONCLUSION

It appears that a 'soft codification' of international investment law is already taking place primarily through the coherent interpretation of investment law instruments by investment tribunals. This trend could be reinforced and a harmonious interpretation strengthened by a soft law instrument providing guidance to users of the systems, such as arbitrators, litigators, negotiators, scholars, and others.

But a soft law instrument may be of use not only in the actual application of investment law, but also in the phase of its creation. Such an instrument could assist governments in the negotiation and renegotiation of existing BITs where the trend is to incorporate (or react to) investment arbitral jurisprudence by adding much more detail to the hitherto quite open-ended treaty obligations. Finally it could, if a window of political opportunity were to emerge, provide an early model and drafting text for another attempt at a legally binding multilateral investment convention.

Index

Added to the page reference 'n' denotes a footnote.